D1594347

NEW YORK'S BURNED-OVER DISTRICT

NEW YORK'S BURNED-OVER DISTRICT

A DOCUMENTARY HISTORY

EDITED BY
SPENCER W. MCBRIDE AND
JENNIFER HULL DORSEY

CORNELL UNIVERSITY PRESS
Ithaca and London

First published 2023 by Cornell University Press

Library of Congress Cataloging-in-Publication Data

Names: McBride, Spencer W., editor. | Dorsey, Jennifer Hull, 1969– editor.
Title: New York's burned-over district : a documentary history / edited by Spencer W. McBride and Jennifer Hull Dorsey.
Description: Ithaca [New York] : Cornell University Press, 2023. | Includes bibliographical references and index.
Identifiers: LCCN 2023004876 (print) | LCCN 2023004877 (ebook) | ISBN 9781501770531 (hardcover) | ISBN 9781501770548 (paperback) | ISBN 9781501770555 (pdf) | ISBN 9781501770562 (epub)
Subjects: LCSH: Christianity—New York (State)—Influence. | Social reformers—New York (State)—History—19th century. | New York (State)—Church history—19th century.
Classification: LCC BR555.N7 N49 2023 (print) | LCC BR555.N7 (ebook) | DDC 261.09747/1—dc23/eng/20230418
LC record available at https://lccn.loc.gov/2023004876
LC ebook record available at https://lccn.loc.gov/2023004877

For our teachers

CONTENTS

Editorial Method

In publishing a volume of primary source documents that is selective rather than comprehensive, there is inevitably a degree of subjectivity in the document selection process. Nevertheless, in compiling this volume we established criteria to guide that process. In terms of geography and chronology, we expanded the boundaries of the Burned-over District as described by historian Whitney Cross in his seminal work on the subject. Cross defined the district as the portion of New York lying west of the Catskill and Adirondack Mountains, between 1800 and 1850. In this documentary history, we have included the communities that lay within those mountainous areas and the Mohawk Valley that divides them. Furthermore, we have expanded the chronology to encompass the years between 1790 and 1860. We selected many documents created in the Burned-over District but also selected many that describe the events in the region but were produced or published elsewhere.

Topically, our goal was to select documents that cover a broad range of subjects related to the religious, social, and cultural developments that characterized this place at this time. These topics include settlement patterns that contributed to a culture wherein religious enthusiasm could flourish; the religious developments themselves, as well as people's reactions to them; and the outgrowths of these developments that endured even after the religious revivalist flame had dimmed. In instances where only portions of a featured document are relevant to the Burned-over District, we have published just the pertinent excerpts. If a document is too long to feature in its entirety, we have included representative excerpts. We have favored documents that capture the different ways people, groups, and movements were perceived by residents of New York. For instance, when we have included documents pertaining to groups that elicited controversy in the public square such as the Latter-day Saints, the Millerites, and members of the Oneida Association, we have attempted to include documents that portray these differing views. We have included documents that were published in polished prose as well as rough personal records. In addition to these stated guidelines, we have leaned on our combined experience as educators and researchers to carefully consider the usefulness of documents in classroom instruction and to independent research.

The documents are organized into eight parts as described in the introduction to this volume. The parts vary in length, but we do not intend this to reflect the relative significance of each part. Working within limitations of space on the printed page, we considered what documents are most essential and useful for readers to get a complete enough picture of each part's themes so as to understand the themes illuminated in the parts that follow, and balanced that judgment with a desire for a variety of document types and considerations of a document's accessibility outside the archive in which it is preserved. Within each part we ordered the documents topically with the thematic congruence of the reader's experience in mind.

Annotation Conventions

Every featured document is annotated to provide the context that we, as editors, deemed essential for readers to understand its scope and significance. A source note accompanies each document, identifying the location of the original document from which the featured transcript was created. A brief historical introduction precedes each document, explaining the context of the document's creation and identifying, when possible, the intended audience. The annotation is not, however, designed to be comprehensive or to draw overly broad analytical conclusions about the documents and their subject matter.

Rules of Transcription

To ensure accuracy in representing texts, transcripts were verified twice, using either the original document or high-resolution images of the same. Both verifications were independent visual collations of the manuscript images with the transcripts.

Formatting is standardized throughout, but original paragraphing is retained. In transcripts of printed sources, typeface, type size, and spacing have been standardized. The formatting of tables, such as those included in church trustee minutes, is standardized to be more legible. Editorial judgments about capitalization, original spelling, and punctuation defer to the usual capitalization, spelling, and punctuation of the author or scribe. In cases where such are ambiguous, we have favored modern spelling and punctuation. Canceled words are typographically rendered with the strike-through bar, while inserted words are enclosed within angle brackets. When a word was changed by strike-through or insertion of an individual or multiple letters, then the first word is rendered with a strike-through bar, with the intended word following after.

Single instances of periods, commas, apostrophes, and dashes are all faithfully rendered without regard to their grammatical correctness. Dashes of various lengths are standardized. In the nineteenth century, Americans frequently used underscore marks as punctuation, most commonly as periods. In this volume we have rendered underscore marks as punctuation based on their respective locations in the documents. Decorative inscriptions are not reproduced or noted. Punctuation is never added silently.

Where words or phrases are especially difficult to understand, editorial clarifications or corrections are inserted in brackets. Correct and complete spellings of words and personal names are supplied in brackets the first time each incorrect spelling or incomplete name appears in a document, if the correct spelling or complete name can be determined. In instances in which the original document features text in square brackets, we have replaced those brackets with parentheses so that it is clear that the text is in the original document. When an excerpt of a document is featured, an ellipsis in square brackets denotes text not included. Lists and signatures that appear in columns in original documents are rendered in a single column in the transcription.

Transcription Symbols

[roman]   Brackets enclose editorial insertions that expand, correct, or clarify the text. This convention may be applied to the abbreviated or incorrect spelling of a word or personal name if the abbreviation or misspelling makes the word incomprehensible or the named subject unidentifiable, to maintain the sense of a sentence without more extensive editorial insertion.

[roman?]   A question mark is added to conjectural editorial insertions. This includes instances where an entire word was accidentally omitted or where it is difficult to maintain the sense of a sentence without some editorial insertion.

[*italic*] Significant descriptions of the textual medium, especially those inhibiting legibility, are italicized and enclosed in brackets. Examples include [*hole burned in paper*] and [*page torn*].

[*illegible*] An illegible word is represented by the italicized word [*illegible*] enclosed in brackets.

<u>Underlining</u> Underlining is typographically reproduced. Individually underlined words are distinguished from passages underlined with one continuous line.

^{superscript} Superscription is typographically reproduced.

~~canceled~~ A single horizontal strike-through bar is used to indicate any method of cancellation.

<inserted> Insertions in the text, whether interlinear, intralinear, or marginal, are enclosed in angle brackets. Letters and other characters individually inserted at the beginning or end of a word are distinguished from words inserted in their entirety.

[. . .] An ellipsis in square brackets indicates that the text is extracted from a larger text and that there is additional text in the original document before or after the text that is featured.

NEW YORK'S BURNED-OVER DISTRICT

Introduction

Nineteenth-century travelers in central and western New York frequently commented on the region's beauty. One man who had passed through the state in 1830 recalled a terrain "filled with flourishing farms and dwellings" that featured "pine-clad mountains" and towns "nestling among the hills."[1] A European visitor described the area's lush forests as "a vast dome of vegetation" containing "trees of all ages, foliage of all colours, plants, fruits and flowers of a thousand species, entangled and intertwined."[2] Yet another tourist exclaimed, "The whole scenery cannot be described in words that can convey an adequate description nor can it be conceived by those, who have not witnessed it."[3] Indeed, the serene towns, rolling hills, sprawling pastures, and dense forests of New York State still inspire artists, musicians, and poets alike. How this picturesque region of the United States obtained a moniker as dreary as the "Burned-over District," then, is a complex and fascinating story.

---

1. Parley P. Pratt, *The Autobiography of Parley Parker Pratt* (New York: Russell Bros., 1874), 44.

2. Alexis de Tocqueville, *Journey to America*, ed. J. P. Mayer (London: Faber and Faber, 1960), 321–22.

3. William Strickland, *Journal of a Tour in the United States of America, 1794–1795* (New York: New-York Historical Society, 1971), 139, 142–46.

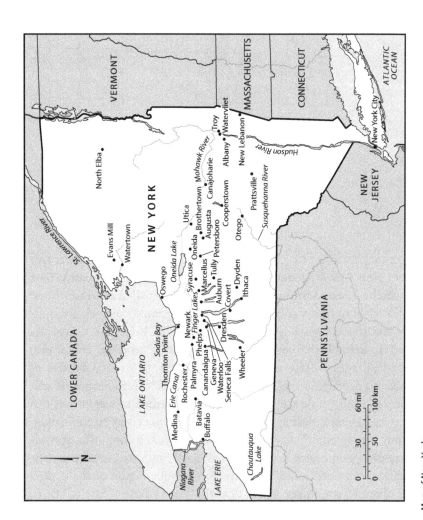

MAP 1. Map of New York

When historians speak of the Burned-over District, we are typically referring to an area in central and western New York that experienced a high level of religious enthusiasm during the first half of the nineteenth century. In the 1780s and 1790s, hundreds of thousands of white settlers started pouring into the area. They were followed by Protestant Christian missionaries and itinerant preachers. Waves of revival meetings resulted in a dramatic increase in church membership and a corresponding rise in the number of societies dedicated to moral and social reform.

While these trends in American religion and reform occurred throughout the United States, New York hosted them in particularly high concentration. This book tells the story of how and why New York became such a hotbed of religious revivalism and reform movements. It tells that story through historical documents curated and transcribed to help readers view this pivotal moment in history through the eyes of some of the men and women who lived it and helped make it so. It argues that the story of the Burned-over District is integral to understanding the social and cultural development of New York and, by extension, the United States in the nineteenth century.

Revivals, Awakenings, and Reform

The revivals that swept nineteenth-century New York were part of a widespread socioreligious movement called the Second Great Awakening.[4] During this movement that spanned from approximately 1790 to 1840, rates of American church attendance rose rapidly. Every mainline Protestant denomination sponsored missionary efforts, but the Baptists and Methodists particularly flourished during this era of revivalism. The Second Great Awakening also gave rise to new denominations and sects such as the Church of Jesus Christ of Latter-day Saints and

---

4. While the label "Second Great Awakening" is widely used by historians, there are some who object to it because they do not think that there was a "First Great Awakening" (1730–1750), or because they think it an artificial and arbitrary label that does not fully account for revivals that occurred in the 1790s. See, for examples, Frank Lambert, *Inventing the "Great Awakening"* (Princeton, NJ: Princeton University Press, 2001), and Jon Butler, *Awash in a Sea of Faith: Christianizing the American People* (Cambridge, MA: Harvard University Press, 1990), 220–24. Others, such as Thomas S. Kidd, have argued that there was a singular, uninterrupted religious awakening consisting of a "long First Great Awakening" that abutted a new round of religious growth that became known as the "Second Great Awakening." See Thomas S. Kidd, *The Great Awakening: The Roots of Evangelical Christianity in Colonial America* (New Haven, CT: Yale University Press, 2007), xiv.

the Adventist (or Millerite) movement. At the same time, the Shakers and the Oneida Association, two alternative religious groups, organized new intentional communities for the spiritual benefit of their followers.

The engines driving this awakening were revival meetings in which traveling and stationed ministers alike preached to large crowds in a manner designed to elicit strong emotional responses from their audiences. Ideally these genuine responses included the confession and forsaking of personal sins and a commitment to more actively participate in one of the many churches that claimed to teach the gospel of Jesus Christ.[5] Whether affiliated with the Baptists, Methodists, Presbyterians, or another denomination, these evangelists actively competed with one another for potential converts. Equally important, spiritual seekers eagerly responded to these efforts and sampled the many options available to them in this unusual religious "marketplace." The result was a greater openness among the public to different religious beliefs and expressions of faith.[6]

Why this spiritual awakening occurred in the time, places, and way it did is a point of great debate among historians. There was certainly an element of the movement that was reacting against the rise of religious skepticism and deism in the post-Revolutionary United States, as well as a popular inclination to more firmly unite republican principles with Christian theology.[7] Moving beyond this basic reactionary explanation, however, some historians have argued that the uptick in religious enthusiasm was the consequence of an increasingly democratic society—that in a country where white men could seemingly move geographically, socially, and economically with greater ease than ever before, Americans naturally sought and created religious communities that better met their personal needs and did so outside the leadership of society's educated elite.[8] Yet a different interpretation maintains that the disruption of the Revolutionary War, coupled with the political and

---

5. On the role of revival meetings in the Second Great Awakening see Nathan O. Hatch, *The Democratization of American Christianity* (New Haven, CT: Yale University Press, 1994); Mark A. Noll, *America's God: From Jonathan Edwards to Abraham Lincoln* (New York: Oxford University Press, 2002), 179–86; and Butler, *Awash in a Sea of Faith*, 220–24.

6. On nineteenth-century ecclesiastical controversy and competition in the United States, the creation of new denominations and sects in their wake, and the movement of Americans between these different faith communities see R. Lawrence Moore, *Selling God: American Religion in the Marketplace of Culture* (New York: Oxford University Press, 1994), 118–45.

7. Noll, *America's God*, 53–92.

8. Hatch, *Democratization of American Christianity*, 3–16.

economic turmoil of the 1780s, generated a high degree of division and uncertainty among the American public, and that burgeoning evangelical Christian groups manipulated this division and uncertainty to expand their memberships and to extend the reach of their cultural authority and political influence.[9]

Whether reflecting reactionary impulses, newfound freedom, or denominational opportunism, the movement spread across the country and had the lasting impact of diversifying the American religious landscape.[10] The documents featured in this volume support several different explanations for the Second Great Awakening. Some demonstrate a reaction to religious skepticism, others the democratization of American Christianity, and still others the coordinated efforts of religious groups to make use of the uncertainty underlying an American society in flux to bolster church membership. Collectively, the documents featured in this volume simultaneously support and complicate commonly shared assumptions about the history, progress, and meaning of the Second Great Awakening.

While the Second Great Awakening was national in scope, it did not affect all parts of the country equally. Precise measurements of religious fervor or "awakenings" are difficult—if not impossible—to ascertain. However, certain geographic areas appear to have experienced more frequent and intense waves of revivalism than others. For instance, Vermont, western Massachusetts, Kentucky, Ohio, and the Delaware River Valley each provide well-documented examples of religious hotbeds during the Second Great Awakening.[11] Nevertheless, whether statisti-

9. Amanda Porterfield, *Conceived in Doubt: Religion and Politics in the New American Nation* (Chicago: University of Chicago Press, 2012), 1–13.

10. Some historians have also suggested that developments in preaching style helped create and perpetuate the Second Great Awakening, that in an effort to distinguish their denomination's doctrinal tenets from those of all others, Christian preachers exaggerated such differences, thereby eliminating subtlety from theological discussion and producing more effective preaching. See, for example, Sydney E. Ahlstrom, *A Religious History of the American People* (New Haven, CT: Yale University Press, 1972), 438–39.

11. Hatch, *Democratization of American Christianity*, 49–66; Noll, *America's God*, 179–86; Paul K. Conkin, *Cane Ridge: America's Pentecost* (Madison: University of Wisconsin Press, 1990); Shelby M. Balik, *Rally the Scattered Believers: Northern New England's Religious Geography* (Bloomington: Indiana University Press, 2014); Bridget Ford, *Bonds of Union: Religion, Race, and Politics in a Civil War Borderland* (Chapel Hill: University of North Carolina Press, 2016); Linda K. Pritchard, "The Burned-Over District Reconsidered: A Portent of Evolving Religious Pluralism in the United States," *Social Science History* 8, no. 3 (Summer 1984): 243–65; and Stephen J. Fleming, "'Congenial to Almost Every Shade of Radicalism': The Delaware Valley and the Success of Early Mormonism," *Religion and American Culture: A Journal of Interpretation* 17, no. 2 (Summer 2007): 129–64.

cally real or merely the product of Americans' cultural imagination and historical memory, central and western New York boast the reputation of topping all these areas where nineteenth-century religious fervor is concerned.[12]

Three waves of particularly intense revivalism occurred in New York between 1800 and 1850. The first, sometimes called "the time of the Great Revival," occurred in 1799–1800, about the same time a more famous series of revivals swept the state of Kentucky.[13] This revivalism was widespread in New York but was strongest in Genesee, Oneida, and Otsego Counties, precipitated by a surge of migrants to the region. In one year, the Methodists made an estimated fifteen hundred converts.[14] After a brief and minor resurgence in 1807–1808, a second wave of revivalism swept the state in the wake of the War of 1812, lasting from approximately 1815 to 1820. According to historian Whitney Cross, this wave surpassed all previous experiences in the area and reached farther west—beyond the eastern shore of Lake Erie—than had previous episodes of revivalism.[15] The third wave crested in 1826, when famed itinerant preacher Charles G. Finney was evangelizing in the area. Historians estimate that this final wave of revivalism continued in western New York until 1837.[16] Growth in church membership and the total number of faith communities active in this area was continuous, but these demonstrable waves indicate that the rate of such growth was unsteady.

The early nineteenth-century history of revivalism in New York stands out even more when we consider the rise of alternative Christian movements in that state. During the first half of the nineteenth century, central and western New York witnessed the creation of three new Christian movements deemed radical by their critics: the Millerites, the Latter-day Saints, and the Oneida Association.[17] New religious

12. Whitney R. Cross, *The Burned-Over District: The Social and Intellectual History of Enthusiastic Religion in Western New York, 1800–1850* (Ithaca, NY: Cornell University Press, 1950), vii, 3–13; Pritchard, "Burned-Over District Reconsidered," 243–65; and Judith Wellman, "Crossing Over Cross: Whitney Cross's Burned-Over District as Social History," *Reviews in American History* 17, no. 1 (March 1989): 159–74.

13. Conkin, *Cane Ridge*.

14. Cross, *Burned-Over District*, 9–10.

15. Cross, 10–12. Also see Paul E. Johnson, *A Shopkeeper's Millennium: Society and Revivals in Rochester, New York, 1815–1837* (New York: Hill & Wang, 1978).

16. Cross, *Burned-Over District*, 12–13, and Johnson, *Shopkeeper's Millennium*, 4–5.

17. For a detailed history of Joseph Smith and the Mormons in New York see Richard Bushman, *Joseph Smith, Rough Stone Rolling: A Cultural Biography of the Founder of Mormonism* (New York: Knopf, 2005), 30–126. On William Miller and the Millerites see David L. Rowe,

communities also appeared in the Hudson River Valley, where Robert Matthews, who claimed at one point to be the reincarnated biblical apostle Matthias, established a short-lived settlement he called "the Kingdom." More famously, the Shakers built a network of intentional communities devoted to the teachings of their English-born spiritual leader, Mother Ann Lee, who claimed God had anointed her "the first Mother of all souls in the regeneration." From their central ministry in Mount Lebanon, New York, the American-born Shakers organized additional communal settlements (popularly known as "Shaker villages") throughout the state.[18] Thus, while the Second Great Awakening occurred nationally, this book presents documents from a region where the social, cultural, and political influence of the religious movement was particularly concentrated. For as prevalent as religious revivalism was in the hotbeds of Vermont, western Massachusetts, Kentucky, Ohio, and the Delaware River Valley, only New York appears to have given rise to so many different and enduring forms of alternative religious communities at one time.

Finally, this book includes documents that bear witness to the strong reform impulse that emerged from this period of religious revival, the effects of which were felt by New York residents long after 1837. Movements aimed at the advancement of temperance (abstinence from alcoholic drink) and Sabbatarianism (observation of the Sabbath), and even to curb the influence of secret societies such as the Freemasons, all proliferated and gained traction in the state. Some of these movements existed prior to the Second Great Awakening, or grew out of separate social and cultural conditions, but the strong religious and democratic impulses of the era gave additional momentum to a wide variety of moral, social, political, and economic reform efforts.[19] Accordingly, the

---

God's Strange Work: William Miller and the End of the World (Grand Rapids, MI: Eerdmans, 2008). The belief system that led to the founding of the Oneida Association began in Vermont before moving to New York, but the formal association was organized in the latter place. On John Humphrey Noyes and the Oneida Association see George Wallingford Noyes, *Free Love in Utopia: John Humphrey Noyes and the Origin of the Oneida Community* (Urbana: University of Illinois Press, 2001).

18. On Robert Matthews see Paul E. Johnson and Sean Wilentz, *The Kingdom of Matthias: A Story of Sex and Salvation in Nineteenth-Century America* (New York: Oxford University Press, 1994). On the Shakers in the United States see Stephen J. Stein, *The Shaker Experience in America: A History of the United Society of Believers* (New Haven, CT: Yale University Press, 1992).

19. On the impact of the Second Great Awakening generally, and the Burned-over District particularly, on nineteenth-century American abolition, anti-Masonry, temperance, and the women's rights movements see Judith Wellman, *Grass Roots Reform in the Burned-Over District of Upstate New York* (New York: Garland, 2000); David M. Fahey, *Temperance and Racism: John*

documents featured in the pages that follow demonstrate the lasting impact of religious movements on matters that are not inherently religious in nature. The ultimate significance of New York's Burned-over District on the development of American society and culture in the nineteenth century extends far beyond the creation and growth of different religious groups. The history of the Burned-over District demonstrates the vital link between concentrated religious enthusiasm and the willful actions many nineteenth-century Americans took to reshape the world in which they lived.

Where—and When—Is the Burned-over District?

The Burned-over District has fluid geographic and chronological boundaries. In his influential work *The Burned-Over District* (1950), historian Whitney R. Cross assigned the label to the fifteen New York counties west of the Catskill and Adirondack Mountains between 1800 and 1850.[20] Of course, the high level of religious enthusiasm that characterized this region in the first half of the nineteenth century spilled over county and state lines, and it hardly ceased altogether after 1850. Furthermore, neighboring territory in Vermont and Massachusetts to the east, Pennsylvania to the south, and Ohio to the west experienced similar concentrations in the frequency of religious revivals and in the intensity of religious enthusiasm.[21] There were, in this sense, multiple "burned-over districts" in the United States, all deserving the attention of scholars. Yet New York's Burned-over District is the focus of this book, and the religious experiences that occurred in that district as described in the documents featured herein demonstrate the ways in which the district was simultaneously typical and unique within a national movement.

Bull, Johnny Reb, and the Good Templars (Lexington: University Press of Kentucky, 1996), 10–11; Glenn C. Altschuler and Jan M. Saltzgaber, *Revivalism, Social Conscience, and Community in the Burned-Over District: The Trial of Rhoda Bement* (Ithaca, NY: Cornell University Press, 1983); Nancy Isenberg, *Sex and Citizenship in Antebellum America* (Chapel Hill: University of North Carolina Press, 1998), 82–101; Sally G. McMillen, *Seneca Falls and the Origins of the Women's Rights Movement* (New York: Oxford University Press, 2008); and Cross, *Burned-Over District*, 173–284.

20. These counties are, in alphabetical order, Allegany, Cattaraugus, Chautauqua, Erie, Genesee, Livingston, Monroe, Niagara, Ontario, Orleans, Seneca, Steuben, Wayne, Wyoming, and Yates. Cross excluded the Adirondacks, the Catskills, and the Mohawk Valley from the Burned-Over District. Cross, *Burned-Over District*, 3–4.

21. For example see Shelby Balik, *Rally the Scattered Believers: Northern New England's Religious Geography* (Bloomington: Indiana University Press, 2014).

Since the publication of Cross's work historians have debated the precise geographical and chronological boundaries of New York's Burned-over District. As a result, scholars can make cases for an assortment of different sets of boundaries.[22] Limiting the boundaries to the fifteen New York counties west of the Catskill and Adirondack Mountains omits several significant and relevant events that took place in the various towns situated within these mountainous regions and those in and near the Mohawk River Valley, which served as a vital corridor to the western territory of the state. In fact, when we examine the presence and impact of religious revivalism and the subsequent rise of an intense reform impulse in these additional counties to the east, it is easy to see that the Second Great Awakening's influence in these places was consistent with that of the counties to the west. For the purpose of setting the geographic and chronological parameters of this documentary history, we define New York's Burned-over District as the region of New York starting at Albany in the east and including the Catskills to the south, the Adirondacks to the north, and the counties west of these areas during the first half of the nineteenth century.

The Evolution of a Dreary Name

Charles Finney was the first to apply the "burnt" label in print to central and western New York. The famed revivalist preacher did so in 1876 when he recalled his extensive interactions with the people of this district in a lengthy autobiography. Finney, whose theological beliefs mixed tenets of Presbyterianism and Congregationalism, actively preached in this region during the 1820s and 1830s and experienced noteworthy success in converting men and women to his evangelical brand of Christianity. Still, in his reminiscence, he recalled the difficulty he experienced in certain towns where recent series of revivals had left populations unresponsive to his preaching. "I found that region of the country what, in the western phrase, would be called, 'a burnt district,'" Finney wrote, explaining that "there had been, a few years previously, a wild excitement passing through that region, which they called a revival of religion . . . and resulted in a reaction so extensive and

22. For example, Michael Barkun uses a slightly more restrictive geographic description than Cross, claiming that the southern boundary of the district was the northern shores of the Finger Lakes. See Michael Barkun, *Crucible of the Millennium: The Burned-Over District of New York in the 1840s* (Syracuse, NY: Syracuse University Press, 1986), 2–3.

profound, as to leave the impression on many minds that religion was a mere delusion."[23] To Finney, the region was "burnt" because decades of religious revivals had, in his opinion, left residents jaded and wary of traveling preachers such as himself.

In 1950, Whitney Cross altered Finney's "burnt" description, applying the "burned-over" label to the region. However, Cross used it with a far more positive view of the district than Finney had expressed in his later years. To Cross, the "fire" of religious enthusiasm that passed through the region left in its wake social "soil" conditioned for the rise of several important reform movements. As a cultural analogue to slash-and-burn farming practices, the region became incredibly fruitful. Like grass, flowers, bushes, and saplings sprouting out of earth scorched by wildfire, the aforementioned reform movements of abolitionism, temperance, anti-Masonry, and advocacy for women's rights all took root and flourished in central and western New York during and after its early nineteenth-century religious awakenings.[24]

Still, if we look to the way many of the residents of the Burned-over District described the several waves of religious enthusiasm that swept the area, we catch a softer and less fiery view of the district. Rather than describe the series of revival meetings as a smoldering fire, several who recorded their religious conversion experiences opted instead for analogies of precipitation.[25] One man rejoiced that the revivals had acted as dews from heaven "watering our parched fields, and making them bring forth abundantly."[26] A New York Shaker described the spiritual effects of a recent revival in similar terms, writing that "since the latter rains and those refreshing showers from heaven descended, the drooping spirits have revived, and the withered plants spring up, and as it were the dry forest begins to bud and blossom, and leap for joy."[27] To such observers, the effects of religious revivalism were more comparable

---

23. Charles G. Finney, *Memoirs of Rev. Charles G. Finney* (New York: A. S. Barnes, 1876), 77–78.

24. Cross, *Burned-Over District*, 3–4; Wellman, "Crossing Over Cross," 163–64.

25. Rachel Cope, "'In Some Places a Few Drops and Other Places a Plentiful Shower': The Religious Impact of Revivalism on Early Nineteenth-Century New York Women" (PhD diss., Syracuse University, 2009), 24–30.

26. Cornelius C. Cuyler, "Revival of Religion in the Reformed Dutch Church at Poughkeepsie under the Pastoral Care of Rev. Cornelius C. Cuyler," *Utica Christian Magazine* 3, no. 1 (July 1815), 17; and Cope, "'In Some Places a Few Drops,'" 28.

27. Grove Write to Ministry New Lebanon, November 16, 1837, quoted in a letter from Ministry New Lebanon to Ministry South Union, December 13, 1837, Western Reserve Historical Society, Cleveland. Also see Cope, "'In Some Places a Few Drops,'" 28.

to the fertile soil that results from steady rainfall than they were to the scorched earth left in the wake of an all-consuming fire.

The background and connotations associated with the name assigned to a region are important. This book uses the Burned-over District label popularized by Cross, understanding its somewhat anachronistic origins but drawn to its valuable connotations. In a historical examination of this region of New York in such a pivotal historical period and of its influence on the rest of the country in the decades that followed, Cross's label remains apt and identifiable to a wider historical community.

Walking the "Burned-over" Fields of History

This book invites students, researchers, and all other readers to figuratively walk the fields of New York's social, cultural, and religious history, to examine—through primary source documents—the unfolding of a religious awakening that had a lasting and consequential influence on the culture of New York and the American nation at large. It contains transcripts of documents that depict the creation, development, and evolution of the Second Great Awakening—and the reform movements that grew out of it—as they were experienced, observed, and remembered by the men and women who participated therein. Publishing in a single volume every document associated with the Burned-over District is impossible. Accordingly, we have selected a sample of the historical documents associated with this place and time. People and experiences in the Burned-over District were diverse, and in selecting documents for this volume, we actively sought to represent that diversity. For instance, we feature documents describing revival meetings from the perspectives of both preachers and attendees; we showcase documents created by men and women to promote new religious groups along with documents created by those groups' critics. We capture the voices and experiences of women in the Burned-over District along with those of their male counterparts. While Native Americans quickly became minorities in their traditional homeland, we feature documents that help illuminate their perspectives and continued presence in the area as it related to religion. Similarly, while white evangelists, worshippers, and reformers outnumbered their Black peers in the Burned-over District, the excerpts from two Black clergymen, Rev. Thomas James of the African Methodist Episcopal Zion Church and Rev. Samuel Ringgold Ward of the Congregationalist Church, and the Black female evangelist

Sojourner Truth, shed light on how some Black men and women experienced spiritual awakening, revivalism, and reform. Thus, while a collection of selected documents can never paint a *complete* portrait of a historical time and place, in this collection we attempt to accurately reflect a representative portion of the same.[28]

The documents included in this book take readers through the history of the Burned-over District in eight topical parts. The first part, titled "Settlement," showcases the demographic composition of the region and the area's strong draw for migrating New Englanders. The second part, "Missionaries," features documents that depict the efforts of missionary societies in the eastern United States to ensure the continued religious devotion of western settlers, as well as the creation of local missionary societies. "Revivals" is the third part and illuminates the origins and effects of religious revivals in central and western New York. "Church Development," the fourth part, consists of documents depicting the founding, expansion, and regulation of different denominations in the region, focused particularly on the Baptists, Methodists, and Presbyterians. Many of these documents are local church records that are sometimes difficult to read and focused on minute details, but they reveal the pragmatic concerns and work required to develop and maintain church communities.

The fifth part, titled "Kingdoms of God," focuses on documents surrounding three new Christian groups that originated in—or drew participation from—the Burned-over District: the Latter-day Saints, the Millerites, and the Kingdom led by Robert Matthews. Similarly, the sixth part, "Intentional Communities," features documents pertaining to the Shakers and the Oneida Association, groups that moved to New York to extend their respective separations from mainstream Protestantism to separations from mainstream American communities and social norms. "Religion and New York Politics," the seventh part, explains how the rising religious fervor and prevailing democratic spirit contributed to the reform impulse that swept antebellum New York State. The final part, "Abolition and Ultraism in the Burned-over District," considers abolitionism in central and western New York as an example of the ultraism that grew out of the age of revivalism and reform. Each part includes a brief introduction to better contextualize the documents for readers. This organization is designed for convenient classroom use, as

---

28. For a detailed description of the document selection criteria adopted by the editors of this volume see "Editorial Method" at the beginning of this book.

a starting point in a research project, or as an entryway for interested readers into the historical records of such a significant time and place.

New York's Burned-over District is integral to understanding the social, cultural, and even political history of the United States. The rise of American religious pluralism, increases in Americans' geographic and social mobility, the development of a more democratic society and political system, and the quest of women and racial minorities for civil rights are all key components in the story of nineteenth-century America. Yet we cannot completely understand or fully appreciate these developments without the history of New York's Burned-over District, where the social, religious, cultural, and political forces that contributed mightily to these developments were found in such a high concentration.

PART I

Settlement

The rate of white settlement in central and western New York rose rapidly between 1790 and 1860. Hundreds of thousands of pioneers dramatically transformed the landscape west of the Adirondack and Catskill Mountains as they cleared old-growth forests to establish new farms and settlements. Amid this migration, the completion of the Erie Canal in 1825 connected many of these settlers—and their goods—to people and markets on the Eastern Seaboard.

Several factors account for this massive movement of people. Politically, the American Revolution opened the territory west of the Appalachian Mountains for white settlement where British imperial policies had previously banned such migration. Economically and socially, many of the migrants were drawn to inexpensive land in New York. This was a particular motivation for young men whose familial lands had been divided numerous times over several generations to the point that they would inherit no land of their own. The new settlers came from several different places, but most were New Englanders. Between 1790 and 1820, approximately eight hundred thousand men, women, and children left New England, most of them for New York.[1] The migration was so

---

1. David Maldwyn Ellis, "The Yankee Invasion of New York, 1783–1850," *New York History* 32, no. 1 (January 1951): 3–17; James W. Darlington, "Peopling the Post-Revolutionary New

immense that, in the 1820s, the president of Yale, Timothy Dwight, wrote that New York is "to be ultimately regarded as a colony from New England."[2]

Environmental factors often compounded these political and economic motives for moving to central and western New York. For instance, in New England, 1816 became known as "the year without a summer," when temperatures dropped dramatically during the summer months. In parts of Vermont, snow fell in June, and the lakes and ponds in the state were topped by several inches of ice. New Englanders had no way of knowing at the time that the aberrant weather was the result of a deadly volcanic eruption in Indonesia in 1815 that had spewed so much ash into earth's atmosphere that it altered weather patterns around the world, sometimes with devastating results. Throughout New England, farmers experienced massive crop failure and financial ruin. In many instances, moving was the only option for starting over. In 1817, an estimated 10 percent of Vermont's population migrated west to New York.[3] In the first half of the eighteenth century, central and western New York represented a fresh start for many Americans.

Of course, humans had started settling in the region thousands of years earlier. This mass migration of white Americans in the eighteenth and nineteenth centuries contributed to the continued displacement and decimation of Native American communities. What Americans called New York had long been part of the homelands of the Six Nations of the Haudenosaunee Confederacy: the Mohawks, Oneidas, Onondagas, Cayugas, Senecas, and Tuscaroras. Following the American Revolution, the Six Nations lost much of their land to the Americans in a 1784 treaty and still more in a 1794 treaty. While white Americans saw their migration to central and western New York as opening new opportunities to them, the Haudenosaunee Confederacy saw it as a dire threat to their homes, their culture, and their very lives.[4]

York Frontier," *New York History* 74, no. 4 (October 1993): 341–81. See also Cross, *Burned-Over District,* 4–6.

2. Timothy Dwight, *Travels in New-England and New-York,* 4 vols. (London: William Baynes and Son, Ogle, Duncan, and Co., 1828), 3:252.

3. William K. Klingaman and Nicholas P. Klingaman, *The Year without Summer: 1816 and the Volcano That Darkened the World and Changed History* (New York: St. Martin's, 2014), 116–18; C. Edward Skeen, "The Year without a Summer: A Historical View," *Journal of the Early Republic* 1, no. 1 (Spring 1981): 51–67.

4. William N. Fenton, *The Great Law and the Longhouse: A Political History of the Iroquois Confederacy* (Norman: University of Oklahoma Press, 1998), 622–40; Matthew Dennis, *Seneca*

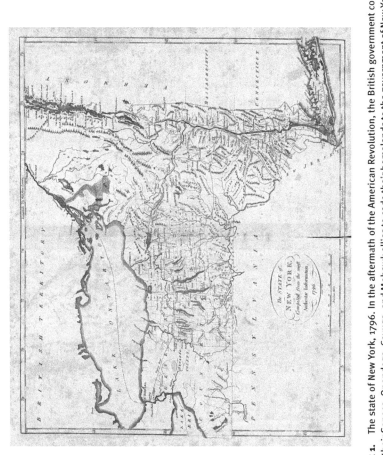

FIGURE 1. The state of New York, 1796. In the aftermath of the American Revolution, the British government compelled their Seneca, Onondaga, Cayuga, and Mohawk allies to cede their homelands to the government of New York State. The neatly parceled plots depicted on this early map indicate the government's aspirations for the orderly settlement of this expansive frontier. (Library of Congress)

The process of white settlement of central and western New York is important to understanding the high concentration of religious fervor that came with it. The migration coincided with a surge in Christian evangelism in the United States. As documents in later parts of this book will demonstrate, the population of central and western New York, removed from well-established towns and cities with well-established denominations and traditions, was fertile ground for the seeds of religious fervor spread by evangelists.[5]

This part consists of four documents. The first is the 1794 treaty signed between the United States and the Haudenosaunee Confederacy regarding the latter's lands in New York and neighboring territories. The second document comments on the origins of the settlers from New England and the effect they had on New York society in general. The third provides the statistics for the state's growing population between 1790 and 1855. Finally, the fourth document describes how this period of intense settlement changed the society and environment of central New York.

Possessed: Indians, Witchcraft, and Power in the Early American Republic (Philadelphia: University of Pennsylvania Press, 2010).

5 Cross, *Burned-Over District*, 3–13.

ONE

Treaty with the Six Nations

Source: Treaty of Canandaigua, 794, Record Group 11: General Records of the United States Government, 1778–2006, Indian Treaties, 1789–1809, National Archives and Records Administration, Washington, DC.

On November 11, 1794, leaders of the Six Nations of the Haudenosaunee Confederacy agreed to a treaty with the United States of America. More than fifty sachems and war chiefs represented the Cayuga, Mohawk, Oneida, Onondaga, Seneca, and Tuscarora nations; Massachusetts statesman Timothy Pickering represented President George Washington. The parties agreed to the treaty at a time when the number of white Americans moving into the region was rapidly increasing.[1] Washington's administration hoped that this treaty would create lasting peace where two previous treaties had failed.[2]

---

1. The population in Ontario County increased from 1,075 people in 1790 to 15,218 in 1800. See "New York Population Growth," document 3 herein. The populations of the Six Nations were approximately nineteen hundred Senecas, three hundred Tuscaroras, six hundred Oneidas, four hundred Cayugas, five hundred Onondagas, and eight hundred Mohawks. See Michael Leroy Oberg, *Peacemakers: The Iroquois, the United States, and the Treaty of Canandaigua, 1794* (New York: Oxford University Press, 2016), 122.

2. On the failures of the Treaty of Fort Stanwix (1784) and the Treaty of Fort Harmar (1789) see Jack Campisi and William A. Starna, "On the Road to Canandaigua: The Treaty of

In addition to establishing "peace and friendship" between the Six Nations and the United States, the treaty defined the lands that belonged to the Oneida and Seneca nations, set forth the parameters for the management of a wagon road to be constructed on Seneca lands, promised a $4,500 annual allowance to the Haudenosaunee Confederacy, and included a provision requiring any future conflict between the Haudenosaunee Confederacy and the United States to be settled peacefully through diplomatic channels. Pickering signed the treaty, and each of the Native American representatives inscribed the document with an *X* as their mark. A wax seal was then placed next to each name on the official copy of the treaty, indicated in the transcript below by "[L.S.]" (for *logus sigilli*, a Latin term meaning "place of the seal"). The United States Senate ratified the treaty on January 2, 1795.[3]

✦ ✦ ✦

A Treaty Between the United States of America, and the Tribes of Indians called the Six Nations

The President of the United States having determined to hold a conference with the Six Nations of Indians, for the purpose of removing from their minds all causes of complaint, and establishing a firm and permanent friendship with them; and Timothy Pickering being appointed sole agent for that purpose; and the agent having met and conferred with the Sachems, Chiefs and Warriors of the Six Nations, in a general council: Now, in order to accomplish the good design of this conference, the parties have agreed on the following articles; which, when ratified by the President, with the advice and consent of the Senate of the United States, shall be binding on them and the Six Nations.

Article I

Peace and friendship are hereby firmly established, and shall be perpetual, between the United States and the Six Nations.

Article II

The United States acknowledge the lands reserved to the Oneida, Onondaga and Cayuga Nations, in their respective treaties with the state

---

1794," *American Indian Quarterly* 19, no. 4 (Autumn 1995): 467–90. Also see Oberg, *Peacemakers*, 33–34.

3. Campisi and Starna, "On the Road to Canandaigua," 484. On the legacy of the Treaty of Canandaigua see Oberg, *Peacemakers*, 144–59.

of New-York, and called their reservations, to be their property; and the United States will never claim the same nor disturb them or either of the Six Nations, nor their Indian friends residing thereon and united with them in the free use and enjoyment thereof: but the said reservations shall remain theirs, until they chose to sell the same to the people of the United States, who have the right to purchase.

Article III

The land of the Seneka nation is bounded as follows: Beginning on Lake Ontario, at the north-west corner of the land they sold to Oliver Phelps, the line runs westerly along the lake, as far as O-yong-wong-yeh Creek, at Johnson's Landing-place, about four miles eastward from the Fort of Niagara; then southerly up that creek to its main fork, then straight to the main fork of Stedman's creek, which empties into the River Niagara, above Fort Schlosser, and then onward, from that fork, continuing the same straight course, to that River; (this line, from the mouth of O-yong-wong-yeh Creek to the River Niagara, above Fort Schlosser, being the eastern boundary of a strip of land, extending from the same line to Niagara River, which the Seneka nation ceded to the King of Great-Britain, at a treaty held about thirty years ago, with Sir William Johnson;) then the line runs along the River Niagara to Lake Erie; then along Lake Erie to the north-east corner of a triangular piece of land which the United States conveyed to the state of Pennsylvania, as by the President's patent, dated the third day of March, 1792; then due south to the northern boundary of that state; then due east to the south-west corner of the land sold by the Seneka Nation to Oliver Phelps; and then north and northerly, along Phelps's line, to the place of the beginning on Lake Ontario. Now, the United States acknowledge all the land within the aforementioned boundaries, to be the property of the Seneka Nation; and the United States will never claim the same, nor disturb the Seneka Nation, nor any of the Six Nations, or of their Indian Friends thereon and united with them, in the free use and enjoyment thereof: but it shall remain theirs, until they choose to sell the same to the people of the United States, who have the right to purchase.

Article IV

The United States having thus described and acknowledged what lands belong to the Oneidas, Onondagas, Cayugas and Senekas, and engaged never to claim the same, nor to disturb them, or any of the Six Nations, or their Indian friends residing thereon and united with them, in the free use and enjoyment thereof: Now, the Six Nations, and each of them, hereby engage that they will never claim any other lands within the boundaries of the United States; nor ever disturb the people of the United States in the free use and enjoyment thereof.

Article V

The Seneka Nation, all others of the Six Nations concurring, cede to the United States the right of making a wagon road from Fort Schlosser to Lake Erie, as far south as Buffaloe Creek; and the people of the United States shall have the free and undisturbed use of this road, for the purpose of travelling and transportation. And the Six Nations, and each of them, will forever allow the people of the United States, a free passage through their lands, and the free use of their harbors and rivers adjoining and within their respective tracts of land, for the passing and securing of vessels and boats, and liberty to land their cargoes where necessary for their safety.

Article VI

In consideration of the peace and friendship hereby established, and of the engagements entered into by the Six Nations; and because the United States desire, with humanity and kindness, to contribute to their comfortable support; and to render the peace and friendship established, strong and perpetual; the United States now deliver to the Six Nations, and the Indians of the other nations residing among and united with them, a quantity of goods of the value of ten thousand dollars. And for the same considerations, and with a view to promote the future welfare of the Six Nations, and of their Indian friends aforesaid, the United States will add the sum of three thousand dollars to the one thousand five hundred dollars, heretofore allowed them by an article ratified by the President, on the twenty-third day of April 1792; making in the whole, Four Thousand Five Hundred Dollars; which shall be expended yearly forever, in purchasing clothing, domestic animals, implements of husbandry and other utensils suited to their circumstances, and in compensating useful artificers, who shall reside with or near them, and be employed for their benefit. The immediate application of the whole annual allowance now stipulated, to be made by the superintendent appointed by the President for the affairs of the Six Nations, and their Indian friends aforesaid.

Article VII

Lest the firm peace and friendship now established should be interrupted by the misconduct of individuals, the United States and Six Nations agree, that for injuries done by individuals on either side, no private revenge or retaliation shall take place; but, instead thereof, complaint shall be made by the party injured to the other: by the Six Nations or any of them, to the President of the United States, or the Superintendent by him appointed: and by the Superintendent, or other person appointed by the President, to the principal chiefs of the Six Nations, or of the nation to which the offender belongs: and such prudent measures shall then be pursued as shall be necessary to preserve our peace and friendship unbroken; until the legislature (or Great Council) of the United States shall make other equitable provisions for the purpose.

Note: It is clearly understood by the parties to this Treaty, that the annuity stipulated in the Sixth Article is to be applied to the benefit of such of the Six Nations and of their Indian Friends united with them as aforesaid, as do or shall reside within the boundaries of the United States: For the United States do not interfere with Nations, Tribes or Families elsewhere resident.

In witness whereof, the said Timothy Pickering, and the Sachems and War-Chiefs of the said Six Nations, have hereto set their hands and seals.

Done at Kon-en-daigua [Canandaigua], in the State of New-York, the eleventh day of November, in the year one thousand seven hundred and ninety-four.

Timothy Pickering [L.S.]
O-no-ye-ah-nee, X [L.S.]
Kon-ne-at-or-tee-ooh, X, or Handsome Lake [L.S.]
Tokenhyouhau, X, alias Captain Key [L.S.]
O-nes-hau-ee, X [L.S.]
Hendrick Aupaumut, [L.S.]
David Neesoonhuk, X [L.S.]
Kanatsoyh, alias Nicholas Kusik [L.S.]
Soh-hon-te-o-quent, X [L.S.]

Oo-duht-sa-it, X [L.S.]
Ko-nooh-qung, X [L.S.]
Tos-song-gau-lo-luss, X [L.S.]
John Sken-en-do-a, X [L.S.]
O-ne-at-or-lee-ooh, X [L.S.]
Kus-sau-wa-tau, X [L.S.]
E-yoo-ten-yoo-tau-ook, X [L.S.]
Kohn-ye-au-gong, X, alias Jake Stroud [L.S.]
Sha-qui-ea-sa, X [L.S.]
Teer-oos, X, alias Captain Printup [L.S.]
Soos-ha-oo-wau, X [L.S.]
Henry Young Brant, X [L.S.]
Sonh-yoo-wau-na, X, alias Big Sky [L.S.]
O-na-ah-hah, X [L.S.]
Hot-osh-a-henh, X [L.S.]
Kau-kon-da-nai-ya, X [L.S.]
Non-di-yau-ka, X [L.S.]
Kos-sish-to-wau, his X mark, [L.S.]
Oo-jau-gent-a, X, alias Fish Carrier [L.S.]
To-he-ong-go, X [L.S.]
Oot-a-gaus-so, X [L.S.]
Joo-non-dau-wa-onch, X [L.S.]
Ki-yau-ha-onh, X [L.S.]
Oo-tau-je-au-genh, X, alias Broken Axe [L.S.]
Tau-ho-on-dos, X, or Open the Way [L.S.]
Twau-ke-wash-a, X [L.S.]
Se-quid-ong-quee, X, alias Little Beard [L.S.]
Ko-djeoto, X, or Half Town [L.S.]
Ken-jau-au-gus, X, or Stinking Fish [L.S.]
Soo-noh-qua-kaum, X [L.S.]
Twen-ni-ya-na, X [L.S.]
Jish-kaa-ga, X, or Green Grasshopper, alias Little Billy [L.S.]
Tug-geh-shot-ta, X [L.S.]
Teh-ong-ya-gau-na, X [L.S.]
The-ong-yoo-wush, X [L.S.]
Kon-ne-yoo-we-sot, X [L.S.]
Ti-oo-quot-ta-kau-na, X, or Woods on Fire [L.S.]
Ta-oun-dau-deesh, X [L.S.]
Ho-na-ya-wus, X, alias Farmer's Brother [L.S.]

Sog-goo-ya-waut-hau, X, alias Red Jacket [L.S.]
Kon-yoo-tai-yoo, X [L.S.]
Sauh-ta-ka-ong-yees, X, or Two Skies of a Length [L.S.]
Oun-na-shatta-kau, X [L.S.]
Ka-ung-ya-neh-quee, X [L.S.]
Soo-a-yoo-wau, X [L.S.]
Kau-je-a-ga-onh, X, alias Heap of Dogs [L.S.]
Soo-nooh-shoo-wau, X [L.S.]
Tha-og-wau-ni-as, X [L.S.]
Soo-nong-joo-wau, X [L.S.]
Ki-ant-whau-ka, X, alias Corn Planter [L.S.]
Kau-neh-shong-goo, X [L.S.]
Witnesses:

> Israel Chapin.
> William Shepard, jr.
> James Smedley.
> John Wickham.
> Augustus Porter.
> James H. Garnsey.
> William Ewing.
> Israel Chapin, jr.
> Horatio Jones,
> Joseph Smith,
> Jasper Parish,

Interpreters.

> Henry Abeele.

Two

A General View of New York

Source: Horatio Gates Spafford, "A General View of New York,"
in *A Gazetteer of the State of New York* (Albany: H. C. Southwick,
1813), 35–36.

In 1813 Horatio Gates Spafford published
A Gazetteer of the State of New York. The book described the history,
geography, and economy of New York, as well as the state's shifting
demographics since the American Revolution. Spafford included in the
gazetteer a section titled "A General Overview of New York," in which he
described New England as the principal source of the people who were
rapidly settling the frontier of New York State. He explained in positive
terms how these new settlers were altering the society and economy of
the state. Excerpts from that section are featured here.

❧ ❧ ❧

[…]
  But the revolution produced great changes in this state, which was
constantly a principal theatre of the war, and often that of its sangui-
nary conflicts. No part of the union, felt more of its immediate consequences or better sustained its American character in that period. And
the changes produced by the revolution, were, in general, favorable to
the character of the state at large. That the principles of civil government and rational liberty were well understood here, the Constitution,

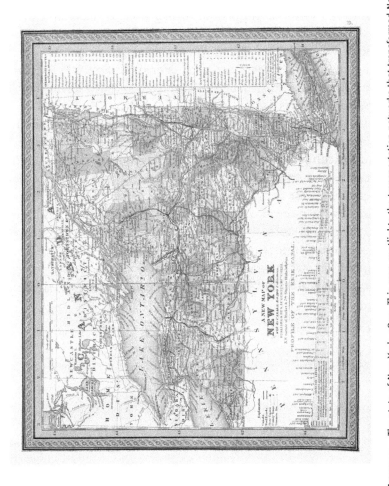

Figure 2. The state of New York, 1849. This map spotlights the transportation networks that transformed New York's landscape and made it the most populous state in antebellum America. (Library of Congress)

and its adoption at that early period, furnish conclusive evidence. To diffuse and perpetuate this knowledge, the municipal plan of the government, became a most efficient mean—for dignity of character is a natural consequence of self-knowledge, and individual consideration. The prosperity that succeeded the peace, widely diffused a spirit of enterprize and of emigration; and the successive increase of population and wealth in this state, is without parallel in modern history. Of the immigrants added to our population during this period, a large portion have come from the eastern states, principally agriculturalists, to settle the new lands of the western region, though many others are mechanics, merchants, traders, and professional characters. Every part of the state has received them; and Europe has also yielded considerable numbers, from all parts. [. . .]

The new character imparted by the influx of imigrants, is beneficial to the whole—and with the New-England people, have come their improved agriculture, their enterprize, their ingenuity in the arts, and their social habits. And through their perseverance and zeal, they are rapidly gaining a vast ascendancy in the state. From these, much has been learnt by the more ancient inhabitants, and something has been added to the general stock of knowledge from all those, who have come from many nations. And while we allow each its share of merit, candor will see in the distinct preservation of national character, the best guarantee for public health, and general and national prosperity. [. . .]

THREE

New York Population Growth

Source: New York State, *Census of the State of New York for 1855* (Albany: C. VanBenthuysen, 1857), xxxiii–xxxiv.

The compilers of the *Census of the State of New York for 1855* documented the rapid population growth of the state since 1790. In the introduction to the published census, the compilers highlighted this growth over time in several charts, including one that lists the population of each county in each of the twelve censuses taken since adoption of the United States Constitution. That chart is featured here.[1]

Although the United States Constitution only requires the federal government to take a census every ten years—and it does so at the end of each decade—in 1825 New York started conducting its own census every ten years, taken in the middle of the decade.[2] Unfortunately, the censuses prior to 1845 did not record the place of birth for the men and women counted and therefore do not indicate the origins of the growing population.[3] However, the chart demonstrates the geography

---

1. To aid the reader, this chart has been reproduced here with a few minor alterations, including the inclusion of the top row at the top of each page. In the published version of the *Census of the State of New York for 1855*, this chart is printed on a single page.

2. New York State, *Census of the State of New York for 1855*, xi; Second Constitution of the State of New York, 1821, Article 1, Section 2.

3. Darlington, "Peopling the Post-Revolutionary New York Frontier," 343–44.

of this population boom, particularly its effects in the western part of the state. For example, Ontario County grew 1,415 percent between 1790 and 1800; 276 percent between 1800 and 1810; and 210 percent between 1810 and 1820. And this growth occurred even as the state created fourteen new counties from the territory that comprised Ontario County in 1790.

* * *

COUNTIES.	1790	1800	1810	1814	1820	1825	1830	1835	1840	1845	1850	1855
Albany,	75,736	34,043	34,661	33,885	38,116	42,821	53,520	59,762	68,593	77,268	93,279	103,681
Allegany,	....	....	1,942	3,834	9,330	18,164	26,276	35,214	40,975	40,084	37,808	42,910
Broome,	....	....	8,130	9,581	14,343	13,893	17,579	20,190	22,338	25,808	30,660	36,650
Cattaraugus,	....	....	458	....	4,090	8,643	16,724	24,986	28,872	30,169	38,950	39,530
Cayuga	....	15,871	29,843	37,318	38,897	42,743	47,948	49,202	50,338	49,663	55,458	53,571
Chautauque,	....	....	2,381	4,259	12,568	20,640	34,671	44,869	47,975	46,548	50,493	53,380
Chemung,	....	....	....	....	....	....	....	....	20,732	23,689	28,821	27,288
Chenango,	....	15,666	21,704	24,221	31,215	34,215	37,238	40,762	40,785	39,900	40,311	39,915
Clinton,	1,614	8,514	8,002	7,764	12,070	14,486	19,344	20,742	28,157	31,278	40,047	42,482
Columbia,	27,732	35,322	32,390	33,979	38,330	37,970	39,907	40,746	43,252	41,976	43,252	44,391
Cortland,	....	....	8,869	10,893	16,507	20,271	23,791	24,168	24,607	25,081	25,140	24,575
Delaware,	....	10,228	20,303	21,290	26,587	29,565	33,024	34,192	35,396	36,990	39,834	39,749
Dutchess,	45,266	49,775	51,363	43,708	46,615	46,698	50,926	50,704	52,398	55,124	58,992	60,635
Erie,	....	....	....	....	....	24,316	35,719	57,594	62,465	78,635	100,993	132,331
Essex,	....	*	9,477	9,949	12,811	15,993	19,287	20,699	23,634	25,102	31,148	28,539
Franklin,	....	....	2,617	2,568	4,439	7,978	11,312	12,501	16,518	18,692	25,102	25,477
Fulton,	....	....	....	....	....	....	....	....	18,049	18,579	20,171	23,284
Genesee,	....	....	12,588	23,975	58,093	40,905	52,147	58,588	59,587	28,845	28,488	31,034
Greene,	....	12,584	19,536	20,211	22,996	26,229	29,525	30,173	30,446	31,957	33,126	31,137
Hamilton,	....	....	....	....	1,251	†	1,325	†	1,907	1,882	2,188	2,543
Herkimer,	....	14,479	22,046	20,837	31,017	33,040	35,870	36,201	37,477	37,424	38,244	38,566
Jefferson,	....	....	15,140	18,564	32,952	41,650	48,493	53,088	60,984	64,999	68,153	65,420

(Continued)

31

(Continued)

COUNTIES.	1790	1800	1810	1814	1820	1825	1830	1835	1840	1845	1850	1855
Kings,	4,495	5,740	8,303	7,655	11,187	14,679	20,535	32,057	47,613	78,691	138,882	216,229
Lewis,	.....	.....	6,433	6,848	9,227	11,669	15,239	16,093	17,830	20,218	24,564	25,229
Livingston,	.....	.....	.....	.....	.....	23,860	27,729	31,092	35,140	33,193	40,875	37,943
Madison,	.....	.....	25,144	26,276	32,208	35,646	39,038	41,741	40,008	40,987	43,072	43,687
Monroe,	.....	.....	.....	.....	.....	39,108	49,855	58,085	64,902	70,899	87,650	96,324
Montgomery,	28,848	21,700	41,214	40,640	37,569	40,902	43,715	48,359	35,818	29,643	31,992	30,808
New York,	33,131	60,489	96,373	95,519	123,706	166,086	197,112	270,089	312,710	371,223	515,547	629,904
Niagara,	.....	.....	8,971	7,477	22,990	14,069	18,482	26,490	31,132	34,550	42,276	48,282
Oneida,	.....	22,047	33,792	45,228	50,997	57,847	71,326	77,518	85,310	84,776	99,566	107,749
Onondaga,	.....	7,406	25,987	30,801	41,467	48,435	58,973	60,908	67,911	70,175	85,890	86,575
Ontario,	1,075	15,218	42,032	56,892	88,267	37,422	40,288	40,870	43,501	42,592	43,929	42,672
Orange,	18,492	29,345	34,347	34,908	41,213	41,732	45,366	45,096	50,739	52,227	57,145	60,868
Orleans,	.....	.....	.....	.....	.....	14,460	17,732	22,893	25,127	25,845	28,501	28,435
Oswego,	.....	.....	.....	.....	12,374	17,875	27,119	38,245	43,619	48,441	62,198	69,398
Otsego,	.....	21,636	38,802	40,587	44,856	47,898	51,372	50,428	49,628	50,509	48,638	49,735
Queens,	16,014	16,893	19,336	19,269	21,519	20,331	22,460	25,130	30,324	31,849	36,833	46,266
Rensselaer,	.....	30,442	36,309	36,833	40,153	44,065	49,424	55,515	60,259	62,338	73,363	79,234
Richmond,	3,835	4,563	5,347	5,502	6,135	5,932	7,082	7,691	10,965	13,673	15,061	21,389
Rockland,	.....	6,353	7,758	7,817	8,837	8,016	9,388	9,696	11,975	13,741	16,962	19,511
St. Lawrence,	.....	.....	7,885	8,252	16,037	27,595	36,354	42,047	56,706	62,354	68,617	74,977
Saratoga,	.....	24,483	33,147	31,139	36,052	36,295	38,679	38,012	40,553	41,477	45,646	49,379
Schenectady,	.....	.....	10,201	11,203	13,081	12,876	12,347	16,230	17,387	16,630	20,054	19,572

COUNTIES.	1790	1800	1810	1814	1820	1825	1830	1835	1840	1845	1850	1855
Schoharie,	.....	9,808	18,945	19,323	23,154	25,926	27,902	28,508	32,358	32,488	33,548	33,519
Schuyler,	.....	.....	.....	.....	.....	.....	.....	.....	.....	.....	.....	18,777
Seneca,	.....	.....	16,609	21,401	23,619	20,169	21,041	22,627	24,879	24,972	25,441	25,358
Steuben,	.....	1,788	7,246	11,121	21,989	29,245	33,851	41,435	46,138	51,679	63,771	62,965
Suffolk,	16,440	19,464	21,113	21,368	24,272	23,695	26,780	28,274	32,469	34,579	36,922	40,906
Sullivan,	.....	.....	6,108	6,233	8,900	10,373	12,364	13,755	15,629	18,727	25,088	29,487
Tioga,	.....	6,889	7,889	10,438	19,971	19,971	27,690	33,999	20,527	22,456	24,880	26,962
Tompkins,	.....	.....	.....	.....	20,681	32,908	36,545	38,008	37,948	38,168	38,746	31,516
Ulster,	29,397	24,855	26,576	26,428	30,934	32,015	36,550	39,960	45,822	49,907	59,384	67,936
Warren,	.....	.....	.....	7,838	9,453	10,906	11,796	12,034	13,422	14,908	17,199	19,669
Washington,	14,042	35,574	44,289	36,359	38,831	39,280	42,635	39,326	41,080	40,554	44,750	44,405
Wayne,	.....	.....	.....	.....	.....	26,761	33,643	37,788	42,057	42,515	44,953	46,760
Westchester,	24,003	27,428	30,272	26,367	32,638	33,131	36,456	38,690	48,686	47,578	58,263	80,678
Wyoming,	.....	.....	.....	.....	.....	.....	.....	.....	.....	27,205	31,981	32,140
Yates,	.....	.....	.....	.....	.....	13,214	19,009	19,796	20,444	20,777	20,590	19,812
Total,	340,120	588,603	961,888	1,035,910	1,372,812	1,614,456	1,913,131	2,174,517	2,428,921	2,604,495	3,097,394	3,466,212

* Reported with Clinton † Reported with Montgomery

FOUR

New York's Environmental Transformation

Source: [Susan Fenimore Cooper], *Rural Hours* (New York: George P. Putnam, 1850), 189–90.

In 1850, Susan Fenimore Cooper anonymously published *Rural Hours*, which documented rural life in the Mohawk Valley during the first half of the nineteenth century. Cooper was the daughter of the famed American writer James Fenimore Cooper and the granddaughter of William Cooper, who had founded the Village of Otsego (now Cooperstown, New York) in 1785. *Rural Hours* is based on a journal in which Susan Fenimore Cooper described in rich detail the environment in New York.[1] She also wrote romantically about the transformation of the landscape as large waves of white Americans moved into the area and dismissively about the Native Americans they displaced. The selection below from *Rural Hours* represents some of Cooper's reflections on the rapid change that occurred in the area during her lifetime.

🌿 🌿 🌿

[. . .]

---

1. Rochelle L. Johnson and Daniel Patterson, eds., *Susan Fenimore Cooper: New Essays on "Rural Hours" and Other Works* (Athens: University of Georgia Press, 2001), xiii–xviii.

Figure 3. Cooperstown from Three Mile Point, 1850–1860. This oil painting by landscape artist Louis Rémy Mignot—a contemporary of Susan Fenimore Cooper—depicts the village of Cooperstown on the edge of Otsego Lake. (Courtesy Fenimore Art Museum, Cooperstown, New York)

At length, nearly three long centuries after the Genoese had crossed the ocean, the white man came to plant a home on this spot, and it was then the great change began; the axe and the saw, the forge and the wheel, were busy from dawn to dusk, cows and swine fed in thickets whence the wild beasts had fled, while the ox and the horse drew away in chains the fallen trunks of the forest. The tenants of the wilderness shrunk deeper within its bounds with every changing moon; the wild creatures fled away within the receding shades of the forest, and the red man followed on their track; his day of power was gone, his hour of pitiless revenge had passed, and the last echoes of the war-whoop were dying away forever among these hills, when the pale-faces laid their hearth-stones by the lake shore. The red man, who for thousands of years had been lord of the land, no longer treads the soil; he exists here only in uncertain memories, and in forgotten graves.

Such has been the change of the last half century. Those who from childhood have known the cheerful dwellings of the village, the broad and fertile farms, the well beaten roads, such as they are to-day, can hardly credit that this has all been done so recently by a band of men, some of whom, white-headed and leaning on their staves, are still among us. Yet such is the simple truth. This village lies just on the borders of the tract of country which was opened and peopled immediately after the Revolution; it was among the earliest of those little colonies from the sea-board which struck into the wilderness at that favorable moment, and whose rapid growth and progress in civilization have become a byword. Other places, indeed, have far surpassed this quiet borough; Rochester, Buffalo, and others of a later date, have become great cities, while this remains a rural village; still, whenever we pause to recall what has been done in this secluded valley during the lifetime of one genera-tion, we must needs be struck with new astonishment. And throughout every act of the work, those old pines were there. Unchanged them-selves, they stand surrounded by objects over all of which a great change has passed. The open valley, the half-shorn hills, the paths, the flocks, the buildings, the woods in their second growth, even the waters in the different images they reflect on their bosom, the very race of men who come and go, all are different from what they were; and those calm old trees seem to heave the sigh of companionless age, as their coned heads rock slowly in the winds. [. . .]

PART II

Missionaries

Missionaries from New England had prose-
lytized among Native Americans in central and western New York in the
eighteenth century. While those missionary efforts continued in the
nineteenth century, Protestant evangelists increasingly directed their
attention to the white Americans who settled the region.

The rise in the number of missionaries in the area was driven in part
by concern that people in New England felt for their distant friends
and relatives. Some worried that once on the American frontier and
away from the communities and churches to which their families had
belonged for generations, these transplanted New Englanders would
forsake their religious devotion.[1]

Others saw opportunity in the massive migration from New England.
For instance, Methodist and Baptist missionaries recognized that
physical distance from New England—and the religious traditions of
their families and former communities—would result in a population
ready to consider joining a denomination they may not have considered
before. This expansion in the religious marketplace and shift in denominational affiliation happened throughout the United States, but

---

1. Cross, *Burned-Over District*, 7–8.

the mass migration of New Englanders and the corresponding increase in the number of missionaries appear to have made the trend especially pronounced in New York.[2]

This part features six documents. The first is the journal that Timothy Mather Cooley kept during his eighteen-week mission to New York in 1803, which includes reports on the number of converts from his preaching and the condition of churches in the region's various settlements. It is a long journal, but it is likely the most detailed overview of the state of religion in those settlements near the start of the nineteenth century. This part also includes a brief published account of the Reverend Jacob Cram's mission to New York and the published response of a Native American leader, Sagoyewatha (also known as Red Jacket), to Cram's request to preach to the Six Nations. That document is followed by the constitution of the Waterloo Missionary Society, a record that demonstrates the commitment to missionary work of Christians in western New York and the people's organizing efforts to support missionaries in the region and beyond. Finally, this part features reports on the evangelizing efforts of Episcopalians in the Burned-over District and a report of the American Bethel Society, which worked to convert to Christianity men working on the Erie Canal.

---

2. Cross, 14–29.

FIVE

Timothy Mather Cooley's Missionary Journal

Source: The original journal is held by the Manuscript Division of the William L. Clements Library at the University of Michigan. The transcript featured here was made from a manuscript copy of that journal in the New York State Library. See "Timothy M. Cooley Missionary Journal, 1803, 1876, 1886," New York State Library, SC10255.

In June 1803 Timothy Mather Cooley left his home in East Granville, Massachusetts, for a mission in New York that lasted eighteen weeks. A Congregationalist minister, Cooley served with the support of the Hampshire Missionary Society in Oneida, Chenango, and Onondaga Counties. A significant component of missionary work at this time was the distribution of religious literature, and Cooley recorded the number of books he left in each place he visited.[1] Throughout his journal Cooley inserted notes marked by the pound symbol (#) in which he specified the population of the settlements he

---

1. According to his journal, the books that Cooley carried with him on his mission included Philip Doddridge, *The Rise and Progress of Religion in the Soul* (Leeds: J. Binns, 1795); Andrew Fuller, *The Gospel Worthy of All Acceptation* (Northampton, MA: T. Dicey, 1785); Joseph Lathrop, *Two Sermons on the Christian Sabbath, for Distribution in the New Settlements of the United States* (Northampton, MA: William Butler, 1803).

visited and the state of religion therein, sometimes with references to numbers on a corresponding map of the area.

❧ ❧ ❧

Missionary Journal

June 5.1803.

This day after committing my family to the care of a kind providence, I set out for a Missionary tour of eighteen weeks by appointment of the Hampshire Missionary Society. I rode to Northampton and received my commission and other necessary papers from Rev. Mr. Williams. When I arrived at Albany I paid attention to the books for distribution which belong to the Society and sent them on to Utica by the Stage.

I found that Mr. Knott could not procure so many of <u>Dodridge's rise and progress of religion</u> as was expected. Obtained 18 <u>Fuller's Gospel</u> &c. and 12 Dodridges and enclosed them safely in a box and sent them with our other books to Utica.

Note—paid to a layman 18 cents. To Stage owners for transporting books $3.50

June 12.

Rode to Esq. Braylon's in Deerfield on the Mohawk and at his request conclude to spend the Sabbath here. Last night I was very unwell, owing to fatigue and a change of air and water.

To day I feel better and hope to gain strength enough to preach to this people to-morrow.

All God's dealings are right.

I have been too confident that my health would be good, but God is showing me that my dependence must be wholly in Him.

June 13. Lord's day.

I preached at Deerfield. The Audience were mostly Baptists and Methodists. Their behaviour was decent. But such a Sabbath I never witnessed before.

The road is thronged with teams and travelers and the house with company.

My Landlady is apparently pious, but I think it must be difficult to live a life of religion in a public house where the Sabbath is so little regarded.

June 14.

Rode to Utica to attend to the Books. They have arrived, but to my great mortification I find that some of them have been injured. The manner of transporting our books by the Stage is expensive and unsafe.

They might be sent on by water from Albany with one third of the expense and with greater security.

The damage done the books is not so great. The covers of some of the pamphlets are worn off and some of the Bibles have been slightly injured.

Rode on to Trenton to unite in Missionary labors with Rev. Mr. Fish and find him a very amiable man. We visited a school. Made arrangements for our future labors. I agree to take a tour of four weeks to the settlements on Black river.

June 16.

In the morning I commenced my tour to the Black river. Rode to Remsen # and visited two schools and left 14 pamphlets with one and 21 with the other. The people appeared kind and needy. At 4 o'Clock preached a lecture. Here they have a Mr. Alexander who officiates as preacher. He is not a professor of religion and some doubt whether that is his real name. The ignorant people of the place are attached to him.

They say he preaches better than they practise and I believe better than he practises himself.

Last Sabbath he disappointed his audience. He went a fishing Saturday and did not return till after the Sabbath!!

Note Remsen is situated near the source of Black River. contains 45 families. 2 schools. no church and but few professors of religion. People poor, stupid and ignorant. Some baptists.

June 17.

visited a rich family.

Prayed and conversed with parents and children. They appeared serious. Rode to Leyden # and preached at Mr. Southwell's.

Note Leyden was first settled 1796. Divided into Storm's patent and Boon's upper settlement. High Falls on Black river in the corner of the Town, 50 feet. contains 150 families. a church formed by Mr. Ely. now in a broken state.

June 20. Lord's day

The weather rainy and the meeting in the forenoon was thin. Afternoon preached from Rev. 2, 17.

There is a Baptist meeting within two miles of me and a Methodist meeting within a quarter of a mile.

The latter failed for want of hearers.

After my exercises were closed a Methodist by the name of [*space left blank by author*] was introduced by two or three of that order. He preached a shocking sermon and displeased his own employers. Two hours before sunset I preached a lecture at Mr. Roice's and baptized

Noble Squire

Betsy Roice

Polly Roice

Hannah Roice

June 21.

At Shalor's Mills in Turin # preached a lecture and about 40 were present. Appearances were favorable.

<u>Note</u> Turin lies on Black River. comprises No. 3 and 4. soil excellent. contains 120 families. In 1802 a church was formed consisting of 18 members. Here is a Baptist church But few Methodists. The people are desirous of settling a minister.

June 22.

Spent the forenoon in visiting several families and conversing on eternal concerns. visited a school. Afternoon preached a lecture at Mr. Underwood's. The house was filled and many were about the door.

June 23.

Visited several families and one school. At 4 o'Clock preached a lecture at the school house near Capᵗ Clap's. About 60 present.

Some came 6 or 7 miles to attend the lecture. After lecture in company with Major Bush and Major Barns I ascended Prospect Hill (so named by Col. Taylor) This eminence commands an extensive prospect of woods. In the days of the Millenium It will unquestionably command a prospect of unnumbered houses and churches, where the duties of family and public worship will be performed in a degree of purity unknown in the present age of stupidity and corruption.

June 24.

Rode through #Martinsburgh and appointed to attend a lecture on my return. Rode to Lowville and called on Deacon Kelly a Baptist teacher. Told him I was a Missionary. He appeared cold. Found some fault with Missionaries for propagating their own peculiar persuasion and sentiments. I told him their object was to preach the gospel of Christ.

I enquired of whether the people in his vicinity would attend a lecture if one were appointed. He said they were not very warm in religion. He appeared to be a most bigotted Baptist pleading for candor in others but possessing none himself. He has in some instances treated Missionaries with shameful neglect. His treatment of me was barely civil.

At last I told him if he thought the people would not attend a lecture I should pass on to the next town.

This appeared to startle him. He was unwilling to have the dust of Missionaries shaken off through his means, tho' I have reason to believe it was his choice I should not preach in the place. Upon this he directed me to the North part of the town and I rode on four miles and found a number of pious people thirsting for Missionary labors. I found afterwards that a number of people in the neighbourhood of Deac[n] Kelly were much displeased that he did not invite me to spend a day with them. And preach a lecture. He is opposed to the formation of a church in this town and will probably be a great damage to the people whenever they contemplate the settlement of a Minister. I visited a school which was under the care of a man of Deistical sentiments. Gave the children 15 Henry's life. Rode to the Northern part of the town. visited a school and left 7 Henry's to be given to the best proficients in the Catechism at the close of the summer school. A little before sunset preached a lecture.

In the evening conversed till a very late hour with a number of pious people. Lodged at Mr. Water's.

Mr. Woodward a Missionary spent four months in the Black river Settlements and left them without knowing that he had in a single instance, been the means of saving good but in this family (Mr. Water) is a pious girl who was a fixed universalist, but by his conversation she was alarmed and has become a hopeful convert. Ministers may be the means of converting souls and not know it, till they meet them as their joy and crown of rejoicing at the day of Judgement.

Martinsburg alias <u>the Triangle</u> was first settled in 1801. contains 20 or 30 families. People stupid and vicious. no church. no meetings held on the Sabbath.

June 25.

Left Lowville # and rode through # Harrisburgh where I made an appointment to preach a lecture to-morrow, then rode to Champion. Preached a preparatory lecture at 4 o'clock. But few attended.

Lowville was settled first 1798. now contains 160 families. many pious people. no church. Some Baptists. People flourishing. will soon be able to support the Gospel.

Harrisburgh was settled 1800. contains No. 5 and 10.50 families. no church. People of different denominations. In the West part of the town, the people meet on the Sabbath read and [*blank*] but have no prayers.

June 26.

Rode back to Harrisburgh where I had yesterday notified a lecture and preached at 4 o'Clock. There was a general attendance and the people appeared kind and thankful. Several came 5 miles to attend the lecture. Left with them one Dodridge's address. One Trustees Address. Sent them one Dodridge's rise and progress.

June 27. Lord's day.

I preached at Champion and administered the sacrament. Took two members into the church by letters of recommendation.

Baptized Polly Warner. There was a decent assembly and they appeared solemn and attentive.

In the intermission of public worship it was mentioned to me that there was a child in the room who had hopefully experienced religion. He was 9 years old. I called him to me and enquired into the state and exercises of his mind, by the following questions. Do you love religion? "yes". Did you always love religion? "No." How long since you loved religion? Not being able to calculate time his mother answered for him that it was about seven or eight weeks since she first discovered any special impressions on his mind. Do you love God and Christ? "yes". Why do you love Christ? "Because he is true". Do you love good folks? "Yes". Do you love wicked folks? "yes". "I want to [do?] 'em good". Do you ever pray to God? "yes". Why do you pray, do pray do you think your prayers will save you from hell and carry you to heaven? "No. I love to pray. I love God and I love to pray". How do you spend the Sabbath day, do you play with your mates on the Sabbath? "No I had rather pray."

In many other questions he answered to the great astonishment of all who heard him. I then gave him a little book entitled extracts from Henry's life.

He asked me what the book told about? I told him it gave an account of a pious Minister who was serious when he was ten years old.

He said he should love to read it.

He went to meeting in the Afternoon and seated himself near me and was as attentive as any one in the Assembly.

I was informed that there were four other children in the neighbour-hood with this one who had become hopefully pious. I directed this little child to notify his mates to meet the next day at nine o'Clock and I would ride to the neighbourhood and meet with them.

June 28.

This morning I travelled four miles to a lovely neighbourhood near the banks of the Black river, where these pious little children lived. I found them collected. As soon as I entered the house I was struck with the solemnity which appeared in their countenances. To see a number of little children discovering in their countenances a deep sense of eter-nal things, was a sight truly striking and pleasing.

I then enquired into the experiences and exercises of each of them. Their answers to my questions were rational and modest.

They gave as great evidence of being Christians as could be rationally expected from children of their age. Two were 9 years old. one eleven. one twelve and one thirteen.

I made enquiry into the first rise of this work among these children and found the particulars to be as follows:

Sometime in May last Josiah Townsend the child first mentioned as his mother was preparing to go to a meeting asked leave to go with. She discouraged him. He was very urgent, which led his mother to ask what he wished to go for? He said, "To hear the Minister preach". She told him he might have a Meeting at home. Upon this he with two or three other children met and attended to some religious duties.

The next evening the children in [the] neighbourhood all met. The meeting was a very solemn one. These meetings have been continued twice a week ever since. They read, pray and sing hymns. In the second meeting Betsy Townsend a girl about 9 years was struck down and lay about two hours helpless. I asked the following questions. Did you feel greatly distressed just before you was struck down? "No." Did you feel great joy? "No. I felt happy." Could you help being struck down? "No." Did you know any thing what took place; or any thing which your parents did to you while in this situation? "No."

When she revived, she began in whispers and afterwards in loud cries, Glory to God! Glory to God! In the course of three or four weeks two others were struck down and exhibited similar symptoms with the one mentioned above. One of them lay about 12 hours in this situation and all the exertions of her parents were ineffectual to bring her to her right mind.

I told these children that they must not conclude they were Christians because they had experienced these bodily convulsions.

They were no evidence of true grace. I told them religion consisted in right exercises of heart toward God and duty.

It is singular that these children should be awakened to attend to the concerns of their souls, when there is no awakening around them.

They did not perform these duties in invitation of others, for they rarely have a meeting in the neighborhood.

They now appear steady and modest and choose to say but little to strangers except to answer questions.

I have stated facts and leave the reader to determine concerning this singular work for himself.

Rode to Rutland and preached a lecture to a decent collection of people.

People contributed $1.79

Champion lies on the bend of Black river near the long falls. Was first settled 1798. contains 100 families. A church of 20 members. They have pitched upon the ground for an Academy; which for a while is to answer for a meeting.

Rutland first settled 1799. contains 100 families. 3 schools. no church.

Memorandum.

Gave each of the pious children one of Henry's life. Left at Champion one Trustees address. 2 Dodridges' Address. 1 Plain truths to be circulated among the people. 6 Henry's life to the school.

June 29.

Rode to Brownville and felt dejected, little expecting a kind reception. The place is vicious. Put out my horse at the Hotel. Sat down and felt discouraged. At length walked over to Brown's, the chief man of the settlement and to my disappointment found him a Quaker. Revealed my Missionary character and he treated me kindly. He engaged to notify a lecture and procured a room in the Hotel for our meeting. I thought there could be nothing good in this place, but to my agreeable disappointment Mr. Brown soon brought in a man of eminent piety and he spent the afternoon with me, till the time of meeting. I found a <u>Lot</u> even in Sodom. At six o'Clock I preached a lecture and was enabled to preach with freedom to sinners. 50 attended. After lecture was invited to take lodgings at Mr. Brown's and found his family hospitable. I proposed to attend prayers in his family. He declined!!!!

June 30.

Sat out for Sachets Harbour and lost my way in the woods. Spent half the day to no purpose wandering among sloughs and woods. At noon found the road and went to Sachets Harbour. At 6 o'Clock preached a lecture. 45 were present. Almost every man, woman, and child in the settlement attended.

<u>Satchets Harbour.</u> situated on Lake Ontario at the mouth of Black river. contains 12 families. rapidly increasing by immigration. People Presbyterians if anything.

<u>Brownville</u> lies North of Black river, the settlement at the Bridge contains 30 families. Baptists and Presbyterians. At Fish Creek 6 miles distant about the same number of families.

July 1.

I found two hopefully pious women who anxiously wished to take upon themselves a profession of religion and give up their children in Baptism. As there was no prospect of a church being formed at present in this neighbourhood; I proceeded to examine these Candidates respecting their experimental acquaintance with religion. I prepared a covenant and confession of faith and in a solemn manner led them into covenant with God.

To the covenant I added this article that as soon as circumstances would admit, they should unite with some Christian church.

Admitted into the church, <u>Mrs. Sherwin</u> and Baptized,

<u>Azariah P. Sherwin</u>
<u>Limri Sherwin</u>
<u>Betsey Sherwin</u>
<u>Rhoda Sherwin</u>

Also admitted Mrs. Minerva Sachet wife of Esq. Sachet and Baptized her son Elisha C. Sachet. I gave to each of these women a certificate that they were members of the church of Christ in full communion.

This procedure I think is justified by apostolic example.

Left Sachets Harbour and rode on to Adams No. 7 on Big Sandy Creek. The roads so bad I did not arrive till dusk.

Adams comprises No 7 & 8. No. 7 contains 90 families. No. 8, 20 families. Presbyterians mostly. greatly need Missionary labors.

July 2

Rode to No. 3 and preached a lecture to nearly 50 people.

No. 2. contains 80 families. Rev. Mr. Lazel has lately moved in here and is about to organize a church. No. 3. contains 70 families.

In these two settlements there are Baptists, Methodists and Presbyterians.

July 3

Rode to Harrisburgh on Deer river and preached to a considerable collection of people on "Ezekiel's vision of the Valley of dry bones" and the very bones of which I discoursed could not be more stupid than my audience appeared to be. Gave them one Dodridge's rise.

N.B. I left in Brownville 6 Plain truths. At Sachet's harbour 10 Henry's life. Sent to Perch river one Dodridge's rise and progress to be read on the Sabbath.

Rode to Lowville.

July 3. Lord's day.

The day was pleasant and a large congregation assembled. Said to be the largest ever seen in the town. Preached two sermons in the North part of the Town and then rode to the South settlement and preached a sermon two hours before sunset. Baptized Kata Snell child of Adam Snell.

Betsey Faunetta do of Sam¹ Faunetta

Mary M. Faunetta do of Frances F.

The parents of these children were Dutch people and brought testimony of their good conduct and regular standing in a Dutch reformed church at Polatine [Palatine].

July 4

Visited several families. At 4 o'Clock I preached a lecture at widow Weller's. The house was filled and the people appeared very solemn and much affected. After the close of the usual exercises I urged some particular duties upon them and took leave of them expecting to see them no more. It was an affectionate parting.

Memorandum.

The people in Lowville contributed 1.50

Mr. Waters	25
Mrs. Waters	50
Lucy Sabins	25
Total	2.50

July 5. Rode to Martinsburgh and preached agreeably to appointment. This is the first sermon ever preached in this place. People generally attended. About 60 present. I proposed to the people to set up meetings on the Sabbath and gave them one of Dodridge's rise and progress to be read in their assemblies. Rode to Turin.

July 6. In the forenoon I visited several families and one school. At 4 o'Clock preached a lecture at the school house near Shalor's Mills. About 90 assembled and appeared to be earnest hearers of the word. Baptized <u>Richard Rockwell</u> son of Joshua R. <u>Lucretia Ives</u> child Esq. <u>Ives</u>
<u>John H. Ives</u>
<u>Sherlock Ives</u> children of Levi Ives
<u>Hannah Ives</u>
<u>Hendrick C. Bail</u>, child of H.C. Bail.

July 7. Visited several families and then rode on to Leyden. Visited and cathechised a school. I find that my former visit to this school 3 weeks ago has had a good effect. They have acquired some knowledge of the Catechism. At 4 o'Clock I preached a lecture to about 50 people.

In the evening attended a conference meeting. Gave 11 <u>plain truths</u> to the school.

July 8. Visited several families and a school in Leyden. Rode to Remsen. visited a school and find they have made a pleasing proficiency in the catechism since my last visit. Left one Hemmenway's discourses with the school to be given to the best in the catechism. Gave one to a little child as a reward for learning a hymn.

At 4 o'clock preached a sermon and the people were very attentive.

July 9. Visited a sick child in a Welsh family. There are a number of this people in the neighbourhood. They are ignorant, inoffensive and indigent.

Rode on to Boon's Settlement in Trenton and put up with Col. Mappa the Dutch. The family are very kind and courteous to me. Spent the afternoon in examining a Dutch Bible and Commentary in which I have the kind assistance of Col. Mappa, as my interpreter. In the Bible I found an impression of the shekel for which Christ was sold.

July 10. Lord's day.

Preached at Boon's patent in Trenton. The house was crowded and behaviour decent. This Village is corrupt and regardless of the Sabbath. The latter part of the Sabbath is generally devoted to visiting &c. a corrupt practise!

In the evening I visited and prayed with a sick woman. Her life hangs in a doubtful suspense. She says she has no comfort in religion.

July 11. Visited the sick woman this morning. She is better. Visited a school. And left 6 Hemenway's to be given next September to the best in the Catechism. Left one Hemenway at Col. Mappa's. In Bensen I gave a Bible to a poor family which had lately had their house burnt and one Bible to a poor family which had bought a testament because the expense of a Bible was too great.

Contributed at Boon's patent $3.31

Rode on to Rev. Mr. Fish's on Holland Patent. I have now completed my tour to the Black river settlements and am pleased with the people and the Country. Settlements are rapidly forming and they stand in great need of assistance from Missionary Societies. Now is the time while settlements are forming for Missionaries to lay a foundation for the permanent establishment of the Gospel before erroneous teachers gain influence among them.

July 12. I preached a lecture at Holland Patent to a crowded house perhaps 90 present. The people appeared serious and very attentive. There are some favorable appearances of a revival of religion in this place.

July 13. Rode to Stuben.# Visited a school and left 7 Hemenway's for those that shall excel in the Catechism. Gave one Lathrop on the Sabbath to Dea[n] Mitchell to be circulated. At 4 o'Clock preached a lecture and 60 present. By particular request I preached an evening lecture. And at a late hour retired to rest worn out with riding, conversing, preaching &c. Gave one Hemenway to Mr. Ball's children.

#Stuben contains near 600 souls. 2 churches. one Congregationalist and one Baptist. Equally divided. Baptists are breaking. This place has been favored with a very great revival of religion.

July 14. I visited a sick woman apparently on her death bed. She expects to die but feels unprepared. Rode to Western and visited two schools. Left 8 Hemenway's with one of the schools. Preached a lecture at the schoolhouse near Gen. Floyd's, but few present. Gave one Hemenway to Mr. Church.

July 15. Rode in company with Esq. Hall to Deac^n Barlow's where I conclude to spend the rest of the week and the Sabbath.

July 16. Spent the day in studying and visiting families which were formerly from Granville. Gave a Hemenway to children.

July 17. Lord's day.
My horse is gone. Mr. Miller rode three miles in pursuit of it but returned without it. Before nine o'Clock my horse was found and brought. I preached in the schoolhouse near Deac^n Barlow's. The house though large was filled and numbers about the door. All persuasions attended and appeared solemn. Baptized Cloe Miller
I preached a third sermon at the school house near Dr. Hutchinson's. It was filled and people were very attentive.

July 18. Spent the day in visiting a number of families and conversing on religious subjects. Lodged Esq Weeks'.

July 19. Visited a school of about 80 children. At 2 o'clock I attending a meeting in which different denominations proposed to meet. 200 were present tho' in the busy season of Harvest.
Mr. Nelson a Missionary preached a sermon. I then preached a sermon and there was a fixed attention thro' the whole exercises. Rode on and lodged with Capt Donely. And as he expected me to administer baptism to his family next Sabbath, I spent the evening in catechising and instructing his children. Gave them one of Hemmenway's discourses.

July 20. I rode to Floyd. Visited a school. Went to the lecture and thought nobody would attend. Began with seven or eight adults. But before the close of the meeting the house was considerably filled with and people were attentive.
Left three pamphlets with Mr. Bacon to be circulated.
Floyd has been settled 13 years, named from Gen. Floyd. Contains about 80 families, mostly Methodists, some Baptists, but few Presbyterians. People ignorant, bigoted and vicious.

July 21. Rode to Stuben and visited a school of about thirty children. They are ignorant of the catechism. Advised the teacher to instruct them in it.

Gave 3 Hemmenway's to be adjudged to the best in the catechism at the close of the Summer school.

At 4 o'Clock preached a lecture, which on account of a misunderstanding relative to the appointment was but thinly attended.

July 22. Rode to Holland patent expecting to find letters from my family but am disappointed.

July 23 Returned to Stuben and visited several families on the way. Visited Capt. Starr who was formerly a professor of Christianity but is now an avowed Deist. I attended a conference meeting with the church preparatory to the sacrament. Recommended the duty of self-examination. Answered a number of questions which were proposed on the subject of church discipline.

I visited the Grave of the Great Baron Stuben. He lies by the Highway under a Hemlock whose branches hang like the weeping willow. This he called his umbrella and often said in his lifetime he meant to be buried under it. He desired that none might see his face after it had become pale in death. A few rough boards nailed from tree to tree guard the spot from the foot of the intruders!! "Ici transit gloria mundi".

July 24. Lord's day. Received letters from my family and thro' the goodness of God all are well. I preached in the school house in Stuben and all denominations attended. Administered the sacrament to the Church.

I baptized Eleazar Donely, George G. Donely, Joseph W. Donely, John Donely, Bettey Donely, Martha Donely, children of Capt. Donely Also Levi Fowler child of Levi Fowler

One person with his wife and child rode 12 miles to attend meeting. He has formerly been Deistical. In the intermission he came to me and with a solemn countenance requested me to Answer this question "What shall I do to be saved." He informed me that his wife and several young people were very anxiously concerned for their souls and would be profited by hearing that interesting question explained.

About nine days ago I visited this man and he suggested some cavils against the Bible; but his conversation is now greatly changed. Whether this change will result in saving good, is known only to Him who has all hearts in his hands.

After meeting rode to Mr. Ingham's and a number of Christian people came in and spent the rest of the day in profitable conversation.

July 25. Rode to Mr. Wells' and dined. Left one Lathrop on the Sabbath. Rode with kind friends to Mr. Church's in an obscure neighbourhood in Western. In the evening his children who are settled around him, came in and we had a solemn meeting. After conversing for three hours on the concerns of the soul, I put the question to each of them, whether they were willing to become the followers of Christ? They all appeared to wish for religion. May God give them His grace.

July 26. Rode a circuit of 6 miles through the woods to visit two sick persons. One of them before I reached the house was in eternity. He died a papist. While he was expiring the family kneeled around the bed and with tears implored the Virgin Mary and the saints to intercede for them. I conversed with the family and found them extremely ignorant. I asked for their testament which they gave me.

The translation is different from ours, but sense as far as my examination extended was the same. Within an hour after leaving this family of papists I was sent for to preach the funeral sermon. At 2 o'Clock preached a sermon and the Catholic people were serious and attentive. After the exercises were closed I rode a mile through the woods and preached a lecture which I had previously appointed. People appeared to really to feel divine truth. Spent the evening to a very late hour in conversing with pious people who came in. At a late hour retired to rest, worn out with the pleasing labors of the day. Left one Bible. 2 Dodridge's address. 4 Hemmenway's to different persons in this neighbourhood.

July 27. Rode five miles and attended the funeral of [a] child. Preached a sermon. The father of the child has been a Deist. He appears to be much affected with this call. Took leave of kind friends in Western and rode to Rome. Esq. Hathaway's. Rome is not Missionary ground.

July 28. Rode to Verona # near Oneida Castle and was very kindly received by Mr. Langdon.
Verona has been settled six years. contains 70 families. Industrious and moral. Congregationalists. A church formed the present summer consisting of 22 members happily united. It lies between Fort Stanwix and Oneida Castle. deserves the notice of Missionaries.

July 29. Visited a school. Left one Hemenway's for the best proficient in the catechism. Visited several families. In the evening a very encouraging number collected to hear the lecture. Rev. Mr. Fish came in just before the exercises commenced and assisted.

July 30. Visited several families. Visited a school of 30 scholars. Gave them 3 Hemenway's.

July 31. Lord's Day.
I preached to a decent assembly and their appearance was favorable. In the intermission the professors met and conversed on the subject of forming a church. All agreed that they were ripe for so important a step.

After meeting at night, those who felt interested in the formation of a church were requested to sit after the Congregation had retired. It was agreed to meet on friday next to attend to the preparatory steps for the formation of a church.

Mr. Starr a pious man called on me and stated a difficulty wh. [which] had long labored in his mind. About 8 years ago he with another young man formed a resolution to offer themselves for baptism. He said with an oath he would go and get himself baptized. The other declared with an oath he was as fit for baptism as he was. Upon this they both stupid and thoughtless rushed on to the solemn ordinance of Baptism. It was administered by an Episcopalian Clergyman whose character has since proved bad. Since this Mr. Starr has been awakened and hopefully converted and now questions the validity of his Baptism. First because his own views were corrupt. Secondly because the person who administered the ordinance was immoral.

I told him that his own wrong views or the corrupt character of the person who administered the ordinance did not destroy the nature of it. If the baptisms of unholy ministers were null of course multitudes would live unbaptized and not know it &c. I told him it was unwarrantable to rebaptize him if the minister was in regular standing.

He concludes to rest satisfied with his baptism and came forward to unite with the rest at the formation of the church.

August 1. I visited a number of families and find a greater number of pious people in this place than I expected.

In this neighbourhood are three families which have taken up the duty of family prayer in consequence of conviction derived from reading Doddridge's Address, left by Rev. Mr. Jaggart the last year. At 4 o'Clock

I preached a lecture at Esq. Clark's barn. 70 present. Appearances agreeable. I conversed with the people after lecture and was heard with attention.

Aug. 2. Left Esq. Clark's and went on for a short visit to Rev. Mr. Sargeants, Stockbridge, about 9 miles from this place.

Passed by Oneida Castle and spent an hour or two among the Indians. They live in huts covered with bark.

They have an unfinished meeting in wh. Mr. Kirtland preaches to them once in a while. They raise a little corn but are not fond of husbandry.

Their gardens are irregular and poorly cultivated. They are 750 in numbers and each receives an annuity from the state of 7 dollars which keeps them drunk a number of months. I visited several of the Indians, but having no interpreter could not converse with them.

Rode on to Stockbridge Rev. Mr. Sargeants He has 450 Indians under his care.

His church consists of 27 members mostly females. The meeting house is well finished with a steeple. As soon as I arrived, he requested me to preach a lecture. Upon a very short notice about 50 collected. I preached to them on the day of Judgment and they heard with listening attention.

They carried the parts of singing with a pleasing softness and harmony.

To see these natives arise and carry on this part of worship with such regularity was very delightful. After the usual exercises were closed, they sung a number of tunes and closed with an Indian psalm.

Aug. 3. Returned from Stockbridge to Verona.

Aug. 4. I visited several families and conversed with them on eternal things and numbers appeared to be much affected. Afternoon Rev. Mr. Fish arrived and rode with me and preached the lecture which I had appointed. Baptized two children of Mr. Samuel Pratt viz: Judith Pratt Major Pratt

We spent the evening at Mr. Devoreaux's in pleasing and profitable conversation.

Aug. 5 We visited several families and conversed with them on religious subjects. At two o'Clock we met with those persons who expected to be organized into a church.

The Candidates gave a relation of their experiences and by their judicious conversation gained our charity and the charity of each other. We presented them with a confession of faith and covenant to which they unanimously agreed.

Aug. 6. Visited. 4 o'Clock preached a lecture. A large number assembled perhaps 100, notwithstanding the travelling was very difficult on account of a shower of rain.

Baptized a child.

Aug. 7. Lord's Day.

After the close of the forenoon exercises The following persons were organized into a church of Christ.

Ithamar Day
Martin Langdon
Lydia Langdon
Sam¹ Whaly
Elisha Devoreaux
Jemima Devoreaux
Solomon Bishop
Samuel Pratt
Hannah Pratt
David Forester
Polly Forester
Cyrus Thompson
James Sharon
Rebecca Sharon
Stephen Stillson
Keeber Starr
Mary Starr   baptized
Stephen Baxter   baptized
Thankful Hichcock
Phebe Langdon
Calvin Adams

The Audience seemed to be much affected with the solemn transaction. The sacrament was then administered.

Afternoon I preached from Jonah 1. and numbers appeared to be melted under the truths of Gods word.

There are favorable appearances of a revival of religion in this place. some are pricked to the heart and begin to enquire what they shall do to be saved.

I baptized Jabes W. Langdon, Lucy Langdon, Betsey Langdon, Therina Langdon, children of Noah Langdon

Alvin Thompson, Cyrus Thompson, children of Cyrus Thompson

Clarissa Starr, child of Keeber Starr

I rode three miles and in the evening attended to the admission of a member who was confined by sickness. Examined and baptized <u>Charlotte Thurston</u>. Then baptized her family.

Sarah Thurston, Abigail Thurston, Hannah Thurston, Daniel Thurston, Betsey Thurston,

Children of Daniel Thurston

Asahel Baxter, Reuben Baxter, Polly Baxter, Stephen Baxter, Lucy Baxter, children of Stephen Baxter

Then rode half a mile through the woods so dark that I could scarcely see my pilot, at a late hour retired to rest much fatigued with the labors of the day. I have reason to notice with gratitude the goodness of God in in giving me strength equal to my labors.

I distributed in Verona 11 Hemmenway's discourses, 6 Doddridges Address one Bible to Mr. Sargeant to be given to a pious youth who is in want. Verona contributed, $5.75

Aug. 8. I left Verona and wish to recommend it to the attention of Missionaries. Rode to Westmoreland.# Rode to Utica to attend to the Books belonging to the Society.

Westmoreland contains perhaps 200 people. rich and flourishing. A large church. There has lately been a revival of religion here. They are seeking to settle a minister. 'tis an inviting vacancy.

Aug. 9. Mr. Fish met me at Utica & we took an exact inventory of the Society's Books and find that none are missing.

Agreed with Mr. Fish that he should have the care of half and I would take the other, that the orders we may give need not interfere. Wrote a letter to Rev. Mr. Williams and gave a brief account of my Missionary labors. wrote letters to my family. Received information that my people were likely to be unsupplied with preaching.

Wrote to my Father and requested him to apply to the Trustees to recall me from my Mission if my people thought best.

[note] <u>Utica and Whitesborough</u> are 4 miles apart. Rev. Mr. Dod supplies them alternatively. In Utica there has lately been a little revival of religion. A few individuals have become hopeful converts. The place is meliorating in morals.

Aug. 10. Parted with Mr. Fish and conclude agreeable to instructions to visit the countries of Chenango and Onondago. Passed through New Hartford an elegant Village, supplied by Rev. Mr. Snowdon. rode

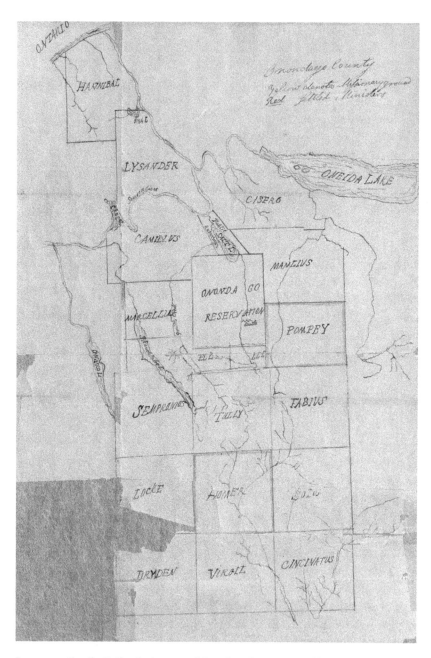

Figure 4. Timothy Mather Cooley, map of Onondaga County, 1803. This pen-and-ink map denotes township divisions within Onondaga County. Cooley's map, which accompanied his journal, separated townships with "established ministries" from "missionary ground." The Onondaga Reservation, home to the Seneca Indians, sits at the center of the map. (Courtesy New York State Library, Manuscripts and Special Collections, Albany)

to Bridgewater. Mr. Southward is settled here. There has of late been a very great reformation in this place and the church consists of about 60 members. They are erecting a new meeting house.

Aug. 11. Rode to Dr. Farrels in Brookfield# in Chenang [Chenago] County. In this little neighbourhood of one mile in extent are Presbyterians, Quakers, Seventh day Baptists, first day Baptists, Methodists & Universalists!!!!!! Left with Elder Clark one Dodridge's addresses, one Lathrop on the Sabbath, one Trustees Lust and address.
[note] Brookfield LB 14 miles 9. contains No 19, 18, 17. People are much divided. There is a seventh day Baptist church under Elder Clark. A first day Baptist church of 50 members under Elder Brown. Another of 80 members under Elder Marsh. There are a few Presbyterians who ought to be collected into a church & society. 500 families in this town.

Aug. 12. Visited families. visited a school of 20 children. gave them 7 addresses from a stranger.
At 4 o'Clock I passed the [*blank*] and preached in Plainsfield. people were very attentive and thankful.

Aug. 13. It being the Sabbath of the seventh day people, I was invited by Elder Clark to preach to his people.
I complied and found them a very pious people.

Aug. 14. Lords Day.
I preached in the Meeting house wh. belongs to the Seventh day people. There were 130 present. The people were not very attentive. The families of Presbyterians took pains to ride several miles to get to meeting. They feel like scattered sheep without a shepherd. This place has been neglected by Missionaries but deserves attention.
Mem. Dr. Israel Farril contributed $1.
I left two Doddridges Address Vivians Dialogues. Two Whitaker's address, one visit to the house of mourning, one Hemmenway's discourses, to be circulated for the good of families in this place.

Aug. 15. Dr. Farril and his wife accompanied me 5 miles through the woods to Esq. Butters. I preached a lecture and christians appeared to rejoice in another opportunity of hearing the gospel.
In the evening a number of pious people came in and we spent the time in conversation and prayer.

I left in the neighbourhood of Esq. Butter 2 Hemmenway's, 2 Whitakers one Doddrige's Address, 2 Addresses from a stranger, 2 Vivians. some of these I gave to the school, some to individuals and some for circulation.

Aug. 16. Took leave of kind christian friends and rode to Hamilton. Mr. Payne an amiable young man was so kind as to accompany me the whole distance. Rode to No. 4 in Hamilton and lodged at Rev. Mr. Knap's. At his request I preached a lecture to his people who appeared quite attentive. Left one Hemmenway for a child, one address from a stranger to a pious woman.

N.B. Deac^n Butter got my horse shod and insisted upon paying the bill.

Rode on to the 5 Town in Hamilton and providentially fell in with company to pilot me thro' the woods.

Left with Mr. Jones on[e] Doddridge's Address, one Whittaker, one Vivian, 3 address from a stranger to be circulated for the good of the people.

Note. Hamilton No. 4 contains 180 families a church of 35 members under Rev. Mr. Knap. a baptist church und. Elder Kosmer. There has been a revival of religion in this place. First settled in 1792.

No. 2 in Hamilton contains above 100 families. stupid. vicious. divided. no church. some baptists. ought to be noticed by Missionaries.

Hamilton No. 5 contains above 100 families. A church of 20 members harmonious. All Presbyterians and happily united. They want Missionary notice. are indigent. place new.

Aug. 17. At 3 o'Clock I preached a lecture and had about 60 present. There was a most encouraging attention. Lodged at Mr. Webster's and spent the evening agreeably in conversation on the things of godliness with the family.

Left with Mr. Webster 2 Doddridge's Address. one Hemmenway. one address from a stranger. one Vivian Dialogues. To be read and lent. 2 Whitakers to the school I visited yesterday to be given to those who make the best progress in learning the Catechism.

Aug. 19. Rode on with a view to spend the approaching Sabbath in Pompey Hollow. accompanied several miles thro' the woods by christian friends. Rode to Cazenovia Rev. Mr. Leonard. He is settled here among a stupid, vicious, infidel people.

It has been my object to spend the next Sabbath at Pompey but find that they are supplied.

Aug. 20. conclude to take a Southern course and spend the Sabbath in #Woodstock Southern part of Cazenovia. Upon arriving here I find they are supplied with baptist preaching. conclude to go 4 miles further to Dreyton, but here I find them all baptists and expect Elder Roots to-morrow.

I am perplexed and hardly know what to do with myself. The people here desired me. stay and preach to them a part of the Day.

Upon enquiry I find there is a settlement 5 miles distant in the edge of Fabius wher the gospel is seldom preached. I immediately rode on through mire and woods and at sunset Saturday night arrived. Disclosed my business and general joy spread through the settlement. This day they buried one of their number. His death was attended with some affecting circumstances and the minds of the people were prepared to receive the truth.

[note] Woodstock settlement in Cazenovia contains 100 families. one half presbyterians. one half baptists. Baptists have a preacher.

Aug. 21. Lord's Day.

The people assembled at nine in the morning and I preached two sermons to them with an intermission of only 20 minutes. The people were much affected and many were in tears.

After exercises I rode back to attend the lecture I had appointed at 2 hours before sunset. Passing by Elder Root's meeting I went in and at his request preached to his people. Then rode 7 miles father and found the people gathered for the lecture I had appointed.

Preached with freedom and some were evidently affected with the truth. I have this day preached four sermons and rode eleven miles. I left one Doddridge's address for the people in Moss's settlement one Whitaker's address to a pious girl who is a cripple. 2 address from a stranger to a school.

Aug. 22. Preached a lecture at Mr. Cole's in Cazenovia. Visited a school. Rode to Dareiter [Deruyter] and preached an evening lecture. A large collection assembled.

Aug. 23. I rode five miles to Moss's settlement where I spent the last Sabbath. And at 9 o'clock in the morning a greater number of people were collected than on the Sabbath. I never preached to a more solemn Assembly. Many were in tears. I rode on with company through the woods to the upper part of Solon# and preached at Esq. Hedges. Left one Vivian's Dialogues with Mr. Eager family and one Hemmenway to a couple of families of children. one Vivian at Esq. Hedges'. One Vivian to Mr. Benedict.

[note] <u>Solon</u> is in Onondaga County. Contains 40 families mostly Baptists. on the borders of Solon and Fabius is a settlement of Congregationalists which desires missionary notice. No church in this town.

Aug. 24. Rode 9 miles thro' the woods to the Southern part of Solon and preached at Mr. Beebe's. Gave to the people and to children 3 addresses from a stranger. 1 Doddridge's Address. 4 Vivians Dialogues.

[August] 25. Mr. Benedict has spent two days to accompany me through the blind roads. Without his company I should never have found the way. I passed on through a solitary desert to Cincinatus. The little neighbourhood soon collected and were attentive to my preaching. At their request I preached to them in the evening and we had a very solemn meeting.

Gave to the people one Whitaker. One address from stranger. one Vivian. Gave Dr. Hunt an order for. 1 Doddridge's Address, 1 Repository tracts No. 7, 1 Do. No. 8, 1 Doddridge's rise and progress, 1 Lathrop on the Sabbath.

All for the use of the people in this settlement.

[note] Cincinatus is 10 miles square and contains 60 families. some Baptist people. Near the <u>Onondago</u> branch is an Indian Burying ground on a little hill. Their mode of burial was to dig a deep round hole and place the corpse upright or sitting in the grave. They laid rafters over the corpse and covered them with dirt, forming a little mound perhaps 3 or 4 feet high.

When the rafters failed the dirt sunk in and the graves are now lower than the common level. The people of the neighbourhood informed me they had dug into these graves and found human bones almost mouldered to dust. In digging they first come across the skull bone which shows that they buried their dead, in an erect or sitting position.

I counted the grains of an <u>Ash</u> which had been fell on this ground and its age was 220. Hence tis probable this was improved as a burying ground 300 years ago.

Aug. 26. Dr. Hunt accompanied me through the woods and I rode to Virgil# and arrived at Esq. Ball's at sunset.

Virgil 10 miles square. contains 40 families. United. No church. Meet on the Sabbath.

Aug. 27. I have a violent cold this morning owing to my sleeping in a house with little or no roof.

The night air in this country is very pernicious to health. At 4 o'Clock I preached a lecture and had perhaps 40 hearers.

Aug. 28. Lords Day

Most of the people in the settlement and some from a neighbouring Town convened. They heard with a degree of attention.

I preached an evening lecture and nearly as many convened as in the day time.

Aug. 29. I visited several families and then rode on to Homer.#

Note. Homer contains 150 families and a church of above 30 members.

Rev. Mr. Darrow is settled here in the ministry. Southwest of Homer lies the Town of Dryden in Cayuga County. A singular sect have arisen in this place.

Their leader is one Ballard who has been excommunicated from the Methodist priesthood. a man of a wretched character. He stiles himself a free willer. Holds to dipping and Armenian [Arminian] doctrines.

He has been the means of influencing the people with a fiery zeal.

Men and women exhort and pray and often several are at once. Loud laughing is practiced in the midst of their pretended worship of God. Nearly 20 have been initiated into their communion by immersion!! I did not visit them because they were out of my missionary limits and there was no prospect of collecting them together to hear one of our denomination.

Aug. 31. Left Tully# and travelled a very bad road till I reached the Castle of the Onondaga Indians.

They are 100 in numbers and abstain from spiritous liquors. Rode to ##Onondaga Hollow, but find the people in no situation to be collected for a lecture, as they are making preparations for a training. Rode to Marcellus at the nine mile creek. Arrived at sunset, myself and horse worn out with excessive bad roads and daily fatigues.

Tully contains 100 families. No church. people vicious. But few friends to religion.

Onondago is the capital of the country. Contains 900 inhabitants. No church. People stupid and vicious. Here are the famous salt springs.

Sept. 1. Spent the day in resting and visiting families.

Sept. 2. I was made acquainted with an unhappy difficulty in the church in this place, which threatened the peace of the church and society. In the evening I visited the offenders and found them very respectable people and free to converse on the subsisting difficulty.

Sept. 3. Wrote an address to the people of my Parish.

Sept. 4. <u>Lords day</u>. After the usual exercises of the day, the offending members came forward and made a confession which was satisfactory to the church.

And thus a difficulty which bid fair to disturb the good order of this flourishing people was harmoniously settled. I preached an evening lecture.

People at Marcellus contributed $2.50

Sept. 5. Rode to Geneva.

Sept. 6. Rode to [*blank*]

Sept. 7. Preached 2 lectures and visited a number of friends in [*blank*]

Sept. 8. Rode to Geneva.

Sept. 9. Rode to Marcellus at the Skaneateles lake and preached a lecture and but few attended.

Sept. 11. Lord's Day.
I preached at the Skaneateles lake and about 300 convened.
Administered the sacrament.
In the evening preached a lecture.

Sept. 12. Rode to the nine mile creek and preached a lecture which I had before appointed a crowd of people attended and were serious. The people unanimously voted an address of thanks to our Missionary society.

Sept. 13. Received letters from my family and hear they are well.
Rode to Marcellus II, and preached an evening lecture and a considerable number came together tho' they had but an hours notice.
Note. Marcellus contains 300 families and 3 churches. one at nine mile creek. one at Skaneateles and one at the II.
People are well united and flourishing.
Able and desirous to support a minister to preach to each church in rotation.

Sept. 14. Visited families. Preached a lecture at 4 o'Clock. At the request of the people I preached an evening lecture. People were very attentive and some came 5 miles thro' the woods to attend the lecture. This people deserves the notice of Missionaries.
Left 3 address. from a stranger.

Sept. 15. Took leave of kind friends at the Ell [Marcellus?] and rode on through the woods to Tully. It was rainy and the road very obscure. sometimes the path failed me and I had no guide but marked trees. In the midst of the woods equidistant from Inhabitants I lost my road. For sometime I wandered in search of it without effect.

I got from my horse and narrowly searched for the marked trees and at last a favourable providence brought me right again.

I arrived at Tully, soaked with rain and every kindness was shown me. Before I could dry my clothes I was necessitated to attend my lecture at the school house.

The rain continued and the travelling difficult, yet to my surprise a decent number of men, women & children collected and were very solemn.

They appeared unwilling to leave the place after the exercises were closed.

The attention of the people in this stupid place is an ample reward for the fatigues I have undergone to get to them.

Gave Capt. Mason an order for 1 Lathrop on the Sabbath. 1 Do. 6 Sermons, 1 Repository tracts No. 7, 1 Do. No. 8, 1 Williams Convertion sermon.

Sept. 16 My work is all laid out before me. As I pursue my way homewards I shall attend to the appointments which I made as I came on. I visited several families. rode to the South part of Tully and preached a lecture. the people stupid. In the evening visited and discoursed with a Deist.

Sept. 17. Rode on through the woods to Solon. In the afternoon preached a lecture.

N.B. Directed to the people at Solon 1 Rise & progress. 1 Lathrops 6 sermons. 1 Fuller's Gospel. 1 Lathrop on the Sabbath. 1 Williams convention sermons. 1 Lyman's do.

Sept. 18. Lords Day. A full assembly collected. In the forenoon I preached to parents.

In the Afternoon to youth from Eccl. 11.9. A young man a few days before had be. [been] instantly killed by the discharge of a gun. I pressed them to consider this call of providence and hope it was a word in season. The assembly appeared much affected.

Sept. 19. Rode to Moss's settlement in Fabius# and preached a lecture at 9 o'Clock. The people appeared to feel the weight of truth.

Rode to Dereiter## in Chenango County and preached a lecture at 4 o'Clock to a full assembly. At their request preached an evening lecture to a larger audience than in the day time. A text was given me just before exercises commenced Prov. 8.4. People were very attentive. Some rode 8 miles to attend the afternoon lecture.

#Fabius is populous, but much divided. mostly baptists & Methodists. one Baptist church. Elder Roots supplies them a part of the time.

##Dereiter contains 100 families mostly Baptists.

Sept. 20. I am not well. My constant preaching and riding have increased the severe cold I took last thursday by riding in the rain. Rode to Woodstock in Cazenovia. Preached a lecture at 4 o'Clock to about 60 people. There is evidently some serious attention to religion in this place.

About 5 weeks I preached in this place and God has been pleased as I am informed to bless what was said, to the awakening of some stupid sinners. After lecture I rode 2 miles and preached in the evening. It was rainy. but the rain did not hinder people from attending. About 60 present.

Sept. 21. I rode on to the second# town in Hamilton and preached a lecture to a very small collection of people. This place needs a missionary for several days. My appointments are such I must leave them to-morrow.

[Note] Hamilton No. 2 contains 100 families divided, loose, stupid people. place unhealthy. need missionary labors.

Sept. 22. In the afternoon I attended a funeral. then rode to the 5th In Hamilton.

Sept. 23. Visited several families.

In the afternoon preached a lecture and about 100 attended. The people of settlement generally convened. In the evening a number of people came in and the time was spent in religious conversation and prayer.

I have heard from Verona that since the formation of the church in that place, there has been some serious attention to religion and some have been hopefully converted.

Sept. 24. Rode to Sherburne# No. 8 and preached a preparatory lecture.

[note] Sherburne settled 1793. contains No. 8 and 9. 2500 inhabitants. A church of 70 members, An unhappy division respecting the place for a meeting house bids fair to destroy the peace of this flourishing town.

Sept. 25. Lords Day.

In the forenoon preached in the West Meeting house. Afternoon rode 2 miles and preached in a large school house. The house was filled and as many about the door as within the house. Administered the sacrament. Baptized <u>Oprah Northrop</u>, child of Stephen Northrop, <u>Sophronia Lathrop</u>, child of Ezra Lathrop.

Preached an evening lecture in the school house.

Sept. 26. Rode to Paynes Settlement in Hamilton No. 4. In the evening preached a lecture, the people were mostly Baptists. They were attentive and thankful.

Sept, 27. Rode on thro' No #3 in Hamilton. and Sangerfield## to Paris Rev Mr. Steels and find him a very sensible pious man.

[#] No. 3 contains 150 families. A new meeting house. a settled minister by the name of Woodworth.

Sangerfield. A flourishing place. They have a Presbyterian and Baptist preacher. Hamilton

Sept. 28. Rode to Holland Patent Rev. Mr. Fishs.

Sept. 29. Spent a part of the day in visiting families in company with Mr. Fish. In the evening preached a lecture. About 70 collected.

Sept. 30. Visited several persons who are under serious impressions.

It was our object to form a church in this place, but some difficulties render it inexpedient at present.

Took leave of Mr. Fish's family where I have experienced the kindest treatment. rode to Whitesborough in company with Mr. Fish.

Oct. 1. Rode with Rev. Mr. Fish to Utica to attend to our Books.

After making arrangements I took an affectionate leave of my fellow laborer Mr. Fish, expecting next Monday to leave missionary ground. Rode to German Flats. Here I met with Mr. Hart a missionary from Connecticut.

Both of us had appointed to spend the Sabbath here. It was a very unhappy circumstance that two of us should meet and be necessitated to spend the Sabbath together, where the harvest was so great and the laborers so few. We concluded to view it a providential direction.

Oct. 2. Lords day.

In the forenoon I preached a sermon. In the afternoon Mr. Hart preached. people appeared to listen with great attention.

In the evening I preached and people appeared solemn. After exercises we were invited by eight or ten young people to visit and converse with them. They were evidently awakened. They were in tears most of the time during our conversation.

Oct. 3. We spent some time in conversing with the youth, prayed with them and I took leave of them expecting to see them no more till we meet in another world. Gave them our Dodriges rise & progress.

Took leave of friends and rode on towards home.

Memorandum

One half of a contribution at German Flats. $2.16.

Oct. 5. At Albany. The <u>Sinod</u> is now in session at this place and 'tis inconvenient adjusting the Society's acc^ts with Rev. Mr. Knott.\

Oct. 7. Arrived at Northampton Rev. Mr. Williams' and gave him a brief sketch of my Missionary labors.

Oct. 8. Reached my own house in safety and found my family well. The goodness of God in preserving my health and that of my family during my long absence from them deserves my notice and gratitude.

I have now completed a missionary tour of eighteen weeks.

People have very affectionately expressed their gratitude to the missionary society and to the benevolent people who have contributed for their good. They have generally received me with a degree of kindness and cordiality which scarcely admits of description.

They have taken great pains to get to meeting and often travel several miles, in bad roads to hear the words of life. In my missionary tour I have rode 1380 miles. preached 108 times. Visited 27 schools. Administered the Lord's supper 5 times. Admitted 26, including those who were received by letters into churches.

Baptized 53 persons. 3 of whom were adults, the others were baptized through profession of their parents.

My labors were mostly in the counties of Oneida, Chenango and Onondaga. I preached 55 sermons in the county of Oneida, 23 in that of Chenango 26 in Onondaga and 5 in neighbouring counties.

I formed one church in the Town of Verona in Oneida county.

SIX

Rev. Jacob Cram's Mission

Source: "Summary Report of Mr. Cram's Late Mission," *Massachusetts Missionary Magazine*, March 1806, 383–86.

In July 1805, the Reverend Jacob Cram left his home in Exeter, New Hampshire, on a six-month mission to New York and Pennsylvania. Cram kept a journal in which he recorded much of his travels and preaching. Upon his return home, the *Massachusetts Missionary Magazine* published Cram's missionary journal over three issues, prefaced with the summary featured here.

Cram's report of his mission described the state of settlement in central and western New York, the dependence on missionaries for preaching, and the increasing occurrence of revivals in the region. Cram referenced "awakenings in several places" and reported on the need of missionaries to preach to Native Americans. However, he did not mention his meeting with leaders of the Seneca in which his request to preach among the Seneca was declined.[1] Cram was one of dozens of missionaries preaching in the area each year at this time, and in many ways his report is representatives of missionaries' experiences in the region.

❧ ❧ ❧

---

1. "Sagoyewatha's Reply to Rev. Jacob Cram," document 7 herein.

Summary Report of Mr. Cram's Late Mission

July 26, 1805. Left Exeter in New Hampshire, and proceeded on a mission from the Massachusetts Missionary Society, to the States of New York and Pennsylvania. Travelled a westerly direction through the western parts of New Hampshire and Vermont, near the south end of Lake Champlain. Crossed the North River, eight miles from Lake George in the State of New York. Proceeded on, through Saratoga, Johnstown, German-flats to the county of Oneida, where I spent some time in visiting the different settlements of Indians and others, inhabiting those parts. From thence I proceeded on, and near the great turnpike and western road to the Genesee river.

On this route I visited a number of settlements of white people; some of which are near the south shore of Lake Ontario. Visited several Indian settlements in a southerly direction on the Genesee river. Leaving this river, I proceeded on south to the Alleghany river. Here I spent some days, attending to a settlement of the Seneca Indians. From this, I went into the State of Pennsylvania, and visited most of the settlements in the counties of Warren and Erie, and one settlement on Lake Erie in the State of Ohio. This was the extent of my travels west, being 500 miles from Boston. Returned down Lake Erie, by Presque Isle, Catoragus and Buffaloe Creeks to the outlet of the Lake at Black Rock. Visited the settlements in the British dominion, between the Lake Erie and Ontario. Came on eastward through the Tuscarora villages, to a settlement of Seneca Indians at Tarawanda Creek, and thence to the Genesee River. After visiting different settlements in the county of Ontario, came in a direct course to the county of Oneida, where I visited the different settlements again. After this I came on by the way of Boston to my place of residence in New Hampshire, which I reached February 1, 1806.

Every where on this route I experienced the kind attention of the people whom I visited, and much good will to the object of my travels. Beside conversing with numbers, who were deeply impressed with a sense of the worth of their souls, I was witness to special awakenings in several places, and heard of revivals of religion in many other places where they had preachers residing with them. Canterbury in New Hampshire, several towns in the vicinity of Dartmouth College, Fair Haven in the west part of Vermont, Stockbridge, Vernon and Verona, in the county of Oneida, and the east of Pompey and Marcus Ell [Marcellus?], in the county of Onondaga in the state of New York, may be deemed among the principal places, which shared in special divine influences in the course of last year.

Since the year of 1800, not far from thirty regular preachers of the word of life have come to reside in the western counties of New York, in places, which have been visited by Missionaries from the Massachusetts Missionary Society, and are now supported by the inhabitants. Many churches have been gathered, and several meeting-houses have been erected since that period.

Most of the inhabitants in these counties were emigrants, or descendants from New England. Those who are acquainted with the new settlements in New England, will be able to form a judgment, of the state of society, and of controversies, civil and religious, unless the controversy respecting Presbyterianism may be an exception. It may be just however to remark, that there is less disposition to inquire into distinguishing truths, than what there was in settlements of the same age, some years since, in New England, or than what there was in these counties, when the Missionaries from the Massachusetts Missionary Society, first visited the State of New York.

The counties, which I visited in the State of Pennsylvania, were very destitute of the stated preaching of the word. The inhabitants are chiefly Presbyterians. There is one minister of that denomination in these counties, who is nearly sixty miles from any other of his order. In these counties there are emigrants from New England. It was thought one fourth of the settlers in the county of Erie were from New England. The state of society in these counties has been very unpleasant, by reason of land disputes, which have much affected their civil and religious concerns. The counties, however, south, on the same side of the Alleghany and Ohio rivers, have been greatly favoured in the effusions of the Holy Spirit.

In a report respecting the state of religion, published in the Western Missionary Magazine, printed at Washington, in Pennsylvania, February, 1805, they say, respecting these settlements, "Thus we see in the course of five years, a Presbytery, consisting of fourteen ministers, settled in that country, where ten years ago we could scarcely see the face of a white man."

Some of these western settlements never had had preaching in them of any kind, before I visited them. On this route individuals heard me, who had not heard preaching for years before. The borough of Erie, where the county courts are held, and which is the principal place of business in the country, had been destitute of preaching for about a year. The New England emigrants in these parts were exceedingly pleased that the good people in New England did not forget their spiritual concerns. They were very desirous of having preachers from New England.

New Connecticut has great credit for the sober and regular conduct of a great proportion of the inhabitants of that district, and for the exertions they have made and are making to promote and preserve the good customs of their ancestors. The Congregational churches, which are 7 in number in those settlements, held a convention last fall. It was a subject of inquiry whether they should have general sacraments after the manner of the Presbyterians.

Visiting these western settlements, a person would have great opportunity of contemplating the wonderful wisdom, grace, and providence of the Great Ruler of nations, in leading our ancestors to settle on this continent, in giving them vast tracts of goodly western lands, which will probably contribute greatly to the advancement of the kingdom of the Great Redeemer of the utmost parts of the earth.

None of the Indian villages west of Oneida, appear to be ready to receive Missionaries to reside with them, excepting the Wyandots in the State of Ohio, who probably by this time are provided by for the Synod of Pittsburg, and the Delawares on the waters of the Wabash, of whom accounts have been given by the Rev. Mr. Sergeant, Missionary to the Mohehunuch [Mohegan?] Indians; who considers it very important that the eastern Missionary Societies should assist in forwarding a mission to them the next season.

The different nations of Indians in the county of Oneida, which contains more than 1500 souls, stand in need of missionary aid. Could proper assistance be afforded the Oneidas, so great and easy is the intercourse betwixt them, and others of the Six Nations, that probably as soon as proper missionary characters could be obtained, the way would be prepared for residents westward.

Jacob Cram.

SEVEN

Sagoyewatha's Reply to Rev. Jacob Cram

Source: *Monthly Anthology and Boston Review*, April 1809, 221-24.

In November 1805, the Reverend Jacob Cram of the Massachusetts Missionary Society met with Haudenosaunee leaders in the hopes of gaining their approval to allow missionaries to preach among them. The United States Indian agent Erastus Granger was present, as was an interpreter. Haudenosaunee leaders, after hearing Cram's request and consulting as a group, selected Sagoyewatha, a skilled orator, to respond to Cram. Sagoyewatha was also known as Red Jacket.

The account of the meeting demonstrates the motivations for Christians to preach to the Haudenosaunee, as well as Cram's disdain for the Haudenosaunee's existing religious practices. Sagoyewatha's reply reflects his people's resentment of their treatment by white men and their determination to defend their religious autonomy by refusing to permit the missionaries to preach in their communities.

Although the published transcript states that the meeting occurred in the summer, the date of Cram's arrival in the area indicates that the meeting likely occurred in November.[1] The transcript was sent

---

1. Granville Ganter, ed., *The Collected Speeches of Sagoyewatha, or Red Jacket* (Syracuse, NY: Syracuse University Press, 2006), 138.

to the *Monthly Anthology and Boston Review* in 1809 by an anonymous correspondent and published in that publication's April issue.[2] It is unknown who made the record of the meeting and the editorial comments that occasionally appear in parentheses.[3] Several other publications subsequently reprinted the account, in some instances with additions to the text. The earliest published version is featured here.

🌑 🌑 🌑

Indian Speech

(In the summer of 1805, a number of the principal Chiefs and Warriours of the Six Nations of Indians, principally Senecas, assembled at Buffalo Creek, in the State of New York, at the particular request of a gentleman Missionary from the State of Massachusetts. The Missionary being furnished with an Interpreter, and accompanied by the Agent of the United States for Indian affairs, met the Indians in Council, when the following took place.)

First, by the Agent

"BROTHERS OF THE SIX NATIONS; I rejoice to meet you at this time, and thank the Great Spirit, that he has preserved you in health, and given me another opportunity of taking you by the hand. "BROTHERS; The person who sits by me, is a friend who has come a great distance to hold a talk with you. He will inform you what his business is, and it is my request that you would listen with attention to his words."
MISSIONARY. "My Friends; I am thankful for the opportunity afforded us of uniting together at this time. I had a great desire to see you, and inquire into your state and welfare; for this purpose I have travelled a great distance, being sent by your old friends,

---

2. *Monthly Anthology and Boston Review*, March 1809, 158.
3. Some scholars have questioned the authenticity of this document in part because of the transmission of the document to a publisher four years after the meeting occurred. However, Granville Ganter argues that the Seneca "were very conscious of what was circulated about them" and did not object to the publication of the meeting account. Furthermore, Ganter notes that "mention of the attendance of the U.S. Indian agent Erastus Granger would have made misrepresentation of federal consequence." See Harry Robie, "Red Jacket's Reply: Problems in the Verification of Native American Speech Text," *New York Folklore* 12, nos. 3–4 (1986): 99–117; Christopher Densmore, "More on Red Jacket's Reply," *New York Folklore* 13, nos. 3–4 (1987). 121–22, Ganter, *Collected Speeches of Sagoyewatha*, 138.

the Boston Missionary Society. You will recollect they formerly sent missionaries among you, to instruct you in religion, and labour for your good. Although they have not heard from you for a long time, yet they have not forgotten their brothers the Six Nations, and are still anxious to do you good.

"BROTHERS; I have not come to get your lands or your money, but to enlighten your minds, and to instruct you how to worship the Great Spirit agreeably to his mind and will, and to preach to you the gospel of his son Jesus Christ. There is but one religion, and but one way to serve God, and if you do not embrace the right way, you cannot be happy hereafter. You have never worshipped the Great Spirit in a manner acceptable to him; but have, all your lives, been in great errours and darkness. To endeavour to remove these errours, and open your eyes, so that you might see clearly, is my business with you.

"BROTHERS; I wish to talk with you as one friend talks with another; and if you have any objections to receive the religion which I preach, I wish you to state them; and I will endeavour to satisfy your mind, and remove the objections.

"BROTHERS; I want you to speak your minds freely; for I wish to reason with you on the subject, and, if possible, remove all doubts, if there be any on your minds. The subject is an important one, and if it is of consequence that you give it an early attention while the offer is made you. Your friends, the Boston Missionary Society, will continue to send you good and faithful ministers, to instruct and strengthen you in religion, if, on your part, you are willing to receive them.

"BROTHERS; Since I have been in this part of the country, I have visited some of your small villages, and talked with your people. They appear willing to receive instruction, but, as they look up to you as their older brothers in council, they want first to know your opinion on the subject.

"You have now heard what I have to propose at present. I hope you will take it into consideration, and give me an answer before we part."

(After about two hours consultation amongst themselves, the Chief commonly called, by the white people, Red Jacket, rose and spoke as follows:)

"FRIEND AND BROTHER; It was the will of the Great Spirit that we should meet together this day. HE orders all things, and has given us a fine day for our Council. HE has taken his garment from before the sun, and caused it to shine with brightness upon us. Our eyes are opened, that we may see clearly; our ears are unstopped, that we have been able to hear distinctly the words you have spoken. For all these favours we thank the Great Spirit; and HIM *only*.

"*BROTHER*; This council fire was kindled by you. It was at your request that we came together at this time. We have listened with attention to what you have said. You requested us to speak our minds freely. This gives us great joy; for we now consider that we stand upright before you, and can speak what we think. All have heard your voice, and all speak to you now as one man. Our minds are agreed.

"*BROTHER*; You say you want an answer to your talk before you leave this place. It is right you should have one, as you are a great distance from home, and we do not wish to detain you. But I will first look back a little, and tell you what our fathers have told us, and what we have heard from the white people.

"There was a time when our forefathers owned this great island. Their seats extended from the rising to the setting sun. The Great Spirit had made it for the use of Indians. HE had created the buffalo, the deer, and other animals for food. HE had made the bear and the beaver. Their skins served us for clothing. HE had scattered them over the country, and taught us how to take them. HE had caused the earth to produce corn for bread. All this HE had done for his red children, because HE loved them. If we had some disputes about our hunting ground, they were generally settled without the shedding of much blood. But an evil day came upon us. Your forefathers crossed the great water, and landed on this island. Their numbers were small. They found friends and not enemies. They told us they had fled from their own country for fear of wicked men, and had come here to enjoy their religion. They asked for a small seat. We took pity on them, granted their request; and they sat down amongst us. We gave them corn and meat, they gave us poison (alluding, it is supposed, to ardent spirits) in return.

"The white people had now found our country. Tidings were carried back, and more came amongst us. Yet we did not fear them. We took them to be friends. They called us brothers.

We believed them, and gave them a larger seat. At length their numbers had greatly increased. They wanted more land; they wanted our country. Our eyes were opened, and our minds became uneasy. Wars took place. Indians were hired to fight against Indians, and many of our people were destroyed. They also brought strong liquor amongst us. It was strong and powerful, and has slain thousands.

"*BROTHER*; Listen to what we say.

"*BROTHER*; Our seats were once large and yours were small. You have now become a great people, and we have scarcely a place left to spread our blankets. You have got our country, but are not satisfied; you want to force your religion upon us.

"*BROTHER*; Continue to listen.

"You say that you are sent to instruct us how to worship the Great Spirit agreeably to his mind, and, if we do not take hold of the religion which you white people teach, we shall be unhappy hereafter. You say that you are right and we are lost. How do we know this to be true? We understand that your religion is written in a book. If it was intended for us as well as you, why has not the Great Spirit given to us, and not only to us, but why did he not give to our forefathers the knowledge of that book, with the means of understanding it rightly? We only know what you tell us about it. How shall we know when to believe, being so often deceived by white people?

"*BROTHER*; You say there is but one way to worship and serve the Great Spirit. If there is but one religion; why do you white people differ so much about it? Why not all agreed, as you can all read the book?

"*BROTHER*; We do not understand these things.

"We are told that your religion was given to your forefathers, and has been handed down from father to son. We also have a religion, which was given to our forefathers, and has been handed down to us their children. We worship in that way. It teaches us to be thankful for all the favours we receive; to love each other, and to be united. We never quarrel about religion.

"*BROTHER*; The Great Spirit has made us all, but he has made a great difference between his white and red children. HE has given us different complexions and different customs. To you HE has given the arts. To these HE has not opened our eyes.

We know these things to be true. Since HE has made so great a difference between us in other things; why may we not conclude that HE has given us a different religion according to our understanding? The Great Spirit does right. HE knows what is best for his children; we are satisfied.

"*BROTHER*; We do not wish to destroy your religion, or take it from you. We only want to enjoy our own.

"*BROTHER*; We are told that you have been preaching to white people in this place. These people are our neighbors. We are acquainted with them. We will wait a little while, and see what effect your preaching has upon them. If we find it does them good, makes them honest and less disposed to cheat Indians; we will then consider again what you have said.

"*BROTHER*; You have now heard our answer to your talk, and this is all we have to say at present.

"As we are going apart, we will come and take you by the hand, and hope the Great Spirit will protect you on your journey, and return you safe to your friends."

As the Indians began to approach the missionary, he rose hastily from his seat and replied, that he could not take them by the hand; that there was no fellowship between the religion of God and the works of the devil.

This being interpreted to the Indians, they smiled, and retired in a peaceable manner.

It being afterwards suggested to the missionary that his reply to the Indians was rather indiscreet; he observed, that he supposed the ceremony of shaking hands would be received by them as a token that he assented to what they had said. Being otherwise informed, he said he was sorry for the expressions.

EIGHT

Constitution of the Waterloo Missionary Society

Source: "Constitution of the Individual or Branch Society established in Waterloo for the aid of Missions," in Waterloo Missionary Society proceedings, #6051, Division of Rare and Manuscript Collections, Cornell University Library.

Christians organized dozens of missionary societies in the United States during the nineteenth century. Some supported foreign missions, while others supported domestic missions. Some missionary societies were affiliated with a specific denomination, while others were amenable to providing monetary support for any Protestant missionaries. Missionary societies in New England frequently dispatched missionaries to New York during the first decades of white settlement in that place. As these settlements stabilized, community members organized churches and secured permanent clergy, thereby reducing their dependence on itinerant missionaries for religious instruction. Still, many Christians desired to aid ongoing missionary efforts in the state and beyond. Accordingly, in the early 1800s Christians in central and western New York organized several missionary societies of their own.

On October 27, 1817, several citizens of Waterloo, New York, formed a missionary society as a branch of the General Missionary Society of the Western District of the State of New York. The society was open to both men and women, and each member paid twenty-five cents to join the society and one dollar per year in dues. Most, if not all, of the money raised was given to the General Missionary Society to fund the missions of Congregationalists or Presbyterians. In addition to the money that it raised to support missions, the Waterloo Missionary Society held quarterly meetings at which members or visitors would speak about Christian missions. The membership roll near the front of the society's minute book lists eighty-three members.[1] The constitution of the branch in Waterloo featured here is representative of similar missionary societies formed throughout the Burned-over District as the area began to rely less on the preaching of missionaries and could devote more attention to aiding missions elsewhere.

❧ ❧ ❧

Constitution of the Individual or Branch Society established in WATERLOO for the aid of Missions

Article 1

This Society shall be composed of People of both sexes and called "The society for the aid of Missions."

Article 2

Every person shall pay 25 cents on entering this society; also a quarterly tax of twenty five cents.

Article 3

All officers of this society shall be chosen from the Juvenile members except one Delegate who may be chosen from the elder members of the Society.

Article 4

Any person or persons wishing to withdraw from this Society may receive a dismission from the same of the secretary, provided they sustain none of its officers and owe it no debts.

---

1. For the membership roll and the minutes of the society's quarterly meetings see Waterloo Missionary Society proceedings, #6051, Division of Rare and Manuscript Collections, Cornell University Library.

Article 5

No impeachment shall be brought against any officer of this Society unless signed by five of its members.

Article 6

At the annual meeting of the Society which shall be held at least one week previous to the meeting of the Delegates, there shall be chosen by Ballot a President Vice President Secretary and one or more Delegates as directed by the constitution of the Society General: all of whom shall hold their offices untill the next annual election

Article 7

It shall be the duty of the President and in his absence of the Vice President to preside in the meetings and to preserve order. He shall be authorized to give orders on the Delegate in the name of the Society for monies to defray all necessary expenses and shall also have power to call extra meetings, if requested, by causing notifications to be affixed in three of the most public places in the vicinity, three days previous to said meeting.

Article 8

It shall be the duty of the secretary to record the transactions of the society; keep a list of its members and perform all necessary writing for the Society, which does not devolve on other officers.

Article 9

It shall be the duty of the senior delegate to receive all initiations and taxes of this Society, and all donations and contributions made to it and deliver the same except what may be requisite for necessary expenses to the Treasurer of the Society General. He shall also keep an account of his receipts and expenditures and exhibit the same to the society at the expiration of his office.

Article 10

If any meeting of this society both the President and Vice President or Secretary be absent, a person shall be chosen to supply the vacancy; who shall continue in office untill the return of the absent officers.

Article 11

No officer or member of this society shall receive any compensation for personal services. Necessary expenses shall be defrayed from the treasury.

Article 12

This Society (extra meetings excepted) shall meet once in three months, vis. On the last Wednesdays in January, April, July and October in each year. And the last Wednesday in Januy shall be deemed the annual Meeting.

Article 13

All meetings of this society shall be introduced and concluded by prayer.

Article 14

At each stated meeting there shall be one or more persons appointed to address the society at the next stated meeting on the subject of Missions, the christian public, and spread of the gospel.

Article 15

Conversations of a moral or religious nature may be introduced if time permit after the usual business of the society shall be transacted.

Article 16

Any article of this constitution may be dispensed with for the time being by the consent of three fourths of the members present, provided the omission do not counteract any article in the Constitution of the society general.

Article 17

Allocations and amendments not infringing on the laws of the society general, may be made to this constitution by the consent of two thirds of the members.

(Adopted at Waterloo 27. Oct. 1817.)

NINE

Reports of Episcopal Missionaries

Source: *Journal of the Convention of New-York, 1835,* in Episcopal Church, Diocese of New York, Convention, *Journal of the Annual Convention, Diocese of New York* (New York: The Diocese, 1785-), 82–104.

Historians of the Burned-over District have not always associated the Protestant Episcopal Church of the United States with a high interest in evangelism, but in actuality, New York Episcopalians shared the same zeal as Baptists, Presbyterians, and Methodists for missionary work.[1] Rev. John Henry Hobart, the third Episcopal bishop of New York, greatly expanded the church's missionary efforts during his tenure (1816-1830). He championed the organization of the General Theological Seminary (1817), the first Episcopal seminary, and actively promoted the New-York Protestant Episcopal Young Men's Missionary Society. His efforts made it possible for the Episcopal Diocese of New York to train and sponsor dozens of missionary priests and deacons in western New York during the 1820s and 1830s.[2]

---

1. Cross, *Burned-Over District,* 67.
2. Diana Hochstedt Butler, *Standing against the Whirlwind: Evangelical Episcopalians in Nineteenth-Century America* (New York: Oxford University Press, 1995).

The following document includes select reports prepared by Episcopal missionaries to the Education and Missionary Society of the Protestant Episcopal Church in the State of New York. The reports include statistical information such as the number of communicants and their monetary offerings to the church, and they also describe some difficulties that were unique to Episcopal missionaries. For example, the missionaries reported that church rules prohibiting deacons from administering Holy Communion undermined church growth. Limited access to church buildings or appropriate worship space also compromised their work. Lastly, a few clergymen acknowledged that some of the people they encountered were still prejudiced against a church with ties to the Church of England and governed by bishops.

* * *

[...]
From the report of the Rev. Orange Clark, Missionary at Lockport, Niagara county.

On assuming the station assigned me on the 26th of July, 1834, I found its condition in many respects very undesirable. It had been for a long period vacant; the church edifice not entirely finished, and the corporation deeply involved in debt, which was fast accumulating, and its friends growing disheartened. But I found here materials and members of a church, of all in the world, calculated to enlist the feelings and affections of a Missionary. Upon careful inquiry it was found, that the debt of the church exceeded two thousand dollars, and that a further sum of one or two hundred dollars ought to be forthwith expended on the church. The congregation was very limited, and subject to large drafts on their liberality, as is the case in all our new villages; and it seemed truly an Herculean task to put the affairs in a safe, unincumbered, and healthy condition. But, with much gratitude to God, we now find ourselves able to report the whole accomplished. Foreign aid, to the amount of one thousand dollars, was obtained; and the residue, according to the statement we shall give below, has been cheerfully contributed by a few gentlemen, with a liberality to which I have never known a parallel. Our church, with the spacious lot of ground on which it stands, is now the unincumbered property of the corporation. The lot will be beautifully enclosed before winter, the fixtures about the church complete, and arrangements are making to procure a bell as large as the tower will sustain.

In addition to the current expenses of sustaining public worship *all the time*, this little congregation have raised, within the last year, *among themselves* the following sums of money, viz:—

To extinguish debt on church,	$1000.00
To enclose, finish, and furnish church,	$280.00
For Sunday School Library, &c.,	$52.00
Domestic and Foreign Missionary Society,	$3.00
New-York Missionary Society,	$32.00
Episcopal Fund,	$2.00
Education Fund,	$10.00
Diocesan Fund,	$9.37
	$1386.60

I have assisted in organizing Grace Church in the upper ward of the village of Lockport, and have held a third service there, generally on Sunday evenings, both before and after their organization since I came here, until within a few weeks. The Rev. Mr. McBurney, who will report that church more particularly, has preached for them half the time, thereby affording me an opportunity of holding a third service on half the Sunday evenings, whenever I could collect congregations in the neighboring new settlements.

Our present number of communicants is 31—6 have removed, and 5 have been added. We have lost none by death.

Baptisms 20—Marriages 3—Burials 10.

The present aspect of things we think, warrants the hope that future reports will be far more cheering. In our pecuniary embarrassment, as above detailed, we have been painfully absorbed with things temporal, and I fear our spiritual interests have suffered. If the increase to our communion be small, yet in looking over the congregation your Missionary is not at all inclined to despond. He finds much to cheer him. But it is to the Missionary Society that this part of our Zion owes its existence. The Church would have had no name here but for that. [. . .]

From the report of the Rev. Burton H. Hickox, Missionary at Watertown, Jefferson county.

Baptisms (infants) 7—Marriages 1—Deaths 3—Communicants (added 5, removed 2) present number 37.

Collections—Episcopal,	$2.00
Diocesan,	$3.00
Missionary,	$19.00

Your Missionary has occupied his present field of labor for the last six months only. He has confined his services on Sunday exclusively to Watertown, which has a population of 3000 or 4000, and is an important point to the Church in this section of the Diocese. There are at present forty-four families connected with the parish, besides a fair representation of young gentlemen. The parish are respectfully attentive to the public services of the Church, and exceedingly kind and liberal. Additions to our communion we have had, but no deep and awakening influence has been felt under the preaching of your Missionary. He has maintained a weekly lecture, the average attendance on which has exceeded one hundred. The Sunday school has been regularly conducted, and has about fifty scholars. In addition to these services I have preached three times in our county jail, once in our county poor-house, four times at Pierrponts' Manor, one at Brownville, one at Evan's Mills, and once at Chaumont. Pierrpont Manor is the most encouraging field of my missionary efforts, in which I have been a coadjutor with the Rev. Mr. Treadway, who will give a full history of its prospects, and the liberal efforts of the individual who has alone sustained this station. I am compelled to say, that in this section of our Diocese, there is much apathy on the subject of religion, and much skepticism. Multitudes call themselves Universalists, and not a few of them from what are denominated the respectable walks in life. All that your Missionary can say, or dare say, is, that he hopes his labors have not been altogether in vain. [. . .]

From the report of the Rev. Timothy Minor, Missionary at Moravia, Cayuga County.

During the last year I have performed the regular services of this station, and frequently, a third service on Sunday, in several of the adjoining towns.

Some peculiarities connected with this church render its immediate prosperity somewhat doubtful. Being long destitute of regular clerical services, many of the former congregation, particularly the youthful part of it, have been led abroad by popular sentiments in search of something new. Still, the church, though small, seems to unite in an onward course.

There has been but little alteration in the state of the church within the year last past.

Communicants (added 2) whole number 19—Marriages 1—Funerals 2. Contributions, five dollars, to be appropriated as follows:

Missionary and Education society,	$3.00
Bishops' fund,	$1.00
Diocesan fund,	$1.00

From the report of the Rev. Thomas Morris, Deacon, Missionary at Ellicottville and Olean, Cattaraugus county.

Baptisms (adults 4, infants 4) 8—Marriages 3—Communicants 24.

Collections—Episcopal,	$3.00
Diocesan,	$4.00
Missionary,	$11.87

Had it been possible for us to have the ordinance of the Lord's Supper administered at Ellicottville, our number of communicates would have been increased at least four; but the distance from this place to the nearest clergyman in Priests' Orders, is upwards of fifty miles, which renders it very difficult to obtain a change; as it is, however, with all our difficulties we feel much encouraged in reviewing the events of the past year. At Olean there is, I think, a better prospect than at any period since my appointment to the mission; prejudices which formerly existed, are in many cases, either entirely removed, or at least so far as to give place to a degree of attention to the ordinances of religion which seems to promise for the future some lasting good. At this place we have lately organized a Sunday School, which promises much usefulness. Having had to make collections, to the amount of eleven dollars, for books for the school, I was under the necessity of omitting all the canonical collections this year, except the missionary collection. [. . .]

From the report of the Rev. George H. Norton, Missionary at Allen's Hill, Ontario county.

Baptisms (adults 2, infants 2) 4—Marriages 4—Deaths 2—Communicants (added 2, died 1) present number 41.

Collections—Missionary, $8 00.

For the year past I have devoted the greatest part of my time to St. Paul's Church, Richmond. In this parish no very essential change has taken place since the date of my last report. In reference to its spiritual condition, it gives me pain to acknowledge that for many months past we have been in a very Laodicean state. I have been abroad five Sundays during the summer past; two of them were spent at Trinity Church, Geneva, which parish has been for some time vacant. The other three were given to Trinity Church, at Centerfield, in this county, which has not for some time past received the stated services of any clergyman. For the present, and until they can be more frequently supplied, I have given the promise of being with them at least one Sunday in each month and I am happy to learn that the Rev. Mr. Staunton, of Palmyra, has made a similar engagement with them. In the absence of a minister, they uniformly have the service performed by a layman; and I will take this opportunity to remark, that in no congregation with which I am acquainted is the solemn worship of our Church conducted with more propriety and apparent devotion. It is indeed reviving to any clergyman who is not accustomed to an animated performance of our Liturgy, to visit a people like those who comprise this parish, who are so spiritually minded, and sustain with such admirable effect the responsive parts of our public service. In conclusion, and by way of encouragement to those who feel interested in extending the limits of our Zion, it may be added that the people above referred to, until about four years ago, were entire strangers to our Church, and had imbibed from education the strongest prejudices against us as a religious community. [. . .]

From the report of the Rev. Amos Pardee, Missionary at Malone, Franklin county.

Baptisms (adults 1, infants 9) 10—Marriages 2—Communicants (added 2, removed 2) 30.

Collections—Episcopal,	$1.00
Diocesan,	$4.00
Missionary,	$6.00

Your Missionary reports that he has spent a large portion of his time in the last year, as in the former year, in the village of Malone; but in the midst of summer and winter he has officiated about one quarter of the time in Hogansburgh, and one quarter in Duane, besides lectures in other places. In the early part of the year, on account of the change of property and removal from Malone of some of the most important and useful members of the church, our prospects were much darkened, but in the latter part of the year, on account of the addition to our congregation, our prospects have improved.

On account of the protracted sickness of the sheriff's family, who reside in a part of the courthouse, we have been unable for nearly six months past to occupy the court-room at all, or procure any other place which we could steadily occupy; and being unable to build a church, we have suffered great inconvenience for the want of a convenient place to hold Divine service. A contract, however, has now been made for the fitting up of a large room which will be commodious and eligibly situated. There is also a Sunday school and successful operation.

In Duane the attendance of the people is generally good, and there is lay reading in their chapel every Lord's day when there is no clergyman present.

In Hogansburgh there has been but little done to the chapel erected by Judge Hogan, except the laying the floor, the furnishing of some comfortable seats, and the building of a temporary reading desk. [. . .]

From the report of the Rev. James O. Stokes, Missionary at Medina, Orleans county.

Your missionary is sorry to inform you that his report must partake rather of the gloomy than of the cheering cast; this, he hopes, is not the result of his own inattention to the important duties of his office. This congregation during the past year has suffered greatly by the removal of families from the village. He apprehends no difficulty in stating that during the two years of his residence in Medina, as many people have left the village which were regarded as belonging to his congregation, as composed it when he first commenced his labors among them, and few, very few have come into the village favorably disposed toward the Church. Thus circumstanced, the congregation has had its influence in the village and neighborhood put to the severest test. He is happy, however, in perceiving that its influence has been adequate to its own preservation, as the congregation and support are much the same as for the last few years. And having thus maintained its strength under circumstances the most trying, he hopes there is reason to conclude that future prosperity may be reasonably anticipated. Your Missionary indulges in this hope also from the favorable receptions with which his services meet in the villages around, in which he preaches on Sunday evenings. Another circumstance of an encouraging nature arises from the prospect of a speedy completion of their new church edifice. And he feels it his duty on his occasion, to state his gratitude to the many friends of the Church, particularly in New-York, for the kind reception he met with in his appeal to their benevolence for pecuniary aid for the above purpose. Among the hundreds to whom he appealed, he does not remember more than two that treated him ungentlemanly or unkindly; and almost all attended to his case with promptitude and pleasure. And this statement he feels it is his duty gratefully to make, not only as an act of justice to his friends, but also as illustrative of true love and zeal for the Church in the great metropolis of the United States.

Your Missionary has the past year baptize 3 children—married 2; but has received no fresh additions to communion. The number of communicants he cannot exactly state.

TEN

Missionaries to Sailors and Canal Workers

Source: "The Western Waters," *Sailor's Magazine* (New York, NY),
September 1, 1838.

The Buffalo-based American Bethel Society
ministered to the sailors and canal workers who labored on American
waterways. The society published and distributed religious tracts, hym-
nals, and bibles. It also underwrote the salaries of maritime missionaries, who ministered to watermen from "floating chapels" commonly
known as Bethels. The following document appeared in an 1838 issue
of the *Sailor's Magazine*, a publication of the American Seaman's Friend
Society. In this report, the Bethel Society justified their distinctive ministry and described the unique social and spiritual needs of sailors, canal
workers, and their families. The report particularly focused on the society's desire to help watermen observe the Sabbath.

❦ ❦ ❦

The Western Waters

The American Bethel Society held their second annual meeting at Buffalo, June 13, 1838. We learn from their annual report, that the society

FIGURE 5. Masthead of the *Sailor's Magazine*, 1847. Missionaries and chaplains stationed in floating chapels hoisted Bethel flags like the one depicted in the masthead of the *Sailor's Magazine*. They distributed bibles and religious tracts and led visiting sailors in worship services. (Courtesy New Bedford Whaling Museum)

has had to encounter many difficulties, such as are attendant on a new enterprize, and in a time of general embarrassment.

The Bethel stations now supplied with chaplains are Troy, Utica, Rochester, Buffalo, Cleveland, and Pittsburgh. A new effort is making to revive this cause. We make the following extracts from the report, as exhibiting in vivid colours the importance of the object, which cannot fail deeply to affect every benevolent mind:

Extent of our Inland Negotiations

No quarter of the world presents so many beautiful, extensive, and navigable lakes and rivers, and affords facilities for forming so many canals, and sustaining so much inland navigation as the United States. And during a few years past, foreign nations have been surprised with the rapid progress of our internal improvements. Not long since, when the Erie canal was contemplated, many supposed such a "herculean task" could never be accomplished. But already there are about seventy canals finished in the United States; and more than one hundred others being excavated, or in contemplation.

And the Rapid advance of our navigation has been equally surprising. More than a year since, according to the most accurate calculations, the American steamboat tonnage was three times as much as that of Great Britain, and twice as much as all the rest of the world.

Watermen employed

In New-York state alone there are 3500 canal boats,* and in connection with these boats there are 20,000 waterman employed;† and besides, there are 10,000 more following some collateral employment, (lock tenders, those engaged in warehouses, &c.,) making in all 30,000.

And if we add those employed upon our steamboats, packet, and sail vessels, the number is at least 50,000. This calculation does not include their families of wives and children, and a multitude of others following some other business in connection with this, though not immediately upon the waters, but who equally need the aid of our society.

Passing by other states—if we cast our eye upon Lake Erie, we behold fifty steamboats and three hundred sail vessels, and five thousand watermen.

Passing by our other lakes—if we cast our eye upon the Mississippi river and its tributaries, we behold 638 steamboats and 50,000 watermen.

And casting our eye over the 30,000 miles of inland navigation, we behold, at least, 100,000 watermen, 100,000 more following some collateral employment, and 200,000 emigrants and passengers annually sailing upon our inland waters. A "nation of watermen."

Their temporal condition calls for our commiseration and our efforts. Exposed in a pecuniary manner to hardships, dangers, epidemics, damps, and dews, the inclemencies of the seasons, heat and cold, storms and tempests, by night and day—having no Sabbaths to rest and refresh their systems, and form the principles of life-preserving virtue—but exposed to intemperance, and hurried into the whirlpool of dissipation; they become reckless and prodigal of life, and in a few years are here no more—their lives shorter than the lives of other classes, and do not, on an average, exceed twelve years after they embark in the watermen's employment.

A great proportion of these evils can and ought to be removed.

Their moral condition is still more deplorable.

"The watermen are an abandoned class of men," has become a proverb. But why are they abandoned? As a general thing, they have no Sabbaths, are driven from our sanctuaries, driven along upon our canals and highways on the Lord's day, exposed to intemperance and all its kindred evils—and should we not expect them to become abandoned?

Let the interesting youth in our communities, who now promise fair to become useful and ornamental members of society; an honor to their parents and a blessing to the world; be placed in like circumstances; drive them from the sanctuary and the means of grace, hurry them into the whirlpool of vice and dissipation—and should we not expect them soon to become abandoned?

And the consequences of depriving the multitude of young men upon our canals and public thoroughfares, of the Sabbath and the means of moral and religious instruction, are both affecting and alarming—and we would make our appeal, by arguments drawn from our state prisons. By the last report of Auburn states prison, on the first of January, 1838, we learn that no less than three hundred and one criminals had been sentenced to that prison, "who had followed the canals," and also one hundred and forty-six more, "who had been sailors," making four hundred and forty-four watermen sentenced to that prison; which is more than one-third of the whole number of convictions. And we also learn that of 1232 criminals sentenced to that prison, 1206 had been habitual Sabbath breakers!! Ought not these facts to awaken the slumbering energies of the church and the nation?

Only give watermen the Sabbath and the means of grace; and then they can have moral and religious captains, boatmen, and drivers, (now the moral and religious class are driven away from the employment,) and the scene will be changed. Then parents will not be afraid to pass along with their little children upon our inland navigation; lest seeing so much wickedness and hearing so much profane language, should prove their ruin. Then too, a happy effect would be produced upon the multitude of emigrants as they pass along our inland waters, and then, too, and extensive shock would be given to licentiousness, and the cause of moral purity receive an impulse heretofore unknown.

Now this great and important work can be done, and must be done. Their spiritual condition is most affecting to the christian, who views this world, and the world to come, in the mirror of the Bible.

True there are a few who have embarked in heaven's life boat—but the great multitude are evidently sailing upon a foundering wreck down the rapid stream of time to the gulf of endless woe. And neither their own security, nor the inactivity of others, makes their danger less, but renders their condition still more alarming.

And when we review our own individual history, we are reminded that under God it has been through the means of grace which we have enjoyed, that we are now permitted to anticipate the kingdom of heaven; and when we contemplate the condition of this multitude, destitute of Sabbaths, and the means of grace, and reflect that each possesses a soul as vulnerable as that of Peter or James, or John, or Andrew; (who once were watermen,) we confess we are almost overwhelmed with the magnitude of the work to be accomplished, and in view of the responsibility devolving upon us, are ready to exclaim, "who is sufficient for these things?"

But this is not all. The importance of the Bethel enterprise will be seen still more clearly by looking at the *Influence of Watermen*. This must be great, for good, or for evil. During the season of navigation they come in contact constantly, night and day, with fellow-men, and exert an influence over tens and hundreds of thousands. And when navigation closes, this neglected and consequently, as a general thing, abandoned multitude, are scattered all through our communities and counties, remote from our canals and commercial places; and spread abroad moral desolation—instances have been known of their breaking up our schools, and often they influence little youth to leave their parents, apprentices to run away from their masters, the fatherless to forsake their mothers, and little orphans to desert their protectors, to become watermen or drivers on the canals, and then they are deprived of religious principles, hurried to the vortex of dissipation, and many are soon ripened for state prison. The startling and affecting fact is proclaimed in the last report of the Auburn states prison; that four hundred and twenty-four had been sentenced to that prison, who either left or lost their parents before they were sixteen years of age!

The best interests of our nation are intimately connected with the success of the Bethel cause.

The business arrangement of our steamboat and canal navigation, is rolling a wave of Sabbath desecration over our land and bringing in a flood of vice and iniquity, which threaten to despoil us of every thing fair and sacred.

Here let facts speak. According to the testimony of those who had the best opportunity of making accurate observations; on the first Sabbath a steamboat run between Albany and New-York, there were 50,000 more Sabbath breakers thronging wharves, &c., than on the previous Sabbath. And one effect produced by this arrangement has been to blind the eyes of the church as well as the community, to the evils and guilt of Sabbath desecration. It is not viewed now as it was fifteen or twenty years ago. And the scene which our christian land presents is both affecting and alarming.

Go to the city of New Orleans, and behold the Lord's day desecrated, by military parade, horse racing, and closed with theatrical plays, &c.

Go to Philadelphia, and on the holy Sabbath of the Lord, behold 6,000 sailing in steamboats, riding upon railroad cars, steamboats, and parties of pleasure.

Go to New-York city, and behold 4,000 more upon the Lord's day than upon any other day of the week, riding upon railroad cars, steamboats, and parties of pleasure.

Then pass along the line upon our inland navigation, and at large and commercial places, on the Sabbath, when the packets and steamboats arrive and depart, the scene which is presented resembles a general military parade.

On a single Sabbath nine steamboats have started away from Buffalo, with 3,000 Sabbath breakers on board.

Again, take another extensive excursion, and enter the churches in our large commercial cities on the Sabbath, and in many instances their sanctuaries are much depopulated—less are attending upon the means of grace in proportion to the number of the population than formerly.

Next examine the calendar of crime—take up the statistics reported in the city of New-York for the year ending Sept. 1, 1837, and mark the increase of 3,068 criminal cases above the number of the preceding year; and making in all 18,956 criminal complaints upon which the police officers acted, besides many others which were dismissed.

Notice also the places where the least regard is paid to the Sabbath—and there we find the greatest number of suicides, murders, assassinations, &c.

Foreign nations begin to give us the name of a Sabbath-breaking nation, and are prophesying our ruin!

Many of our statesmen begin to see the evils threatened, and our land begins to feel the desolation.

Now suppose all the canals in the United States, which thousands of labourers are now excavating, and those which have been chartered and surveyed; should be finished, and brought into Sabbath-breaking arrangements, and the multitude of watermen employed should be destitute of the means of grace, and consequently given up to vice and dissipation, and should then spread abroad through the community the contagion of their wicked and deadly influence—might we not tremble for the result? Would not our just and equitable laws be powerless—mobs reign—more states prisons be needed—our property be insecure—and our lives endangered!!!

And ought not our slumbers to be broken—our fears excited—and our efforts enlisted, when authors in England are writing upon the importance of giving the gospel to the watermen of the United States, and warning us of the fearful consequences which must result from neglecting the Bethel cause.

And, with the Bible in our hands, should Sabbath desecration and all its kindred evils, continue to roll their threatening and desolating waves over our fair land, we can predict the destiny of our nation. "The kingdom and nation that will not serve thee, shall perish; yea, those nations shall be utterly wasted."

[*] According to the register at the comptroller's office in Albany, where the names of all the canal boats in the state must be recorded, there were 3501 canal boats in New-York state alone on the 2d of April, 1838.

† Each boat is manned out with the following crew: one captain, two steersmen, one bowsman, one cook or chamber-maid, (and some both,) and generally two drivers. This makes 24,507 hands employed upon the line boats in New-York state alone.

PART III

Revivals

Early Christian missionaries in central and western New York often wrote of "revivals of religion" in general terms to indicate a community's renewed interest in religion. But the term soon came to indicate an orchestrated resurgence of religious devotion, often associated with prolonged outdoor meetings or a series of such meetings over a period of time. In New York and elsewhere, many religious leaders honed their ability to evoke emotional responses from revival participants, and the result was a dramatic increase in the number of Christian converts.

In New York one name quickly became synonymous with planned religious revivals: Charles Grandison Finney. As a missionary in New York, Finney became a popular preacher as thousands of men and women flocked to hear him. Yet Finney did more than exemplify revival preaching; he packaged it so that his revivals could be duplicated elsewhere. In his book *Lectures on Revivals of Religion* Finney created a step-by-step guide to carrying out successful revivals.[1] In addition, followers such as Theodore Weld zealously spread Finney's brand of revivalism by traveling the region to help plan and carry out such events. Finney did not invent the revival—and such events occurred throughout central

---

1. Charles G. Finney, *Lectures on Revivals of Religion* (New York: Leavitt, Lord, 1835).

and western New York prior to his arrival there in 1825—but he system-
atized revival meetings and consciously propagated them.[2]

The popularity of revivals did not preclude controversy. Many leaders
of mainline Protestant Christian denominations objected to Finney's
tactics. Part of this contention may have been competitive, as the evangelical message Finney preached threatened the preeminence—and
membership numbers—of more traditional churches. While all denominations in central and western New York experienced rapid growth
during the early 1800s, the Baptists and Methodists benefited the most
from this spirit of revivalism. In addition, some religious leaders complained that the camp meetings so often associated with revivals promoted an irreverent decorum, a departure from the staid environment
of traditional Christian worship.[3]

Perhaps the most controversial point of contention was the participation of women in revivals. Such events afforded women a voice that
they did not have in traditional Christian worship. Nearly every Christian denomination of the day featured an all-male priesthood with
severe restrictions—and sometimes outright prohibitions—on women
preaching.[4] Still, women featured prominently in many revival meetings in the Burned-over District. They publicly professed their faith,
related the spiritual experiences that had brought about their conversion, and exhorted audiences to seek their own conversion, or renewal
of faith. Revivals in central and western New York empowered women
in a male-dominated society and, as a result, became an arena in which
some reformers challenged the traditional exclusion of women from
the public square.[5]

Many of the women who claimed their public voices in these settings
recognized that it was only one step on the road to gender equality. For
instance, sisters Sarah and Angelina Grimké observed that women were
demonstrating in revival meetings that they could speak as well, if not
better, than men. Yet churches still denied women formal ordination

---

2. Howard Alexander Morrison, "The Finney Takeover of the Second Great Awakening
during the Oneida Revivals of 1825–1827," *New York History* 59, no. 1 (January 1978): 27–53.

3. "A Convention to Regulate Revivals," document 16 herein.

4. On the history of women preaching in colonial America and the early United States
see Amanda Porterfield, *Feminine Spirituality in America: From Sarah Edwards to Martha Graham*
(Philadelphia: Temple University Press, 1980), and Catherine A. Brekus, *Sarah Osborn's World:
The Rise of Evangelical Christianity in Early America* (New Haven, CT: Yale University Press, 2013).

5. "The Grimké Sisters on the Limits of Revivalism and Reform," document 19 herein. Also
see Nancy Isenberg, *Sex and Citizenship in Antebellum America* (Chapel Hill: University of North
Carolina Press, 1998), 95–99.

and careers in the priesthood. Even men who fought for women's rights to speak in revivals at times expressed hesitation to extend those rights much further. Accordingly, revivalism aided the woman's cause within limits.[6]

Eventually, these contentions came to a head. In 1827, a group of clergymen convened in New Lebanon, New York, to develop regulations for revival meetings. The conference included Finney, some of his supporters, and many of his critics. The result was a series of resolutions but no clear means for enforcement.

Thus, revivals in central and western New York amid the Second Great Awakening were more complex than many have thought. At one level, they were grassroots events, called for and carried out by regular men and women in their own communities. Yet eventually most revivals followed the general organization prescribed by Finney, with policies negotiated by elite clergymen. In one sense, revivals were democratizing, giving regular Americans greater independence in charting a path to salvation and, in the case of many women, a public voice for the first time. Yet these developments were contested, and even many who championed revivalism sought to constrain its more liberal impulses.

It is important to note that while the documents in this part are focused on the religious revivals organized by Christians in New York, the state experienced a Native American religious revival at this time as well. Ganiodaio, a Native American prophet also known as Handsome Lake, sought to simultaneously revive and reform traditional Seneca religious practices. As part of the revival process, Ganiodaio worked with Quaker agents to address some of the major problems that Seneca communities were facing in the wake of white colonization, such as poor health, alcohol abuse, and economic turmoil. Observers dubbed the movement "Handsome Lake's Revival," and many, including President Thomas Jefferson, praised the development in western New York. Among the Seneca, however, the revival was polarizing. While some welcomed the reforms, others rejected them, either because they saw them as corrupting their own religious practices or as prohibiting widespread Seneca conversion to Christianity.[7]

---

6. "Theodore Weld on Revivals and Women's Rights," document 18 herein; "The Grimké Sisters on the Limits of Revivalism and Reform," document 19 herein.

7. Matthew Dennis, *Seneca Possessed: Indians, Witchcraft, and Power in the Early American Republic* (Philadelphia: University of Pennsylvania Press, 2010); Thomas Jefferson to Brother Handsome Lake, November 3, 1802, in Thomas Jefferson, *Writings*, ed. Merrill D. Peterson (New York: Library of America, 1984), 556.

The ten documents featured in this part illuminate the complexity of religious revivals in western New York. They include an excerpt from Finney's autobiography in which he recounted his arrival in Oneida County, as well as an excerpt from Finney's book on revivals, which became a manual of sorts. The part also includes newspaper accounts of revivals, as well as reflections of men and women who participated in them. It features the published minutes of the 1827 meeting of clergymen in New Lebanon, New York, who sought to regulate revivals, and letters between reformers Theodore Weld, Sarah Grimké, and Angelina Grimké on the role of women in revivalism. The same letters speak to the connection between revivalism and the contemporary antislavery and women's rights movements.

ELEVEN

Charles Finney's Argument for Religious Revivals

Source: Charles G. Finney, *Lectures on Revivals of Religion* (New York: Leavitt, Lord, 1835), 9–20.

In 1835 Charles Grandison Finney published *Lectures on Revivals of Religion*, a book that argued for the efficacy of religious revivals and functioned as an instruction manual for planning such meetings. The first essay in that book, titled "What a Revival of Religion Is," is featured here. In a later edition of his *Lectures*, Finney succinctly defined a religious revival as "the renewal of the first love of Christians, resulting in the awakening and conversion of sinners to God." He added that "in the popular sense, a revival of religion in a community is the arousing, quickening, and reclaiming of the more or less backslidden church and the more or less general awakening of all classes, and insuring attention to the claims of God."[1] The lecture demonstrates Finney's definition of and advocacy for revival meetings.

☙ ☙ ☙

1. Charles G. Finney, *Lectures on Revivals of Religion* (New York: F. H. Revell, 1868), 14.

Lecture I

What a Revival of Religion is

TEXT.—O Lord, revive thy work in the midst of the years, in the midst of the years made known; in wrath remember mercy. —Hab. iii. 2.

It is supposed that the prophet Habakkuk was contemporary with Jeremiah, and that this prophecy was uttered in anticipation of the Babylonish captivity. Looking at the judgments which were speedily to come upon his nation, the soul of the prophet was wrought up to an agony, and he cries out in his distress, "O Lord, revive thy work." As if he had said, "O Lord, grant that thy judgments may not make Israel desolate. In the midst of these awful years, let the judgments of God be made the means of reviving religion among us. In wrath remember mercy."

Religion is the work of man. It is something for man to do. It consists in obeying God with and from the heart. It is man's duty. It is true, God induces him to do it. He influences him by his Spirit, because of his great wickedness and reluctance to obey. If it were not necessary for God to influence men—if men were disposed to obey God, there would be no occasion to pray, "O Lord, revive thy work." The ground of necessity for such a prayer is, that men are wholly indisposed to obey; and unless God interpose the influence of his Spirit, not a man on earth will ever obey the commands of God.

A "Revival of Religion" presupposes a declension. Almost all the religion in the world has been produced by revivals. God has found it necessary to take advantage of the excitability there is in mankind, to produce powerful excitements among them, before he can lead them to obey. Men are so spiritually sluggish, there are so many things to lead their minds off from religion, and to oppose the influence of the Gospel, that it is necessary to raise an excitement among them, till the tide rises so high as to sweep away the opposing obstacles. They must be so excited that they will break over these counteracting influences, before they will obey God. Not that excited feeling is religion, for it is not; but it is excited desire, appetite and feeling that prevents religion. The will is, in a sense, enslaved by the carnal and worldly desires. Hence it is necessary to awaken men to a sense of guilt and danger, and thus produce an excitement of counter feeling and desire which will break the power of carnal and worldly desire and leave the will free to obey God.

Look back at the history of the Jews, and you will see that God used to maintain religion among *them* by special occasions, when there would be a great excitement, and people would turn to the Lord. And after they had been thus revived, it would be but a short time before there would be so many counteracting influences brought to bear upon them, that religion would decline, and keep on declining, till God could have time—so to speak—to convict them of sin by his Spirit and rebuke them by his providence, and thus so gain the attention of the masses to the great subject of salvation, as to produce a widespread awakening of religious interest, and consequently a revival of religion. Then the counteracting causes would again operate, and religion would decline, and the nation would be swept away in the vortex of luxury, idolatry, and pride.

There is so little *principle* in the church, so little firmness and stability of purpose, that unless the religious feelings are awakened and kept excited, counter worldly feeling and excitement will prevail, and men will not obey God. They have so little knowledge, and their principles are so weak, that unless they are excited, they will go back from the path of duty, and do nothing to promote the glory of God. The state of the world is still such, and probably will be till the millennium is fully come, that religion must be mainly promoted by means of revivals. How long and how often has the experiment been tried, to bring the church to act steadily for God, without these periodical excitements. Many good men have supposed, and still suppose, that the best way to promote religion, is to go along *uniformly*, and gather in the ungodly gradually, and without excitement. But however sound such reasoning may appear in the abstract, *facts* demonstrate its futility. If the church were far enough advanced in knowledge, and had stability of principle enough to *keep awake*, such a course would do; but the church is so little enlightened, and there are so many counteracting causes, that she will not go steadily to work without a special interest being awakened. As the millennium advances, it is probable that these periodical excitements will be unknown. Then the church will be enlightened, and the counteracting causes removed, and the entire church will be in a state of habitual and steady obedience to God. The entire church will stand and take the infant mind, and cultivate it for God. Children will be trained up in the way they should go, and there will be no such torrents of worldliness, and fashion, and covetousness, to bear away the piety of the church, as soon as the excitement of a revival is withdrawn.

It is very desirable it should be so. It is very desirable that the church should go on steadily in a course of obedience without these excitements. Such excitements are liable to injure the health. Our nervous system is so strung that any powerful excitement, if long continued, injures our health and unfits us for duty. If religion is ever to have a pervading influence in the world, it cannot be so; this spasmodic religion must be done away. Then it will be uncalled for. Christians will not sleep the greater part of time, and once in a while wake up, and rub their eyes, and bluster about, and vociferate a little while, and then go to sleep again. Then there will be no need that ministers should wear themselves out, and kill themselves, by their efforts to roll back the flood of worldly influence that sets in upon the church. But as yet the state of the Christian world is such, that to expect to promote religion without excitements is unphilosophical and absurd. The great political, and other worldly excitements that agitate Christendom, are all unfriendly to religion, and divert the mind from the interests of the soul. Now these excitements can only be counteracted by *religious* excitements. And until there is religious principle in the world to put down irreligious excitements, it is vain to try to promote religion, except by counteracting excitements. This is true in philosophy, and it is a historical fact.

It is altogether improbable that religion will ever make progress among *heathen* nations except through the influence of revivals. The attempt is now making to do it by education, and other cautious and gradual improvements. But so long as the laws of mind remain what they are, it cannot be done in this way. There must be excitement sufficient to wake up the dormant moral powers, and roll back the tide of degradation and sin. And precisely so far as our own land approximates to heathenism, it is impossible for God or man to promote religion in such a state of things but by powerful excitements. This is evident from the fact that this has always been the way in which God has done it. God does not create these excitements, and choose this method to promote religion for nothing or without reason. Where mankind are so reluctant to obey God, they will not act until they are excited. For instance, how many there are who know that they ought to be religious, but they are afraid if they become pious they shall be laughed at by their companions. Many are wedded to idols, others are procrastinating repentance, until they are settled in life, or until they have secured some favorite worldly interest. Such persons will never give up their false shame, or relinquish their ambitious schemes, till they are so excited by a sense of guilt and danger that they cannot contain themselves any longer.

These remarks are designed only as an introduction to the discourse. I shall now proceed with the main design, to show,

I. What a revival of religion is not;
II. What it is; and,
III. The agencies employed in promoting it.

I. A Revival of Religion is Not a Miracle

1. A miracle has been generally defined to be, a Divine interference, setting aside or suspending the laws of nature. It is not a miracle in this sense. All the laws of matter and mind remain in force. They are neither suspended nor set aside in a revival.

2. It is not a miracle according to another definition of the miracle—*something above the powers of nature*. There is nothing in religion beyond the ordinary powers of nature. It consists entirely in the *right exercise* of the powers of nature. It is just that, and nothing else. When mankind become religious, they are not *enabled* to put forth exertions which they were unable to put forth. They only exert the powers they had before in a different way, and use them for the glory of God.

3. It is not a miracle, or dependent on a miracle, in any sense. It is a purely philosophical result of the right use of the constituted means—as much so as any other effect produced by the application of means. There may be a miracle among its antecedent causes, or there may not. The apostles employed miracles, simply as means by which they arrested attention to their message, and established its divine authority. But the miracle was not the revival. The miracle was one thing; the revival that followed it was quite another thing. The revivals in the apostles' days were connected with miracles, but they were not miracles.

I said that a revival is the result of the *right* use of the appropriate means. The means which God has enjoined for the production of a revival, doubtless have a natural tendency to produce a revival. Otherwise God would not have enjoined them. But means will not produce a revival, we all know, without the blessing of God. No more will grain, when it is sowed, produce a crop without the blessing of God. It is impossible for us to say that there is not as direct an influence or agency from God, to produce a crop of grain, as there is to produce a revival. What are the laws of nature according to which it is supposed that grain yields a crop? They are nothing but the constituted manner of the operations of God. In the Bible, the word of God is compared to grain, and preaching is compared to sowing seed, and the results to the springing up and growth of the crop. And the result is just as philosophical in the one case, as in the other, and is as naturally connected with the cause; or, more correctly, a revival is as naturally a result of the use of the appropriate means as a crop is of the use of its appropriate means. It is true that religion does not properly belong to the category of cause and effect; but although it is not *caused* by means, yet it has its occasion, and may as naturally and certainly result from its *occasion* as a crop does from its *cause*.

I wish this idea to be impressed on all your minds, for there has long been an idea prevalent that promoting religion has something very peculiar in it, not to be judged of by the ordinary rules of cause and effect; in short, that there is no connection of the means with the result, and no tendency in the means to produce the effect. No doctrine is more dangerous than this to the prosperity of the church, and nothing more absurd.

Suppose a man were to go and preach this doctrine among farmers, about their sowing grain. Let him tell them that God is a sovereign, and will give them a crop only when it pleases him, and that for them to plow and plant and labor as if they expected to raise a crop is very wrong, and taking the work out of the hands of God, that it interferes with his sovereignty, and is going on in their own strength: and that there is no connection between the means and the result on which they can depend. And now, suppose the farmers should believe such doctrine. Why, they would starve the world to death.

Just such results will follow from the church's being persuaded that promoting religion is somehow so mysteriously a subject of Divine sovereignty, that there is no natural connection between the means and the end. What *are* the results? Why, generation after generation has gone down to hell. No doubt more than five thousand millions have gone down to hell, while the church has been dreaming, and waiting for God to save them without the use of means. It has been the devil's most successful means of destroying souls. The connection is as clear in religion as it is when the farmer sows his grain.

There is one fact under the government of God, worthy *of* universal notice, and of everlasting remembrance; which is that the most useful and important things are most easily and certainly obtained by the use of the appropriate means. This is evidently a principle in the Divine administration. Hence, all the *necessaries* of life are obtained with great *certainty* by the use of the simplest means. The luxuries are more difficult to obtain; the means to procure them are more intricate and less certain in their results; while things absolutely hurtful and poisonous, such as alcohol and the like, are often obtained only by torturing nature, and making use of a kind of infernal sorcery to procure the death-dealing abomination. This principle holds true in moral government, and as spiritual blessings are of surpassing importance, we should expect their attainment to be connected with *great certainty* with the use of appropriate means; and such we find to be the fact; and I fully believe that could facts be known, it would be found that when the appointed means have been *rightly* used, spiritual blessings have been obtained with greater uniformity than temporal ones.

II. I am to Show What a Revival Is

It presupposes that the church is sunk down in a backslidden state, and a revival consists in the return of a church from her backslidings, and in the conversion of sinners.

1. A revival always includes conviction of sin on the part of the church. Backslidden professors cannot wake up and begin right away in the service of God, without deep searchings of the heart. The fountains of sin need to be broken up. In a true revival, Christians are always brought under such convictions; they see their sins in such a light, that often they find it impossible to maintain a hope of their acceptance with God. It does not always go to that extent; but there are always, in a genuine revival, deep convictions of sin, and often cases of abandoning all hope.
2. Backslidden Christians will be brought to repentance. A revival is nothing else than a new beginning of obedience to God. Just as in the case of a converted sinner, the first step is

a deep repentance, a breaking down of heart, a getting down into the dust before God, with deep humility, and forsaking of sin.

3. Christians will have their faith renewed. While they are in their backslidden state they are blind to the state of sinners. Their hearts are as hard as marble. The truths of the Bible only appear like a dream. They admit it to be all true; their conscience and their judgment assent to it; but their faith does not see it standing out in bold relief, in all the burning realities of eternity. But when they enter into a revival, they no longer see men as trees walking, but they see things in that strong light which will renew the love of God in their hearts. This will lead them to labor zealously to bring others to him. They will feel grieved that others do not love God, when they love him so much. And they will set themselves feelingly to persuade their neighbors to give him their hearts. So their love to men will be renewed. They will be filled with a tender and burning love for souls. They will have a longing desire for the salvation of the whole world. They will be in an agony for individuals whom they want to have saved—their friends, relations, enemies. They will not only be urging them to give their hearts to God, but they will carry them to God in the arms of faith, and with strong crying and tears beseech God to have mercy on them, and save their souls from endless burnings.

4. A revival breaks the power of the world and of sin over Christians. It brings them to such vantage ground that they get a fresh impulse towards heaven. They have a new foretaste of heaven, and new desires after union with God; and the charm of the world is broken, and the power of sin overcome.

5. When the churches are thus awakened and reformed, the reformation and salvation of sinners will follow, going through the same stages of conviction, repentance, and reformation. Their hearts will be broken down and changed. Very often the most abandoned profligates are among the subjects. Harlots, and drunkards, and infidels, and all sorts of abandoned characters, are awakened and converted. The worst among human beings are softened, and reclaimed, and made to appear as lovely specimens of the beauty of holiness.

III. I am to Consider the Agencies Employed in Carrying Forward a Revival of Religion.

Ordinarily, there are three agents employed in the work of conversion, and one instrument. The agents are God,—some person who brings the truth to bear on the mind,—and the sinner himself. The instrument is the truth. There are *always two* agents, God and the sinner, employed and active in every case of genuine conversion.

1. The agency of God is two-fold; by his Providence and by his Spirit.
   (1.) By his providential government, he so arranges events as to bring the sinner's mind and the truth in contact. He brings the sinner where the truth reaches his ears or his eyes. It is often interesting to trace the manner in which God arranges events so as to bring this about, and how he sometimes makes every thing seem to favor a revival. The state of the weather, and of the public health, and other circumstances concur to make every thing just right to favor the application of truth with the greatest possible efficacy. How he sometimes sends a minister along, just at the time he is wanted! How he brings out a particular truth, just at the particular time when the individual it is fitted to reach is in the way to hear!
   (2.) God's special agency by his Holy Spirit. Having direct access to the mind, and knowing infinitely well the whole history and state of each individual sinner, he employs that truth which is best adapted to his particular case, and then sets it home with Divine power. He gives it such vividness, strength, and power, that the sinner quails, and throws down his weapons of rebellion, and turns to the Lord. Under his influence, the truth burns and cuts its way like fire. He makes the truth stand out in such aspects, that it crushes the proudest man down with the weight of a mountain. If men were *disposed* to obey God, the truth is given with sufficient clearness in the Bible; and from preaching they could learn all that is necessary for them to know. But because they are wholly *disinclined* to obey it, God clears it up before their minds, and pours in a blaze of convincing

light upon their souls, which they cannot withstand, and
they yield to it, and obey God, and are saved.

2. The agency of men is commonly employed. Men are not mere
    instruments in the hands of God. Truth is the instrument.
    The preacher is a moral agent in the work; he acts; he is not
    a mere passive instrument; he is voluntary in promoting the
    conversion of sinners.

3. The agency of the sinner himself. The conversion of a sinner
    consists of his obeying the truth. It is therefore impossible
    it should take place without his agency, for it consists in *his*
    acting right. He is influenced to this by the agency of God,
    and by the agency of men. Men act on their fellow-men,
    not only by language, but by their looks, their tears, their
    daily deportment. See that impenitent man there, who has
    a pious wife. Her very looks, her tenderness, her solemn,
    compassionate dignity, softened and moulded into the image
    of Christ are sermon to him all the time. He has to turn his
    mind away, because it is such a reproach to him. He feels a
    sermon ringing in his ears all day long.

Mankind are accustomed to read the countenances of their neighbors. Sinners often read the state of a Christian's mind in his eyes. If his
eyes are full of levity, or worldly anxiety and contrivance, sinners read it.
If they are full of the Spirit of God, sinners read it; and they are often
led to conviction by barely seeing the countenance of Christians.

An individual once went into a manufactory to see the machinery.
His mind was solemn, as he had been where there was a revival. The
people who labored there all knew him by sight, and knew who he
was. A young lady who was at work saw him, and whispered some foolish remark to her companion, and laughed. The person stopped and
looked at her with a feeling of grief. She stopped, her thread broke, and
she was so much agitated she could not join it. She looked out at the
window to compose herself, and then tried again; again and again she
strove to recover her self-command. At length she sat down, overcome
with her feelings. The person then approached and spoke with her; she
soon manifested a deep sense of sin. The feeling spread through the
establishment like fire, and in a few hours almost every person employed there was under conviction, so much so, that the owner, though
a worldly man, was astounded, and requested to have the works stop

and have a prayer meeting; for he said it was a great deal more important to have these people converted than to have the works go on. And in a few days, the owner and nearly every person employed in the establishment were hopefully converted. The eye of this individual, his solemn countenance, his compassionate feeling, rebuked the levity of the young woman, and brought her under conviction of sin: and this whole revival followed, probably in a great measure, from so small an incident.

If Christians have deep feeling on the subject of religion themselves, they will produce deep feeling wherever they go. And if they are cold, or light and trifling, they inevitably destroy all deep feeling, even in awakened sinners.

I knew a case, once, of an individual who was very anxious, but one day I was grieved to find that her convictions seemed to be all gone. I asked her what she had been doing. She told me she had been spending the afternoon at such a place, among some professors of religion, not thinking that it would dissipate her convictions to spend an afternoon with professors of religion. But they were trifling and vain, and thus her convictions were lost. And no doubt those professors of religion, by their folly, destroyed a soul, for her convictions did not return.

The church is required to use the means for the conversion of sinners. Sinners cannot properly be said to use the means for their own conversion. The church uses the means. What sinners do is to submit to the truth, or to resist it. It is a mistake of sinners, to think they are using means for their own conversion. The whole drift of a revival, and every thing about it, is designed to present the truth *to* your mind, for your obedience or resistance.

Remarks

1. Revivals were formerly regarded as miracles. And it has been so by some even in our day. And others have ideas on the subject so loose and unsatisfactory, that if they would only *think*, they would see their absurdity. For a long time, it was supposed by the church, that a revival was a miracle, an interposition of Divine power which they had nothing to do with, and which they had no more agency in producing, than they had in producing thunder, or a storm of hail, or an earthquake. It is only within a few years that ministers generally have supposed revivals were to be *promoted*, by the use of means designed

and adapted specially to that object. Even in New England, it has been supposed that revivals came just as showers do, sometimes in one town, and sometimes in another, and that ministers and churches could do nothing more to produce them than they could to make showers of rain come on their own town, when they were falling on a neighboring town.

It used to be supposed that a revival would come about once in fifteen years, and all would be converted that God intended to save, and then they must wait until another crop came forward on the stage of life. Finally, the time got shortened down to five years, and they supposed there might be a revival about as often as that.

I have heard a fact in relation to one of these pastors, who supposed revivals might come about once in five years. There had been a revival in his congregation. The next year, there was a revival in a neighboring town, and he went there to preach, and staid several days, till he got his soul all engaged in the work. He returned home on Saturday, and went into his study to prepare for the Sabbath. And his soul was in an agony. He thought how many adult persons there were in his congregation at enmity with God—so many still unconverted—so many persons *die* yearly—such a portion of them unconverted—if a revival does not come under five years, so many adult heads of families will be in hell. He put down his calculations on paper, and embodied them in his sermon for the next day, and with his heart bleeding at the dreadful picture. As I have understood it, he did not do this with any expectation of a revival, but he felt deeply, and poured out his heart to his people. And that sermon awakened *forty heads of families*, and a powerful revival followed; and so his theory about a revival once in five years was all exploded.

Thus God has overthrown, generally, the theory that revivals are miracles.

2.   Mistaken notions concerning the sovereignty of God have greatly hindered revivals.

Many people have supposed God's sovereignty to be some thing very different from what it is. They have supposed it to be such an arbitrary disposal of events, and particularly of the gift of his Spirit, as precluded a rational employment of means for promoting a revival of religion.

But there is no evidence from the Bible that God exercises any such sovereignty as that. There are no facts to prove it. But everything goes to show that God has connected means with the end through all the departments of his government—in nature and in grace. There is no *natural* event in which his own agency is not concerned. He has not built the creation like a vast machine that will go on alone without his further care. He has not retired from the universe, to let it work for itself. This is mere atheism. He exercises a universal superintendence and control. And yet every event in nature has been brought about by means. He neither administers providence nor grace with that sort of sovereignty that dispenses with the use of means. There is no more sovereignty in one than in the other.

And yet some people are terribly alarmed at all direct efforts to promote a revival, and they cry out, "You are trying to get up a revival in your own strength. Take care, you are interfering with the sovereignty of God. Better keep along in the usual course, and let God give a revival when he thinks it is best. God is a sovereign, and it is very wrong for you to attempt to get up a revival, just because *you think* a revival is needed." This is just such preaching as the devil wants. And men cannot do the devil's work more effectually than by preaching up the sovereignty of God, as a reason why we should not put forth efforts to produce a revival.

3. You see the error of those who are beginning to think that religion can be better promoted in the world without revivals, and who are disposed to give up all efforts to produce religious awakenings. Because there are evils arising in some instances out of great excitements on the subject of religion, they are of opinion that it is best to dispense with them altogether. This cannot, and must not be. True, there is danger of abuses. In cases of great *religious* as well as all other excitements, more or less incidental evils may be expected of course. But this is no reason why they should be given up. The best things are always liable to abuses. Great and manifold evils have originated in the providential and moral governments of God. But these *foreseen* perversions and evils were not considered a sufficient reason for giving them up. For the establishment of these governments was on the whole the best that could be done for the production of the greatest amount of happiness. So

in revivals of religion, it is found by experience, that in the present state of the world, religion cannot be promoted to any considerable extent without them. The evils which are sometimes complained of, when they are real, are incidental, and of small importance when compared with the amount of good produced by revivals. The sentiment should not be admitted by the church for a moment, that revivals may be given up. It is fraught with all that is dangerous to the interests of Zion, is death to the cause of missions, and brings in its train the damnation of the world.

FINALLY.—I have a proposal to make to you who are here present. I have not commenced this course of Lectures on Revivals to get up a curious theory of my own on the subject. I would not spend my time and strength merely to give you instructions, to gratify your curiosity, and furnish you something to talk about. I have no idea of preaching *about* revivals. It is not my design to preach so as to have you able to say at the close, "We *understand* all about revivals now," while you do *nothing*. But I wish to ask you a question. What do you hear lectures on revivals for? Do you mean that whenever you are convinced, what your duty is in promoting a revival, you will go to work and practise it?

Will you follow the instructions I shall give you from the Word of God, and put them in practise in your lives? Will you bring them to bear upon your families, your acquaintance, neighbors, and through the city? Or will you spend the winter in learning *about* revivals, and do nothing *for* them? I want you, as fast as you learn any thing on the subject of revivals, to put it in practice, and go to work and see if you cannot promote a revival among sinners here. If you will not do this, I wish you to let me know at the beginning, so that I need not waste my strength. You ought to decide *now* whether you will of this or not. You know that we call sinners to decide on the spot whether *they* will obey the Gospel. And we have no more authority to let you take time to deliberate whether *you* will obey God, than we have to let sinners do so. We call on you to unite now in a solemn pledge to God, that you will do your duty as fast as you learn what it is, and to pray that He will pour out his Spirit upon this church and upon all the city this winter.

TWELVE

Revivals at Marcellus and Amber

Source: "Revivals at Marcellus and Amber," *Onondaga Register*, February 1, 1826.

New York newspapers frequently published reports of revivals that occurred throughout the country but paid special attention to those in the state. In February 1826, the *Onondaga Register* reprinted such a report from the *Western Recorder* (Utica, NY) detailing revivals in the towns of Marcellus and Amber, including the construction of a new church.

✄ ✄ ✄

From the Western Recorder

Revivals and Marcellus and Amber.—A correspondent writes us from the village of Amber, that an unusual season of religious attention has existed in one school district in the town of Marcellus, the fruits of which are the hopeful conversion of about twenty souls.

"This cloud of mercy," adds the writer, "has extended to Amber, and for four weeks has *fallen in a shower*! Our village is small; but O, what a change! Four weeks since, there was not a praying family here, except our Methodist minister's and my own. Now, more than half the heads of families are hoping in divine mercy: and most of them we can say *behold they pray.* The work seems to be extending around us. Churches of different orders participate in it, and almost every day we hear of one or more hopeful conversions.

"Yesterday, a well finished house, 50 feet by 40, just built in this village, was dedicated to the service of God. When the corner stone was laid last spring, not one, I believe, who engaged in helping forward the work, indulged the hope of a saving change. Several of these are now rejoicing in the Lord. These circumstances combined to render the dedication service solemn & interesting. Truly the Lord has done, and is still doing many things for us, whereof we are glad."

Thirteen

Report of New York Revivals

Source: "Revivals of Religion," *Onondaga Register*, July 19, 1826.

On July 19, 1826, the *Onondaga Register* published a compilation of reports on religious revivals in New York and northern Pennsylvania from the *Western Recorder* (Utica, NY). The report indicated a large number of men and women converting to the different denominations in the region. Such reports were common in New York newspapers at this time, and this particular report is featured here as another example of the continued spread and growing popularity of revivals in the region.

❦ ❦ ❦

Revivals of Religion

Utica.—Last Sabbath week, 59 persons were admitted into Christian communion by profession, in Mr. Aikin's church. About 40 have joined Mr. Brace's church, and nearly the same number Mr. Everett's.—Many have also united with the Baptist and Methodist churches. All of the above, however, comprise but a part of the subjects of the present revival.

FIGURE 6. Methodist camp meeting, 1836. Americans sometimes used the term "revival" to refer to camp meetings in which preaching occurred outdoors over the course of several days. This painting by Edward Williams Clay depicts a Methodist camp meeting in 1836. (Harry T. Peters "America on Stone" Collection, National Museum of American History, Smithsonian Institution)

Canandaigua.—A letter from Canandaigua mentions, that last Sabbath week, 48 were received by profession into the communion of the Presbyterian church in that place; and that probably a more interesting Sabbath was never before witnessed there. *Western Recorder.*

An interesting work of grace has been commenced in the village of *Herkimer.*—The "still small voice" of God has been heard there; and within three weeks, about twenty persons indulge a hope that they have passed from death to life. Herkimer is an important section of our presbytery, and on many accounts a revival in that place appears to be doubly interesting. The work is still going on; the church and other professors are much aroused: and the fervent prayers of all our christian friends are desired, that God would deepen, extend and perfect the work.

From *Fairfield,* also, we have cheering accounts. Much attention to the concerns of the soul is excited there—and a number have very recently obtained hope in Christ. The same also may be said of the village of *Frankfort.*

While Christians have so much to animate and cheer them—while almost every part of our presbytery is thus watered from on high, how great is the responsibility of our churches, and how criminal are their members, for their great want of faith in the promises, and confidence in the faithfulness of God. Surely the divine love and mercy exhibited in the conversion of such a multitude of souls, should lead every follower of Christ to instant and persevering prayer, that every church within out bounds may receive the influences of the Holy Spirit—and that neither the unfaithfulness nor the *unbelief* of christians, should operate to prevent a universal outpouring of that Spirit.

A Revival commenced in the church of Gravel Run, Crawford co. Pa. last autumn, and about the same time in the congregation of Springfield, near Ohio. It continued during the winter, and issued in the hopeful conversion of a number of young persons, and elder ones. The Rev. Mr. Chamberlain, a zealous laborer in the Lord's vineyard, tho' of delicate health, has been with these congregations in the commencement and progress of the work. *ib.*

FOURTEEN

Bradford King's Conversion

Source: Bradford King Diary, 1811–1833, King Family Papers, A.K52, Rare Books, Special Collections, and Preservation, River Campus Libraries, University of Rochester.

Bradford King experienced his religious conversion after hearing Charles Finney preach in Rochester, New York, in 1830. In his journal, King recorded his feelings upon hearing Finney's sermon and how his reflections on the sermon ultimately led to what he described as his actual moment of conversion several days later. King also mentioned the conversion of Artemesia Perkens at an "anxious meeting."[1] In revivals, "anxious benches" or separate "anxious meetings" were designed to help the unconverted experience the manifestations of the Holy Spirit. Preachers instructed revival attendees to pray specifically for those seated on the "anxious bench" during the meeting. The prose in King's journal entry is difficult to understand in places, but it represents the conversion experience of an average man at one of Finney's revival meetings.

❧ ❧ ❧

1. In a later insertion in the diary, King noted that Perkens "died April 24 1832 her last words were she never had forgot the time when she was first converted it shows the above to be true that she always could say Blessed be the name of Jesus."

[...] Some time in the month of October <1830> I herd the Rev^d Mr Finney Preach It awakened in me a sense of my being in Rebellion to God & of my total inability to do any thing without him I yielded to the call & as I hope & trust gave myself to God & Expect to find pardon & Acceptan [acceptance] only in the Merits of the Bleeding Savior Lord Strengthen me in this my Dedication

Friday Evening Oct 29th <1830> (twenty ninth) I formally Gave myself to God in the 2nd Presbyterian Church <Rochester> Likewise Artemesia Perkens & on Saturday Evening Artemesia at the anxious meeting could say Blessed Be the name of Jesus with such clearness & light that she never can forget it

I did not get Relief until the Thursday Wednesday following at or near one oclock in the morning. When I went to bed & thought the Bed never Before felt so soft & comfortable & I sung many times over with that Ease & satisfaction which astonished me these words which I Recollect I am Going to the Kingdom will you Go along with me. & some others with Equal Ease But they are Gone from me I did not get Entire Relief untill I went to the anxious Meeting & there Related some of My Exercises I was told to go home & commence Family Worship which I never had Done after having Done that the Monday following as soon as I got home. I felt Relief in full Excepting occasionally felt some dout [doubt] as to my sins being forgiven But was decided that as for me & my House we would serve the Lord [. . .]

FIFTEEN

Nancy Alexander Tracy's Conversion

Source: Nancy Alexander Tracy, Autobiography, L. Tom Perry Special Collections, Brigham Young University, Provo, Utah.

In her autobiography, Nancy Alexander Tracy reminisced about the religious experiences of her youth. She recalled attending religious meetings—including a Methodist revival—in Herkimer County, New York, and seeking Christian conversion privately. She did not unite, however, with the Methodists or any of the other Protestant Christian denominations in the area. Instead, she joined with the Mormons after hearing some of their missionaries preach. The excerpt from Tracy's account featured here is illustrative of those who were not converted by revival meetings, despite their desires for it, and instead found spiritual fulfillment among newer religious movements outside mainline Protestant Christianity. A page of the manuscript is severely torn. However, the missing text is supplied based on a typescript made of the autobiography before the manuscript was damaged.[1]

❧ ❧ ❧

---

1. Nancy Alexander Tracy Autobiography, typescript, L. Tom Perry Special Collections, Brigham Young University, Provo, Utah.

[. . .]

I was born in the town of Henderson, Jefferson Co., New York. I was born of goodly parents, Aaron and Betsey L. Alexander, on the 14th of May, 1816. My father died when I was four years old. He left my Mother in comfortable circumstances on a farm. There were four small children, the oldest six years of age. Mother felt that she could not take care of the place, so she sold the farm and was to receive money for it, but the man who bought it failed in business and never paid her. Consequently it left her destitute and she had to put out her three oldest children. I was the second child, so it fell to my lot to go to my Grandfather's home, on Mother's side, to live in Herkimer Co. one hundred miles from Mother. I was now five years old. My uncles and aunts were all grown and most of them married, so I was quite a favorite in the family. I was kept in school most of the time, but as I grew up I learned to spin flax and wool and weave cloth. This I did in the summer and I went to school in the winter.

When I was 13 years old, there was quite a revival in the town among the Methodists. I had been trained to always go to their church and Sunday schools, in which I took a great delight for I had a religious turn of mind. When this reformation broke out I felt as though I wanted to get religious and be happy as others seemed to be. I tried to get a change of heart and would go off alone by myself and take the bible and read and pray, but I could feel no different, so I never joined their church.

When I was 15, my Mother came to see me and stayed one year. I became so attached to her that I could not bear the idea of being separated from her again. When she was preparing to leave I told her I wanted to go with her. She finally consented. I knew I was leaving a good home, where I had been kindly cared for, and I knew too that Mother had no home of her own, still I had a great anxiety to go and take the chance of a home. I was going to school at the time, so I bid the school and my teacher good-bye and went with Mother.

When we arrived in Jefferson Co., I was again placed in school for the winter. In the spring I was offered a school to teach, but declined as I thought I was too young, being only 16 years old so I went to live with Abram Tracy, his wife was Mother's cousin. While there I became acquainted with his brother, Moses Tracy. An attachment sprang up between us and on the 15th of July we were married. This was in the year of 1832. My husband then took me to his Father's home to live, until we could get a home of our own. In the fall we went keeping house. The winter passed off very pleasantly for us.

In the spring of 1833 there was quite a sensation created by a new sect of ministers that came around preaching. They were called Mormons. We heard all sorts of stories and did not know what to think of them, such frightful stories were told. At length we heard of an appointment, that one David W. Patten was going to preach about two miles from where we lived. A curiosity seized me and I felt I must go and hear him so 3 of us went, Ensign Tracy's wife, Lydia, Margaret Minor, and myself. Two our astonishment we beheld a tall, stately looking man, with piercing black eyes. He arose and gave out a hymn. We expected to see some one hardly in human form, from what we had heard, but instead I could at a glance see the noble spirit he possessed beaming in his countenance, and when he began to speak it was with such force and power. Before he was half through I could have borne my testimony of the truth of the gospel and doctrine he was preaching. Never before had I heard the true gospel as the Saviour and his apostles had taught it while they were on the earth, but this man had now given us a pure gospel sermon and I believed it with all my heart and would have gladly gone down into the waters of baptism, but I wanted my husband to hear first and come along with me. These elders preached often in the neighborhood and many became convinced of the truth of the gospel and were baptized. Finally quite a large branch was organized in the town of Ellisburg. My husband as yet did not seem to believe as readily as I would have liked, but I still believed when he would give himself up to investigate the gospel, he would embrace it, for I knew he was honest hearted.

In Nov. the 24th, 1833, our first son was born and for a long time I lay as it were, at death's possessive door. The presiding elders of the branch used to come to our house and would talk about the gospel and its ordinances, and I felt a great desire to be administered to, but I was [page torn] [surrounded by unbelievers] and had [page torn] [not obeyed the ordinance of baptism as I had felt constrained] to do [page torn] [and felt that I] was unworthy to ask for the blessings, but I determined if the Lord would let me live, to go forth in the discharge of what I knew was my duty. In spring my husband seemed to take hold, commenced going to meetings and studying the Bible and finally to my great satisfaction said he was ready to be baptized. I had measurably regained my health and on the tenth day of May, 1834, we were both baptized by Elder Thomas Dutcher.

At the early day the opposite power was at work, filling the minds of people with prejudice. The pulpit and press had commenced a tirade against the Mormons. My relatives thought I had brought a great stain upon myself and them, in embracing such a delusion, as they called it. They would send me the papers of the day [*page torn*] [with the most vile] slanders and falsehoods [*page torn*] [to see if they] could not reclaim me, but I was not moved. I felt humble and thought to thank God that my soul was at last satisfied thus far that I had embraced truth instead of error and it was marvelous to me how I had escaped while in tender year, of uniting with some of the religions of the day. I was brought up so strictly amongst them, I felt to acknowledge the hand of God, that I had been preserved with my heart pure to listen to the voice of the good sheperd. [. . .]

SIXTEEN

A Convention to Regulate Revivals

Source: "For the Troy Sentinel," and "Important Convention," *Troy Sentinel*, August 14, 1827.

The revival meetings in the Burned-over District stirred up controversy among many Christians. Some saw the meetings as a departure from the decorum they expected from Christian worship services, and for many the prayers offered at these revivals by women violated social norms. Accordingly, on July 18, 1827, nearly thirty Presbyterian and Congregationalist ministers from New York, Connecticut, and Massachusetts convened in New Lebanon, New York. The convention lasted for nine days as the ministers debated what resolutions they would adopt to regulate revivals.

🕊 🕊 🕊

From the New York Observer.
Important Convention

It is generally known to the Christian public, that a Convention of Presbyterian and Congregational ministers have been several days in session at New Lebanon, to consult on certain differences of opinion which were supposed to exist among themselves and their brethren, in respect to revivals of religion. Not that any doubted the reality and unspeakable importance of these refreshings, or had ceased to pray that they might become co-extensive with the earth; for here, let the enemy know, there has been, and is, a perfect unanimity. Indeed, it is *on account* of this strong feeling in favor of revivals, that so tender an anxiety has been awakened to preserve them from all extravagancies.

When the project of such a Convention was first rumored, there were many who prophesied evil rather than good from its deliberations; because, they said, it would be perfectly easy, by inviting men of a particular stamp, to make its results just what the projectors might please.—Concerning this we remark, in the first place, that no such partiality appears to have been observed in selecting the members,—and secondly, that though this were the case, still the meeting would have accomplished one important good, by showing to the public that we are the *real* sentiments of this and that man, this and that party, (if such they may be called,) on the points in dispute. But we trust other benefits will result from the measure; and that the spirit of Christian tenderness and supplication, which seems to have pervaded the meeting, will be diffused through all our congregations, allaying every improper excitement, and preparing them for new blessings from the overflowing fountain of mercy.

NEW LEBANON, July 18, 1827.

At a Convention of Ministers of the Gospel, assembled at the house of Mr. Betts, by letters of invitation from Mr. Beman and Dr. Beecher, Rev. Heman Humphrey, D. D. was chosen Moderator, and Rev. William R. Weeks and Rev. Henry Smith, Scribes.

The meeting was opened with a prayer by the Moderator.

After some conversation respecting the list of persons who had been originally agreed upon to compose this meeting, voted to have a recess, till half past two o'clock.

After recess, met and proceeded to business.

Of the brethren who were considered as duly invited, there were *present*, Rev. Asahel S. Norton, D.D. of Clinton, N.Y. Lyman Beecher, D. D. Boston, Mass. Moses Gillet, Rome, N.Y. Nathan S. S. Beman, Troy, N.Y. Dirck C. Lansing, D. D. Auburn, N. Y. Heman Humphrey, D. D. Amherst College, Mass. John Frost, Whitesborough, N.Y. Asahel Nettleton, Connecticut; William R. Weeks, Paris, N.Y. Justin Edwards, Andover, Mass. Henry Smith, Camden, N.Y. and Charles G. Finney, Oneida co. N.Y. *Absent*, Rev. David Porter, D. D. Catskill, N.Y. Alvin Hyde, D.D. Lee, Mass. Samuel Tomb, Salem, N.Y. Joel T. Benedict, Chatham, N.Y. Eliphalet Nott, D. D. Union College, N.Y. Thomas

M'Auley, D. D. New York, Gardiner Spring, D. D. New York, James Patterson, Philadelphia, Henry R. Weed, Albany, N.Y. Samuel C. Aikin, Utica, N.Y. Thomas H. Skinner, D. D. Philadelphia, and Edwin Dwight, Richmond, Mass.

The Rev. Caleb J. Tenney, of Wethersfield, and the Rev. Joel *Hawes*, of Hartford, Conn. being present by invitation from Dr. Beecher—the Rev. George W. Gale, of the Oneida Academy, N.Y. being present by invitation from Mr. Frost, and the Rev. Silas Churchill, Minister of the place—it was voted that they be invited to take a seat as members of this Convention.

The Convention united in a season of prayer, interspersed with singing.

Voted that those of our brethren who are in the place, be requested to spend as much of their time as convenient, in special prayer for the divine blessing on the deliberation of this meeting.

After the brethren who had called the meeting had made an exposition of its origin, it was moved and seconded, that we proceed to see in what respects there is an agreement between brethren from different sections of the country, in regard to principles and measures in conducting and promoting revivals of religion:—which motion was under discussion till seven o'clock, when the Convention adjourned, to meet tomorrow morning, at eight o'clock. Concluded with prayer.

Thursday Morning, July 19.

Met according to adjournment, and opened with prayer. Present the same as yesterday, with the addition of the Rev. Mr. Aikin.

The minutes of yesterday was read.

The motion under discussion yesterday was taken up, and after further discussion, it was carried—*fourteen* voting in the affirmative, *one* in the negative, and *two* declining to vote, as follows: *For the affirmative,* Messrs. Norton, Beecher, Churchill, Gillet, Tenny, Lansing, Humphrey, Nettleton, Hawes, Weeks, Gale, Edwards, Smith, and Finney. *For the negative,* Mr. Beman. *Declined voting,* Messrs. Frost and Aikin.

Mr. Frost entered the following as his reason for declining to vote:— "That he understood the object of the meeting to be, to correct misapprehensions, and restore peace among brethren."

The Convention then proceeded to attend to the subject proposed; and, on motion of Mr. Edwards, the following propositions were agreed to:

"That revivals of true religion are the work of God's Spirit, by which, in a comparatively short period of time, many persons are convinced of sin, and brought to the exercises of repentance towards God and faith in our Lord Jesus Christ." *Voted in the affirmative unanimously.*

"That the preservation and extension of true religion in our land have been much promoted by these revivals." *Voted unanimously.*

"That, according to the Bible, and the indications of Providence, greater and more glorious revivals are to be expected, than have ever yet existed." *Voted unanimously.*

"That, though revivals of religion are the work of God's Spirit, they are produced by means of divine truths and human instrumentality, and liable to be advanced or hindered by measures which are adopted in conducting them. The idea that God ordinarily works independently of human instrumentality, or without any reference to the adaptation of means to ends, is unscriptural." *Voted unanimously*

"There may be some variety in the mode of conducting revivals, according to local customs, and there may be relative imperfections attending them, which do not destroy the purity of the work and its permanent and general good influence upon the church and the world; and, in such cases, good men, while they lament these imperfections, may rejoice in the revival as the work of God." *Voted unanimously.*

Recess till three o'clock. Then met, and resumed the consideration of general principles. On motion of Mr. Edwards, the following propositions were agreed to:

"There may be so much human infirmity, and indiscretion, and wickedness of man, in conducting a revival of religion, as to render the general evils which flow from this infirmity, indiscretion, and wickedness of man, greater than the local and temporary advantages of the revival; that is, this infirmity, indiscretion, and wickedness of man, may be the means of preventing the conversion of more souls than may have been converted during the revival." *Voted unanimously.*

"In view of these considerations, we regard it as eminently important, that there should be a general understanding among ministers and churches, in respect to those things which are of a dangerous tendency, and are not to be countenanced." *Voted unanimously.*

Mr. Edwards then introduced the following proposition:

"In social meetings of men and women, for religious worship, females are not to pray."

After some discussion, adjourned to meet tomorrow morning, at eight o'clock. Concluded with prayer.

Friday, July 20.

Met according to adjournment, and opened with prayer.

Present the same as yesterday. The minutes of yesterday were read.

The consideration of the proposition under discussion yesterday, was resumed. After further discussion, united in a season of prayer. Then attended further to the discussion of the subject, till one o'clock, and adjourned to meet at half past two o'clock. Concluded with prayer.

Friday Afternoon.

Met according to adjournment, and opened with prayer.

The consideration of the proposition, which had been under discussion, was resumed.

It was moved by Mr. Aikin, and seconded by Mr. Finney, that the further consideration of the proposition be postponed, till we shall have gone into an enquiry into matters of fact.

After some discussion, united in a season of prayer.

After further discussion, Mr. Aikin asked and obtained to leave to withdraw his motion for postponement, and it was withdrawn.

The Rev. Mr. Weed appeared in Convention, and took his seat as a member.

After further discussion, the question was taken, and *nine* voted in favor of the proposition, and *nine* declined voting, as follows: *For the proposition*, Messrs. Norton, Beecher, Tenney, Humphrey, Nettleton, Hawes, Weeks, Weed, and Edwards. *Decline voting*, Messrs. Churchill, Gillet, Beman, Lansing, Frost, Gale, Aikin, Smith, and Finney.

It was moved by Mr. Frost, and seconded by Mr. Finney, that the following question be answered, to wit:

"Is it right for a woman in any case to pray in presence of a man?"

After some discussion, it was moved by Mr. Edwards that the further consideration of this question be indefinitely postponed. The motion was seconded, and after some discussion, Mr. Edwards asked and obtained leave to withdraw his motion, and it was withdrawn.

It was moved by Mr. Lansing, that that further consideration of the question be postponed, for the purpose of introducing a substitute, which he read. The motion was seconded, and after discussion, it was carried.

Mr. Lansing then introduced the following proposition, as a substitute for the question of Mr. Frost, to wit:

"There may be circumstances in which it may be proper for a female to pray in the presence of men."

The motion was seconded, and after discussion, the question was taken, and *eight* voted in favor of the proposition, and *ten* declined voting, as follows: *For the proposition*, Messrs. Churchill, Gillet, Beman, Lansing, Frost, Gale, Aikin, and Finney. *Decline voting*, Messrs. Norton, Beecher, Tenney, Humphrey, Nettleton, Hawes, Weeks, Weed, Edwards, and Smith.

Adjourned to meet to-morrow morning, at eight o'clock. Concluded with prayer.

Saturday, July 21.

Met according to adjournment, and opened with prayer. Present the same as yesterday. The minutes of yesterday were read.

Mr. Edwards introduced the following proposition:

"It is improper for any person to appoint meetings in the congregations of acknowledged ministers of Christ, or to introduce any measures to promote or conduct revivals of religion, without having first obtained the approbation of said ministers."

The motion was seconded, and after considerable discussions, the question was taken, and *thirteen* voted in favor of the proposition, and *five* declined voting, as follows: *For the proposition*, Messrs. Norton, Beecher, Churchill, Tenney, Humphrey, Nettleton, Hawes, Weeks, Weed, Gale, Edwards, Smith, and Finney.—*Declined voting*, Messrs. Gillet, Beman, Lansing, Frost and Aikin.

Those who declined voting, entered the following as their reason, to wit: "That *there may be some cases*, where the elders or members of a minister's own church may appoint and conduct prayer meetings, without having consulted the minister or obtained his approbation; but in no case ought such elders or members to appoint or conduct such meetings contrary to the will of the pastor: and these meetings ought to be *occasional,* and not *stated.*"

Mr. Edwards introduced the following proposition:

"Those meetings for social religious worship, in which all speak according to their own inclinations, are improper; and all meetings for religious worship, ought to be under the presiding influence of some person or persons."

The motion was seconded, and after discussion, it was *voted unanimously in the affirmative.*

Mr. Edwards introduced the following proposition:

"The calling of persons by name in prayer ought to be carefully avoided."

The motion was seconded, and after some discussion, it was moved and seconded that it be so amended as to read as follows:

"The calling of persons by name in social circles for prayer ought to be carefully avoided." This amendment did not prevail.

Mr. Edwards moved that the proposition be so amended as to read as follows:

"The calling of persons by name in social prayer ought to be carefully avoided."

The motion was seconded, and the amendment prevailed.

Mr. Lansing then moved that the proposition be so amended as to read as follows:

"The calling of persons by name in public prayer ought to be carefully avoided."

The motion was seconded, and after some discussion, the question was put by lifting the hands, and *nine* were counted in favor of the amendment, and *eight* against it; upon which the Moderator declared it *not a vote,* being understood to vote against it. It was questioned whether it was usual for the Moderator to vote in such cases; upon which, he declined voting, and declared the amendment carried.

After some remarks, it was moved, that it is the sense of this body that the Moderator has a right to vote, in all cases before us, as any other member. The motion was seconded and carried.

It was then agreed to take the question on Mr. Lansing's amendment over again, by ayes and noes, when the amendment prevailed, *ten* voting in the affirmative, *seven* in the negative, and *one* declining to vote, as follows: *For the affirmative.* Messrs. Churchill, Gillet, Beman, Lansing, Frost, Weed, Gale, Aikin, Smith, and Finney. *For the negative,* Messrs. Norton, Beecher, Tenney, Nettleton, Hawes, Weeks, and Edwards. *Declined voting,* Mr. Humphrey.

The question was then taken on the proposition, as amended, and all voted in favor of it, except that Mr. Edwards declined voting, and Mr. Nettleton was absent.

Mr. Edwards again introduced the following proposition:

"The calling of persons by name in social prayer ougt to be carefully avoided."

The motion was seconded, and the question being taken, *eight* voted in favor of the proposition, and *nine* declined voting, as follows: *For the proposition*, Messrs. Norton, Beecher, Tenney, Humphrey, Hawes, Weeks, Weed, and Edwards. *Declined voting*, Messrs. Churchill, Gillet, Beman, Lansing, Frost, Gale, Aikin, Smith, and Finney. *Absent*, Mr. Nettleton.

Mr. Beman introduced the following proposition:

"The calling of persons by name in prayer may take place in small social circles."

The motion was seconded, and after some discussion, it was moved and seconded that the proposition be so amended to read as follows:

"The calling of persons by name in prayer may take place in small social circles; but in all cases ought to be practised with great caution and tenderness."

The amendment prevailed.

After further discussion of the proposition as amended, adjourned to meet on Monday next, at ten o'clock in the forenoon. Concluded with prayer.

Monday, July 23.

Met according to adjournment, and opened with prayer. Present the same as before.

The minutes of last week were read and corrected.

The proposition under discussion on Saturday was taken up. After further discussion, Mr. Beman asked and obtained leave to withdraw it, and it was withdrawn.

Mr. Edwards introduced the following proposition:

"Audible groaning, violent gestures, and boisterous tones, in prayer, are improper."

The motion was seconded, and after some discussion, Dr. Beecher moved an amendment, inserting the words "and unusual postures," which motion was seconded, and the amendment prevailed. After further discussion, those words were struck out.

Adjourned to meet at half past two o'clock.—Concluded with prayer. *Monday Afternoon.*

Met according to adjournment, and opened with prayer.

After further discussion, Mr. Lansing moved to amend the proposition, so that it read as follows:

"Audible groaning in prayer is improper."

The motion was seconded, and after some discussion, Mr. Beman moved the postponement of the motion under consideration, for the purpose of introducing a substitute, which he read. The motion was seconded, and carried.

Mr. Lansing then proposed the substitute offered by Mr. Beman, as follows:

"Audible groaning in prayer, is, in all ordinary cases, to be discouraged; and violent gestures, and boisterous tones, in the same exercise, are improper."

The motion was seconded, and the question being taken, *fourteen* voted in favor of the proposition, and *three* declined voting, as follows: *For the proposition*, Messrs. Beecher, Churchill, Gillet, Beman, Tenney, Lansig, Humphrey, Frost, Weed, Gale, Aikin, Edwards, Smith, and Finney. *Declined voting*, Messrs. Norton, Hawes, and Weeks. *Absent*, Mr. Nettleton.

Mr. Edwards introduced the following proposition:

"Speaking against ministers of the Lord Jesus Christ, in regular standing, as cold, stupid, or dead, as unconverted, or enemies to revivals, as heretics, or enthusiasts, or disorganizers, as deranged or mad, is improper."

The motion was seconded, and the amendment prevailed.

Mr. Edwards then moved to strike out all the epithets, so that it read as follows:

"Speaking against Ministers of the Lord Jesus Christ, in regular standing, is improper."

The motion was seconded, and after discussion, it was lost.

The question was then taken on the proposition as amended, and all voted in favor of it, except that Mr. Edwards declined voting, and Mr. Nettleton was absent.

Mr. Edwards introduced the following proposition:

"To receive persons as converted, merely on the ground of their own judgment, without opportunity for examination, and time to afford evidence of real conversion, is improper."

The motion was seconded; and after discussion, the mover asked and obtained leave to withdraw the same, and it was withdrawn.

Mr. Lansing introduced the following propositions:

"The writing of letters to individuals in the congregations of acknowledged ministers, complaining of measures supposed to have been employed in revivals of religion, being calculated to im-pair the confidence of members of such congregations in their ministers, and to encourage the wicked to oppose, ought to be carefully avoided."

The motion was seconded, and after some discussion, the mover asked leave to withdraw the proposition for the present, with the un-derstanding that it shall come up hereafter. Leave was granted accord-ingly, and it was withdrawn.

Adjourned to meet to-morrow morning, at eight o'clock. Concluded with prayer.

Tuesday, July 24.

Met according to adjournment, and opened with prayer.

Present the same as yesterday, except Mr. Nettleton. The minutes of yesterday were read.

Mr. Edwards introduced the following proposition:

"The existence in the churches of evangelists, in such numbers as to constitute an influence in the community, separate from that of the settled pastors, and the introduction, by evangelists, of measures, without consulting the pastors, or contrary to their judgment and wishes, by an excitement of popular feeling which may seem to render acquiescence unavoidable, is to be carefully guarded against, as an evil which is calculated, or at least liable, to destroy the institution of a settled ministry, and fill the churches with confusion and disorder."

The motion was seconded, and after some discussion, the Convention united in a season of prayer.

After further discussion, the question was taken, and all voted in favor of the proposition, except Mr. Churchill, who was absent.

Mr. Edwards *introduced* the following proposition:

"Language adapted to irritate, on account of its manifest personality, such as describing the character, designating the place, or any thing which will point out an individual or individuals before the assembly, as the subjects of invidious remark, is, in public prayer and preaching, to be avoided."

The motion was seconded, and after some discussion, Mr. Lansing moved to amend the proposition, by striking out the words, "on account of its manifest personality, such as,"—which motion was seconded, and after discussion, was lost.

After further discussion, the question was taken, and twelve voted in favor of the proposition, and five declined voting, as follows: *For the proposition*, Messrs. Norton, Beecher, Churchill, Gillet, Tenney, Humphrey, Frost, Hawes, Weeks, Weed, Edwards, and Smith. *Declined voting*, Messrs. Beman, Lansing, Gale, Aikin, and Finney.

Messrs. Lansing and Aikin entered the following, as their reason: "The undersigned do decline voting on the foregoing particular not because they do not most unequivocally condemn such personality in preaching as makes an invidious exposure of individuals, but because they suppose that the article in question may be liable to such construction, as to lead many to say, that such *characteristic* preaching is condemned by this Convention, as is adapted to make sinners suppose that their individual case is intended. *D.C. Lansing, S.C. Aikin.*

On the motion of Mr. Edwards, the following propositions were agreed to:

"All irreverent familiarity with God, such as men use towards their equals, or which would not be proper for an affectionate child to use towards a worthy parent, is to be avoided." *Voted unanimously.*

"From the temporary success of uneducated and ardent young men, to make invidious comparisons between them and settled pastors; to depreciate the value of education, or introduce young men as preachers without the usual qualifications, is incorrect and unsafe." *Voted unanimously.*

"To state things which are not true, or not supported by evidence, for the purpose of awakening sinners, or to represent their condition as more hopeless than it really is, is wrong." *Voted unanimously.*

"Unkindness and disrespect to superiors in age or station, is to be carefully avoided." *Voted unanimously.*

"In promoting and conducting revivals of religion, it is unsafe, and of dangerous tendency, to connive at acknowledged errors, through fear that enemies will take advantage from our attempt to correct them." *Voted unanimously.*

"The immediate success of any measures, without regard to its scriptural character, or its future and permanent consequences, does not justify that measure, or prove it to be right."—*Voted Unanimously.*

"Great care should be taken to discriminate between holy and unholy affections, and to exhibit with clearness the scriptural evidences of true religion." *Voted unanimously.*

"No measures are to be adopted in promoting and conducting revivals of religion, which those who adopt them are unwilling to have published, or which are not proper to be published to the world." *Voted unanimously.*

Adjourned to meet at half-past 2 o'clock.—Concluded with prayer.

Tuesday Afternoon.

Met according to adjournment, and opened with prayer. The minutes of the morning were read.

Mr. Beman introduced the following proposition, to wit:

"As human instrumentality must be employed in promoting revivals of religion, some things undesirable may be expected to accompany them: and as these things are often proclaimed abroad and magnified, great caution should be exercised in listening to unfavorable reports."

The question being taken, eleven voted in favor the proposition, and six declined voting, as follows: *For the proposition,* Messrs. Churchill,

Gillet, Beman, Lansing, Humphrey, Frost, Hawes, Gale, Aikin, Smith, and Finney. *Declined voting*, Messrs. Norton, Beecher, Tenney, Weeks, Weed, and Edwards.

Those who declined voting, entered the following as their reason, to wit: "As the above does not appear to us to be, in the course of Divine Providence, called for, we therefore decline to act."

Mr. Beman introduced the following proposition, to wit:

"Although revivals of religion may be so improperly conducted, as to be attended with disastrous consequences to the church and the souls of men; yet, it is also true, that the best conducted revivals are liable to be stigmatized and opposed by lukewarm professors and the enemies of evangelical truth.["]

The question being taken, eleven voted in favor of the proposition, and six declined voting, as follows: *For the proposition*, Messrs. Churchill, Gillet, Beman, Lansing, Humphrey, Frost, Hawes, Gale, Aikin, Smith, and Finney. *Declined voting*, Messrs. Norton, Beecher, Tenney, Weeks, Weed, and Edwards.

Those who declined voting, entered the following as their reason, to wit: "As the above does not appear to us to be, in the course of Divine Providence, called for, we therefore decline to act."

Mr. Beman introduced the following proposition, to wit:

"Attempts to remedy evils existing in revivals of religion, may, through the infirmity and indiscretion and wickedness of man, do more injury, and ruin more souls, than those evils which such attempts are intended to correct."

The question being taken, nine voted in favor of the proposition, and eight declined voting, as follows: *For the proposition*, Messrs. Churchill, Gillet, Beman, Lansing, Frost, Gale, Aikin, Smith, and Finney. *Declined voting*, Messrs. Norton, Beecher, Tenney, Humphrey, Hawes, Weeks, Weed, and Edwards.

Those who declined voting, entered the following as their reason, to wit: "As the above does not appear to us to be, in the course of Divine Providence, called for, we therefore decline to act."

Mr. Beman introduced the following proposition, to wit:

"In public meetings for religious worship, composed of men and women, females are not to pray."

The question being taken, nine voted in favor of the proposition, and eight declined voting, as follows: *For the proposition*, Messrs. Churchill, Gillet, Beman, Lansing, Frost, Gale, Aikin, Smith, and Finney. *Decline voting*, Messrs. Norton, Beecher, Tenney, Humphrey, Hawes, Weeks, Weed, and Edwards.

Those who declined voting, entered the following as their reason, to wit: "As we have expressed our views on the subject in a previous proposition, we therefore decline to act."

Mr. Lansing introduced the following proposition, to wit:

"The writing of letters to individuals in the congregations of acknowledged ministers, or circulating letters which have been written by others, complaining of measures which may have been employed in revivals of religion; or visiting the congregations of such ministers, and conferring with opposers, without conversing with the ministers of such places, and speaking against measures which have been adopted; or for ministers residing in the congregations of settled pastors to pursue the same course; thus strengthening the hands of the wicked, and weakening the hands of settled pastors, are breaches of Christian charity, and ought to be carefully avoided."

The question being taken, nine voted in favor of the proposition, and eight declined voting, as follows: *For the proposition*, Messrs. Churchill, Gillet, Beman, Lansing, Frost, Gale, Aikin, Smith, and Finney. *Declined voting*, Messrs. Norton, Beecher, Tenney, Humphrey, Hawes, Weeks, Weed, and Edwards.

Those who declined voting, entered the following as their reason, to wit: "As the above does not appear to use to be called for, and is, in our view, liable to great misapprehension and abuse, and may not be, in all respects correct, we therefore decline to act; there being cases when it is the duty of ministers of the Gospel freely to communicate, by letter or otherwise, with one another, and with private Christians, and give notice of approaching danger; to do which, they are bound by their office, and the impropriety of neglecting it is in proportion to the magnitude of the interests involved."

Mr. Beman introduced the following proposition, to wit:

"In preaching the Gospel, language ought not to be employed with the intention of irritating or giving offence; but, that preaching is not the best adapted to do good and save souls, which the hearer does not perceive to be applicable to his own character."

The question being taken, ten voted in favor of the proposition, and seven declined voting, as follows: *For the proposition*, Messrs. Churchill, Gillet, Beman, Lansing, Humphrey, Frost, Gale, Aikin, Smith, and Finney. *Declined voting*, Messrs. Norton, Beecher, Tenney, Hawes, Weeks, Weed, and Edwards.

Those who declined voting, entered the following as their reason, to wit: "As the above does not appear to us to be, in the course of Divine Providence, called for, we therefore decline to act."

On motion of Mr. Frost, the following propositions were agreed to:

"Evening meetings continued to an unseasonable hour, ought to be studiously avoided." *Voted unanimously.*"

"In accounts of revivals of religion, great care should be taken that they be not exaggerated." *Voted unanimously.*"

The Convention united in a season of prayer, and then attended to the reading of sundry documents, till half-past six o'clock, and had a recess till eight o'clock.

After recess, met and had a season of free conversation; and then adjourned to meet tomorrow morning at eight o'clock. Concluded with prayer.

Wednesday, July 25.

Met according to adjournment, and opened with prayer. Present the same number as before. The minutes of yesterday were read.

Attended to further free conversation on the documents of yesterday.

It was moved and seconded, that we proceed to the reading of other documents, without further conversation on those which have been read.

The Rev. Mr. Benedict appeared in convention and took his seat as a member.

After some discussion, united in a season of prayer.

After further discussion, the question was put, and the motion was lost.

Attended further to free conversation on the documents of yesterday, till one o'clock, and then adjourned to meet at half-past two o'clock.— Concluded with prayer.

Wednesday afternoon.

Met according to adjournment, and opened with prayer.

Attended further to free conversation on the documents previously read, and to the reading of some others.

Recess till eight o'clock.

After recess, met, and attended to the reading of other documents. Adjourned to meet to-morrow morning at eight o'clock. Concluded with prayer.

Thursday, July 26.

Met according to adjournment, and opened with prayer. Present the same as before. The minutes of yesterday were read.

Attended further to the reading of documents. United in a season of prayer.

Attended further to free conversation on the documents. Adjourned to meet at half-past 2 o'clock. Concluded with prayer.

Thursday afternoon.

Met according to adjournment, and opened with prayer.

Attended further to free conversation.

Recess till eight o'clock.

After recess, met, and attended further to free conversation.

After which it was voted that the minutes of this Convention be forwarded to the Editors of the New York Observer, for insertion in their paper.

Voted, that the Rev. Mr. Churchill express to the people of New Lebanon our grateful sense of their kindness and hospitality, and our best wishes for their present and everlasting welfare.

By order of the Convention,

HEMAN HUMPHREY, *Moderator.*

WM. R. WEEKS, *Scribe.*

SEVENTEEN

Theodore Weld on a Revival's Aftermath

Source: Charles Grandison Finney Presidential Papers, 1814–
1878, Oberlin College Archives, Oberlin, OH.

In April 1828 reformer Theodore Weld
wrote from his home in Fabius, New York, to Charles Finney. Weld had
befriended Finney in 1825 following a revival in Utica, New York. Since
then Weld worked with others in Finney's so-called "Holy Band" to assist with revival meetings and then to propagate them in different communities.[1] He frequently referred to Finney as his "spiritual father" or
his "father in Christ." In addition to updating Finney on his health and
the health of his family, Weld wrote of the ongoing efforts to continue
the spread of revival meetings throughout New York. He asked Finney,
who was at this time preaching in Philadelphia, if the revival meetings
had become so commonplace to him that he now approached them as
a trade more than as a religious cause.

Weld also apprised Finney of the state of religious devotion in Oneida
County. According to Weld, the spirit of Christian conversion promoted
by earlier revivals had given way to heated debates over the particulars of

---

1. Benjamin P. Thomas, *Theodore Weld: Crusader for Freedom* (New Brunswick, NJ: Rutgers
University Press, 1950), 14–16.

Christian devotion. Weld attributed some of this contention to preachers who disagreed with Finney's methods and some of his tenets. These preachers were generally opposed to the use of Finney's "new measures," such as inviting women to pray in meetings and to profess their religious beliefs and his use of the "anxious bench," a bench placed near the front of a crowd during a revival whereon men and women uncertain of the truth of what was being taught could sit while others in attendance prayed for their conversion. Many also attacked Weld for his criticism of those who used the Calvinist "Hopkinsian Triangle" (the emphasis on belief in original sin, the inability of men and women to save themselves, and the Atonement) as a test of orthodoxy.[2] Weld also acknowledged that many who had converted at revivals soon thereafter returned to old habits of which he did not approve, such as drinking and dancing.

❧ ❧ ❧

Fabius [N.Y.] 22nd April 1828
My dear father in Christ.

I received your very kind letter three weeks after date. I had left Whitesboro' a day or two before it reached there to be absent a week on a visit to my friends.

Upon the evening of my arrival [I] was seized with bilious fever, occasioned by exposure and fatigue. For a few days the fever raged round my system with great violence. My friends expressed the strong apprehension that dust must return to dust. But God in great mercy rebuked, and now all is calm again. My dear sister was seized with the same fever before I had entirely recovered. It has already run 15 days. She is still very low, but we think the fever formed a crisis yesterday, and today she seems decidedly better; so you see dear brother how our cup runs over. What shall we render to the Lord? My wretched cold heart hardly rejoices at all at the glorious conquests of the Lord Jesus in Phila. 'Tis true—I know it—and with shame and confusion of face, confess it. I do feel something that the Devil would have me call joy, but it deserves not even the nickname; it just moves over the soul's surface but so gently as scarsely to ruffle it. Oh for that joy unspeakable, that full-of-glory-joy, that would stir the sluggish spirit and trouble the dead water of my stagnant soul.

---

2. Gilbert H. Barnes and Dwight L. Dumond, eds., *Letters of Theodore Dwight Weld and Angelina Grimké Weld and Sarah Grimké, 1822–1844*, 2 vols. (New York: D. Appleton-Century, 1970), 1:10n3.

FIGURE 7.   Theodore Weld, 1803–1895. Weld traveled throughout western New York to help communities hold revivals patterned after the method established by Charles G. Finney. Weld also became active in several reform movements, including the abolition of slavery. (Library of Congress)

Dear brother Finney—I make slow headway beating up against the wind and tide of my wicked heart. My easy besettings are strong besettings. Pride you know is one of the chiefest with me. It makes dreadful havoc in my soul. It would lay it in ruins every day, but for Christ's strengthening. Thanks be to God who giveth us the victory thro our Lord Jesus Christ. Now brother beloved how is it with your own soul? Has no sin any dominion over you? Are you laying aside every weight, every easily besetting sin? Are you running the race with patience? Are you digging your way deeper and deeper into the dust? Do you feel the power of sin waxing weaker and weaker? Are you remembering the command which claimed the whole heart and soul and mind and strength, all the time? Dear brother do tell me what mark you are pressing towards? The same that Paul did? Perfect sinlessness? Have you resolved thro Christ to reach it? And do you expect to reach [it]? Can you see from day to day that you are nearing it? My dear father in Jesus, you are in such a maddening whirl of care, responsibility and toil, I do dreadfully fear that you neglect the culture of personal holiness. Father, listen patiently to the prattlings of a child whose ready soul yearns for you and who would feign pour into your ear his fears and his sorrows and his prayers. Your letters to Oneida County friends (I have seen no others) during the winter and spring have distressed me exceedingly. I do think there has been in most of them head enough tis true, but no soul. In my estimation your theory is in the main faultless "without spot or wrinkle" but the warm vitality of practicals where is it? And Echo answers where is it? I thought I saw when at Stephentown—and I have more clearly discerned it in your letters this winter—(unless I strongly mistake) that revivals have become with you matters of such every day commonness as scarcely to throw over you the least tinge of solemnity. I fear they are fast becoming with you a sort of trade, to be worked at so many hours every day and then laid aside. Dear brother do you not find yourself running into formality, a round of formality in the management of revivals? I mean of feeling. The machinery all moves on, every wheel and spring and chord in its place; but isn't the main spring waxing weaker?

There has been in your letters a strain of light sarcastic remark particularly on the subject of the [Hopkinsian] triangle, etc., etc. The triangular errors have slain their ten thousands and, in view of their wide wasting destructiveness to souls, and, standing as you now do in the midst of the wrecks and ruins it has made, when you speak of it, oh! Dip not your pen in the gall of sarcasm, nor dip it [in] tears and write with a trembling hand and a soul of sorrow. Brother, if there is a man on earth whose countenance ought to spread over with the hues of eternity continually, you are that man. Where ought we to look for solemnity of demeanor—speaking advisedly with the lips—and I may add tenderness of conscience, and brokenness of heart, a hungering after righteousness, a thirsting after the Living God, and an ever growing assimilation to his blessed character, if not in you dear brother? Who on the footstool has seen such displays of grace and glory as you have? Who has witnessed such exhibitions of almightiness in Gods moral kingdom as you? When did Jobs kindred soul break out in the exclamation—I abhor myself! 'Twas when his eyes saw God. What then my brother becometh you? If Moses reverently drew off his shoes when only a little bush shone with the presence of God, what then becometh you who have long stood in midst of a blaze of Gods glory, Heaven and earth and air lighted up around you? But I have not room to dilate. Oh could I see you face to face I would unlode my burdened spirit. Oh dear Finney had I not rather go to the stake than to see you shorn of your locks. "And he wist not the Lord was departed from him". The opposition with which you meet from the church and the world is with me comparatively a nameless nothing. All that I throw away into forgetfulness. But I am distressed to death at the thought of your heart hardening under the influence of those scenes and that truth which God makes so gloriously effectual in breaking the hearts of others. Now my spiritual father, suffer a child who loves you as he loves his own soul to utter in your ear this one importunate beseeching: Do retire alone at least for an hour, shake off all the entanglements of company and business and all your variety of care, and enter into the secret chambers [of] your soul and solemnly debate this matter with your conscience in the fear of God. Oh break up the fallow ground of your heart and desist not from effort till satan is bruised under your feet. I long to see you rise to the full stature of a perfect man in Christ Jesus. I long to see you renew your strength and mount on the wings of eagles, and run and weary not in the way of Gods commandments.

The state of feeling in Oneida County is dreadfully low. Christians have talked themselves to death. Instead of throwing themselves on our faces in the dust, we have been talking and disputing and taking sides, with not a little I fear of that spirit which saith I am of Paul, etc. I fear we have forgotten that memorable declaration of Jehovah: "I will be exalted in the earth". For my own part I do know that I have indulged in a wicked asperity of feeling against Mr. Nettleton, Beecher, etc. I know I have often advocated brother Finney's cause, and those called "new measures", with much of the unhallowed feeling of a political partisan. May God in mercy humble me for this sin, and enable me to break off from it by righteousness. Oh it would make your heart ache to see many of those praying young converts in Utica rushing back tumultuously to the beggarly elements of this world. Many of the most engaged have frequently danced till a late hour at parties this winter. [I] have not room for the particulars. Some of the young people have set their faces like a flint against this conformity of the world. Brayton and Parmele have taken the fore front of the hottest battle, and they have acquitted themselves like men. Blessed be our God, there are not a few others who have defiled their garments. Yet all over the county, except at Rome and Verona, the pulse beats faintly. Oh brother pray for Oneida.

Our Academy at Whitesboro flourishes. If my dear sister continues to recover as she has yesterday and today, I shall the Lord willing return there next week. I [if] you can filch away half an hour from the pressure of your duties, do sit down and tell me how it is with you, with your dear wife, the blessed work of God in Phila., etc. Direct to me at Whitesboro. Have you seen my dear brother L[ewis] since his return from Washington? How does he feel? If you should see him, remember us with much affection; and now my beloved brother, I commend you to God praying that his strength may be perfected in your weakness, and that He will pour upon your soul and your labors the full horn of his blessing.

Father Nash is in Brookfield, Madison County—Powerful revival there—brother Foote is in Verona. By the way where are brother Norton and his wife? I do not know that they have been heard from here these three months. Kellogg in Salina—Hotchkiss to be settled in Fairlie.

My parents, brother and sister present their affectionate salutations. Give my best love to your dear wife and believe yours in bonds that bind closer than a brothers

T.D. Weld

P.S. Brother, if you ever studied the strength of the Lord Jehovah, you will during the session of the General Assembly. Probably the great question will be settled then, whether or not revivals shall sweep from the Atlantic to the Rocky Mounts.

EIGHTEEN

Theodore Weld on Revivals and Women's Rights

Source: Weld-Grimké Family Papers, William L. Clements Library, University of Michigan.

On August 26, 1837, Theodore Weld wrote to fellow reformers sisters Sarah and Angelina Grimké about the relationship between the abolition movement and the nascent movement for women's rights.[1] Weld supported women's rights, and he maintained that revival meetings provided a forum where women experienced authentic gender equality. Weld observed that in the context of a revival, women spoke and prayed publicly and, in the process, opened the minds of many men who would have previously objected to such acts by women.

While Weld supported the cause of women's rights, he also thought that it was expedient to prioritize the cause of abolition, arguing in this letter that women's rights would naturally follow once the abolitionist movement succeeded. A month later the Grimké sisters wrote to Weld in response to this letter and another one that Weld had sent.[2]

༄ ༄ ༄

---

1. Weld first met Sarah and Angelina Grimké in 1836 when the Grimkés arrived in New York to work as agents for the antislavery cause that Weld helped lead. Weld and Angelina Grimké would marry in May 1838, but their relationship was platonic at the time he wrote this letter (Thomas, *Theodore Weld*, 133–34, 150–64).

2. See "The Grimké Sisters on the Limits of Revivalism and Reform," document 19 herein.

[*First page or pages of the manuscript missing*] Prayer meetings and conferences of both sexes; and the very week that I was converted to Christ
in the city of Utica during a powerful revival of religion under brother
Finney—and the first time I ever spoke in a religious meeting—I urged
females both to pray and speak if they felt deeply enough to do it, and
not to be restrained from it by the fact that they were females. I made
these remarks at a meeting when not less than two hundred persons
were present of both sexes, and five ministers of the gospel at least,
and I think more. The result was that seven females, a number of them
the most influential female Christians in the city, confessed their sin
in being restrained by their sex, and prayed publickly in succession at
that very meeting. It made a great deal of talk and discussion, and the
subject of female praying and female speaking in public was discussed
throughout western New York. As I was extensively acquainted west of
Utica I had opportunity to feel the pulse of the ministry and church
generally, and I did not find one in ten who believed it was unscriptural, fully. They grieved and said perhaps, and they didnt know, and
they were opposed to it, and that it [was] not best; but yet the practice
of female praying in promiscuous meetings grew every day and now all
over the region nothing is more common in revivals of religion. I found
wherever the practice commenced first it always held its own and fained
over crowds; but where it was first laid down as a doctrine and pushed,
it always went hard and generally forestalled the practice and shut it
out. 2. The feeling of opposition to female praying, speaking, etc., which
men generally have is from a stereotyped notion or persuasion that they
are not competent for it. It arises from habitually regarding them as
inferior beings. I know that the majority of men regard women as silly.
The proposition that woman can reason and analyze closely is to them
an absurdity. They are surprised greatly if a woman speaks or prays to
edification, and in this state of mind it is not strange that they stumble
at Paul. But let intelligent woman begin to pray or speak and men begin
to be converted to the true doctrine, and when they get familiar with it
they like it and lose all their scruples. True there is a pretty large class
of ministers who are fierce about it and will fight, but a still larger class
that will come over if they first witness the successful practice rather
than meet it in the shape of a doctrine to be swallowed. Now if instead
of blowing a blast thro' the newspapers, sounding the onset and sum-
moning the ministers and churches to surrender, you had without any
introductory flourish just gone right among them and lectured when
and where and as you could find opportunity and paid no attention

to criticism, but pushed right on without making any ado about "attacks" and "invasions" and "opposition" and have let the barkers bark their bark out, within one year you might have practically brought over 50,000 persons of the very moral elite of New England. You may rely upon it, your specimens of female speaking and praying will do fifty times as much to bring over to womans rights the community as your indoctrinating under your own name thro' the newspapers those who never saw you.

Another point: you say "anti slavery men are trying very hard to separate what God has joined together"; you then say that "the different moral reformations can only be successfully advanced by combining them together. They are bo[u]nd in one like the sciences, are parts of a whole to be raised together" etc. Now there is a sense in which this is true philosophy and religion, but in the sense in which you use it, tho' very plausible and taking, it is a most fatal fallacy. Since the world began, Moral Reform has been successfully advanced only in one way, and that has been by uplifting a great self evident central principle before all eyes. Then after keeping the principle in full blaze till it is admitted and accredited and the surrounding mass of mind is brought over and committed to it, then the derivative principles which radiate all directions from this main central principle have been held up in the light of it and the mind having already embraced the central principle, move spontaneously outward over all its relations. No moral enterprise when prosecuted with ability and any sort of energy EVER failed under heaven so long as its conductors pushed the main principle and did not strike off until they got to the summit level. On the other hand every reform that ever foundered in mid sea was capsized by one of these gusty side winds. Nothing more utterly amazes me than the fact that the conduct of a great, preeminently great moral enterprise should exhibit so little of a wise, farsighted, comprehensive PLAN. Surely it is almost plain enough to be called self evident, that the only common sense method of conducting a great moral enterprise is to start with a fundamental plain principle, so fundamental as to involve wide relations and so plain that it cannot be denied; then push the principle—the whole principle, as a whole (not split up into fractions) push it in its most obvious import and bearing; push it till the community see it, feel it, and so far as the thinking portion are concerned surrender to it. Then when you have drawn them up to the top of the general principle, you can slide them down upon all the derivative principles, all at once; but if you attempt to start off on a derivative principle from any other point than the summit level of the main principle you must beat up stream—yes up a cataract. It reverses the order of nature and the laws of mind. Further, being throughout indoctrinated in the main principle in the first place clears the vision to see a great many relations of it which before were not seen at all or only through clouds, and is a preparative absolutely indispensable to most minds to enable them to see clearly and feel the intense force of the constituent principles involved in the main one. The truth is, the place to begin anything is where it begins and if you begin anywhere else your work is shabbily done and must be done over again.

What was it that gave the Reformation a momentum that carried it triumphant over the dome of St. Peters? Ans. Martin Luther made the sale of indulgences his fulcrum and lever too, and in the light of that monarch abomination, whose roots made net work round the whole system, he showed up a thousand other perversions which could not have been seen except in that strong light. Suppose Luther had begun with some remote collateral or struck off upon such a collateral before its bearings could be strongly appreciated—where had the reformation gone! What has given to Reform in Great Britain an impulse that will soon toss the nation from the aristocratic moorings of centuries? Ans. Slavery was discussed for years in every corner; the whole English mind was soaked with it. It became keen sighted and deep-impulsed on the question of human rights, and acquired such a head as to carry everything before it. Then the Temperance Reformation started with the great anti alcoholic doctrine—the strongest and most obvious form of the grand anti stimulant principle—that was pushed for years, till the mass surrendered. Now we sweep by the board with tremendous force the whole tribe of stimulants in meat and drink. The whole preaching and operations of the apostles illustrate the same principle most strikingly. The whole teaching of Christ is a great reflector flashing this principle everywhere. Pray have you ever read the New Testament!! "I have many things to say unto you but ye cannot hear them now" said Jesus to his disciples. Now he meant by this SOMETHING. What was it? Not what time servants and trucklers and poor poltroons say who wish to cover their cowardice with the mantle of Divinity. Not that he was afraid the truth would make them mad. Not that he refrained because they hated the truth so that he thought it would be bad policy to tell it to them; but they could not hear it, that is, fully comprehend it, appreciate it in its relations, see its truth and consistency; they would be in a haze and quandary. They had not sufficiently mastered the general principles out of which they spring to run out the remote relations or even many obvious ones. Now what is plainer than that the grand primitive principle for which we struggle is HUMAN rights, and that the rights of woman is a principle purely derivative from the other? HUMAN rights—analyze, sift, explain, trace, enforce; show their origin, responsibilities, sacredness; perforate the indurated mind of the church all over with them, and you have done nine tenths of the work necessary to bring over the community to womans rights. See what had been done already by abolition doctrines. I know personally hundreds of our leading abolitionists who 3 years ago would have demurred stoutly to the doctrine of womens preaching and divers other particulars of womens rights, but have been brought right on the whole subject by their general principles of human rights. How? Ans. By lodging in the public mind a principle that involves womans rights and leads to them and gives eyes to see them and prepares hearts to welcome them. Four fifths of the abolitionists now are for womans rights or so far on the road that they will get there soon. Your womans rights! You put the cart before the horse; you drag the tree by the top in attempting to push your womans rights, until human rights have gone ahead and broken the path. Well, here I am at the end of the second sheet. What I have written I have written. I have run on and on here in the office of Wight, Stanton, and Leavitt jabbering all the time and [illegible] they buzz—hum, hum, buzz, buzz, all the time. I have left unsaid most that I designed. Among other things 20 different reasons why you should let alone womans rights except to exercise them—but must stop.

Adieu! My sisters most dearly beloved. God bless you and speed the right. Your own brother Theodore

NINETEEN

The Grimké Sisters on the Limits of Revivalism and Reform

Source: Weld-Grimké Family Papers, William L. Clements Library, University of Michigan.

On September 20, 1837, Sarah and Angelina Grimké responded to two letters from Theodore Weld, including a letter in which he argued that reformers should prioritize the antislavery movement over women's rights.[1] The Grimké sisters first met Weld in 1836 when he was training new antislavery agents. The three of them maintained a close relationship thereafter.[2]

Sarah was the primary writer of the letter, and Angelina added to it before they mailed it. The excerpt from the letter featured here is Sarah's response to Weld's argument that women speaking and praying in revival meetings in western New York would ultimately lead to universal women's rights. She argued that while men tolerated women speaking and praying, most would oppose women who sought formal ordination as ministers in Protestant Christian denominations. This excerpt

---

1. See "Theodore Weld on Revivals and Women's Rights," document 18 herein.
2. Thomas, *Theodore Weld*, 133–34. Also see Gerda Lerner, *The Grimké Sisters from South Carolina: Pioneers for Women's Rights and Abolition*, 2nd ed. (Chapel Hill: University of North Carolina Press, 2004).

demonstrates that while revivals contributed to the women's rights movement in some meaningful ways, those contributions were limited.

✷ ✷ ✷

[. . .]

I do not think women being <u>permitted</u> to pray & tell their experience in revivals is any proof that Christians do not think it wrong for women to preach. This is the touchstone, to presume to teach the brethren. Let a woman who has prayed in a revival claim to be an appointed minister of Jesus & to exercise that office by teaching regularly on the sabbath, & she will at once be regarded as a fanatic, or a fool. I know the opposition

FIGURE 8.   Angelina Emily Grimké, 1805–1879. Angelina Grimké joined her older sister Sarah on the abolitionist lecture circuit and collaborated with her in advocating for several other social reforms. In 1836, she married fellow reformer Theodore Weld. (Library of Congress)

FIGURE 9.   Sarah Moore Grimké, 1792–1873. Sarah Grimké was an advocate for several reform movements in nineteenth-century New York, including women's suffrage and the abolition of slavery. (Library of Congress)

"arises <(in part)> from habitually regarding women as inferior beings" but chiefly, I believe, from a desire to keep them in unholy subjection to man, & one way of doing this is to deprive us of the means of becoming their equals, by forbidding us the privileges of education to fit us for the performance of duty. I am greatly mistaken if most men have not a desire that women should be silly. Thou says I have summoned the ministers & churches to surrender. Not I truly. I do not believe, if I remember right, that I have said one word yet in my letters on the subject of womens preaching; we have done exactly what thou sayest we ought to have done, gone right among the ministers & lectured just when & where we could. I agree with thee that moral reform is successfully advanced "by uplifting a great self-evident principle before all eyes". This has been done by proclaiming human rights & thus the way was prepared for the reception of womans rights. I have read the New Tes[tament] my dear brother, I tho't to edification; but I cannot agree with thee in the application of that text, "I have many things to say", &c. I do not suppose Christ had allusion to the truth of the gospel, these he had declared again & again, but to the sufferings which awaited his disciples after his death; these sufferings he left time & circumstances to unfold as they were strengthened to bear them. If Jesus alluded to any great & important truth, why is none such revealed in the scripture after his ascension? I rejoice with thee that the cause of the slave cannot be destroyed by our misconception of duty, if indeed we have misconceived it, but we believe that if women exercised their rights of thinking & acting for themselves, they would labor ten times more efficiently than they now do for the A[nti] S[lavery] cause & all other reformations. Do not wrong us by supposing that in our movements the slave is overlooked. [. . .]

PART IV

Church Development

Most Christian denominations were pres-
ent in central and western New York between 1790 and 1860, but three
denominations—the Baptists, Methodists, and Presbyterians—experienced particularly rapid growth in the region during this period, just
as they did throughout the rest of the United States. Consequently,
new congregations of these denominations sprang up in towns and
settlements throughout the Burned-over District. The documents in
this part illuminate this growth in church membership, the founding
of new churches, and the way that members of these churches regulated
their respective religious communities.

Such regulation often included the establishment of constitutions
for religious societies, specified confessions of belief, and set the selection of trustees. Church trustee records may not strike the casual
observer as particularly exciting historical sources, but they are remark-
ably illuminating. Church trustees would weigh in on the admission
of new church members to their respective societies and, at times, the
disfellowship or excommunication of others. They would hire clergymen, appoint choristers to lead choirs, arrange for the construction of
chapels, determine the permissible public use of those buildings, plan
revival meetings, and more. Often, when a congregation split because it

had grown too large—or too divided on doctrinal or social issues—the resulting break generated even more work for church leaders.[1]

While this part primarily focuses on the church communities in New York built and maintained by the Baptists, Methodists, and Presbyterians, two documents herein illuminate matters of race and broader denominational affiliation in the Burned-over District. The first is a letter from the residents of Brothertown, a settlement created by Christian Indians of the Mohegan, Pequot, Niantic, Narragansett, Montaukett, and Tunxis tribes of New England who migrated to central New York at the end of the eighteenth century. When New York appointed a Quaker schoolteacher for Brothertown, the multidenominational community expressed concern to their state-appointed superintendents that because all the men appointed to oversee the settlement were Quakers, the community members felt like Quaker proselytes. The other document in this part related to race and mainline Protestant Christian denominations is an excerpt from the autobiography of Samuel Ringgold Ward, a Black Congregationalist minister who led a predominantly white congregation in South Butler, New York. Ward's experience was exceptional for the time and place, and it complicates our understanding of racial attitudes in the Burned-over District.

It is easy to think of the church communities of mainline Protestant denominations in purely statistical terms—as rising and falling membership numbers. In fact, building and maintaining religious communities was hard, ever-present work in a region experiencing dramatic demographic shifts. The records presented here reveal the variety of pragmatic—even mundane—work required of church members and some of the social conflicts that such work brought to a head.

---

1. Cross, *Burned-over District*, 252–67.

TWENTY

Brothertown and Religious Autonomy

Source: Thomas Eddy and Edmund Prior to the Brothertown Peacemakers, April 10, 1798, Brothertown Indians Collection, 1788–1810, microfilm, New York State Library.

In early 1799 conflict arose between the residents of Brothertown and their state-appointed superintendents. The Brothertown Indian community was organized by Algonquian-speaking Christian Indians and led by the famous Presbyterian minister Samson Occom of the Mohegan nation. Beginning in 1774, the Brothertown Indians began migrating from New England to settle on land granted to them by the Oneida Nation. On their arrival, the state of New York arranged an annuity for the community, and while the community was led internally by a group called "Peacemakers," the governor appointed superintendents who resided in New York City to manage Brothertown's finances. By 1795, Brothertown's population was 137.[1]

In 1798, the superintendents, Thomas Eddy and Edmund Prior, had appointed a new schoolmaster for Brothertown. Both Eddy and Prior

---

1. Anthony Wonderley, "Brothertown, New York, 1785-1796," *New York History* 81, no. 4 (October 2000): 457–92.

were Quakers, as was the man they selected, John Dean.[2] In September 1798, the Brothertown Peacemakers sent a petition to Governor John Jay objecting to the selection of Dean, arguing that their Quaker superintendents had selected a fellow Quaker as an act of proselytizing. They desired to select their own schoolmaster and objected to the idea that a white schoolmaster must be chosen to reside among them.

The September 1798 petition from the Brothertown Peacemakers is apparently not extant. However, its contents are summarized in a letter that Eddy and Prior wrote to the Peacemakers in April 1799 in which the superintendents chastised them for their petition and defended their own actions. The conflict reveals an aspect of settlement and church development in the Burned-over District that is quite different from those experienced by white settlers in the area. Whereas moving from New England to New York had freed many white settlers to adopt new religious traditions, the residents of Brothertown believed that their state-appointed superintendents restricted both their religious freedom and their political sovereignty.

★ ★ ★

New York 4th mo. [April] 10th 1799
Esteemed Friends,

We found by a letter from Joseph Kirtland that in the case of Pendleton against David Fowler jun. & thirteen other Inhabitants of Brothertown, the Court & Jury had awarded for Costs & Damages One Hundred & seventeen Dollars & sixty two Cents and there is allso a further charge paid David Fowler Junior for expence of Witnesses of Eleven Dollars & twenty five Cents—as this has arisen in consequence of measure adopted <by a majority of you> in your Town Meetings, it is consistent with the Law and right reason that the whole Town should bear the Expenses, and we have therefore agreed to pay and charge it to your Annuity.

You send us certificates of services rendered by one of your People, and of each has no date and the other does not mention the day when the services began and when they end—in order that you may know how to draw proper certificates we send you a form that you may now draw proper ones and send us them we will order the Money to be immediately paid you.

---

2. Wonderley, 489.

David Fowler in a letter he wrote us some time in September last, mentions that you had agreed to try John Dean as a school master and this Spring you send a Petition to the Governor in which you say as you live in a Land of Liberty you would not wish to be made Proselites by any people, but ought to have the liberty of acting according to the dictates of your own Consciences, both in Religion & in Teaching your Children, and ask for Liberty of choosing your own School Master.

The office we hold as your Superintendents is a good deal of trouble and would not continue but that we have a sincere desire to help and as[sist] ~~you towards getting~~ in improving your Town and morally to promote your good if however [*page torn*] and you continue to be jealous & foolishly suspic[ious] [th]at we are actuated by motives of interest or [*page torn*] improper influences over you we shall be gla[d] [*page torn*] resign and leave it with the Governor to appoint [*page torn*] other persons in our room.

We are very sorry to discover in you a disposition so jealous, a number of you know the solicitude we have felt & the care & industry we have used to procure for you in a suitable sober person to teach your children to motivate you further in the necessary branches of husbandry, to become your assistant in ~~becoming~~ in procuring the necessary supplies for you, thereby saving you a very considerable expense of commission, ~~are in~~ <and> allso capable of overseeing the building of a mill or any other useful Building and procuring Timber Boards Rails &c. a person in whom <we> could place full confidence to <set you an example of sobriety and> act for you as if one of ourselves were on the spot.

It is absolutely necessary for such a person to reside amongst you, as we reside a great distance, and you might then have him to advise with on all occasions—if such a person had been with you the Business with Pendleton might have been settled without going to Law, and subjecting you to pay above One Hundred and twenty Dollars Costs.

In looking for such a person our views were far from being to a person of our own Religious Persuasion. We allso took great pains to enquire among those of other Religious Denominations without the least anxiety about what Religion the man professed, which indeed is of the least consequence provided he was a pious good man, and we know there are such among all kinds of people, whether Presbyterian, Baptist, Church or others—we have sent some of our Children to school masters Presbyterians or other Religious Denominations and such foolish jealousys as you take up never came unto our minds.

[*Page torn*] w̶a̶s̶ addressed with the Governor w̶a̶s̶ <and he> much [*page torn*] approved of what we have mentioned to [*page torn*] he observed that by having such a man as John Dean there would be much trouble saved to yourselves as well as to us for he instead of writing down or sending to us <for money or advice> would be able to act for the superintendents and be allways ready to pay such Moneys as [*page torn*] for [t̶h̶r̶e̶e̶ ̶i̶l̶l̶e̶g̶i̶b̶l̶e̶ ̶w̶o̶r̶d̶s̶]̶ p̶e̶r̶s̶o̶n̶s̶ No [*two illegible words*] Clerks a̶n̶d̶ ̶o̶t̶h̶e̶r̶ salary or other wages laid out amongst you—give stronger proofs of disinterested desires than we have in hopes that we might [*page torn*] as to your choosing your own [i̶l̶l̶e̶g̶i̶b̶l̶e̶ ̶w̶o̶r̶d̶] School master, we would wish to remind you have done it in two Instances and as soon as those School masters of your own choosing got their money for their services they got Drunk and became idle, and set very bad examples to your other young men.

John Dean is the only person we have been able to prevail on to reside amongst you that we thought a suitable character, and the Governor is of opinion with us that he may be of great use to you and act in assisting you with advice and in managing your concerns the same as if he was one of your Superintendents. The Governor observed that by having such a man as John Dean among you there would be much trouble saved to yourselves as well as us—for then instead writing down or sending to us for Money or advice he would be able to act as if he was a Superintendent and allways be ready to pay such Money as may be due for Town Clerks Salary or otherwise paid out amongst you.

No persons would give stronger proofs of disinterested Friendship than we have without <desiring> any Award except the satisfaction of seeing you do well and become a sober Religious & Industrious people. We are sorry to say you have acted often in such a way as to discourage us in our hopes and expectations yet we are well satisfied if you would stay aside all foolish suspicions & jealousys and every man set down to mind his own business & study to be quiet you would soon find John Dean fully equal to all the purposes we have in view and as he kept a school with good Reputation in his own town w̶e̶ you will find your children would be well instructed in school learning & sobriety, which with suitable Industry on your parts would soon render your town a flourishing & happy settlement. How many poor people are there who went into the wilderness without any property, had their lands to buy and pay for, and by their own Labours & Industry have now got in easy circumstances and live with Reputation & Comfort.

It would ~~give us much~~ make us exceedingly sorry should you continue in poverty & want notwithstanding all the advantages you possess of having such fine land that cost you nothing, and allso a very handsome yearly income. But without care & Industry all the advantages you ~~possess~~ have with all the pains we take to promote your Interest & welfare will be of no account.

When we see foolish jealousys & disorderly conduct amongst you, instead of improving in Religious Sober & Industrious lives, our wish [is] to be clear of having the Superintendence of your affairs and have it for some other persons to act who possibly might be more successful.

As soon as your accounts for Town clerk & School keeping come properly stated they shall be ordered [*remainder of the page is missing*].

TWENTY-ONE

A Baptist Constitution

Source: First Baptist Church of Prattsburg records, #6134, Division of Rare and Manuscript Collections, Cornell University Library.

During the first half of the nineteenth century the Baptist population grew rapidly throughout the United States. Some areas, however, saw greater growth than others. In 1845, there were 93,855 Baptists in New York, a larger population than in any other state. Baptists accounted for nearly 4 percent of the state's population.[1]

In April 1823 several Baptists in and around Prattsburg, New York, broke away from the Baptist congregation in the nearby town of Wheeler and formed a new religious society. That process included drafting and adopting a constitution that outlined the duties of the society's trustees in procuring money to employ a minister, acquire land, and construct buildings. These were practical concerns for building and maintaining a church, and such constitutions were common among Christian congregations in the United States at this time. Furthermore, a New York statute required such documents as part of the

---

1. "The Baptists," *Freeman's Journal*, October 11, 1845.

legal incorporation process for a church or religious society.[2] This constitution created by the Baptists of Prattsburg is featured as an example of this common type of document.

❧ ❧ ❧

Constitution

Whereas it being a blessing confered on us in this enlightened land to possess the word of God and it being necessary to be taught the ways of wisdom out of the word and it being also necessary to administer to the teacher of the word of our earthly substance in order that he may apply himself to his calling; And it being also necessary to procure lands on which to build houses for worship and for burrying places and all necessary expences in building. Therefore we the subscribers do consider ourselves members of a society for the above mentioned purposes and agree to adopt the following articles by which to be governed to wit.

Article 1st

This society shall be known and distinguished by the name of "The Baptist Religious Society of Prattsburgh["]

Article 2

There shall be ~~seven~~ <five> trustees elected <four at least of whom shall be members of the Chh [church]> to take charge of the estate and property belonging to the society and to transact all the affairs relative to the temporalities thereof <no meeting of Trustees shall be legal except the majority are chh members>

Article 3

Whenever it shall be thought proper by the trustees of said society or a majority of them to employ a preacher of the gospel to purchase lands for Meeting house or buying ground or any other expense they may call

---

2. "An Act to Provide for the Incorporation of Religious Societies [April 5, 1813], *Laws of the State of New York, Revised and Passed at the Thirty-Sixth Session of the Legislature* (Albany: H. C. Southwick, 1813), 212–19; "An Act Supplementary to the Act, Entitled 'An Act to Provide for the Incorporation of Religious Societies,' Passed April 5th, 1813 [April 12, 1822], *Laws of the State of New York, Passed at the Forty-Fifth Session of the Legislature, Begun and Held at the City of Albany, on the First Day of January, 1822* (Albany: Cantine and Leake, 1822), 187.

a special society meeting by giving notice on the Sabbath at the place of public worship at least eight days previous to said meeting

Article 4th

That whenever said society ~~on a majority of their~~ shall be convened at the time and place of which legal notice shall have been given a vote of the majority of the members present shall be considered an act binding on said society

Article 5th

That whatever sum said society may vote to raise to defray any expense in employing ministers buying lands building &c an attempt shall be made to raise the same by subscription and in case the subscription shall prove in sufficient to answer the required object the whole sum shall be averaged on the members of said society (after deducting what may have been signed by those who are not particular members of the society) in proportion to their property and abilities

Article 6th

There shall be three men chosen at each meeting when a tax shall be voted who are regular members of said society whose duty it shall be (where case may require) to assess each member agreeable to the fifth article of this constitution within the space of one month and to deliver the assessment over to one of the trustees of said society.

Article 7th

The trustees shall be considered the collectors of all bills or subscriptions received by them from the assessors and to pay out of such monies on what they may collect all the expences of said society and to make report of the state of the funds of the society at teach annual meeting

Article 8th

That if any member wishes at any time to be dismissed after subscribing his name to the above articles and becoming a regular member, it shall be the duty of the clerk to erase his name after the member applying for a dismission shall pay all averages (if any there be) that he shall formerly have been assessed but shall be considered a member and subject to assessment till all averages are paid

Article 9th

Any article of this constitution may be amended after having obtained the consent of two thirds of the members present at any legal meeting of the society and a majority of all the members shall be required to vote for any amendment before it shall be considered binding

Whitman Smith
Harry Clark
J. Niles
Isaac Barnes
Benj. Vermilya
John Vermilya
Alexander Davis
Riley Clemonon
John S. Koon
Daniel Parks
D.D.W. Foster
Isaac Vermilya
Elvis Simons
Truman Strong
A. Hubbard
John Hoes
Jacob Koons
Lach Horton

TWENTY-TWO

Baptist Trustee Minutes

Source: First Baptist Church of Covert records, #6038, Division of Rare and Manuscript Records, Cornell University Library.

The First Baptist Church of Covert, New York, was founded in 1803 and grew steadily from then. The society's trustees met as needed, sometimes multiple times a year. Their business included managing the church's finances and the appointment of individuals to fill necessary roles such as choristers. But much of their business related to membership matters, such as admitting new Baptists to the church and dismissing others from fellowship. An excerpt from the trustees' minute book from 1832 and 1833 is featured here as an example of the type of issues addressed by the trustees of this church and other Baptist churches in the region.

✧ ✧ ✧

[. . .]

January 7th 1832 church met by special appointment commenct [commenced] by singing and prayer by Elder Woolsey

1st Voted by request of Lewis Porter our former clerk after serving the church as clerk for above twenty years they will receive his resignation from the above office and that Walter Glazier serve this church as the stated clerk until removed

2nd Brothers Silas Gregg and Chapple Close be assistant choristers and that they have the priviledge of going in the galery or stand in front of the Pulpitt as they please

3rd Voted that Brothers John Boorham Samuel Hopkins and Eli Cole be a committee to solicett subscriptions and donations for the foreign Missionary society

4 Voted to receive members of the open communion Baptist that are in good standing and are willing to comply with our custom and regulation

5th Voted letter of dismission to sister Demer Remington

1832

Saturday January 14th the church met commenct by singing and prayer by Elder Woolsey

1st Heard the minds of the brothers and sisters and found peace and union to continue with us and about one hundred and and thirty present

2 Caled [called] up the business of brother John C Hall and brother Daniel Woolsey reported he had visited brother Hall and that he manifested a hardness against the church and the church further agres that brother Lott and Elder Woolsey labour with brother Hall and try to win him to his duty and brother Woolsey further reports that he and brother Eli Cole had visited brother Daniel Hall and he stated he had no hardness against any of the church but his not attending to church and covenant meetings was his coldness of heart and said he was going from home that would disapoint him from attending our first meeting

3rd Brother Isaac Russell present confest his coldness and the church forgave him after he promist to do better.

4th Voted to give letters of dismission to Brother Jesse Denison and his wife Phebe and his daughter Axhsah

5th Voted to receive sister Phebe Ferris by her relating the travail of her mind since she was dropt from the Harmervill church

6th Received sister Eliza Thompson by letter from the first Baptist church in Hector

7th Heard sister Elizabeth Burch relate her christain Experunce and the church voted to receive her for baptism

8th Lords day January 15th sister Burch baptised by Elder Woolsey and the church returned to the meetinghouse and received the emblems of the body and blood of Christ about one hundred and twenty five present

Feb 11th Church met commenct as usual by singing and prayer by Elder Woolsey

1st Inquired in to the ~~mar~~ condition of the church found them in union and fellowship and a good share christian spiritts

2nd Voted that at our next church meeting we take a vote to see if we will have a missionary society in our church or not and as many of the Breathren and sisters join as see proper

3rd Caled up the buisness of brothers Daniel Hall and John C Hall they were both present and answered for themselves and the church forgave them and they promist to be more punctual in the future

4th Withdrew the hand of fellowship from Brother Cyrus Cole

5th Voted and did receive Mary Maynord formerly a member of the Open communion Baptist church by her relating her christain experience

Saturday March 10th 1832 Church met commenct by singing and prayer by Elder Woolsey

1st Church took up the business of employing Elder Woolsey one year from the first of April next and it was voted to continue him and give him two hundred dollars for one year

2nd Brother Lewis Cole came in to the church at our regular covenant meeting and abused the Elders in particular and the church in general brothers Nathan Cole Nathan Hall John Boorham and Daniel Cole gave sutch information to the church that they withdrew the Hand of fellowship from him

3rd Caled up the buisness of the foreign Missionary Society and after hearing the minds of several of the breatheren voted to adjourn the business of forming the society untill our church meeting in May

4th Withdrew the hand of fellowship from sister Mary Adair she having joined the Methodist

5th Voted to give letter of recommendation to sister [blank] Scott closed by prayer by Elder Abbott after hearing from several of the brothers and sisters about one hundred present

1832

Saturday April 14th Church met commenced by singing and prayer by Elder Woolsey.

1st Enquired in to the condition of the Church and found a comfortable union.

2nd Voted to have two sermons at the meeting house during the summer and fall.

3rd Voted to have our Covenant meetings begin at one OClock and that we have an extra Church meeting two weeks from our monthly meetings untill attened by the Church.

4th Voted to give Brother Thomas Maynard and Sister Lucinda Tedd letters of dismissions.

5th Recd a Subcrepton in behalf of Brother Wm States and agree to help him to some provision if a waggon is sent to receive it.

6th Lords day April 15th the Church communed about one hundred present the Breatheren and sisters appeared to have a comfortable season.

Saturday April 14th 1832 Met as usual opened meeting by singing and prayer by Elder Woolsey

1st Enquired in to the condition of the church and found a comfortable Union.

2nd Voted to have Two sermons on the sabbath at the meeting hour during the summer and fall.

3rd Voted to have our Covenant meetings begin at one Oclock and that we have an extra Church meeting two weeks from our monthly meetings untill altered by the Church.

4th Voted to give Brother Thomas Maynard and sister Lucinda Teed formerly (Woolsey) letters of dismission.

5th Received a subscreption in behalf of Brother William States and agree to help him to some provission if a waggon is sent to receive it.

Saturday April 28th 1832 Church met opened meeting by singing and prayer by Elder Woolsey

1st Enquired in to the condition of the Church and found peace and Union with us.

2nd Voted that sister Maynard have a letter of dismission

3rd Voted that Aaron H Cole have a letter of recommendation.

4th Voted that Jacob St John become a member with us that was formerly a member with the Harmervill church by his relating the travail of his mind

Saturday May 12th Church met commenct by singing and prayer by Elder Woolsey enquired in the condition of the church and found peace and union to prevail be with us.

1st Caled up the buisness of forming a missionary society in the church which was adjourned in March last to this meeting and agreed to drop the question in the church and as many or all unite in the missionary society as they can best please them selves.

Saturday May 26th church met opened meeting by singing and prayer by Elder Woolsey.

1st Voted that Elder Woolsey and Brother Thomas Hopkins visit brother Samuel Williams and cite how to attend our next covenant meeting closed by prayer by brother Sears from Delaware

Saturday June 9th 1832 Church met commencd as usual by singing and prayer by Elder Woolsey

1st enquired in to the condition of the Church and found a comfortable union

2nd Voted to give letters of dismission to Sisters Sally King wife of Jeremiah King and Diantha Smith

3rd Voted that there be a subscreption paper circulated in the bounds of the Church to give the society an opportunity of contributing what they wish for the support of Elder Woolsey the present year

4th Voted that sister Juliaen Woolsey be received by letter from the Colchester Church at the Delaware

Saturday June 23rd Church met commenct as usual and enquired into the minds of the Brothers and Sisters and found peace and union to prevail with us to a good degree no buisness to attend to

Saturday July Church met commenced as usual

1st caled for the breatherin and found peace and union

2 Voted to give letters of dismission to sister Hannah Hopkins

Saturday August 11th 1832 Church met opened meeting by Singing and prayer by Elder Woolsey

1st Appointed Silas Gregg Clerk protem

2nd Heard the minds of the breathrin and sisters and found peace and union to dwell among us generally

3 Appointed Elder Richard Woolsey and Lewis Porter delegates to the association

Saturday August 25th commenct as usual

1st Enquired in to the condition of the church and found a comfortable union

2nd Caled up the request in the circular of the association of the last year on the subject of Communion when the assoseation meets and it was voted that we put in our letter we think it in expedient [inexpedient]

Saturday Sept 8th Church met commenct as usual by singing and prayer

1st Enquired into the condition of the church and found a comfortable union and peace among the breatherin

2nd Voted to give letters of dismission to brother Dennis Howler and his wife and daughter Sally and brother George Adair and his wife.

October 13th Church met oppened meeting by singing and prayer by Elder Woolsey enquired into the condition of the church and found peace and union no business.

2nd Voted to hold meeting again 2 weeks from this day at to commence at ten Oclock A.M.

October 27th Church met commenct by singing and prayer by ~~elder progress~~ elder Woolsey

1st Enquired in to the condition of the church and found peace in the body but the feelings of the church rather cool not that life and animation we sometimes have agread to commune on the morrow About seventy five present.

2nd Heared the expercunce [experience] of brothers Asaph Porter and Thomas Fretts and voted to receive them when baptized into our fellowship

Sunday Nov 4th they were both baptised by Elder Woolsey at Little point.

Saturday Nov 10th Church met commenct by Singing and prayer by Elder Woolsey

1st Enquired in to the condition of the church and found peace and union but a few of the breatherin [brethren] present no business.

Saturday Dec 8th The Church met commenct by Singing and prayer by Brother Lewis Johnston

1st Elder Woolsey not present chose Deacon N[.] Cole Moderator.

2nd Enquired in to the condition of the church and peace and union in the body. 3rd Voted to hold a protracted meeting to commence the first day of Jan next, and that the clerk write to the breatherine in the sister churches to attend with us.

4th The church was informed and by the enquiry of brother N Cole found it to be true that sister Abagail Campbell was pregnant and that the child was likely to be born a bastard and on due reflection the church withdrew the hand of fellowship from her

Saturday Dec 22nd 1832 Church met commenct by singing and prayer by Elder Woolsey

1st Enquired in to the condition of the church and found considerable engagedness among the breatheren and peace and union in the boddy and appointed committee to visit delinquent breatheren.

2nd Appointed brother Amibs Wixom to visit Daniel Hall brother Ogden Cole to visit John C Hall brothers Silas Gregg & Lewis Porter or

Zephiniah Lott to visit brother Elias Stilwell and cite them all to appear to our next church meeting.

3rd Appointed brothers Nathan Cole & Cheesman A Hopkins King and Walker Glazier for a committee to attend to the business of our contemplated protracted meeting closed meeting by prayer by brother Daniel Woolsey.

1833 Sunday January 6th Closed a protracted meeting that has continued six days in succession and we think proffitable to the Church many of the brothers and sisters confest their faults one to another and promist to try and live in that manner the Gospel points out as the christian path and several brought to knoledge of the truth and went their way rejoicing A number of Elders and visiting breatherin attended with us and we have reason to believe the most of them went their way satisfied with the goodness of our God and thankful to him for the blessings he has bestowed on us.

Saturday Jan 12th 1833 Church met commenced by prayer by singing and prayer by Elder Woolsey.

1st Brother Daniel Hall appeared and confest his wandiring and appeared to be humbled under a sence of his past life and desired that by the grace of God he might live more of a christian life

2nd The case of brother Jeremiah Robeson put off until the next meeting

3rd Brother Elias Stillwell appeared and promised to be more faithful to his covenant engagement

4th The Church then commenced to hear the breatherenn minds by their voluntary speaking and some spoke and some prayed as they were led the breatherenn seemed to be thankful to God for past favours.

5th Sister [blank] Chambers told her christian experiance and was received for Baptism brother [blank] Nivereon told his christian experience and the church took a vote on his experence and were satisfied but he did not feel satisfied himself   Closed by prayer by brother Nathan Cole

Saturday January 26th church met commenced by singing and prayer.

1st Appointed brother Nathan Hall to visit brother Wm Baxter and sister Betriz Baxter and say [illegible] the reason they dont take letters and join the church where they live and also to see if brother Thomas and sister Louiza Baxter have joined any other church. [. . .]

Twenty-three

Methodist Population Report

Source: *American Journal* (Ithaca, NY), August 15, 1821.

In 1821 the *American Journal* of Ithaca published a table with the Methodist population in the United States. The nearly fifty thousand Methodists in New York were divided between two different conferences—New York and Genesee. Because the boundaries of these two conferences crossed state lines, the precise number of Methodists in New York is difficult to ascertain. However, this table suggests that more Methodists lived in New York than in any other state at this time. This table lists separately the number of white Methodists and the number of Black Methodists. In both New York conferences, the number of Black men and women constituted less than 3 percent of Methodist church membership.

$ $ $

Mr. Mack—The following summary of the number of communicants in the Methodist Episcopal Church in America, is extracted from the minutes of their annual Conference for the year 1821:

	WHITES.	COL. [COLORED]	TOTAL.
Ohio Conference	33957	221	34178
Missouri do	7262	196	7458
Tennessee do	31105	3454	34559
Mississippi do	3443	704	4147
South-Carolina do	22105	12485	34590
Virginia do	18481	6489	24970
Baltimore do	28272	9412	37684
Philadelphia do	26571	8234	34805
New-York do	23134	504	23638
New-England do	19402	248	19650
Genessee do	25355	112	25467
Total	239087	42059	281146
Total last year			259890
Increase this year			21256
Travelling preachers 977			

TWENTY-FOUR

Proposal for a Methodist College

Source: "The New College," *Troy Sentinel*, December 1, 1829.

By the late 1820s the Methodist population in central and western New York had grown to the extent that church leaders appointed a committee to consider establishing a college in Troy, New York. The proposed college would be nonsectarian but operated under the auspices of the Methodist Episcopal Church. In 1829 the *Troy Sentinel* reported on a public meeting about the establishment of the new college, including the statistical justification for such an institution based on the Methodist population in the area and the desire to keep New York Methodists from leaving the state for their education. No such college was established in Troy until 1858, when Troy University was founded. That school closed in 1861.[1]

❧ ❧ ❧

The New College

The General Committee of Troy, appointed for the purpose of arranging measures to procure the location in this city of a College to be

---

1. Joseph Hillman, *The History of Methodism in Troy, New York* (New York: Joseph Hillman, 1888), 154–59.

established under the auspices of the Methodist Episcopal Church, present to the inhabitants of Troy the following considerations on the subject committed to their charge.

In every point of view in which the Committee have been able to view this subject it appears interesting and important; and it is their deliberate and deep conviction, that the inhabitants of Troy are called on, by every consideration growing out of an enlightened regard to their best interests as a community, to employ all just means in their power, to secure the establishment of a respectable College in this city, the opportunity for doing which, is now offered to them.

This opportunity if furnished by the determination of the Methodist Episcopal Church to establish a College somewhere in this northern quarter of the Union.

That Church in North America is divided into jurisdictions, termed Conferences, of which there are eighteen. One of these is chiefly in Canada; the others are all within the limits of the United States. In each of these territorial divisions there is an annual meeting of delegates from the several Districts of which they are composed, who constitute the body in which the jurisdiction of the Conference is vested, and which body is itself styled a Conference.

One of these bodies is the New York Conference, embracing within its territorial jurisdiction the eastern side of this state in its whole extent, with parts of Connecticut, Massachusetts, and Vermont. At the annual meeting of this Conference, in May last, a resolution was adopted that a College should be established somewhere within the bounds of the Conference, and a committee was appointed to take the requisite measures for carrying the resolution into effect. One of the members of that committee visited this city several weeks ago, for the purpose of making the determination of the Conference known to our citizens, & inviting them to become competitors for the location of the contemplated institution.

In pursuance of this invitation, a meeting of our citizens was held at the Court House on the evening of the 28th day of September last, at which the subject was opened, considered, and favorably received. Resolutions were passed declaring the establishment of the proposed institution in Troy to be a desirable object, and a Committee of three citizens from each Ward, exclusive of the Chairman, was appointed, with authority to pursue such course as they should judge expedient for the promotion of that object. That Committee, in conformity with the design of their appointment, now address their fellow-citizens of Troy on this subject.

In the first place, it seems proper to remark that, although the proposed institution is to be established under the auspices of the Methodist Community, yet *it is not desired nor intended to make it a sectarian school.* It is intended that the objects of the College shall be general and liberal, embracing as full a course of study and as free a discipline as are enjoyed at the broadest foundations in the country, and wholly exempt from any sectarian test, or obligation.

The Methodists, in taking measures to found this institution, are only seeking to provide a seat of learning, where they may have officers and teachers in greater or less part of their own persuasion in christian faith, where they may exercise that proper and legitimate kind of influence which springs from a just and efficient administration of the means of learning as well as from the weight of personal character, and whither they may send their young men for the cultivation of knowledge, with the full confidence of their being safe from influences they could not approve. Such is the precise condition of things at most of the collegiate institutions in this country, as it regards the various other sects of christians; and such is all that is sought by the Methodists. To this species of influence and predominance the Committee cannot perceive any just and reasonable objection: it seems to be fair and equal.

To such an institution the patronage of the Methodist Community, throughout all its jurisdictions, especially in the Atlantic and Northern quarters of the Union, it is supposed would be given steadily and efficiently.

As the value of such an institution to the community in which it is established, depends on the number of its students and its generally flourishing condition, it may be well to look at the probable extent of the patronage which it may be fairly expected to receive.

The whole Methodist Community, as has been already observed, is distributed into eighteen Conferences, which are here enumerated, with the number of communicants in each.—This enumeration is made for the twofold purpose of showing the whole extent of that community, as well as the proportions in which it is distributed through the land, and to indicate the sources from which the expected patronage would come. The statement is made on the authority of the published Minutes of the Annual Conferences, at their meetings for the year now running, 1829.

Canada Conference	8753
Pittsburgh "	22583
Ohio "	32700
Missouri "	3257
Illinois "	18724
Kentucky "	23888
Holstein "	17952
Tennessee "	17476
Mississippi "	10948
South Carolina "	38708
Virginia "	28384
Baltimore "	28644
Philadelphia "	34819
New-York "	32789
New England "	20337
Genesee "	13532
Oneida "	19246
Maine "	9939
Total,	382679

In this enumeration the *Whites* only in the several Conferences are included. Besides these, there are 62814 negroes, and 2250 indians, in all, making a grand total of 447743.

The Committee, however, have taken only the whole number of white persons; and these, let it be remembered, are actual communing members of the Methodist Church. But in addition to these, there are large numbers of persons, not strictly members of that denomination, who, nevertheless, worship with them, incline to their opinions, and receive from them their leading social influences. Such is the fact, in greater or less degree, in reference to all various sects in Christendom. If the number of persons associated in this way with the Methodists, be taken at only half of the whole number of their actual members, it will give an increase of 191,339 persons. Add this number to the whole number of communicants and it will give a total of 574,013 souls. Now the population of the state of Massachusetts, by the census of 1820, was 516,419; and suppose it to amount at this time to 550,000. Still we have what may be regarded for the present purpose, as a Methodist population, *more than 20,000 greater than that of the state of Massachusetts, which supports three colleges, embracing, one year with another, say 600 students.*

If it be said that many students from other states resort to the colleges of Massachusetts, the reply is, that many of the youth of Massachusetts go to other states, especially to Connecticut, for their education; so that her own institutions lose, in this way, probably as many as they gain from other communities; and it seems to the committee that the comparison instituted, may be considered as furnishing a reasonable measure for estimating the extent of patronage that might be anticipated, for the contemplated college, from the Methodists and their friends.

TWENTY-FIVE

Building the First Wesleyan Methodist Church of Seneca Falls

Source: First Wesleyan Methodist Church of Seneca Falls records, #6049, Division of Rare and Manuscript Collections, Cornell University Library.

On March 27, 1843, Methodists in Seneca Falls, New York, gathered to organize the First Wesleyan Methodist Society of Seneca Falls. The society elected six trustees, pursuant to New York law.[1] The society's minute book demonstrates that during the ensuing years the trustees gathered donations and pledges for the construction of a meetinghouse. The excerpt of the minute book featured here is an example of how religious societies in the Burned-over District raised the funds for such construction projects and the resolutions they adopted to govern the use and future sale of the building. In addition, the excerpt includes a resolution of the trustees to prohibit use of the meetinghouse for partisan political meetings. However, the resolution did not exclude other public meetings from the space. This seemingly unremarkable decision opened the way for the First Wesleyan Methodist Church to host the 1848 Seneca Falls Convention, one of the most famous meetings of American women's rights activists in the nineteenth century.

❧ ❧ ❧

---

1. "Incorporation of Religious Societies," *Laws of the State of New York* (1813), 212–19; "Supplementary to the Act," *Laws of the State of New York* (1822), 107.

Book No 1

The property of the First Wesleyan M. Church Seneca Falls NY

At a meeting held pursuant to the Revised Statues of the State of New York of the Society worshiping in the School house in District No 1 in Seneca falls for the purposing of organizing themselves into a Religious Society under the Statute on the Evening of March 27.1843.

H.L Worden was Chosen Chairman & A. Failing Secretary

It was Motioned & carried that we proceed to elect 6 Trustees of Said Society. Whereupon the following persons were elected.

John C King & HL. Worden for 3 years

Abram Failing & E.O Lindsley—2 do

Jos Metcalf & Wm Fox

Abram Failing was Chosen Clerk of the Trustees.

The following Resolutions were passed

Resolved that this Society be known [*illegible word*] & distinguished forever as the First Wesleyan Methodist Society of Seneca falls.

Resolved that the Trustees be empowered to Negociate for & purchase a Lot for the establishment of a house of Public Worship & also to circulate a Subscription to raise money to buy [*illegible word*] & the Erection of said house of Worship.

Adjourned A. Failing Clerk

We whose names are hereunto Set promise to pay to the Trustees of the First Wesleyan Methodist Society of Seneca falls or to their successors the Sums Set opposite to our respective names for the purpose of purchasing a lot in the Village of Seneca falls for the erection of a house of Public Worship and for the erection of Said house thereupon to be paid in the following manner. That which is Subscribed to be paid in Some thing besides money is to be paid on demand and that which is Subscribed to be paid in Cash to be paid one half when said house is enclosed and the other half when it shall be completed.

Dated Seneca falls. April 20.1843.

Recd from John C King one hundred Dollars on Wm Fox subscription July. 8.1844.

Recd of Wm Fox six Dollars on his Subscription July 17 1844 by Bille Cay.

Recd of Wm Hap Sixty dollars & forty cents in full of his Subscription June 10.1845   A Failing

Received of William Fox one hundred dollars on the above subscription Sept the 9th 1845

Recd   John C King collection

SUBSCRIBERS NAMES	WHAT TO BE PAID IN $ ¢
Joseph Metcalf	500.00
Elbert O Lindsley <$31.88 pd [paid]>	50.00
Willard Metcalf	50.00
William Fox <$33.60>	20.00
do one hundred in produce	100.00
John C King <6.88 pd 3.07>	50.00
E Partridge	50.00
L. J Hill to Be Paid in Bls	5.00
D Skidmore Be Paid in Tailoring	5.00
Lerenzo Hangdin in brick	12.50
Christerfur Moures—	20.00
Samuel Taylor—	10.00
C.S. Granger to be paid Tailoring if twice the amount	15.00
of tailoring be furnished in the same	5.00
C A Norris Blacksing	5.00
Henry J Beester in Work	5.00
Archable Odell	5.00
Marvin S Baird—	10.00
Joel Bowker <14.50>	5.00
Lemuel Stansbury	5.00
B G. Johnson	5.00
J.W. Dickerson in trimming pulpit	

Received of John C. King forty three Dollars & twelve cents on the [*illegible word*] subscription EO Lindsley collector

—pade [paid] to Joseph Metcalf 50 00
—pade to Joseph Metcalf 10 00
—pade to Joseph Metcalf 5 00
—Pd [paid] Metcalf

David Crowell in Team work	$5.00
William Russel verbel order	$5.00
George Pegler	$5.00
H P. Heerst <paid>	$100.00

At a meeting of the Trustees of the first Wesleyan Society of Seneca Falls according to previous notice given—Present the Whole Board on the 14th day of January 1844 at the Vestry of their Church.

Joseph Metcalf presented his account against the Society for cash advanced in building their house of Worship materials furnished *His* [*illegible word*] Labor performed about the same, amounting to $1770.10 which account was accepted and a final Settlement made with him upon which Settlement there was found due to him from the Society the Sum of $952.65. upon which it was

Resolved That the said Trustees acknowledge the Said Society indebted to Joseph Metcalf to the amount of the said sum of $952.65.

Resolved that the following bills against the Society below stated be allowed and that the same be credited upon the Subscription for building the House of the Said individuals.

Wm Fox	$33.60
John C. King	$6.88
Joel Bowker <in full>	$14.50
E OLindsley	$31.88

Resolved That this House of Worship shall not be opened for the purpose of speaking or preaching in favor of elevating to Power either of the political parties of the country

A true Copy of the minutes.

Attest

A.   Failing Clerk

of Trustees

adjourned

At a meeting of the Trustees of the first Wesleyan Society held at the Office of Wm A. Sackett in Senecafalls May 31.1843 the following Resolution was passed

That the Seal whose impression is hereto impressed be & the same is hereby declared to be the Common Seal of the Trustees of the first Wesleyan Methodist Society in Senecafalls in Seneca County. &

That whereas Harmon Dumond has sold & conveyed by the Deed of himself & wife having date 31. May 1843. to the aforesaid Trustees a Lot of land situated on Lot No 100 in The Village of Seneca falls for a Site for a Church Edifice for the sum of $600 to be paid in Eight years with annual interest & the same to be secured by the Bond & Mortgage of said Corporation bearing even date with said deed. Now therefore Resolved that Abram Failing be & is hereby authorised to Execute such

Bond & Mortgage by affixing thereto the common seal of the said Corporation, & that he attest the Execution of the said Bond & Mortgage by subscribing his name to the same as Clerk & thereupon deliver the said Bond & Mortgage after the same shall have been duly executed & acknowledged to the said Dumont

Adjourned A. Failing Clerk

At a Meeting of the Trustees of this Society held in the Class room of their Chapel Feby 3.1844 it was Resolved

That, the said Chapel should never be sold to any Society, individual, or Company without paying to every individual who has contributed to said building said house the sum so contributed, if required, with the consent of the Trustees

Adjourned A. Failing Clerk

At an annual meeting of the first Wesleyan Society of Seneca falls held at their Class Room of which meeting notice had been given pursuant to Statute on the 27th day of March 1844

Geo Pegler was chosen Chairman & A. Failing Secry

Joseph Metcalf was re elected to serve as Trustee for three years

Joel Bowker was elected for 2 Years.

At the annual meeting of the first Wesleyan Society of Seneca Falls held in the Vestry of said Church on the twenty seventh day of March 1845. C Mowers *was* the Chair

It was motioned & carried that we proceed to ballot for two Trustees to fill the Vacancies which occur this day by the Expiration of the term for which A. Failing & E. O. Lindsley were elected, upon which balloting A. Failing and Norcott were each elected as Trustees of this Society for three years from this day. A. Failing was reelected as Clerk of the Trustees.

A resolution was also passed at said Society meeting in the following words "to wit"

Resolved, that all resolutions heretofore passed by which it was resolved that the Slips in their house of Worship should never be sold or rented and that said house should not be opened for the purpose of Speaking or preaching for the purpose of Elevating to power either of the Political parties of the country be recinded & repealed and that the same from this day hencefoward be repealed & rescinded

~~And also as follows. Resolved that A. Failing be autho~~

The Trustees of said Society also at the same time passed the following resolution "to wit"

Resolved That A. Failing be authorised to call upon William Fox for the payment of the balance of his subscription of $300. towards the purchase of a Lot & building of their house of Worship, and in case he refuses or neglects to pay, that then he the Said Failing be authorized to commence legal proceeding against said Fox for its collection.

TWENTY-SIX

The Growth of Presbyterianism in the Synod of Geneva

Source: "Narrative of the State of Religion within the Bounds of the Synod of Geneva," *Geneva Gazette*, March 3, 1819.

On February 18, 1819, the Presbyterian Synod of Geneva met in Geneva, New York, to draft its annual report on the "state of religion" in the synod. That meeting approved the statement, and the *Geneva Gazette* published it nearly three weeks later. The report celebrates the growth of the church in the area, the installation of standing pastors in new settlements, and the construction of new meetinghouses.

❧ ❧ ❧

Narrative

Of the State of RELIGION within the bounds of the Synod of Geneva: as reported and approved at the Stated Meeting of the Synod, in the village of Geneva, on the 18th day of Feb. 1819.

"The Synod of Geneva think they are not mistaken under the awakening sentiment, that the day in which we live is the time of Zion's solicitude and travail. With such a persuasion, big with hope, the piety of our Churches looks with the deepest interest into the disclosures that may be expected from the annual report of such an extensive ecclesiastical

190

body as the Synod of Geneva: an interest of unfeigned regret for every thing that a Christian would deplore, and of the liveliest sentiments of gratitude and of growing fervor for every and the least indication of the rising prospects of Zion. When the Synod look at the *actual* state of morality and religion within their bounds, they see *much—very* much, over which to drop their tears and offer their prayers: but when they make a *comparative* survey, they feel themselves obliged, in acknowledgment of the favors of the Supreme Head of the Church, in justice to the cause of truth, and as an excitement to future effort,—they feel themselves obliged to say, the condition of their Churches is more prosperous than in years past. As the most efficient methods of restraining the powers of darkness which make their appearance in the varied and combined forms of vice, crime, and religious heresy, the Synod have the satisfaction to state, that during the past year, very extensive and successful efforts have been made within their bounds for the organization of Churches and Religious Societies in the new and destitute settlements; in the installation of Pastors over particular Churches, and in the rearing of Houses of public worship. The Synod have also to rejoice in a confidence of the general fidelity of ministers within their connexion, and of licentiates under their care; and they would not fail to acknowledge the special smiles of heaven in having afforded an animating degree of efficacy to their feeble and instrumental efforts; in confirming many weak hands and feeble knees; in edifying the Churches previously and within the last year organized; in securing a general and increasing harmony of sentiment and of doctrine; in extending the salutary influence of piety and true religion to the shaming of vice and the retiring of infidelity; and in bestowing in many instances the copious effusion of the Holy Spirit. The monthly Concert of Prayer has been generally observed with increasing interest, and it is confidently believed that this harmonious institution will never flag, till Zion has become a praise in the whole earth. Sabbath Schools have been instituted in most of our congregations, and proved extremely useful. Bible Classes also, to a growing extent, have received the attention of ministers.

As a more particular statement, the Synod would observe, that in the extensive region which Niagara Presbytery embraces, (110 miles by 50, Buffalo being a centre,) numerous churches have been collected, considerable missionary labor spent, and great and permanent good, it is believed, effected in bringing that disorganized and scattered mass of population to more regular habits of morality, observance of the Sabbath, and of divine worship. A special attention may be said to have characterized the religious aspects of Lewiston, Clarence, Cayuga-Creek, Pembroke, Gainsville, Le Roy, Fredonia, and what is *particularly interesting*, the *Aborigines* at their villages near Buffalo. By these special favors and the more ordinary attention, the churches within the bounds of Niagara Presbytery have received an animating increase,

The Presbytery of Ontario appears to have been favored with harmony among ministers and churches, a growing influence of piety, and some special attention in the towns of Penfield, Bloomfield and Riga.

The Presbytery of Geneva deplore the lukewarmness of their churches; but, at the same time, report a gradual reformation of the people within their bounds, and a uniform attendance on the means of grace. The town of Ulysses has experienced a copious refreshing, and already reckons about fifty among the professed converts.

Within the bounds of Cayuga Presbytery, the village of Aurora has received an abundant effusion of the Holy Spirit, since August last, and about 50 hopeful subjects of grace are reckoned among its fruits. Their churches are walking in harmony and love.

The Presbytery of Onondaga have many good things, for which to praise the great Jehovah. A deep and general seriousness in the course of the last year has pervaded the first church of Onondaga, the first church of Pompey, the village of Orville, the towns of Sullivan, Lenox, and Lysander; by which the kingdom of the Redeemer, within their limits, has been greatly increased and strengthened.

The Presbytery of Bath presents a truly affecting instance of divine power and grace in the town of Prattsburg. In the adjoining corners of Bath and Prattsburg about thirty have recently been brought to the knowledge of the truth, as it is in Jesus and in the more central parts of Prattsburg, the work within two weeks past has assumed the most interesting features and an overwhelming influence. Between forty and fifty, it is credibly stated, have been hopefully born again within the short compass of ten days; and the present moment with that people is a season big with the prospects of Zion's glory, and travailing for the birth of many souls.

Permitted to close their report with the notice of such an event, so near to them that they can almost hear the cries of awakened sinners, and the praises of those who are rejoicing in the Lord, so promising in its aspects, so affecting in its nature, the Synod feel that they have occasion for the most unfeigned and cordial thanks to the great Head of the Church, and to lift their united prayer to Heaven, that this may be but the small beginning of the first fruits of God's goodness to their Churches the coming year, and to Zion universally, in all future time."

———

To the above general statement, the Stated Clerk takes the liberty to add the following particulars.

From the Reports of the several Presbyteries, it appears that there are now belonging to this Synod, *ninety-two* ordained Ministers, and *eleven* Licentiates: that they have under their care *one hundred and forty-three* Congregations: that, during the last year, 191 adults, and 1099 infants have been Baptized: that, during the same time, 1018 have been added to the number of Communicants; and that the whole number of Communicants is 7084.

This statement is taken from the Presbyterial reports, as presented at the late meeting of the Synod in Geneva, and, so far as relates to the number of Ministers, Licentiates and Congregations, may be considered as accurate; but, with respect to the number of Baptisms and of Communicants, it falls far short of the truth. One reason of this is that, from 40 or 50 churches, (some of them large and respectable,) the Synod have never received *any report*, either of baptisms or of communicants. Another reason is, that many of the churches, (though they have heretofore reported) have neglected to report the number of baptisms and of communicants *added last year*; consequently the number of communicants in those churches is reported by the Synod precisely what it was in their last annual report, though it is well known that in some of them considerable additions have been made since the last meeting of the Synod. If annual reports had been obtained from *all* the churches under the care of the Synod, the number of communicants would probably have amounted to more than 8000. But, taking the number of communicants, of churches, and of ministers, just as they stand in the above statement, the result is highly encouraging, and ought to strengthen our faith and animate our exertions in building up that Church which the Redeemer purchased with his blood.

The increase of the number of Churches and of Ministers of the gospel, within the bounds of this Synod, for a few years past, is almost without a parallel; and must be truly gratifying to all who "pray for the peace of Jerusalem." In the autumn of 1805, the Presbytery of Geneva was formed, and then consisted of only *three* ministers.* This Presbytery then included all the district of country now contained within the boundaries of the *eight* Presbyteries which constitute the Synod of Geneva. *Thirteen years and a half* ago, this district of country contained only one Presbytery, only three regular Presbyterian Ministers, and perhaps eight or ten small Presbyterian Churches:—Now it contains eight Presbyteries;+ 92 Presbyterian Ministers; 11 Licentiates, 143 Presbyterian Congregations, and more than 7000 Communicants in these congregations. And besides this increase in one denomination, there have been considerable additions to the number of ministers, of congregations and of communicants in various other denominations.

Such an immense increase, in so short a time, and in so small a district of country as that embraced by the Synod of Geneva, calls loudly on all the true friends of Zion for expressions of gratitude and praise to Him whose "paths are goodness and truth to all such as keep his covenant"—to Him, who has promised that the gates of Hell shall never prevail against his CHURCH.

Geneva, 22d Feb. 1819.

* The Reverend Messrs. Jedediah Chapman, John Lindsley, and Jabez Chadwick. These were the only regular Presbyterian ministers then in the country.—Their number was soon increased by the addition of the Rev. Messrs. Higgins, Woodruff and Mandeville.

+ Two new Presbyteries were formed at the late meeting of the Synod.

TWENTY-SEVEN

A Presbyterian Congregation's Confession of Faith and Covenant

Source: Presbyterian Church of Newark records, #6116, Division of Rare and Manuscript Collections, Cornell University Library.

In 1825, the founding members of the First Presbyterian Church of Newark, New York, adopted a confession of faith and covenant. The confession lists and summarizes many of the central theological claims of the 1647 Westminster Confession of Faith. The covenant was presumably made by all men who served the congregation as pastors or elders but may have been required of all church members as well. A clerk copied the confession and covenant into the congregation's minute book as one of the church community's founding documents.

🕮 🕮 🕮

Confession of Faith

Adopted by the Presbyterian Church of Newark

I. You Believe, That there is one God, who is infinitely perfect, and is the Creator, Preserver, and Governor of all things: That this one God exists mysteriously in three Persons, the Father, the Son, and the Holy Ghost, who are the same in substance, and equal in all perfections.

II. That the Scriptures of the Old and New Testament are the Word of God, and are the only rule of faith and practice.

III. That our first Parents were made perfectly holy; but, by disobedience, fell from the state in which they were created; in consequence of which. All their posterity are, by nature, entirely sinful.

IV. That God, in his infinite and sovereign mercy, has provided a Saviour, even Jesus Christ, his dearly beloved Son, who having become incarnate, by his obedience honored the law, and by his death made a complete atonement for the sin of the world: So that, all who believe in Him obtain the forgiveness of their sins, and a sure title to eternal life.

V. That salvation is freely offered to all: but that all mankind are naturally so depraved, and such perfect enemies to God and the Saviour, that no one will repent of sin and believe in Christ, until God, according to his eternal purpose give him a new heart by the sovereign and efficacious influence of his Holy Spirit.

VI. That all true believers persevere in faith and holiness, being kept by the power of God through faith unto salvation.

VII. That the Law of God, which requires perfect holiness of heart and life, is the rule which Christians are bound to observe

VIII. That Baptism and the Lord's supper are Christian ordinances: the latter of which is to be administered to professing believers; and the former to them, and to their households.

IX. That, at the end of the world, there will be a Resurrection of the bodies, of all mankind, and a day of Judgment; when Christ, the Judge, will sentence the wicked to endless punishment, and receive the righteous to life everlasting.

COVENANT

You do now, in the presence of the dread Majesty of heaven and earth, the Searcher of all hearts, and before his people solemnly profess to give up yourselves to God, the Father, Son, and Holy Ghost.

You choose Him for your God, your Father, you Saviour and your Sanctifier

You renounce all ways of sin as what you truly abhor; and choose the service of God as your greatest privilege.

You promise, in humble dependence on Divine Grace, to live soberly, righteously and piously, denying all ungodliness and every worldly lust.

You promise and covenant that so long as God, in his holy Providence, should permit you to remain among us, you will treat the Members of this church with Christian watchfulness and brotherly affection; that you will attend upon its Institutions and Ordinances & Submit to its Discipline; Seek its Prosperity, & Peace and that in all your conduct, you will adorn the doctrine of God your Saviour.

TWENTY-EIGHT

Race and Ministry in Wayne County

Source: Samuel Ringgold Ward, *Autobiography of a Fugitive Negro: His Anti-slavery Labours in the United States, Canada, & England* (London: J. Snow, 1855), 28–32 and 80–85.

In the following excerpts from *Autobiography of a Fugitive Negro*, Rev. Samuel Ringgold Ward narrated his experience as a Black pastor in antebellum New York. The excerpts begin with an explanation of how Ward, the son of escaped slaves, entered the ministry and proceeds with a description of his experience ministering to an all-white congregation in western New York. This account highlights how racism shaped Ward's early education, his ministry to both white and Black Christians, as well as his theology and antislavery politics.

✷ ✷ ✷

[...] I grew up in the city of New York as do the children of poor parents in large cities too frequently. I was placed at a public school in Mulberry Street, taught by Mr. C. C. Andrew, and subsequently by Mr. Adams, a Quaker gentleman, from both of whom I received great kindness. Dr. A. Libolt, my last preceptor in that school, placed me under lasting obligations. Poverty compelled me to work, but inclination led me to study; hence, I was enabled, in spite of poverty, to make some progress in necessary learning. Added to poverty, however, in the case of a black lad in that city, is the ever-present, ever-crushing Negro-hate, which hedges up his path, discourages his efforts, damps his ardour, blasts his hopes, and embitters his spirits.

Some white persons wonder at and condemn the tone in which some of us blacks speak of our oppressors. Such persons talk as if they knew but little of human nature, and less of Negro character, else they would wonder rather that, what with slavery and Negro-hate, the mass of us are not either depressed into idiocy or excited into demons. What class of whites, except the Quakers, ever spoke of their oppressors or wrongdoers as mildly as we do? This peculiarly American spirit (which Englishmen easily enough imbibe, after they have resided a few days in the United States) was ever at my elbow. As a servant, it denied me a seat at the table with my white fellow servants; in the sports of childhood and youth, it was ever disparagingly reminding me of my colour and origin; along the streets it ever pursued, ever ridiculed, ever abused me. If I sought redress, the very complexion I wore was pointed out as the best reason for my seeking it in vain; if I desired to turn to account a little learning, in the way of earning a living by it, the idea of employing a black clerk was pre-posterous—too absurd to be seriously entertained. I never knew but one coloured clerk in a mercantile house. Mr. W.L. Jeffers was lowest clerk in a house well known in Broad Street, New York; but never was advanced a single grade, while numerous white lads have since passed up by him, and over him, to be members of the firm. So, if I sought a trade, white apprentices would leave if I were admitted; and when I went to the house of God, as it was called, I found all the Negro-hating usages and senti-ments of general society there encouraged and embodied in the Negro pew, and in the disallowing Negroes to commune until all the whites, however poor, low, and degraded, had done. I know of more than one coloured person driven to the total denial of all religion, by the religious barbarism of white New Yorkers and other Northern champions of the slaveholder.

However, at the age of sixteen, I found a friend in George Atkinson Ward, Esq., from whom I received encouragement to persevere, in spite of Negro-hate. In 1833 I became a clerk of Thomas L. Jennings, Esq., one of the most worthy of the coloured race; subsequently my brother and I served David Ruggles, Esq., then of New York, late of Northamp-ton, Massachusetts, now no more.

In 1833 it pleased God to answer the prayers of my parents, in my conversion. My attention being turned to the ministry, I was advised and recommended by the late Rev. G. Hogarth, of Brooklyn, to the teacher-ship of a school for coloured children, established by the munificence of the late Peter Remsen, Esq., of New Town, N.Y. The most distinctive thing I can say of myself in this my first attempt at the profession of a pedagogue, is that I succeeded Mr., now the Rev. Dr. Pennington. I af-terwards taught for two-and-a-half-years in Newark, New Jersey, where I was living in January 1838, when I was married to Miss Reynolds, of New York; and in October 1838 Samuel Ringgold Ward the younger was born, and I became, "to all intents, constructions, and purposes whatsoever," a family man, aged twenty-one years and twelve days.

In May, 1839, I was licensed to preach the gospel by the New York Congregational Association, assembled at Poughkeepsie. In November of the same year, I became the travelling agent of first the American and afterwards the New York Anti-Slavery Society; in April, 1841, I accepted the unanimous invitation of the Congregational Church of South But-ler, Wayne Co., N.Y., to be their pastor; and in September of that year I was publicly ordained and inducted as minister of that Church. I look back to my settlement among that dear people with peculiar feelings. It was my first charge: I there first administered the ordinances of bap-tism, and the Lord's supper and there first laid hands upon and set apart a deacon; there God honoured my ministry, in the conversion of many and in the trebling the number of the members of the Church, most of whom, I am delighted to know, are still walking in the light of God. The manly courage they showed, in calling and sustain and honouring as their pastor a black man, in that day, in spite of the too general Negro-hate everywhere rife (and as professedly pious as rife) around them, exposing them as it did to the taunts, scoffs, jeers, and abuse of too many who wore the cloak of Christianity—entitled them to what they will ever receive, my warmest thanks and kindest love. But one circumstance do I regret, in connection with the two-and-a-half years I spent among them—that was, not the poverty against which I was struggling during the time, nor the demise of the darling child I buried among them: it was my exceeding great inefficiency, of which they seemed to be quite unconscious. Pouring my tears into their bo-soms, I ask of them and of God forgiveness. I was their first pastor, they my first charge. Distance of both time and space has not yet divided us, and I trust will ever leave us one in heart and mind. [. . .]

The Church and congregation were all white persons save my own family. It was "a new thing under the sun" to see such a connection.

The invitation was unanimous and cordial; and not one incident occurred during my settlement, on the part of the living members, to
make it even seem to be otherwise. Having spoken elsewhere touch-
ing this relation, I choose not here to repeat myself; but I will add,
the novelty of such a settlement attracted a great deal of notice, and a
great many remarks pro and con. I understood it to be a matter of vast
importance, how I should demean myself in so responsible a position;
for I felt it to be such, in two very important points of view—first, in
regard to the anti-slavery cause generally; and secondly, in reference to
the coloured people especially. If I should acquit myself creditably as a
preacher, the anti-slavery cause would thereby be encouraged. Should
I fail in this, that sacred cause would be loaded with reproach. So, if
I were successful or unsuccessful in this charge would encouragement
or discouragement come to the people of colour. In the one case, the
traducers and disparagers of the Negro would say, "Said we not truly
when we affirmed that nothing could be made of, or done with, the
Negro? Such a one was actually placed in such a position; but so invet-
erate and unconquerable were the degrading tendencies of the Negro,
that he could not sustain himself." Then whoever pleaded for Negro
equality would be pointed to my failure as a perfect refutation of his
doctrine, and a complete and triumphant answer to his argument. On
the other hand, if I did succeed, some other young black would feel
encouraged to qualify himself for a position of usefulness among his
own people; but while appropriately serviceable to them, he might also
be so situated as to do good to others and for his own class. I was not
willing to do mischief to the dear anti-slavery cause, nor to that of my
beloved people. I hope God spared me from either—from both. Or, at
any rate, among the many things wherewithal I have been reproached,
this is not one of them.

During my residence in South Butler, I was frequently called upon
to speak, lecture, and preach, elsewhere. Thus were afforded me numerous opportunities of making known to others than my own congregation the gospel of Jesus; and of spreading before others than those of
my own neighborhood what were the doctrines of the abolitionists,
and the duties of American citizens, in regard to those doctrines. I had
the pleasure of seeing principles of importance taking root, springing up, and becoming productive, and scattering seed upon fresh soil.
While I cannot agree with some as to the good results and wide extent
of my labors, I certainly hope that some good was done. That hope is

more based upon the peculiar character of the people of my charge, and those among whom I travelled, than upon anything I was enabled to do. My own people were honest, straightforward, God-fearing descendants of New England Puritans. Living in the interior of the State, apart from the allurements and deceptions of fashion, they felt at liberty to hear, judge, and determine for themselves, and to act in accordance with what the Bible, as they understood it, demanded of them. They heard a preacher: they supposed and believed that he preached God's truth. That was what they wanted, and all they wanted. The mere accident of the colour of the preacher was to them a matter of small consideration. Some might ridicule: indeed, some did. But what of that? They received the truth, and it was of sufficient value to enable them to endure ridicule for its sake. Anti-slavery doctrines were unpopular; anti-slavery practice was still more so. But what said the Bible about these doctrines? Did they agree with the law of love? Were they in agreement with—or, what is more to the point, part and parcel of—what Jesus taught? If so, let rectitude take the place of popularity. They could afford to without the latter. So this honest, right-hearted people loved—so they stood by the pastor—so their influence spread abroad—and so the Lord God of Jacob blessed them, according to his gracious promise.

When in South Butler, also, the people of my own colour called upon me not unfrequently to visit and labour among them. They seemed inclined to take advantage of my position, to make it serviceable; and I was but too happy to accede to their wishes.

In doing so, I always sought to inculcate some truth which would have a direct influence on our character and our condition. Being deprived of the right of voting upon terms of equality with whites—being denied the ordinary courtesies of decent society, to say nothing of what is claimed for every man, especially every freeborn American citizen—I very well know, from a deep and painful experience, that the black people were goaded into a constant temptation to hate their white fellow citizens. I know, too, how natural such hatred is in such circumstances: and all I know of the exhibition of vindictiveness and revenge by the whites against their injurers—and the most perfect justice of the Negro regarding the white man according to daily treatment received from him—caused me to see this temptation to be all the stronger: and convinced me also, that the white had no personal claim to anything else than the most cordial hatred of the black.

How frequently have I heard a Negro exclaim, "I cannot like a white man. He and his have done so much injury to me and my people for so many generations." How difficult, how impossible, to deny this, with all its telling force of historical fact! How natural is such a feeling, in such circumstances! How richly the whites deserved it!

My course was, however, to remind them of the manner in which Christ had been treated by those for whom he died, ourselves included; to direct their attention to the fact, that in the face of bad social customs, and education, and religion, God enabled some whites to do and endure all things for our cause, in its connection with their own; to assure them that the number of such was constantly increasing in our native country, while nearly all of the white race in Europe were our friends, especially the English, the French, and the Germans; and I felt justified in calling attention to my own position, and an example of improved feeling, and a sign of hope and a token of encouragement. Accustomed to be soothed, as are my people, by hopeful, encouraging truth, I never knew these appeals to fail of effect. In addition to the above, I urged that, as Christ forgave, so should we; and that he made our being forgiven depend upon whether we forgave our enemies; that just as surely as the whites were our enemies—a most palpable fact, of every-day illustration—just so surely we must forgive them, or lie down for ever with them, amid the torments of the same perdition! What an aggravation of our temporal torments, to be obliged to be associated with our injurers, and to be partakers with them in an unrepented, unsanctified, more fiendish state, in the pangs of an endless perdition!

I beg to state that I never taught on this subject what I did not then, and do not now, believe. I seriously believe that the prejudice of the whites against Negros is a constant source of temptation to the latter to hate the former. I also believe that the same prejudice will aggravate the perdition of both: and I pray, therefore, that my people may be saved from that hatred, and made forgiving; and for the whites of America, my highest wish is that they may all become like the people of South Butler, thus removing danger from themselves, and, by doing justly, remove the most insidious of temptations from my people, whom, God knows they have injured enough already. [. . .]

PART V

Kingdoms of God

The Latter-day Saints and the Millerites both originated in the Burned-over District. While the groups differed from each other on many points of Christian doctrine, both groups looked to the near future for the biblically prophesied Second Coming of Jesus and the subsequent millennium in which the Kingdom of God would be established on the earth. Accordingly, the Latter-day Saints (who were also called Mormons) and Millerites each felt that it was their mission to prepare all who would listen for the end of the world.

The history of the Latter-day Saints commenced with Joseph Smith, who moved with his family to a farm just south of Palmyra, New York, in 1817. As a series of religious revivals swept through the area, Smith began to worry about the state of his soul. According to Smith's personal history, he began attending the meetings of several churches in the area but grew uncertain about which of all the churches he should join. In fact, years later, when he recalled the revival meetings of his youth, Smith described a scene that evoked both excitement and anxiety among religious seekers in western New York. In 1820, amid his personal confusion, Smith decided to find a secluded spot in the woods near his home in which to pray, and it was in this setting that he had a vision of deity in which God and Jesus Christ appeared to him, instructed him to join none of the churches he had been considering, and informed him that "the fulness of the gospel should at some future time" be revealed to him.[1]

Smith claimed that three years later he was visited by an angel who showed him the location of an ancient record buried in a nearby hill. Smith stated that the record consisted of gold plates with ancient characters inscribed thereon and that he translated them "by the gift and power of God."[2] In 1830, he published the Book of Mormon, which he advertised as a record of God's dealings with the ancient inhabitants of the American continents. That same year, Smith founded the Church of Christ (later renamed the Church of Jesus Christ of Latter-day Saints). But because Smith's followers believed the Book of Mormon was scripture to be read along with the Bible, friends and critics alike soon dubbed them "Mormons."[3]

The Latter-day Saints believed that they were gathering righteous men and women in preparation for the Second Coming of Christ. Chief among their tasks was to establish the city of Zion, which they believed was the "New Jerusalem" prophesied in the New Testament.[4] Accordingly, Smith and many of his followers left New York in 1831 to form new communities in Ohio and Missouri in which they could practice their religious beliefs. In this sense their history fits closely with other religious societies that established utopian communities in nineteenth-century America. Although the Latter-day Saints did not establish such large-scale communities in New York, the state remains significant to the church's history as the birthplace of a movement that its participants viewed as establishing the Kingdom of God on earth preparatory for the second advent of Christ.[5]

About the same time Smith claimed to have had his first interaction with deity, William Miller was deeply engaged in the study of the Bible. A veteran of the War of 1812 who became a Baptist shortly after that conflict ended, Miller fastidiously read the Bible intent on discovering the "primitive church," a quest he shared with many other Americans intent on restoring Christianity as it was taught by Jesus and his

1. Bushman, *Joseph Smith, Rough Stone Rolling*, 30–41.
2. "Joseph Smith's Visions," document 29 herein; Bushman, *Joseph Smith, Rough Stone Rolling*, 41–46.
3. Bushman, *Joseph Smith, Rough Stone Rolling*, 80–112.
4. Revelation 21:1–2.
5. Bushman, *Joseph Smith, Rough Stone Rolling*, 144–76; Spencer W. McBride, "Pilgrimage to History," *New York Archives* 15, no. 1 (Spring 2015): 16–19.

apostles. In 1821, after two years of examining biblical prophecies in both the Old and New Testaments, Miller believed that he had made a monumental discovery. Based largely on his reading of prophecies in the Old Testament book of Daniel, Miller concluded that the Second Coming of Jesus would occur "about the year 1843."[6]

Miller did not immediately publicize his discovery. While he confided in a few close friends and family members, he made his first public declaration of the approximate date of Christ's return in a lecture he gave in Dresden, New York, in 1831. His message elicited both praise and disdain from New York residents, and it had a similarly polarizing response from Americans in general as it spread throughout the United States. Men and women who believed Miller's prediction did not all gather to a central place but formed a scattered community of believers and often referred to themselves as "Adventists"; nonbelievers frequently referred to them as "Millerites."[7] Several of Miller's followers employed his method of interpreting prophecy to ascertain a more precise date for the Second Coming. Eventually, Adventists were instructed in print to make themselves ready for Christ's return between March 21, 1843, and March 21, 1844. When the latter date came and went without any sign of Jesus, the day was labeled "the Great Disappointment."[8]

The disappointment caused many Adventists to seek spiritual direction elsewhere, but many others maintained their faith in Miller's prediction by revisiting their calculations. Several of his followers soon began to prepare for the end of the world and the beginning of the prophesied millennial reign of Christ on October 22, 1844.[9] That day also came and passed without incident. This second "Great Disappointment" proved too much for Miller's leadership, and the movement he started weakened and splintered.[10]

---

6. Daniel 8:14 (KJV) states, "And he said unto me, Unto two thousand and three hundred days; then shall the sanctuary be cleansed." Miller interpreted twenty-three hundred days as twenty-three hundred years and, using Jewish calendars and historical research, narrowed the expected window in which Christians should watch for the Second Coming. William Miller, *Evidence from Scripture and History of the Second Coming of Christ, About the Year 1843: Exhibited in a Course of Lectures* (Troy, NY, 1836); David L. Rowe, *God's Strange Work: William Miller and the End of the World* (Grand Rapids, MI: Eerdmans, 2008), 69–84.

7. Rowe, *God's Strange Work*, 157.

8. Rowe, 176–77.

9. Rowe, 185–91.

10. Rowe, 226–35. The most prominent and enduring religious denomination to grow out of the Millerites is the Seventh-day Adventist Church.

Even as word of William Miller's predictions expanded well beyond New York, ministers preaching his "Adventist" message reported a significant and enduring interest for his biblical calculations in the Burned-over District. And while the Latter-day Saints and Millerites were similar in their respective beliefs that the return of Jesus Christ was imminent, their understanding of the event differed significantly. Whereas the Latter-day Saints believed that they were building the Kingdom of God on earth in preparation for the Second Coming, the Millerites believed that they were preparing themselves for the Second Coming and the establishment of the Kingdom of God on earth that would follow.[11]

Perhaps less well-known than the Mormons and Millerites, but more controversial, was the religious community founded in New York by Robert Matthews. Beginning in 1825, Matthews claimed that he started having visions and receiving the will of God as a prophet. Three years later he announced that a flood would destroy Albany, New York, and he fled the city without his wife and children, who refused to flee with him. Soon thereafter he traveled to New York City, where he met the Presbyterian minister Elijah Pierson, who believed Matthews's prophetic claims. Matthews and Pierson converted several others in the city, including businessmen who financed the founding of an intentional religious community in Sing Sing, New York, called the Kingdom or Mount Zion. The Kingdom was a place for Matthews and his followers to create a society based on their religious beliefs and belief that the ushering in of the prophesied millennial era was at hand. However, that venture was short-lived. By the end of 1834 Pierson was dead, Matthews was imprisoned, and the Kingdom disbanded.[12] While the Kingdom was located in the Hudson River Valley, some of its members came from central and western New York or would be influential in that region after leaving the community.

This part consists of seven documents. Three of them showcase the Latter-day Saints, specifically how Smith declared his prophetic role in building the kingdom of God on earth, the role of the Book of Mormon in attracting converts to his cause, and the way critics challenged both

---

11. For a comparison of Mormon and Millerite forms of millennialism see Grant Underwood, *The Millenarian World of Early Mormonism* (Champaign: Illinois University Press, 1993), 116–26.

12. Paul E. Johnson and Sean Wilentz, *The Kingdom of Matthias: A Story of Sex and Salvation in Nineteenth-Century America*, 2nd ed. (New York: Oxford University Press, 2012).

Smith and his church. Three other documents demonstrate the polarizing nature of Miller's claims: two excerpts from Miller's own works are paired with a passage from one of his contemporary critics. The seventh document is an excerpt from the autobiography of Sojourner Truth, who was a member of the Kingdom and witnessed the beginning of that religious movement.

TWENTY-NINE

Joseph Smith's Visions

Source: "Church History," *Times and Seasons* (Nauvoo, IL), March 1, 1842.

In 1842, Joseph Smith wrote a brief historical sketch of his life and the rise of the Church of Jesus Christ of Latter-day Saints. Chicago newspaper editor John Wentworth requested the sketch on behalf of a friend who wanted to include information on the Latter-day Saints in a history he was writing.[1] Smith wrote of his first vision of deity (what Latter-day Saints have come to call "the First Vision"), the origins of the Book of Mormon, the church's expansion to other states, the persecution church members experienced in Missouri, and the subsequent move of the church's headquarters to Nauvoo, Illinois. He closed the sketch with a summary of the church's theological beliefs.

Ultimately, Smith's historical sketch was not included in the history for which it was intended, but it was published by a Nauvoo newspaper. The portions of the historical sketch pertaining to the church's early history in New York are featured here, as is the conclusion projecting an optimistic future and summarizing the church's beliefs.

❧ ❧ ❧

---

1. "'Church History,' 1 March 1842," in Karen Lynn Davidon, David J. Whittaker, et al., *Histories, Volume 1: Joseph Smith Histories, 1832–1844*, vol. 1 of the Histories Series of *The Joseph Smith Papers*, edited by Dean C. Jessee et al. (Salt Lake City: Church Historian's Press, 2012), 489.

At the request of Mr. John Wentworth, Editor, and Proprietor of the "Chicago Democrat," I have written the following sketch of the rise, progress, persecution, and faith of the Latter-Day Saints, of which I have the honor, under God, of being the founder. Mr. Wentworth says, that he wishes to furnish Mr. Bastow [George Barstow], a friend of his, who is writing the history of New Hampshire, with this document.

FIGURE 10.   Joseph Smith Jr., 1805–1844. In the 1820s, amid the revivalism that swept western New York, Joseph Smith claimed to have had a series of divine visions, which led to the founding of the Church of Jesus Christ of Latter-day Saints. (Courtesy Community of Christ Archives)

As Mr. Bastow has taken the proper steps to obtain correct information all that I shall ask at his hands, is, that he publish the account entire, ungarnished, and without misrepresentation.

I was born in the town of Sharon Windsor co., Vermont, on the 23rd of December, A. D. 1805. When ten years old my parents removed to Palmyra New York, where we resided about four years, and from thence we removed to the town of Manchester [New York].

My father was a farmer and taught me the art of husbandry. When about fourteen years of age I began to reflect upon the importance of being prepared for a future state, and upon enquiring the plan of salvation I found that there was a great clash in religious sentiment; if I went to one society they referred me to one plan, and another to another; each one pointing to his own particular creed as the summum bonum of perfection: considering that all could not be right, and that God could not be the author of so much confusion I determined to investigate the subject more fully, believing that if God had a church it would not be split up into factions, and that if he taught one society to worship one way, and administer in one set of ordinances, he would not teach another principles which were diametrically opposed. Believing the word of God I had confidence in the declaration of James; "If any man lack wisdom let him ask of God who giveth to all men liberally and upbraideth not and it shall be given him," I retired to a secret place in a grove and began to call upon the Lord, while fervently engaged in supplication my mind was taken away from the objects with which I was surrounded, and I was enwrapped in a heavenly vision and saw two glorious personages who exactly resembled each other in features, and likeness, surrounded with a brilliant light which eclipsed the sun at noon-day. They told me that all religious denominations were believing in incorrect doctrines, and that none of them was acknowledged of God as his church and kingdom. And I was expressly commanded to "go not after them," at the same time receiving a promise that the fulness of the gospel should at some future time be made known unto me.

On the evening of the 21st of September, A. D. 1823, while I was praying unto God, and endeavoring to exercise faith in the precious promises of scripture on a sudden a light like that of day, only of a far purer and more glorious appearance, and brightness burst into the room, indeed the first sight was as though the house was filled with consuming fire; the appearance produced a shock that affected the whole body; in a moment a personage stood before me surrounded with a glory yet greater than that with which I was already surrounded. This messenger

proclaimed himself to be an angel of God sent to bring the joyful tidings, that the covenant which God made with ancient Israel was at hand
to be fulfilled, that the preparatory work for the second coming of the
Messiah was speedily to commence; that the time was at hand for the
gospel, in all its fulness to be preached in power, unto all nations that
a people might be prepared for the millennial reign.

I was informed that I was chosen to be an instrument in the hands of
God to bring about some of his purposes in this glorious dispensation.

I was also informed concerning the aboriginal inhabitants of this
country, and shown who they were, and from whence they came; a brief
sketch of their origin, progress, civilization, laws, governments, of their
righteousness and iniquity, and the blessings of God being finally withdrawn from them as a people was made known unto me: I was also
told where there was deposited some plates on which were engraven an
abridgement of the records of the ancient prophets that had existed on
this continent. The angel appeared to me three times the same night
and unfolded the same things. After having received many visits from
the angels of God unfolding the majesty, and glory of the events that
should transpire in the last days, on the morning of the 22d of September A. D. 1827, the angel of the Lord delivered the records into my
hands.

These records were engraven on plates which had the appearance of
gold, each plate was six inches wide and eight inches long and not quite
so thick as common tin. They were filled with engravings, in Egyptian
characters and bound together in a volume, as the leaves of a book with
three rings running through the whole. The volume was something near
six inches in thickness, a part of which was sealed. The characters on
the unsealed part were small, and beautifully engraved. The whole book
exhibited many marks of antiquity in its construction and much skill in
the art of engraving. With the records was found a curious instrument
which the ancients called "Urim and Thummim," which consisted of
two transparent stones set in the rim of a bow fastened to a breastplate.

Through the medium of the Urim and Thummim I translated the
record by the gift, and power of God.

In this important and interesting book the history of ancient America is unfolded, from its first settlement by a colony that came from
the tower of Babel, at the confusion of languages to the beginning of
the fifth century of the Christian era. We are informed by these records that America in ancient times has been inhabited by two distinct

races of people. The first were called Jaredites and came directly from the tower of Babel. The second race came directly from the city of Jerusalem, about six hundred years before Christ. They were principally Israelites, of the descendants of Joseph. The Jaredites were destroyed about the time that the Israelites came from Jerusalem, who succeeded them in the inheritance of the country. The principal nation of the second race fell in battle towards the close of the fourth century. The remnant are the Indians that now inhabit this country. This book also tells us that our Saviour made his appearance upon this continent after his resurrection, that he planted the gospel here in all its fulness, and richness, and power, and blessing; that they had apostles, prophets, pastors, teachers and evangelists; the same order, the same priesthood, the same ordinances, gifts, powers, and blessing, as was enjoyed on the eastern continent, that the people were cut off in consequence of their transgressions, that the last of their prophets who existed among them was commanded to write an abridgement of their prophesies, history &c., and to hide it up in the earth, and that it should come forth and be united with the bible for the accomplishment of the purposes of God in the last days. For a more particular account I would refer to the Book of Mormon, which can be purchased at Nauvoo, or from any of our travelling elders.

As soon as the news of this discovery was made known, false reports, misrepresentation and slander flew as on the wings of the wind in every direction, the house was frequently beset by mobs, and evil designing persons, several times I was shot at, and very narrowly escaped, and every device was made use of to get the plates away from me, but the power and blessing of God attended me, and several began to believe my testimony.

On the 6th of April, 1830, the "Church of Jesus Christ of Latter-Day Saints," was first organized in the town of Manchester, Ontario co., state of New York. Some few were called and ordained by the spirit of revelation, and prophesy, and began to preach as the spirit gave them utterance, and though weak, yet were they strengthened by the power of God, and many were brought to repentance, were immersed in the water, and were filled with the Holy Ghost by the laying on of hands. They saw visions and prophesied, devils were cast out and the sick healed by the laying on of hands. From that time the work rolled forth with astonishing rapidity, and churches were soon formed in the states of New York, Pennsylvania, Ohio, Indiana, Illinois and Missouri; [. . .]

Persecution has not stopped the progress of truth, but has only added fuel to the flame, it has spread with increasing rapidity, proud of the cause which they have espoused and conscious of their innocence and of the truth of their system amidst calumny and reproach have the elders of this church gone forth, and planted the gospel in almost every state in the Union; it has penetrated our cities, it has spread over our villages, and has caused thousands of our intelligent, nobel, and patriotic citizens to obey its divine mandates, and be governed by its sacred truths. It has also spread into England, Ireland, Scotland and Wales: in the year of 1839 where a few of our missionaries were sent over five thousand and joined the standard of truth, there are numbers now joining in every land.

Our missionaries are going forth to different nations, and in Germany, Palestine, New Holland, the East Indies, and other places, the standard of truth has been erected: no unhallowed hand can stop the work from progressing, persecutions may rage, mobs may combine, armies may assemble, calumny may defame, but the truth of God will go forth boldly, nobly, and independent till it has penetrated every continent, visited every clime, swept every country, and sounded in every ear, till the purposes of God shall be accomplished and the great Jehovah shall say the work is done.

We believe in God the Eternal Father, and in his son Jesus Christ, and in the Holy Ghost.

We believe that men will be punished for their own sins and not for Adam's transgression.

We believe that through the atonement of Christ all mankind may be saved by obedience to the laws and ordinances of the Gospel.

We believe that these ordinances are 1st, Faith in the Lord Jesus Christ; 2d, Repentance; 3d, Baptism by immersion for the remission of sins; 4th, Laying on of hands for the gift of the Holy Ghost.

We believe that a man must be called of God by "prophesy, and by laying on of hands" by those who are in authority to preach the gospel and administer in the ordinances thereof.

We believe in the same organization that existed in the primitive church, viz: apostles, prophets, pastors, teachers, evangelists &c.

We believe in the gift of tongues, prophesy, revelation, visions, healing, interpretation of tongues &c.

We believe the bible to be the word of God as far as it is translated correctly; we also believe the Book of Mormon to be the word of God.

We believe all that God has revealed, all that he does now reveal, and we believe that he will yet reveal many great and important things pertaining to the kingdom of God.

We believe in the literal gathering of Israel and in the restoration of the Ten Tribes. That Zion will be built upon this continent. That Christ will reign personally upon the earth, and that the earth will be renewed and receive its paradasaic glory.

We claim the privilege of worshipping Almighty God according to the dictates of our conscience, and allow all men the same privilege let them worship how, where, or what they may.

We believe in being subject to kings, presidents, rulers, and magistrates, in obeying, honoring and sustaining the law.

We believe in being honest, true, chaste, benevolent, virtuous, and in doing good to all men; indeed we may say that we follow the admonition of Paul "we believe all things we hope all things," we have endured many things and hope to be able to endure all things. If there is any thing virtuous, lovely, or of good report or praise worthy we seek after these things.

Respectfully &c., JOSEPH SMITH.

THIRTY

Mormonism's Early Critics

Source: "Mormonism—Religious Fanaticism—Church and State,"
Morning Courier and Enquirer (New York, NY), August 15, 1831.

In August and September 1831, journalist
James Gordon Bennett published a two-part feature story in the *Morning Courier and Enquirer* on the Latter-day Saints. Although that paper
was published in New York City, Bennett wrote the story in Canandaigua, New York, just ten miles south of the farm formerly owned by
Joseph Smith's family. Between June and August of that year, Bennett
traveled throughout the western parts of the state with the prominent
American politician Martin Van Buren. The purpose of their trip was to
interview business and political leaders in the region in order to gauge
public opinion on a variety of controversial subjects, including internal
improvements, the New York Safety Fund Banking System, and Freemasonry. In the course of this "interviewing tour," the Latter-day Saints
apparently became a topic of conversation with several individuals in
the Palmyra area. Bennett recorded several pages of notes on the Saints
in his journal, which he then used to compose this story.[1]

---

1. Leonard J. Arrington, "James Gordon Bennett's 1831 Report on 'The Mormonites,'"
BYU Studies 10, no. 3 (Spring 1970); 353–64

Bennett mocked the Saints. He derided Smith as a fraud, citing as evidence reports of the Smith family engaging in treasure seeking and financial speculation, implying that the rise of Mormonism was merely a ploy to enrich their family. This story is representative of the way many of Smith's first critics dismissed the Latter-day Saints as fanatics. Claims that Smith's ecclesiastical leadership was an outgrowth of his youthful employment as a laborer on treasure hunting expeditions quickly became a staple in the rising cottage industry of anti-Mormon publications.[2] Yet these claims were often exaggerated, and components of them were factually incorrect. For example, those Bennett interviewed had apparently mixed up stories about the Mormons in Ohio in 1831 with their memories of the Smiths in New York in the late 1820s. In these stories they identified Sidney Rigdon (called Ringdon in the text below), a preacher and devotee of Alexander Campbell who was converted by Mormon missionaries in Ohio—but not until 1830—as part of the story of the Book of Mormon's origins in New York in the 1820s. The first part of Bennett's two-part story appears here.

§ § §

Mormonism—Religious Fanaticism—Church and State

Canandaigua, Aug. 15th, 1831.

New York has been celebrated for her parties—her sects—her explosions—her curiosities of human character her fanaticism political and religious. The strangest parties and wildest opinions originate among us. The human mind in our rich vales—on our sunny hills—in our crowded cities or thousand villages—or along the shores of our translucent lakes bursts beyond all ordinary trammels; throws aside with equal fastidiousness the maxims of ages and the discipline of generations, and strikes out new paths for itself. In politics—in religion—in all the great concerns of man, New York has a character peculiarly her own; strikingly original, purely American—energetic and wild to the very farthest boundaries of imagination. The centre of the state is quiet comparatively, and grave to a degree; but its two extremities, Eastern and

2. See J. Spencer Fluhman, *"A Peculiar People": Anti-Mormonism and the Making of Religion in Nineteenth-Century America* (Chapel Hill: University of North Carolina Press, 2012), 39–46; Richard L. Anderson, "Joseph Smith's New York Reputation Reappraised," *BYU Studies* 10, no. 3 (Spring 1970): 283–314; Rodger I. Anderson, *Joseph Smith's New York Reputation Reexamined* (Salt Lake City: Signature Books, 1990).

Western; the city of the Atlantic, and the continuous villages of the Lakes, contain all that is curious in human character—daring in conception—wild in invention, and singular in practical good sense as well as in solemn foolery.

You have heard of MORMONISM—who has not? Paragraph has followed paragraph in the newspapers, recounting the movements, detailing their opinions and surprising distant readers with the traits of a singularly new religious sect which had its origin in this state. Mormonism is the latest device of roguery, ingenuity, ignorance and religious excitement combined, and acting on materials prepared by those who ought to know better. It is one of the mental exhalations of Western New York.

The individuals who gave birth to this species of fanaticism are very simple personages, and not known until this thrust them into notice. They are the old and young Joe Smith's, Harris a farmer, Ringdon a sort of preacher on general religion from Ohio, together with several other persons equally infatuated, cunning, and hypocritic. The first of these persons, Smith, resided on the borders of Wayne and Ontario counties on the road leading from Canandaigua to Palmyra. Old Joe Smith had been a country pedlar in his younger days, and possessed all the shrewdness, cunning, and small intrigue which are generally and justly attributed to that description of persons. He was a great story teller, full of anecdotes picked up in his peregrinations—and possessed a tongue as smooth as oil and as quick as lightning. He had been quite a speculator in a small way in his younger days, but had been more fortunate in picking up materials for his tongue than stuff for the purse. Of late years he picked up his living somewhere in the town of Manchester by following a branch of the "American System"—the manufacture of gingerbread and such like domestic wares. In this article he was a considerable speculator, having on hand during a fall of price no less than two baskets full, and I believe his son, Joe, Junior, was at times a partner in the concern. What their dividends were I could not learn, but they used considerable molasses, and were against the duty on that article. Young Joe, who afterwards figured so largely in the Mormon religion, was at that period a careless, indolent, idle, and shiftless fellow. He hung round the villages and strolled round the taverns without any end or aim—without any positive defect or as little merit in his character. He was rather a stout able bodied fellow, and might have made a good living in such a country as this where any one who is willing to work, can soon get on in the world. He was however, the son of a speculative Yankee pedlar, and was brought up to live by his wits. Harris also one of the fathers of Mormonism was a substantial farmer near Palmyra—full of passages of the scriptures—rather wild and flighty in his talk occasionally—but holding a very respectable character in his neighborhood for sobriety, sense and hard working.

A few years ago the Smith's and others who were influenced by their notions, caught an idea that money was hid in several of the hills which give variety to the country between the Canandaigua Lake and Palmyra on the Erie Canal. Old Smith had in his pedling excursions picked up many stories of men getting rich in New England by digging in certain places and stumbling upon chests of money. The fellow excited the imagination of his few auditors, and made them all anxious to lay hold of the bilk axe and the shovel. As yet no fanatical or religious character had been assumed by the Smith's. They exhibited the simple and ordinary desire of getting rich by some short cut if possible. With this view the Smith's and their associates commenced digging, in the numerous hills which diversify the face of the country in the town of Manchester. The sensible country people paid slight attention to them at first. They knew them to be a thriftless set, more addicted to exerting their wits than their industry, readier at inventing stories and tales than attending church or engaging in any industrious trade. On the sides & in the slopes of several of these hills, these excavations are still to be seen. They Would occasionally conceal their purposes, and at other times reveal them by such snatches as might excite curiosity. They dug these holes by day, and at night talked and dreamed over the counties' riches they should enjoy, if they could only hit upon an iron chest full of dollars. In excavating the grounds, they began by taking up the green sod in the form of a circle of six feet diameter—then would continue to dig to the depth of ten, twenty, and sometimes thirty feet. At last some person who joined them spoke of a person in Ohio near Painesville, who had a particular felicity in finding out the spots of ground where money is hid and riches obtained. He related long stories how this person had been along shore in the east—how he had much experience in money digging—how he dreamt of the very spots where it could be found. "Can we get that man here?" asked the enthusiastic Smiths. "Why," said the other, "I guess as how we could by going for him." "How far off?" "I guess some two hundred miles—I would go for him myself but

I want a little change to bear my expenses." To work the whole money-digging crew went to get some money to pay the expenses of bringing on a man who could dream out the exact and particular spots where money in iron chests was hid under ground. Old Smith returned to his gingerbread factory—young Smith to his financing faculties, and after some time, by hook or by crook, they contrived to scrape together a little "change" sufficient to fetch on the money dreamer from Ohio.

After the lapse of some weeks the expedition was completed, and the famous Ohio man made his appearance among them. This recruit was the most cunning, intelligent, and odd of the whole. He had been a preacher of almost every religion—a teacher of all sorts of morals.—He was perfectly au fait with every species of prejudice, folly or fanaticism, which governs the mass of enthusiasts. In the course of his experience, he had attended all sorts of camp-meetings, prayer meetings, anxious meetings, and revival meetings. He knew every turn of the human mind in relation to these matters. He had a superior knowledge of human nature, considerable talent, great plausibility, and knew how to work the passions as exactly as a Cape Cod sailor knows how to work a whale ship. His name I believe is Henry Rangdon or Ringdon, or some such word. About the time that this person appeared among them, a splendid excavation was begun in a long narrow hill, between Manchester and Palmyra. This hill has since been called by some, the Golden Bible Hill. The road from Canandaigua to Palmyra, runs along its western base. At the northern extremity the hill is quite abrupt and narrow. It runs to the south for a half mile and then spreads out into a piece of broad table land, covered with beautiful orchards and wheat fields. On the east, the Canandaigua outlet runs past it on its way to the beautiful village of Vienna in Phelps. It is profusely covered to the top with Beech, Maple, Bass, and White-wood—the northern extremity is quite bare of trees. In the face of this hill, the money diggers renewed their work with fresh ardour, Ringdon partly uniting with them in their operations.

(To be continued.)

THIRTY-ONE

Parley P. Pratt Encounters the Book of Mormon

Source: Parley Parker Pratt, *The Autobiography of Parley Parker Pratt* (New York: Russell Bros., 1874), 36–40.

Parley Pratt was an early follower of Joseph Smith and quickly rose to a position of prominence in the church's leadership. Born in Burlington, New York, in 1807, Pratt remained in the state until 1826, when he moved with his wife to Ohio. In Ohio, he joined the Reformed Baptist Society—a religious movement led by Thomas and Alexander Campbell that emphasized the reestablishment of the primitive church as described in the Bible.[1] As Pratt recalled in his autobiography, "I began to understand the things which were coming on the earth—the restoration of Israel, the coming of the Messiah, and the glory that should follow. . . . I was all swallowed up in these things. I felt constrained to devote my time in enlightening my fellow men on these important truths, and in warning them to prepare for the coming of the Lord."[2] Accordingly, he sold his land and many of his possessions to perform the work of an

---

1. Terryl L. Givens and Matthew J. Grow, *Parley P. Pratt: The Apostle Paul of Mormonism* (New York: Oxford University Press, 2011), 21–26.
2. Pratt, *Autobiography*, 33.

itinerant preacher. It was in this capacity that he discovered the Book of Mormon and eventually united with Joseph Smith and his followers.

Pratt started writing his autobiography in 1854, by which time he had moved with the Latter-day Saints to Utah Territory.[3] However, Pratt was murdered in 1857 while traveling through Arkansas as a missionary, and his autobiography was published posthumously in 1874.[4] An excerpt from that autobiography appears here. With the advantage of hindsight, Pratt pointed to his discovery of the Book of Mormon as the most pivotal moment in his life. Indeed, his autobiography served a dual purpose: it was simultaneously a record of his life and a religious tract. For present-day readers, however, it provides a first-person account of the religious enthusiasm in the Burned-over District and contextualizes the way many New Yorkers first encountered the Book of Mormon in the years immediately following its publication.

* * *

[. . .]

In August 1830, I had closed my business, completed my arrangements, and we bid adieu to our wilderness home and never saw it afterwards.

On settling up, at a great sacrifice of property, we had about ten dollars left in cash. With this small sum, we launched forth into the wide world, determining first to visit our native place, on our mission, and then such other places as I might be led by the Holy Spirit.

We made our way to Cleveland, 30 miles. We then took passage on a schooner for Buffalo, a distance of 200 miles. We had a fair wind, and the captain, being short of hands, gave me the helm, the sails being all set, and turned in. I steered the vessel the most of the day, with no other person on deck. Of course, our passage cost us little besides my labor. Landing in Buffalo, we engaged our passage for Albany on a canal boat, distance 300 miles. This, including board, cost all our money and some articles of clothing.

Arriving at Rochester, I informed my wife that, notwithstanding our passage being paid through the whole distance, yet I must leave the boat and her to pursue her passage to our friends; while I would stop awhile in this region. Why, I did not know; but it was plainly manifest by the Spirit to me. I said to her, "we part for a season; go and visit our

3. Matthew J. Grow, "A 'Truly Eventful Life': Writing the *Autobiography* of Parley P. Pratt," *Journal of Mormon History* 37, no. 1 (Winter 2011): 153–58.

4. Givens and Grow, *Parley P. Pratt*, 8, 382–84.

friends in our native place; I will come soon, but how soon I know not; for I have a work to do in this region of country, and what it is, or how long it will take to perform it, I know not; but I will come when it is performed."

My wife would have objected to this; but she had seen the hand of God so plainly manifest in His dealings with me many times, that she dare not oppose the things manifest to me by His spirit.

She, therefore, consented; and I accompanied her as far as Newark, a small town upwards of 100 miles from Buffalo, and then took leave of her, and of the boat.

It was early in the morning, just at the dawn of day, I walked ten miles into the country, and stopped to breakfast with a Mr. Wells. I proposed to preach in the evening. Mr. Wells readily accompanied me through the neighborhood to visit the people, and circulate the appointment.

We visited an old Baptist deacon by the name of Hamlin. After hearing of our appointment for the evening, he began to tell of a *book*, a STRANGE BOOK, a VERY STRANGE BOOK! In his possession, which had been just published. This book, he said, purported to have been originally written on plates either of gold or brass, by a branch of the tribes of Israel; and to have been discovered and translated by a young man near Palmyra, in the State of New York, by the aid of visions, or the ministry of angels. I inquired of him how or where the book was to be obtained. He promised me the perusal of it, at his house the next day, if I would call. I felt a strange interest in the book. I preached that evening to a small audience, who appeared to be interested in the truths which I endeavored to unfold to them in a clear and lucid manner from the Scriptures. Next morning I called at his home, where, for the first time, my eyes beheld the "BOOK OF MORMON,"—that book of books—that record which reveals the antiquities of the "New World" back to the remotest ages, and which unfolds the destiny of its people and the world for all time to come;—that Book which contains the fullness of the gospel of a crucified and risen Redeemer;—that Book which reveals a lost remnant of Joseph, and which was the principal means, in the hands of God, of directing the entire course of my future life.

I opened it with eagerness, and read its title page. I then read the testimony of several witnesses in relation to the manner of its being found and translated. After this I commenced its contents by course. I read all day; eating was a burden, I had no desire for food; sleep was a burden when the night came, for I preferred reading to sleep.

As I read, the spirit of the Lord was upon me, and I knew and comprehended that the book was true, as plainly and manifestly as a man comprehends and knows that he exists. My joy was now full, as it were, and I rejoiced sufficiently to more than pay me for all the sorrows, sacrifices and tolls of my life. I soon determined to see the young man who had been the instrument of its discovery.

I accordingly visited the village of Palmyra, and inquired for the residence of Mr. Joseph Smith. I found it some two or three miles from the village. As I approached the house at the close of the day I overtook a man who was driving some cows, and inquired of him for Mr. Joseph Smith, the translator of the *"Book of Mormon."* He informed me that he now resided in Pennsylvania; some one hundred miles distant. I inquired for his father, or for any of the family. He told me that his father had gone a journey; but that his residence was a small house just before me; and, said he, I am his brother. It was Mr. Hyrum Smith. I informed him of the interest I felt in the Book, and of my desire to learn more about it. He welcomed me to his house, and we spent the night together; for neither of us felt disposed to sleep. We conversed most of the night, during which I unfolded to him much of my experience in my search after truth, and my success so far; together with that which I felt was lacking, viz: a commissioned priesthood, or apostleship to minister in the ordinances of God.

He also unfolded to me the particulars of the discovery of the Book; its translations; the rise of the Church of Jesus Christ of Latter-Day Saints, and the commission of his brother Joseph, and others, by revelation and the ministering of angels, by which the apostleship and authority had been again restored to the earth. After duly weighing the whole matter in my mind I saw clearly that these things were true; and that myself and the whole world were without baptism, and without the ministry and ordinances of God; and that the whole world had been in this condition since the days that inspiration and revelation had ceased—in short, that this was a *new dispensation* or *commission*, in fulfillment of prophecy, and for the restoration of Israel, and to prepare the way before the second coming of the Lord.

In the morning I was compelled to take leave of this worthy man and his family—as I had to hasten back a distance of thirty miles, on foot, to fulfill an appointment in the evening. As we parted he kindly presented me with a copy of the Book of Mormon. I had not yet completed its perusal, and was glad indeed to possess a copy of my own.

I travelled on a few miles, and, stopping to rest, I commenced again to read the book. To my great joy I found that Jesus Christ, in his glorified resurrected body, had appeared to the remnant of Joseph on the continent of America, soon after his resurrection and ascension into heaven; and that he also administered, in person, to the ten lost tribes; and that through his personal ministry in these countries his gospel was revealed and written in countries and among nations entirely unknown to the Jewish apostles.

Thus revealed, written, handed down and preserved, till revealed in this age by the angels of God, it had, of course, escaped the corruptions of the great and abominable church; and been preserved in purity.

This discovery greatly enlarged my heart, and filled my soul with joy and gladness. I esteemed the Book, or the information contained in it, more than all the riches of the world. Yes; I verily believe that I would not at that time have exchanged the knowledge I then possessed, for a legal title to all the beautiful farms, houses, villages and property which passed in review before me, on my journey through one of the most flourishing settlements of western New York. [. . .]

THIRTY-TWO

William Miller's Biblical Calculations

Source: William Miller, *Evidence from Scripture and History of the Second Coming of Christ, About the Year 1843: Exhibited in a Course of Lectures* (Troy, NY, 1836), 3–10.

By 1836, word that William Miller had predicted the Second Coming of Jesus to occur "about the year 1843" had spread throughout the United States. In addition to Miller's preaching, many who believed his prediction took it upon themselves to act as missionaries, urging others to repent of their sins and to set their temporal affairs in order in preparation for the end of the world and the establishment of the Kingdom of God. In addition, Miller published several of his lectures in a Vermont newspaper in 1832. Without this network of followers and the attention of newspapers to spread his message, Miller's predictions may have remained a phenomenon confined to the Finger Lakes region of New York.

As a result of the rapid spread of his message, Miller was soon inundated with letters from men and women anxious to hear more about the biblical calculations he used in arriving at his controversial prediction. Responding to each of these letters was a daunting task. At the urging of several of his closest followers, in 1833 he published in a book a series of sixteen lectures he had given on the subject, and then published a revised version of that book in 1836 as *Evidence from Scripture and History of the Second Coming of Christ, About the Year 1843: Exhibited in a Course of Lectures*, so that he could direct all inquirers to that publication.[1] Featured here is the introduction Miller wrote to his published lectures. It describes the methods he used to interpret prophecies recorded in the Bible, his insistence that all biblical prophecies were complementary to each other, and his hope that readers would believe his words and prepare for the imminent arrival of Jesus.

❧ ❧ ❧

In presenting this pamphlet to the public, the writer is only complying with the solicitations of some of his friends, who have requested that his views on the prophecies of Daniel and John, might be made public. The reader is therefore requested to give the subject a careful and candid perusal, and compare every part with the standard of Divine Truth; for if the explanation the writer has given to the scriptures under consideration, should prove correct, the reader will readily perceive that it concerns us all, and becomes doubly important to us; because we live on the eve of one of the most important events ever revealed to man by the wisdom of God—the judgment of the great day.

In order that the reader may have an understanding of my manner of studying the prophecies, by which I have come to the following result, I have thought proper to give some of the rules of interpretation which I have adopted, to understand prophecy.

Prophetical scripture is very much of it communicated to us by figures, and highly and richly adorned metaphors' by which I mean that figures, such as *beasts, birds, air* or *wind, water, fire, candlesticks, lamps, mountains, islands*, &c., are used to represent things prophesied of—such as kingdoms, warriors, principles, people, judgements, churches, word of God, large and smaller governments.—by the most prominent feature or quality of the figure used, as *beasts*; if a *lion*, power and rule; if a *leopard*, celerity; if a *bear*, voracious; an *ox*; submissive; a *man*, proud and independent. *Fire*, denotes justice and judgement in its figure; in the metaphor, denotes the purifying or consuming up the dross or wickedness; as *fire* has a cleansing quality, so will the justice or judgments of God. "For when thy judgments are in the earth, the inhabitants of the world will learn righteousness." Therefore almost all of the figures used in prophecy have their literal and metaphorical meaning; as *beasts*

---

1. Rowe, *God's Strange Work*, 110–12.

denote, literally, a kingdom; so metaphorically good or bad, as the case may be, to be understood by the subject in connection.

To understand the literal meaning of figures used in prophecy, I have pursued the following method—I find the word *"beast"* used in a figurative sense; I take my concordance, trace the word, and in Daniel vii. 17, it is explained to mean "kings or kingdoms." Again, I come across the words *"bird* or *fowl,"* and in Isa. Xlvi 11, it is used meaning a conqueror or warrior, Cyrus. Also, in Ezekiel xxxix. 4-9, denotes armies or conquerors.—Again, I come across the words, *"air* or *wind,"* as used in Rev. ix. 2 and 16, 17, to understand which I turn to Ephe. Ii. 2 and 4-14, and there learn that it is used as a figure, to denote the theories of worldly men or vain philosophy. Again, *"water* or *rivers"* are used as figures in Rev. xvii. 15, it is explained to mean the nation or people living on the river mentioned, as in Rev. xvi. 12. *"Fire"* is often used in a figurative sense; explained in Num. xxi. 27-28: Deut. Xxxii.22: Psal. lxxviii. 21: Heb. Xii. 29: to mean justice and judgment.

As prophecy is a language somewhat different from other parts of scripture, owing to its having been revealed in vision, and that highly figurative, yet God in his wisdom has so interwoven the several prophecies, that the events foretold, are not all told by one prophet, and although they lived and prophesied in different ages of the world, yet they tell us the same things, so you take away one and a link will be wanting. There is a general connection through the whole; like a well regulated community they all move in union, speaking the same things, observing the same rules, so that a bible reader may almost with propriety suppose, let him read in what prophecy he may, that he is reading the same prophet, the same author. This will appear evident to any one who will compare scripture with scripture. For example, see Daniel xii. 1: Math. Xxiv. 21: Isa. Xlvii. 8: Zeph. Ii. 15: Rev. xviii. 7. There never was a book written that has a better connection and harmony than the bible, and yet it has the appearance of a great store house full of all the precious commodities heart could desire, thrown in promiscuously; therefore the biblical student must select and bring together every part of the subject he wishes to investigate, from every part of the subject he wishes to investigate, from every part of the bible; then let every word have its own scripture meaning, every sentence its proper bearing, and have no contradiction, and your theory will and must of necessity be correct. Truth is one undeviating path, that grows brighter and brighter the more it is trodden; it needs no plausible arguments, nor pompous dress to make it more bright; for the more naked and simple the fact, the stronger it appears.

Let it be noticed that God has revealed to his prophets the same events in divers figures, and at different times, as he has to Daniel in the 2d, 7th and 8th chapters concerning the four Kingdoms; or to Peter, see Acts x. 16: also, Isa. And John. Then to get the whole truth, all those visions or prophecies must be concentrated and brought together, that has reference to the subject which we wish to investigate, and when combined let every word and sentence have its proper bearing and force in the grand whole, and the theory or system, as I have before shown, must be correct. I have likewise noticed that in those events, visions and prophecies which have had their fulfillment, every word and every particular has had an exact and literal accomplishment, and that no two events has ever happened that I can learn, which will exactly apply or fulfil the same prophecy: take for instance the prophecies concerning the birth, life and crucifixion of our Saviour, and in his history we find a literal fulfilment; yet in the birth, life or death of any other individual it would be vain to find a parallel. Again, take the prophecies which have been admitted, by protestants, at least, to apply to Cyrus, Alexander, Julius Caesar, destruction of Jerusalem, and the church of Rome, and I have never been able to trace even a resemblance of the prophecies in question, in any historical events except the true ones. If this is true, may we not suppose that the unfulfilled prophecies in their accomplishments will be equally as evident and literal?

There are two important points to which all prophecy seems to centre, like a cluster of grapes upon its stem—the first and second coming of Christ. The first coming to proclaim the gospel, set up his kingdom, suffer for sinners, and bring in an everlasting righteousness. His second coming to which the ardent faith and pious hope of the tried and tempted child of God centres, is for complete redemption from sin, for the justification and glorification promised to all those who look for his appearing, the destruction of the wicked and mystical Babylon the abomination of the whole earth.

His first coming was a man, his human nature being only visible, his Godhead known only in his miracles. His second coming will be as God, his divine Godhead and power being most visible. He comes first, like the "the first man of the earth, earthly;" his second coming is "the Lord from heaven." His first coming was literally according to the prophecies. And so we may safely infer will be his second appearance, according to the scriptures. At his advent, his forerunner was spoken of, "one crying in the wilderness:" The manner of his birth, "a child born of a virgin:" The place where, "Bethlehem of Judea:" The time of his death, "when seventy weeks should be fulfilled:" For what he should suffer, "to make an end of sins, to make reconciliation for iniquity, and to bring in everlasting righteousness, to seal up the vision and prophecy and to anoint the most holy." The *star* that appeared, the *stripes* he received, the *miracles*, he performed, the *tauntings*, of his foes—all were literally fulfilled. Then why not suppose that all the prophecies concerning his second coming will be as literally accomplished as the former? Can any man show a single reason why it will not? If this be true we can obtain much light by reading the scriptures. We are there informed the manner of his second coming, "suddenly, in the clouds, in like manner as he ascended:" The majesty of his coming, "on a great white throne, with power and great glory, and all his saints with him:" The object of his coming, "as the ancient of days, to send his angels into the four winds of heaven, gather his elect, raise the righteous dead, change the righteous living, chain satan, destroy anti-Christ, the wicked and all those who destroy the earth, judge, justify and glorify his people, cleanse his church, present her to his Father, live and reign with her on the new heavens and new earth," the form of the old having passed away.

The time when these things shall take place is also specified by some of the prophets, unto 2300 days (meaning years;) then shall the sanctuary be cleansed, after the anti-christian beast has reigned her "time, times and an half;" after the two witnesses have prophecied "a thousand two hundred and three score days clothed in sackcloth;" after the church captivity in the wilderness, "forty-two months;" after the "gospel should be preached in all the world for a witness, then shall the end come." The signs of the times are also given, when we may know, he is near even at the door. When there is many "lo here's, and lo there's;" when the way of truth is evil spoken of; when many seducers are abroad in the land; when scoffers disbelieve in his coming, and say "where is the promise of his coming;" when the wise and foolish virgins are called to trim their lamps, and the voice of the friend of the bridegroom is, "behold he cometh;" when the city of the nations are divided into three parts; when the power of the holy people is scattered, and the kings of the east come up to battle; when there is a time of trouble, such as never was before and the church in her Laodicean state; when the seventh seal opens, the seventh vial is poured out, the last woe pronounced by the Angel flying through the midst of heaven, and the seventh and last trumpet sounds; then will the mystery of God be finished, and the door of mercy be closed forever, then shall we be brought to the last point, his second coming.

Again, prophecy is sometimes typical; that is, partly fulfilled in the type, but completely only in the anti-type. Such was the prophecy concerning Isaac, partly fulfilled in him, wholly so in Christ; likewise concerning Israel, partly fulfilled in them as a nation, but never fully accomplished until the final redemption of spiritual Israel. Likewise the prophecies concerning the Jewish captivity in Babylon, and their return, are only partly accomplished in the history of past events. The description of those things in the prophets are so august and magnificent, that if only applicable to the literal captivity of the Jews and their return, the exposition would be weak and barren; therefore I humbly believe that the exact fulfillment can only be looked for in the captivity of the church in the wilderness, under the anti-Christian beast, destruction of mystical Babylon, and glorification of the saints in the New Jerusalem state.

There is also in the 24th chapter of Matthew many things prophecied of, which were not fulfilled at the destruction of Jerusalem; such as the coming of the Son of Man in the clouds, the gathering his elect from the four winds of heaven, his taking one and leaving another. This shows a typical meaning in this prophecy, and that it will not all be fulfilled until the end of the world. Also the transfiguration of Christ on the mount, prophesied of by himself eight days before, is noticed by Peter, 2d Epistle, i. 16–18, as being a type or figure of his second coming.

Who that has read the prophecies with any degree of attention, will not acknowledge the great agreement between the old testament prophecies and the new? Almost every prophecy given by Christ and his apostles may be found in the old testament prophets, represented by figure, which were familiar to the writers and readers of those times. The foregoing rules are some of the principal ones which I have observed in attempting to explain the prophecies of Daniel and John, and to give the time when the mystery of God will be finished, as I humbly believe it is revealed to the prophets.

If I have erred in my exposition of the prophecies, the time being so near at hand will soon expose my folly: but if I have the truth on the subjects treated on in these pages how important the era in which we live? What vast and important events must soon be realized, and how necessary that every individual be prepared, that that day may not come upon them unawares, while they are surfeited with the cares and riches of this life, and the day overtake them as a thief? "But ye brethren are not in darkness, that that day should overtake you as a thief." 1. Thes. V. 4. In studying these prophecies, I have endeavored to divest myself of all prepossessed opinions, not warranted by the word of God, and to weigh well all the objections that might be raised from the scriptures, and after fourteen year's study of the prophecies and other parts of the bible, I have come to the following conclusions, and do now commit myself to God as my Judge, in giving publicity to the sentiments herein contained, consciously desiring that this little book may be the means to cite others to study the scriptures and to see whether these things be so, and that some minds may be led to believe in the word of God, and find an interest in the offering and sacrifice of the Lamb of God; that their sins might be forgiven them, through the blood of the atonement, "when the refreshing shall come from the presence of the Lord, and from the glory of his power," "when he comes to be admired in all them that believe in that day."

And now, my dear reader, I beg of you to lay aside your prejudice, examine this subject candidly and carefully for yourselves. Your belief or unbelief will not effect the truth. If it is so, whatever you may think or do will not alter the revealed purposes of God. "Not one jot or tittle of his word will fail:" but you may by your obedience in the faith, secure you an interest in the first resurrection, and a glorious admittance into the New Jerusalem, and an inheritance among the justified in glory; and you may set down with Abraham, Isaac and Jacob, in the Kingdom of God. May this be your lot, is the prayer of your Servant,

WM. Miller

Hampton, Washington County, N.Y.

THIRTY-THREE

William Miller Defends His Prediction

Source: William Miller, *William Miller's Apology and Defense* (Boston: J. V. Himes, 1845), 24–26.

Followers of William Miller eagerly awaited March 21, 1844, with a fervent belief that the Second Coming of Jesus would occur on that day. Miller's detractors also awaited that day, but with an eagerness to discredit Miller once and for all. When March 21 came and passed without incident, several men and women ceased to follow Miller. However, others looked to the Bible to find and correct any errors in Miller's calculations. One group subsequently declared that the Second Coming would occur on October 22, 1844, and Miller eventually supported this group's reasoning.[1] When that date also came and passed without incident, disappointed Adventists and their vindicated critics looked to Miller for a response. He published *William Miller's Apology and Defence* on August 1, 1845. While he admitted that his calculations were clearly wrong in determining a precise date of Christ's Second Coming, he insisted that his biblical interpretation supported his claims that the event was imminent.

☙ ☙ ☙

1. David L. Rowe, *God's Strange Work: William Miller and the End of the World* (Grand Rapids, MI: Eerdmans, 2008), 184–91.

I had never been positive as to any particular day for the Lord's appearing, believing that no man could know the day and hour. In all my published lectures, it will be seen on the title page, "about the year 1843." In all my oral lectures, I invariably told my audiences that the periods would terminate in 1843, if there were no mistake in my calculation; but that I could not say the end might not come even before that time, and they should be continually prepared. In 1842, some of my brethren preached with great positiveness the exact year, and censured me for putting in an IF. The public press had also published that I had fixed upon a definite day, the 23rd of April, for the Lord's Advent. Therefore, in December of that year, as I could see no error in my reckoning, I published my belief, that sometime between March 21st, 1843, and March 21st, 1844, the Lord would come. Some had their minds fixed on particular days; but I could see no evidence for such, unless the types of the Mosaic law pointed to the feast of Tabernacles.

During the year '43, the most violent denunciations were heaped upon me, and those associated with me, by the press, and some pulpits. Our motives were assailed, our principles misrepresented, and our characters traduced. Time passed on: and the 21st of March, 1844 went by, without our witnessing the appearing of the Lord. Our disappointment was great; and many walked no more with us.

Previously to this, in the fall of '43, some of my 25 brethren began to call the churches Babylon, and to urge that it was the duty of Adventists to come out of them. With this I was much grieved, as not only the effect was very bad, but I regarded it as a perversion of the word of God, a wresting of Scripture. But the practice spread extensively; and from that time the churches, as might have been expected, were closed against us. It prejudiced many against us so that they would not listen to the truth. It created a deep feeling of hostility between Adventists and those who did not embrace the doctrine; so that most of the Adventists were separated from their respective churches. This was a result, which I never desired, nor expected; but it was brought about by unforeseen circumstances. We could then only act in accordance with the position in which we were thus placed.

On the passing of my published time, I frankly acknowledged my disappointment in reference to the exact period; but my faith was unchanged in any essential feature. I therefore continued my labors, principally at the West during the summer of '44, until "the seventh month movement," as it is called. I had had no participation in this, only as

I wrote a letter eighteen months previously, presenting the observances under the Mosaic law, which pointed to that month as a probable time when the Advent might be expected. This was written because some were looking to definite days in the Spring. I had, however, no expectation that so unwarranted a use would be made of those types, that any should regard a belief in such mere inferential evidence a test of salvation. I therefore had no fellowship with that movement until about two or three weeks previous to the 22nd of October, when seeing it had obtained such prevalence, and considering it was at a probable point of time, I was persuaded that it was a work of God, and felt that if it should pass by I should be more disappointed than I was in my first published time.

But that time passed; and I was again disappointed. The movement was of such a character, that for a time it was very mysterious to me, and the results following it were so unaccountable that I supposed our work might be completed, and that a few weeks only might elapse between that time and the appearing of Christ. However that might be, I regarded my own work as completed; and that what was to be done for the extension of these views, must be done by younger brethren, except an occasional discourse from myself.

THIRTY-FOUR

A Historical Rebuttal of Millerism

Source: "Millerism," *Spirit of the Times* (Batavia, NY), November 8, 1844.

In 1845, after both of William Miller's predictions of the second advent of Jesus had failed, Miller faced criticism from a variety of sources. Whereas many of his opponents based their arguments in their respective interpretations of biblical philosophy, the editors of the *United States Saturday Post* (Philadelphia) based their rebuff on their interpretation of Western history. Their intent was to demonstrate that Miller's predictions of the end of the world were just the most recent in a long line of such instances. Accordingly, they summarized a series of twelve similar instances, spanning chronologically from the fourth century CE to the late eighteenth century. The chief source for the authors' historical research appears to be the first volume of *The Recreative Life, or Eccentricities in Literature and Life*, a book published in London in 1821. The accounts in this article contain the same information and appear in nearly the same order as they did in that volume's section titled "False Prophets—Fanatics—Coming from the Lord."[1] This article was reprinted in dozens of newspapers in western

---

1. *The Recreative Life, or Eccentricities in Literature and Life* (London, 1821), 199–212.

New York. The version featured here was published in the *Spirit of the Times*, in Batavia, New York, in November 1844.

✶ ✶ ✶

Millerism

We several times proposed to make the delusion of "Millerism," as it is termed, the subject of an article during its former paroxysms; but forbore, partly from a disinclination to meddle with the faith of any man or set of men, and partly because the delusion would, we thought, work its own cure, by the falsification of the prophecy, in the going by of the time at which its consummation was placed. And as that period passed, and "the world and all that it inherits" still remained firm and undestroyed, we looked to see the matter completely at an end, and people returning to their accustomed occupations, and to their sober senses.

FIGURE 11.   "The Salamander Safe," 1843. This cartoon by Thomas S. Sinclair depicts a believer in William Miller's prediction of the end of the world preparing provisions for April 23, 1844, while thumbing his nose at onlookers. (Library of Congress)

But, to our great astonishment, we now find delusion resuming its sway with, if not more general extent, with more extravagance than ever. We learn not only in this city, but at other distant points, the zeal of pseudo-prophets has again blown up this excitement. We find the believers carried into the most strange conduct, and the most pitable [pitiable] perversion of all the rules of duty, and of all the obligations, both of religion and prudence. We hear of women arrayed in "ascension robes," deserting the care of their households, and sitting down in upper rooms, some even in unfinished garrets, to be as near to heaven as possible, and there awaiting the "second Advent." We hear of such crowds besetting the places of evening meeting of the believers, that the arm of civil power is compelled to interpose, and close the places of meeting to save the peace. We find the disciples of Mr. Miller and his followers closing their stores, giving away their goods, and pasting notices on their shutters, that their shops are now closed to wait "the coming of the King of Kings."

Painfully absurd as is such conduct, we have no disposition to make it the subject of ridicule, although the temptation to do so is strong; and although, perhaps, exposure of the absurdity of such conduct, is the best argument against it. But we have collected to-day a list of the most prominent delusions of this nature in the history of the world, and present them as but a part of the experience of the past, in order to show the disappointed in their expectations, that they are not the first in order of time, or the only ones, by many thousands, who have been carried away by such fancies.

Without referring to the delusions of the Jews, who looked for a temporal reign of Christ as an earthly potentate, or the mistaken among the early Christians who confidently predicted the second advent of the Saviour as to occur at the end of the Roman Pagan Empire, giving him also an earthly kingdom; or to the manner in which the end of the crusades, and the victory of the Christian over the Moslem would establish that kingdom; we will look to later manifestations of the consequences of mistaking the promises of the gospel, and confounding things spiritual and temporal.—It is sufficient to say that the later delusions are but a perpetuation of the error of those who, in early times rose, and saying, "I am Christ" deceived many.

In the year 1212, it was predicted and promised that the Mediterranean Sea should be dried up, that believers should pass to Jerusalem on foot, there to build up the new city. After what we have seen in our own time, it will readily be credited that Italy was filled with

pilgrims, waiting the drying up of the sea, to commence their journey; and the misery which these persons suffered, and which they
inflicted on their friends and dependents by their information, will
easily be imagined.

In 1524, John Stoflerus, a mathematician and astrologer of Suabia,
predicted a great deluge, and he was so far believed that those who
owned lands near the sea sold out at great loss. Books were published
giving cheap directions how to escape the inundation; and surveyors
actually consulted the stars, and pointed out what places would be least
exposed to the waters.— Boats were built and placed on the tops of high
pillars, in which the believers sat with their families, waiting for the
water to come up and float them off. Many arches were contrived with
breathing holes in the top, in which men might live, with the waters
around them, until the danger had passed away. The time fixed for the
inundation proved a very dry season, and the water-proof contrivances
were ruined by continued drought. And notwithstanding the failure
of this prediction, we find that Stoflerus did not lose his faith; for he
then set the final destruction of the world for the year 1586, and died
prophesying it.

Meanwhile, Martin Stifelius predicted the end of the world to take
place in 1533, giving the day and the hour. He was in his pulpit preaching on the subject, when the time arrived, and his audience was waiting
the consummation of all things, when a violent storm arose, and for a
short time he and his people were in the full belief that all was over. The
storm passed away—the sky was serene—the day was delightful—and the
preacher was dragged from his desk and beaten to death.

William Hackett, in 1590, predicted the destruction of England, and
had not a few followers. He claimed himself to be Monarch of all Europe, and his followers proclaimed him. He was hanged for sedition—an
argument which is not now used against error.

Walter Gostello, in 1658, foretold the restoration of Charles II., and
the destruction of London. The first part of his prophecy being fulfilled, gave him some credit as a prophet. The second part, it is hardly
necessary to say, is as yet unaccomplished. Thomas Venner, who flourished about the same time, declared the earthly kings were impostors,
and attempting with a crowd of his followers, to take actual possession of the earth, in the name of the Lord, they were opposed by the
soldiery. They fought like tigers, believing themselves invulnerable,
but were overpowered by numbers, and Venner with twelve others, was
hanged.

There were several such prophets in France in the seventh [seventeenth] century—but one of the most remarkable of the seers of that era was John Mason, a minister of Walter Straford, near Buckingham, England. An immense concourse met at the time appointed, and with fiddles and other musical instruments, with dancing and other tumultuous signs of rejoicing, awaited the coronation. Poor Mason died in 1697, a full believer in the delusion that he had frequent conversations with the Saviour, and that his divine mission was confirmed.

Whigton, the mathematician, was a believer in the immediate approach of the millenium, and lived to see the failure of two predictions. Lord Napier, the inventor of the logarithms, also prophesied the end of the world, and outlived its terms, as he had set it. Dr. Lloyd Bishop of Worcester, at ninety years of age, went to Queen Anne, and prophesied that at the end of four years the King of France would turn Protestant, there would be a war of religion, and the papacy would be destroyed.

To come down to a later time. In 1761, two learned men arrived at Cologne, who conversed with the Jesuits of that city in Latin, Greek, Hebrew and Chaldaic. They gave out that they were from Damascus, and were seven hundred years old; and prophesied that Constantinople would be destroyed in 1767, that the whole world would be shook by an earthquake in 1770, that the sun moon and stars would fall in 1771, that the world would be burnt 1772, and the general judgment would take place in 1778.

In the year 1772, a hermit frightened the inhabitants of Triste [Trieste?] into the belief that the destruction of that city was immediately to take place; and so general was the faith in which his predictions were received, that the city was absolutely deserted to escape the destruction. But the day passed over without calamity to any one except the unlucky prophet; for when his disciples returned to resume their business, they found that the predictor of destruction had realized it in his own person. He was hanged by the proper authorities.

Toward the close of the seventeenth [eighteenth?] century, the whole court of France was thrown into terror, and people who had never prayed before, began then, in belief that the immediate destruction of the world was at hand. As the event did not verify their fears, and the world continued to stand, they made up for temporary self-denial by plunging anew into the worst excesses.—The re-action made them infinitely greater sinners than they were before.

We have quoted these facts—few indeed among the very many that might be adduced, to remind the reader that this is "no new thing under the sun." We are inclined to think that with the failure of this last, as fail it must, for people's expectations cannot be kept up forever, delusions of this particular description will cease, and men will no longer strive to be wise above what is written. Whether the end of the world occurs sooner or later is of little individual consequence to any of us; for death must happen at some time, and is as likely to occur soon as late; and death to the individual is an end of the world so far as he or she is concerned. We do not think of preparing for that by waiting in idleness—nor should any think to prepare for the end of all things in any other way than by a continuance of the performance of our duties to our Maker, to our fellows and to ourselves.

Since we wrote the preceding, the following eloquent passage from Moshiem, relative to the state of the Christian world in the tenth century—a period previous to those in which the instances we have quoted above occurred—has fallen under our eye:

"Among the opinions which took possession of the minds of men, none occasioned such an universal panic, nor such dreadful impressions of terror and dismay, as a notion that now prevailed of the immediate approach of the day of judgement. This notion which took its rise from a remarkable passage in the Revelations of St. John, and had been entertained by some teachers in the preceding century, was advanced publicly by many at that time, and spreading itself with amazing rapidity through the European provinces, it threw them into great consternation and anguish. They imagined that St. John had clearly foretold, that after a thousand years from the birth of Christ, Satan was to be let loose from his prison, Anti-Christ to come, and the destruction and conflagration of the world to follow those great and terrible events. Hence prodigious numbers of people abandoned all the civil connections and their paternal relations; and, giving over to the churches and monasteries all their lands, treasures, and worldly effects, repaired with the utmost precipitation to Palestine, where they imagined that Christ would descend from heaven to judge the world. Others devoted themselves by a solemn and voluntary oath to the service of the churches, convents, and priesthood, whose slaves they became in the most rigorous sense of the word, performing daily heavy tasks; all this from a notion that the Supreme Judge would diminish their sentence, and look upon them with more favorable and propitious eye, on account of their having made themselves the slaves of his ministers.—When an eclipse of the sun or moon happened to be visible, the cities were deserted, and their miserable inhabitants fled for refuge to caverns, and hid themselves among the craggy rocks, and under the bending summits of steep mountains. The rich attempted to bribe the Deity by rich donations conferred on the sarcedotal [sacerdotal] and monastic orders, who were looked upon as the immediate viceregents of heaven. In many places temples, palaces, and noble edifices, both public and private, were left to suffer decay, they were deliberately pulled down, from a notion that they were no longer of any use, since the final dissolution of all things was at hand. In a word, no language is sufficient to express the confusion and despair that tormented the minds of these miserable mortals on this occasion. The general delusion was indeed imposed and combatted by the discerning few, who endeavored to dispel these groundless terrors, and to efface the notions from which they arose in the minds of the people. But their attempts were ineffectual: nor could the apprehension of the superstitious multitude be entirely removed before the end of this century. Then, when they saw that the so much dreaded period had passed without the arrival of any great calamity, they began to understand that St. John had not foretold what they so much feared."

THIRTY-FIVE

Matthias the Prophet

Source: Sojourner Truth, *Narrative of Sojourner Truth, a Northern Slave, Emancipated from Bodily Servitude by the State of New York, in 1828* (Boston, 1850), 87–96.

One of Robert Matthews's followers in the Kingdom was Isabella Baumfree, a woman who had been enslaved until 1826 and joined the movement while working as a housekeeper for Elijah Pierson in 1832. When Pierson died in 1834, Baumfree and Matthews were accused of poisoning him. Both were acquitted, but this event ended Baumfree's association with Matthews and the Kingdom. In 1843, Baumfree became a Methodist and changed her name to Sojourner Truth. She soon began traveling the northern United States as a famous evangelist, claiming that she was called by God to speak out in favor of abolition and women's rights. Sojourner Truth later dictated her autobiography—written in the third person—which included the story of how she met Pierson and Matthews, and a sample of Matthews's preaching.[1] That excerpt, which appeared in print under the heading "The Matthias Imposter," is featured here.

🖉 🖉 🖉

1. For a historical account of Truth's relationship with Matthews see Nell Irvin Painter, "In the Kingdom of Matthias," in *Sojourner Truth: A Life, a Symbol* (New York: W. W. Norton, 1996), 48–61.

[. . .]

We now come to an eventful period in the life of Isabella, as identi-fied with one of the most extraordinary religious delusions of modern times; but the limits prescribed for the present work forbid a minute narration of all the occurrences that transpired in relation to it.

After she had joined the African Church in Church street, and during her membership there, she frequently attended Mr. Latourette's meet-ings, at one of which, Mr. Smith invited her to go to a prayer-meeting, or to instruct the girls at the Magdalene Asylum, Bowery Hill, then under the protection of Mr. Pierson, and some other persons, chiefly respect-able females. To reach the Asylum, Isabella called on Katy, Mr. Pierson's colored servant, of whom she had some knowledge. Mr. Pierson saw her there, conversed with her, asked her if she had been baptized, and was answered, characteristically, 'by the Holy Ghost.' After this, Isabella saw Katy several times, and occasionally Mr. Pierson, who engaged her to keep his house while Katy went to Virginia to see her children. This engagement was considered an answer to a prayer by Mr. Pierson, who had both fasted and prayed on the subject, while Katy and Isabella ap-peared to see in it the hand of God.

Mr. Pierson was characterized by a strong devotional spirit, which finally became highly fanatical. He assumed the title of Prophet, assert-ing that God had called him in an omnibus, in these words:—'Thou are Elijah, the Tishbite. Gather unto me all the members of Israel at the foot of Mount Carmel'; which he understood as meaning the gathering of his friends at Bowery Hill. Not long afterward, he became acquainted

FIGURE 12. Sojourner Truth, 1797–1883. Before she rose to national fame as a Christian evan-gelist, Sojourner Truth had been a member of "the Kingdom," an intentional religious community led by Robert "Matthias" Matthews. (Library of Congress)

with the notorious Matthias, whose career was as extraordinary as it was brief. Robert Matthews, or Matthias (as he was usually called), was of Scotch extraction, but a native of Washington County, New York, and at that time about forty-seven years of age. He was religiously brought up, among the Anti-Burghers, a sect of Presbyterians; the clergyman, the Rev. Mr. Bevridge, visiting the family after the manner of the church, and being pleased with Robert, put his hand on his head, when a boy, and pronounced a blessing, and this blessing, with his natural qualities, determined his character; for he ever after thought he should be a distinguished man. Matthias was brought up a farmer till nearly eighteen years of age, but acquired indirectly the art of a carpenter, without any regular apprenticeship, and showed considerable mechanical skill. He obtained property from his uncle, Robert Thompson, and then he went into business as a store-keeper, was considered respectable, and became a member of the Scotch Presbyterian Church. He married in 1813, and continued in business in Cambridge. In 1816, he ruined himself by a building speculation, and the derangement of the currency which denied bank facilities, and soon after he came to New York with his family, and worked at his trade. He afterwards removed to Albany, and became a hearer at the Dutch Reformed Church, then under Dr. Ludlow's charge. He was frequently much excited on religious subjects.

In 1829, he was well known, if not for street preaching, for loud discussions and pavement exhortations, but he did not make set sermons. In the beginning of 1830, he was only considered zealous; but in the same year he prophesied the destruction of the Albanians and their capital, and while preparing to shave, with the Bible before him, he suddenly put down the soap and exclaimed, 'I have found it! I have found a text which proves that no man who shaves his beard can be a true Christian;' and shortly afterwards, without shaving, he went to the Mission House to deliver an address which he had promised, and in this address, he proclaimed his new character, pronounced vengeance on the land, and that the law of God was the only rule of government, and that he was commanded to take possession of the world in the name of the King of kings. His harangue was cut short by the trustees putting out the lights. About this time, Matthias laid by his implements of industry, and in June, he advised his wife to fly with him from the destruction which awaited them in the city; and on her refusal, partly on account of Matthias calling himself a Jew, whom she was unwilling to retain as a husband, he left her, taking some of the children to his sister in Argyle, forty miles from Albany. At Argyle he entered the church and interrupted the minister, declaring the congregation in darkness, and warning them to repentance. He was, of course, taken out of the church, and as he was advertised in the Albany papers, he was sent back to his family. His beard had now obtained a respectable length, and thus he attracted attention, and easily obtained an audience in the streets. For this he was sometimes arrested, once by mistake for Adam Paine, who collected the crowd, and then left Matthias with it on the approach of the officers. He repeatedly urged his wife to accompany him on a mission to convert the world, declaring that food could be obtained from the roots of the forest, if not administered otherwise. At this time he assumed the name of Matthias, called himself a Jew, and set out on a mission, taking a western course, and visiting a brother at Rochester, a skillful mechanic, since dead. Leaving his brother, he proceeded on his mission over the Northern States, occasionally returning to Albany.

After visiting Washington, and passing through Pennsylvania, he came to New York. His appearance at that time was mean, but grotesque, and his sentiments were but little known.

On May the 5th, 1832, he first called on Mr. Pierson, in Fourth street, in his absence. Isabella was alone in the house, in which she had lived since the previous autumn. On opening the door, she, for the first time, beheld Matthias, and her early impression of seeing Jesus in the flesh rushed to her mind. She heard his inquiry, and invited him into the parlor; and being naturally curious, and much excited, and possessing a good deal of tact, she drew him into conversation, stated her own opinions, and heard his replies and explanations. Her faith was at first staggered by his declaring himself a Jew; but on this point she was relieved by his saying, 'Do you not remember how Jesus prayed?' and repeated part of the Lord's Prayer, in proof that the Father's kingdom was to come, and not the Son's. She then understood him to be a converted Jew, and in the conclusion she says she 'felt as if God had sent him to set up the kingdom.' Thus Matthias at once secured the good will of Isabella, and we may supposed obtained from her some information in relation to Mr. Pierson, especially that Mrs. Pierson declared there was no true church, and approved of Mr. Pierson's preaching. Matthias left the house, promising to return on Saturday evening. Mr. P. at this time had not seen Matthias.

Isabella, desirous of hearing the expected conversation between Matthias and Mr. Pierson on Saturday, hurried her work, got it finished, and was permitted to be present. Indeed, the sameness of belief made her familiar with her employer, while her attention to her work, and characteristic faithfulness, increased his confidence. This intimacy, the result of holding the same faith, and the principle afterwards adopted of having but one table, and all things in common, made her at once the domestic and the equal, and the depositary of very curious, if not valuable information. To this object, even her color assisted. Persons who have travelled in the South know the manner in which the colored people, and especially slaves, are treated; they are scarcely regarded as being present. This trait in our American character has been frequently noticed by foreign travellers. One English lady remarks that she discovered, in course of conversation with a Southern married gentleman, that a colored girl slept in his bedroom, in which also was his wife; and when he saw that it occasioned some surprise, he remarked, 'What would he do if he wanted a glass of water in the night?' Other travellers have remarked that the presence of colored people never seemed to interrupt a conversation of any kind for one moment. Isabella, then, was present at the first interview between Matthias and Pierson. At this interview, Mr. Pierson asked Matthias if he had a family, to which he replied in the affirmative; he asked him about his beard, and he gave a scriptural reason, asserting also that the Jews did not shave, and that Adam had a beard. Mr. Pierson detailed to Matthias his experience, and Matthias gave his, and they mutually discovered that they held the same sentiments, both admitting the direct influence of the Spirit, and the transmission of spirits from one body to another. Matthias admitted the call of Mr. Pierson, in the omnibus in Wall street, which, on this occasion, he gave in these words:—'Thou art Elijah the Tishbite, and thou shalt go before me in the spirit and power of Elias, to prepare my way before me.' And Mr. Pierson admitted Matthias' call, who completed his declaration on the 20th of June, in Argyle, which, by a curious coincidence, was the very day on which Pierson had received his call in the omnibus. Such singular coincidences have a powerful effect on excited minds. From that discovery, Pierson and Matthias rejoiced in each other, and became kindred spirits—Matthias, however, claiming to be the Father, or to possess the spirit of the Father—he was God upon the earth, because the spirit of God dwelt in him; while Pierson then understood that his mission was like that of John the Baptist, which the name Elias meant. This conference ended with an invitation to supper, and Matthias and Pierson washing each other's feet. Mr. Pierson preached on the following Sunday, but after which, he declined in favor of Matthias, and some of the party believed that the 'kingdom had then come.'

As a specimen of Matthias' preaching and sentiments, the following is said to be reliable:

'The spirit that built the Tower of Babel is now in the world—it is the spirit of the devil. The spirit of man never goes upon the clouds; all who think so are Babylonians. The only heaven is on earth. All who are ignorant of truth are Ninevites. The Jews did not crucify Christ—it was the Gentiles. Every Jew has his guardian angel attending him in this world. God don't speak through preachers; he speaks through me, his prophet.

'"John the Baptist," (addressing Mr. Pierson), read the tenth chapter of Revelations.' After the reading of the chapter, the prophet resumed speaking, as follows:—

"Ours is the mustard-seed kingdom which is to spread all over the earth. Our creed is truth, and no man can find truth unless he obeys John the Baptist, and comes clean into the church.

"All real men will be saved; all mock men will be damned. When a person has the Holy Ghost, then he is a man, and not till then. They who teach women are of the wicked. The communion is all nonsense; so is prayer. Eating a nip of bread and drinking a little wine won't do any good. All who admit members into their church, and suffer them to hold their lands and houses, their sentence is, "Depart, ye wicked, I know you not." All females who lecture their husbands, their sentence is the same. The sons of truth are to enjoy all the good things of this world, and must use their means to bring it about. Every thing that has the smell of woman will be destroyed. Woman is the capsheaf of the abomination of desolation—full of all deviltry. In a short time, the world will take fire and dissolve; it is combustible already. All women, not obedient, had better become so as soon as possible, and let the wicked spirit depart, and become temples of truth. Praying is all mocking. When you see any one wring the neck of a fowl, instead of cutting off its head, he has not got the Holy Ghost. (Cutting gives the least pain.)

"All who eat swine's flesh are of the devil; and just as certain as he eats it, he will tell a lie in less than half an hour. If you eat a piece of pork, it will go crooked through you, and the Holy Ghost will not stay in you, but one or the other must leave the house pretty soon. The pork will be as crooked in you as ram's horns, and as great a nuisance as the hogs in the street.

'The cholera is not the right word; it is choler, which means God's wrath. Abraham, Isaac, and Jacob are now in this world; they did not go up in the clouds, as some believe—why should they go there? They don't want to go there to box the compass from one place to another. The Christians now-a-days are for setting up the Son's kingdom. It is not his; it is the Father's kingdom. It puts me in mind of a man in the country, who took his son in business, and had his sign made, "Hitch-cock & Son;" but the son wanted it "Hitchcock & Father"—and that is the way with your Christians. They talk of the Son's kingdom first, and not the Father's kingdom.'

Matthias and his disciples at this time did not believe in a resurrection of the body, but that the spirits of the former saints would enter the bodies of the present generation, and thus begin heaven on earth, of which he and Mr. Pierson were the first fruits.

Matthias made the residence of Mr. Pierson his own; but the latter, being apprehensive of popular violence in his house, if Matthias remained there, proposed a monthly allowance to him, and advised him to occupy another dwelling. Matthias accordingly took a house in Clarkson street, and then sent for his family at Albany, but they declined coming to the city. However, his brother George complied with a similar offer, bringing his family with him, where they found very comfortable quarters. Isabella was employed to do the housework. In May, 1833, Matthias left his house, and placed the furniture, part of which was Isabella's, elsewhere, living himself at the hotel corner of Marketfield and West streets. Isabella found employment at Mr. Whiting's, Canal street, and did the washing for Matthias by Mrs. Whiting's permission.

Of the subsequent removal of Matthias to the farm and residence of Mr. B. Folger, at Sing Sing, where he was joined by Mr. Pierson, and others laboring under a similar religious delusion—the sudden, melancholy and somewhat suspicious death of Mr. Pierson, and the arrest of Matthias on the charge of his murder, ending in a verdict of not guilty—the criminal connection that subsisted between Matthias, Mrs. Folger, and other members of the 'Kingdom,' as 'match-spirits'—the final dispersion of this deluded company, and the voluntary exilement of Matthias in the far West, after his release—&c. &c., we do not deem it useful or necessary to give any particulars. Those who are curious to know what there transpired are referred to a work published in New York in 1835, entitled 'Fanaticism; its Sources and Influence; illustrated by the simple Narrative of Isabella, in the case of Matthias, Mr. and Mrs. B. Folger, Mr. Pierson, Mr. Mills, Catharine, Isabella, &c. &c. By G. Vale, 84 Roosevelt street.' Suffice it to say, that while Isabella was a member of the household at Sing Sing, doing much laborious service in the spirit of religious disinterestedness, and gradually getting her vision purged and her mind cured of its illusions, she happily escaped the contamination that surrounded her,—assiduously endeavoring to discharge all her duties in a becoming manner. [. . .]

PART VI

Intentional Communities

This part focuses on two New York–based intentional communities: the United Society of Believers in Christ's Second Appearing, better known as the Shakers, and the Oneida Association, whose members were known as "perfectionists." The Shaker sect traces its origins to the visions of Ann Lee, a woman who had labored in the factories of Manchester, England, before migrating to New York in 1774. From a young age, Lee had shown signs of charismatic gifts, including speaking in ancient and foreign tongues and communicating with spirits. She also grew up at a time when the Church of England was expanding its missionary efforts among the nation's laboring classes. She likely heard Anglican evangelists preach the doctrine of Christian perfection, the belief that by the grace of God faithful Christians could achieve a state of holiness in their lifetime. In this unique context, Lee experienced a spiritual awakening and began preaching in the streets. She discerned that she had achieved a state of divine holiness and that God had called her to lead other Christians in their own quest for holiness. Ann Lee professed that like Christ himself, she had been ordained by God to hear and forgive the sins of faithful Christians and was entrusted with the spiritual care of Christ's disciples on earth. Lee's followers recognized her as the mother of "the family of Christ," divinely empowered to grant men and women "new life" in the present. Accordingly, they addressed her as "Mother Ann Lee."[1]

In 1774, Mother Ann discerned a call from God to bring this new gospel to America. She emigrated with a small cohort of disciples to the city of New York and then settled in Watervliet, just north of Albany. The Shakers, as they were popularly known in both England and America, evangelized in the Housatonic River Valley and greater New England. By the time she died in 1784, Lee had attracted hundreds of new followers who accepted her as the Daughter of God.[2]

Unlike the Shakers, the Oneida perfectionists were relatively late in settling in New York. The perfectionists originated in Putney, Vermont, where Yale graduate John Humphrey Noyes started preaching radical ideas about theology and social order. For instance, he taught that there would be two separate Second Comings of Jesus: one to the Jews, and another to the gentiles. He argued that the former had occurred in 70 CE and that the Second Coming to the gentiles was imminent. As part of his millenarian views, Noyes claimed that traditional monogamous marriage was no longer required of Christians and, in its stead, articulated a system he dubbed "complex marriage." In such a system, free love was the reigning principle; all members of a community were married to one another and could engage in consensual sexual intercourse. Noyes believed that complex marriage matched the social order of heaven and that its implementation would expedite the Second Coming of Jesus to the gentiles.[3]

Noyes's radical teachings also called for a system of communal criticism of individuals designed to enable a man or a woman to excise their faults on a path to perfection. It is because of this practice that many people began to refer to Noyes and his followers as perfectionists. Yet Noyes's teachings did more than elicit new names. They drew the ire of many Vermonters who deemed the group's religious teachings blasphemous and its system of complex marriage adulterous—and criminal.[4]

1. Stephen J. Stein, *The Shaker Experience in America: A History of the United Society of Believers* (New Haven, CT: Yale University Press, 1992), 18–25.

2. Stein, 76–87.

3. Anthony Wonderley, *Oneida Utopia: A Community Searching for Human Happiness and Prosperity* (Ithaca, NY: Cornell University Press, 2017), 38–39, 54–57. Also see Maren Carden, *Oneida: Utopian Community to Modern Corporation* (Baltimore: Johns Hopkins University Press, 1969); *First Annual Report of the Oneida Association; Exhibiting Its History, Principles, and Transactions to Jan. 1, 1849* (Oneida Reserve, NY: Leonard and Co., 1849).

4. Wonderley, *Oneida Utopia*, 41–51.

In 1848, Noyes and his followers left Vermont to join perfectionists already living in New York, and together established an intentional
community in Oneida County. They organized their community as the
Oneida Association, constructed several buildings, including a large
mansion, near the shore of Oneida Lake. They held their property in
common and began to practice Noyes's teachings in the haven they
had created for themselves. Much of their property was held in common, and children born in the community would be raised by the community, freeing individual mothers from the full-time responsibility of
child rearing. By the end of the community's first year, it consisted of
twenty-nine men and twenty-nine women, most of whom were originally from New England.[5]

While the evangelical fervor that had been so concentrated in central and western New York began to fade, the region remained fertile
ground for such socioreligious experiments. Land was available at
affordable prices and provided Noyes and his followers the relative
isolation they sought. The Oneida Association did not seek converts
through proselytizing. Still, many men and women united with the organization in the ensuing years. But the perfectionists also attracted
critics, many of whom abhorred the group's drastic departure from
monogamy, which had long been enshrined as the principal form of
marriage in Western society. Opponents of the association claimed that
Noyes and others only used its religious teachings as a justification for
sexual lasciviousness.

The nine documents featured in this part spotlight the distinctive
doctrines of the Shakers and the Oneida community and their respective models of Christian communalism. Six documents come from the
Shakers and include correspondence from the men and women who
helped organize, settle, and administer intentional communities at Sodus Bay, New York. The description of charitable gifts to Prime Lane,
the map of the Watervliet Shaker Village, and Seth Wells's address on
schooling and education provide examples of how the Shakers engaged
with, and adapted to, the world beyond their villages. The lyrics to a
Shaker hymn offer a concise explanation of Shaker theology and doctrine. The remaining three documents come from the Oneida community and detail the association's core values. The selections from "Home
Talks" elucidate some of John Noyes's most prominent teachings on

---

5. *First Annual Report of the Oneida Association*, 1–2.

sex and communal order. The selections from the Report of the Oneida Association tell us how community members experienced these practices, and the spiritual benefits they gained from them. The critique of the Oneida community by Rev. Hubbard Eastman serves as a reminder of the general hostility that many mainline Christians directed at Americans whose quest for spiritual fulfillment led them to pursue the alternative lifestyles offered by the Shakers, the Oneida perfectionists, and other antebellum-era intentional communities.

THIRTY-SIX

Shaker Charity

Source: "Prime Lane, Papers concerning maintenance of the poor (1825)," Western Reserve Historical Society, Shaker Communities, Shaker Manuscripts, 1723–1952, reel 2, box 3, folder 20.

Shaker evangelism took two forms: traditional evangelism and evangelical charity. In addition to sending missionaries to the frontier, the Shakers advertised their faith and values with charitable acts. The Watervliet and Mount Lebanon Shakers regularly distributed alms to paupers and occasionally responded to large-scale disasters. In 1795, amid a surging yellow fever epidemic, the Shakers donated wagonloads of provisions to the residents of New York City.

Shaker trustees maintained detailed logs of their charitable work, and this document relates their contributions to Prime Lane, a Black man and former slave who lived at Watervliet Village in the 1800s. It includes the types of gifts and the financial value of the giving, and offers insight into the Shakers' motives for assisting the Lane family. It is worth noting that two of Prime's daughters freely joined with the Shakers when they reached adulthood.

❧ ❧ ❧

Prime Lane (colored)

In the spring of the year 1802, Prime Lane with his family came from New-Cornwall, and moved into a small house on the farm then occupied by Aaron Wood, commonly called the Bennet place. The first season <it was proposed for him> he was [illegible] to raise his summer crops on shares, but it was soon found that he could not support his family with any tolerable degree of comfort without our charitable assistance, so that <besides> his planting, rent free, in the course of this season year he received many gratuities, such as articles of cloathing for himself & family, pasture for a cow, fresh meat and many other articles in the provision line, which inclusive of house rent and firewood must at a very moderate calculation amount to 40 Dollars . . . . . 40..00

The next year we put up a house for him containing two dwelling-rooms, with a convenient chamber, kitchen and celler, sufficient to accommodate a family of 8 or 10 persons, and gave him the use of about 12 acres of cleared land, suitable for plowing, mowing, pasture & garden for such a family as Prime then had. These privileges <including> with the additional favor of firewood for the use of his family we judge to be worth, at a moderate price 50 Dollars a year, which for 8 years amount to.   400..00.

Favours & gratuities during the above mentioned time, such as Articles of cloathing, Meat, Butter, Cheese, Lard, fruit, vegetables, milk, Cider, and many other small articles in the provision line, the use of team & farming utensils, the use of a Cow 4 or 5 seasons, pasture, mowing grass, pieces of corn & potatoe ground, &. &. amounting <on an average> at least to $12^{1/2}$$ a year.   100..00

Favors & gratuities from the families during the above mentioned period, amounting in their estimation to 50 Dollars.   50..00

On the most moderate calculation the sum total is—590..00

But we believe there ought to be a deduction of 80 Dollars from this sum, on account of Keziah Wilsey who lived in Prime's family about 2 years, and who was not able to earn her living.

This will leave a Balance of 510 Dollars against Prime for which we have not received a single one cent.

In addition to the foregoing statements we think it not improper to mention some other favours, which though very serviceable to Prime's family, yet they cannot be properly estimated by us.

When Prime first came here with his family, he was poor, and had a family of daughters who were ignorant of most of the branches of business performed by females among us, & all needed instruction. We accordingly taught them to spin, weave, make cloth, Comb worsted—taught them prudence & economy, & how to lay out their business to advantage—how to economize their time, improve their talents, correct evil habits &c. &c. &c. Besides this, they were often greatly assisted by the Deacons, who by doing business for them abroad, such as buying & selling &c. ~~often~~ saved them much time & trouble as well as considerable expence. These services were performed as duties which we owe the poor families <around us> who profess the same faith with us, and whose peculiar circumstances require ~~these~~ such services; and they were more particularly extended towards Prime's <family> because they were ~~black~~ ignorant and black & more liable to be imposed upon by the wicked than white people.

Charity to Prime Lane—amount $~~510~~.00

1802 & after $590.00

Thirty-seven

The Church Family at Watervliet

Source: "Watervliet Church Family Plan by D. A. Buckingham—
map 1838," New York State Museum, Albany.

This 1838 drawing of the Shaker Village at Watervliet, New York, testifies to the economy of this intentional community. The structures in the drawing include workshops, barns, storehouses, offices, mills, and a schoolhouse. On the periphery we see pasturage for livestock, a botanical garden (medicinal garden), and a seed garden. The scale and diversity of the Shakers' economic operations enabled a remarkable degree of independence from the regional economy.

This Shaker village was strategically located on the main roads to the cities of Schenectady, Troy, and Albany, providing the Shakers with easy access to trade and travel. However, the village entrance was double gated, requiring visitors to the Shaker community to stop at the brick office of the trustee (structure 21) before passing through a second gate into the heart of the community. These gates made it known to outsiders that while the Shakers welcomed visitors, they also set their own terms for wider engagement with the world.

✺ ✺ ✺

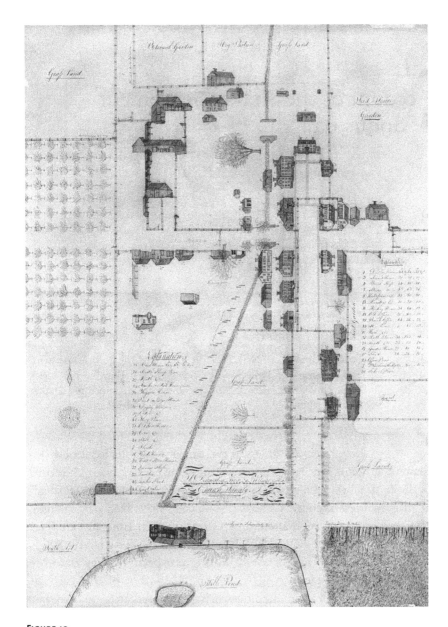

Figure 13.

Thirty-eight

Account of the Shaker Settlement of Sodus Bay

Source: Groveland, New York: "A Record of the commencement, and progress of Believers at Sodus—and Porbay," 1826-1833, Western Reserve Historical Society, Shaker Communities, Shaker Manuscripts, 1723-1952, reel 30, box 92, folder 21.

In 1826 the Shakers established a new settlement at Sodus Bay, New York. The following excerpt from "A Record of the commencement, and progress of Believers at Sodus—and Porbay" is an eyewitness account of how the Shakers organized new villages. It describes Shaker men and women dividing their time and energies between building the village's infrastructure, establishing relationships with their nearest neighbors, and uniting prospective believers to the community. One year into the endeavor, the author of this account took satisfaction in what the Shakers had achieved at Sodus Bay but also acknowledged that the achievements came at a cost.

🐝 🐝 🐝

1826

Feb 23   In the year of our Lord 1826, on the 23ʳᵈ· day of February three Brethren namely, Proctor Sampson of New

	Lebanon, Samuel Southwick of the town of Rose and Joseph Pelham of the town of Galen, by and with the united counsel and consent of Jeremiah Tallcott of New Lebanon went and purchased a tract of land of Robert C. Nicholas (of the County of Ontario) supposed to contain 1296 3/4. Acres, partly in the town of Portbay & partly in the town of Sodus, for the sole purpose of locating and establishing a Society of Believers (commonly called Shakers) took a Deed and gave a Mortgage in security and returned to Joseph Pelham's on the 24th
" " 25	Jeremiah Tallcott and Proctor Sampson went from Joseph Pelham's to Samuel Southwick's.
" " 27	Jeremiah Tallcott & Proctor left Samuel's and went home to New Lebanon, leaving it for Joseph and Samuel to take possession of the above purchased property at the appointed time.
March 1	According to appointment, Samuel S. and Joseph P. met Robert C. Nicholas at Sodus and took formal possession of the aforesaid purchased property. upon which was about 200 Acres of poor improvement, one Grist Mill much out of repair. Two dwelling houses tolerable good, and several others small and poor, all framed buildings. 2 common barns and two small stables. (Also one yoke of oxen and two cows which were given into the bargain) After taking possession in due form Samuel and Joseph went to their respective homes.
" " 13	Joseph and Susannah Pelham and Rollin Cramer who had previously united were with the first Believers that moved on to Sodus to remain.
" " 15	Mary Goodenow a youn woman that united the 23rd day of February last, moved on to remain.
" " 28	Hired a millwright James Valentine by name and commenced repairing the Grist Mill.
April 13	Smith and Sally Tindall who had previously united moved on here with their effects, and four small children, and also Isaac Odle a youth that lived with them; all to remain.
" " 15	Finished repairing the Grist Mill. Began to grind.
" " 20	Two Brethren Proctor Sampson & William Reed arrived here from N Lebanon. Br. William came to remain as a trustee for this Society.

" " 24   Malachi and Elsey Sanford with 2 small children moved on here with their effects to remain.

April 24th.   Daniel and Hannah Dryer who had previously united, now moved on here with
their effects and six children to remain.

" " 29   Seemi and Jerusha Gray who had previously united, now moved on here with their effects and six children to remain.

May 13   Two Brethren and two Sisters arrived here from N. Lebanon. Being sent by the Church, as the leading Elders and Eldresses of this Society namely Jeremiah Tallcott & John Lockwood, Polly Lawrence and Lucy Brown.

        And also another Sister, Roby Bennet to be a Deaconess. Brother Calvin Green came with them to open the testimony to the world awhile, But not to remain.

" "   15 Teams went to Lyons. Brot [Brought] in the Elders effects that they brot from the East.

" "   29 Seemi and Jeursha Gray with their children and effects went to the world.

June 16th   Brother Justus Harwood came and brought two sisters Tina Seaton & Elvira Wells from Watervliet to live here and be helpers. Sister Tina took charge of the little girls.

June 19   Br. Justus Harwood left here and went home to Watervliet.

" " 30   John Kingsley who had previously united moved on here with his unbelieving Katherine and their 3 children.

July 3   Joseph Pelham Sold his farm in Galen for $1000.

" " 15   Jesse and Lucy Leonard having united, moved on here with their effects and two small children.

" " 20   Augustine & Clarissa Leonard moved on here with their effects and five children.

" 23   Elder Archibald Meacham and Br. Andrew Houston called here on their way from Ohio to N. Lebanon made us a good visit, tarried two days & went on their way.

" " 25   Martha, Daughter of Malachi & Elsey Sanford Deceased aged Nine months.

" " 26   Silvia Williams came on here with her four children to be Believers

" 30   Eldress Polly Lawrence taken very sick with the Bilious cholic; every medical aid seemed useless. After every exertion that could be made in the time

Aug 2	She Deceased at Six Oclock this morning, aged 34 years and nine months after three days Severe suffering; which she bore with the greatest fortitude and patience.
Aug. 7	James Martin a young brother from Watervliet came here to live and be a Phisian [physician?].
" " 12	Br. Garret K Lawrence arrived here from N. Lebanon, being sent for on Eldress Polly' account. He is a good phisian, and a natural Brother to Eldress Polly.
" " 15	Elder Jeremiah and Br. Garret went to N. Lebanon.
" " 30	John and Katherine Kingsley & 3 children turned off.
Sept 3	Elder Jeremiah got home from the East brot, Eunice Esther Bennet with him from Watervliet to take the place made vacant by the death of Eldress Polly. And also a brother Abiather Benedict by name to be a help.
" " 20	Commenced building a SawMill by James Valentine Millwright. Ann Lawson United Sept. 9th.
Nov. 29	Elder Jeremiah went to the East again.
Dec. 7	James Valentine the Millwright, having united moved on here with his unbelieving woman and three children.
" " 16	Finished the first SawMill built by Believers, and commenced sawing today.
" 28	Elder Jeremiah returned from N. Lebanon and Br. Proctor Sampson came with him.
" 30	As the deed given by Robert C Nicholas was executed to Proctor Sampson, Samuel Southwick & Joseph Pelham; It was now felt best for them to execute a Deed to the Eastern Believers, which was done according to counsel, to day.
" 31	At the close of this <year> we have 72 Abiding members in this Society including the Elders, Deacons, Brethren and Sisters that came from the East, which number 10. There have 76 united <and> gathered on since the first day of March last; 12 of which have turned off; and two have deceased. One of which was Eldress Polly Lawrence.

THIRTY-NINE

Indenture of Susan Remer to the Shakers of Watervliet

Source: "Indentures of children adopted by Watervliet Shaker families, 1832–1872," New York State Library, Shaker Collection, 1784–1992, SC20330, box 41a, folder 5, Reemer/Remer, Susan, August 18, 1832 (MB/FM,289.8,S527,202-9411 22, reel 5).

Men and women formally united with a Shaker village by signing a covenant, which was both a spiritual and a legal document. By the covenant, the newly united affirmed their faith in the gospel of Christ's second appearing and agreed to live according to the rules of the Shaker faith, including adherence to the principles of celibacy and communalism. Thus, husbands and wives who joined with the Shakers agreed to live separate and apart from one another, and they agreed to put all their real estate and assets (land, tools, etc.) in trust for the benefit of the whole Shaker village.

Early in Shaker history, adult converts to the Shaker faith routinely brought children with them. By law, children were the legal property of their parents and thereby subject to the terms of the covenant signed by their parents. As early as 1795, Shaker leaders expressly required parents who united with the Shakers to place their children under the care of the Shaker leadership. Parents signed indenture papers, like the one included here, that recognized the Shaker leadership (not the parents) as the legal guardians of the children they brought into the Society. On reaching adulthood, these children would decide for themselves whether to unite with the Shakers—and sign their own covenant—or depart the village for the world.

A punishing economic recession in the aftermath of the War of 1812 prompted many struggling households to look for charity from the comparatively prosperous Shaker villages. The uptick in poverty also induced some struggling families to indenture their children to the Shakers. In response to the demand, the Shakers produced a printed indenture form with blank spaces for the handwritten insertion of the relevant information. Accordingly, the following transcript of Susan Remer's indenture to the Shaker community at Watervliet, New York, denotes handwritten insertions in angle brackets.

✻ ✻ ✻

This Indenture, Made the <eighteenth day> of <August> in the year of our Lord one thousand eight hundred and <thirty two> Between <Ephraim B Prentiss> of <Watervliet> in the County of <Albany> and State of New-York, of the first part, and <Abram S Reemer> of the <Town of Peru and County of Huron> of the second part, and <Susan Reemer> an infant under the age of twenty-one years, <the daughter> of the said <Abram S Reemer> of the third part, Witnesseth, That the said parties have, in conformity to the civil institutions of the said State, agreed and covenanted in form as follows, viz: That the said <Susan Reemer> aged <four> years on the <twenty fifth> day of <March last past> by and with the consent of her <Father Abram S Reemer> hath of <her> own free will, placed and bound <herself> unto the said <Ephraim B Prentiss> a member of the United Society (called Shakers) of said <Watervliet> to be under the care and in the employment of the said <Ephraim B Prentiss> as such member, in whatever may be for the present good, or tend to the future benefit and welfare of the said <Susan Reemer> according to the customs, principles and practice, as far as may be lawful, of the aforesaid Society, until <she> the said <Susan Reemer> shall have arrived at the full age of ~~twenty-one~~ <Eighteen years>: Provided nevertheless, That in case <she> the said <Susan Reemer> shall, at any time during <her> said infancy, obstinately refuse to perform and conform, in and to whatever <he> the said <Ephraim B Prentiss> shall or may lawfully require of <her> the said <Susan Reemer> according to the customs, principles and practice aforesaid, then, and in such case, the said <Abram S Reemer> for <himself his> executors and administrators,

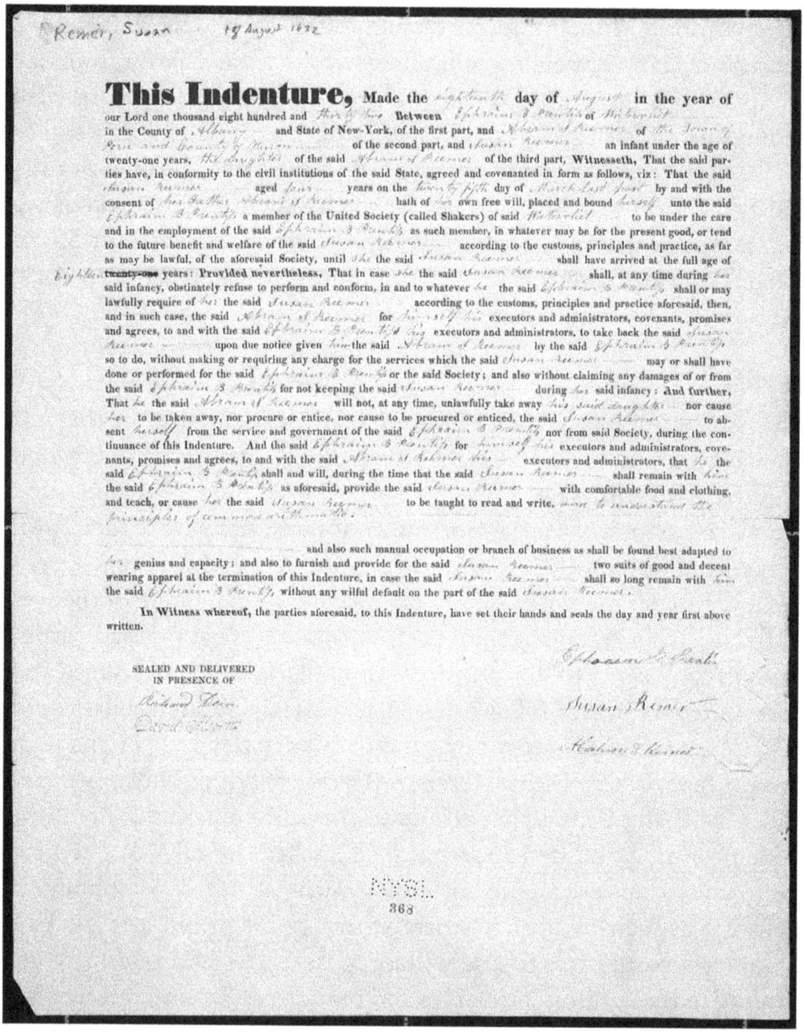

Remer, Susan 18 August 1832

This Indenture, Made the eighteenth day of August in the year of our Lord one thousand eight hundred and thirty two Between Ephraim B Prentiss of Watervliet in the County of Albany and State of New-York, of the first part, and Abram S Reemer of the Town of Peru and County of Huron of the second part, and Susan Reemer an infant under the age of twenty-one years, the daughter of the said Abram S Reemer of the third part, **Witnesseth,** That the said parties have, in conformity to the civil institutions of the said State, agreed and covenanted in form as follows, viz: That the said Susan Reemer aged four years on the twenty fifth day of March last past by and with the consent of her father Abram S Reemer hath of her own free will, placed and bound herself unto the said Ephraim B Prentiss a member of the United Society (called Shakers) of said Watervliet to be under the care and in the employment of the said Ephraim B Prentiss as such member, in whatever may be for the present good, or tend to the future benefit and welfare of the said Susan Reemer according to the customs, principles and practice, as far as may be lawful, of the aforesaid Society, until she the said Susan Reemer shall have arrived at the full age of eighteen ~~twenty-one~~ years: **Provided nevertheless,** That in case she the said Susan Reemer shall, at any time during her said infancy, obstinately refuse to perform and conform, in and to whatever he the said Ephraim B Prentiss shall or may lawfully require of her the said Susan Reemer according to the customs, principles and practice aforesaid, then, and in such case, the said Abram S Reemer for himself his executors and administrators, covenants, promises and agrees, to and with the said Ephraim B Prentiss his executors and administrators, to take back the said Susan Reemer upon due notice given him the said Abram S Reemer by the said Ephraim B Prentiss so to do, without making or requiring any charge for the services which the said Susan Reemer may or shall have done or performed for the said Ephraim B Prentiss or the said Society; and also without claiming any damages of or from the said Ephraim B Prentiss for not keeping the said Susan Reemer during her said infancy: **And further,** That he the said Abram S Reemer will not, at any time, unlawfully take away his said daughter nor cause her to be taken away, nor procure or entice, nor cause to be procured or enticed, the said Susan Reemer to absent herself from the service and government of the said Ephraim B Prentiss nor from said Society, during the continuance of this Indenture. And the said Ephraim B Prentiss for himself his executors and administrators, covenants, promises and agrees, to and with the said Abram S Reemer his executors and administrators, that he the said Ephraim B Prentiss shall and will, during the time that the said Susan Reemer shall remain with him the said Ephraim B Prentiss as aforesaid, provide the said Susan Reemer with comfortable food and clothing, and teach, or cause her the said Susan Reemer to be taught to read and write, and to understand the principles of common arithmatic.

and also such manual occupation or branch of business as shall be found best adapted to her genius and capacity; and also to furnish and provide for the said Susan Reemer two suits of good and decent wearing apparel at the termination of this Indenture, in case the said Susan Reemer shall so long remain with him the said Ephraim B Prentiss without any wilful default on the part of the said Susan Reemer.

In Witness whereof, the parties aforesaid, to this Indenture, have set their hands and seals the day and year first above written.

SEALED AND DELIVERED
IN PRESENCE OF

Richard [illegible]
David [illegible]

Ephraim B Prentiss
Susan Remer
Abraham S Remer

NYSL
368

FIGURE 14. Indenture for Susan Remer. When her parents united with the Shakers in 1832, they followed the community's practice to place her under the guardianship of the Shaker leadership by signing the indenture form featured here. (Courtesy New York State Library, Manuscripts and Special Collections, Albany)

covenants, promises and agrees, to and with the said <Ephraim B Prentiss his> executors and administrators, to take back the said <Susan Reemer> upon due notice given <him> the said <Abram S Reemer> by the said <Ephraim B Prentiss> so to do, without making or requiring any charge for the services which the said <Susan Reemer> may or shall have done or performed for the said <Ephraim B Prentiss> or the said Society; and also without claiming any damages of or from the said <Ephraim B Prentiss> for not keeping the said <Susan Reemer> during <her> infancy: And further, That <he> the said <Abram S Reemer> will not, at any time, unlawfully take away <his said daughter> nor cause <her> to be taken away, nor procure or entice, nor cause or be procured or enticed, the said <Susan Reemer> to absent <herself> from the service and government of the said <Ephraim B Prentiss> nor from said Society, during the continuance of this Indenture. And the said <Ephraim B Prentiss> for himself his executors and administrators, covenants, promises and agrees, to and with the said <Abram S Reemer his> executors and administrators, that he the said <Ephraim B Prentiss> shall and will, during the time the said <Susan Reemer> shall remain with <him> the said <Ephraim B Prentiss> as aforesaid, provide the said <Susan Reemer> with comfortable food and clothing, and teach, or cause <her> the said <Susan Reemer> to be taught to read and write, <and to understand the principles of common arithmetic> and also such manual occupation or branch of business as shall be found best adopted to <her> genius and capacity; and also to furnish and provide for the said <Susan Reemer> two suits of good and decent wearing apparel at the termination of this Indenture, in case the said <Susan Reemer> shall so long remain with him the same <Ephraim B Prentiss> without any wilful default on the part of the said <Susan Reemer>.

In Witness whereof, the parties aforesaid, to this Indenture, have set their hands and seals the day and year first above written.

FORTY

Shakers and the Education of Children

Source: "Seth Y. Wells on the education of children," January 26, 1832, New York State Library, Shaker Collection, 1784–1992, SC20330, box 1, folder 20.

Shaker Seth Young Wells had been a school-teacher when he united with the Watervliet Shakers in 1798. In 1803, Wells assumed the responsibility of mentoring and instructing new converts to the faith (the so-called "gathering order"), and in 1820, as the number of children in the village swelled, Mother Lucy Wright appointed him the superintendent of the Shakers' developing school system. In the following document, Wells explained the Shakers' motivation for establishing schools and his expectation that the whole community of believers would support the school, its teachers, and students.

❧ ❧ ❧

To the Elders, Deacons, Brethren & Sisters of the Society in Watervliet. Beloved Friends,

In union with the Ministry, Elders and Trustees, and in discharge of the duty I owe to the Society as superintendent of the Schools established therein, I now address you on the education of the children under the care of the society, and beg your serious and candid attention to my remarks on this subject.

As the Society is in the habit of receiving children from the world, to be brought up under its care and protection, I consider the responsibility of believers for the faithful discharge of their duty towards such children to be very great. The day must and will come when the great and important charge of supporting the gospel and maintaining the honor, credit and reputation of the Society must devolve on the rising generation. They must occupy our places when we are laid in the dust. It is therefore a duty which now presses upon us, the weight of which we ought to feel, that these children should be instructed, cultivated and brought up in such a manner as to become suitably qualified to fill the responsible stations in which they may hereafter be placed. To accomplish this object various duties are required of the Society, and every individual member may and ought to be a help in fulfilling these duties: for as one and all must finally be accountable to God for the faithful improvement of every talent put into their hands; so their conduct relative to the youth and children under the care of the families in which they respectively reside, must be called to an account.

Example has a much more powerful influence upon the infant and youthful mind than precept. Children are the creatures of imitation. They learn to speak and act by imitation. Their language is the language of imitation, and their actions are formed and brought into use by imitation. Even their ideas and opinions are the effects of imitation, and the society and example of the Brethren & Sisters with whom they are associated, constitute the source and foundation from whence all this imitation proceeds. What they see and hear their superiors say and do, they will say and do; and no admonition will prevent their following a bad example which is daily before their eyes & in their ears. How important then it is, that every Brother & Sister who is in any way connected or associated with the children, should show forth good examples in conduct and conversation. One bad example in word or deed is liable to make a lasting impression on the mind of the child that hears or sees it. Therefore I would seriously and earnestly urge upon every Brother & Sister in the Society the necessity and importance of carefully setting a good example at all times, and in all things, before the youth & children in their respective families, as well as in all places where youth and children are present. I have full confidence in the Elders and Teachers of this Society; but it will be in vain for Elders & Teachers, to instruct reprove or admonish the young, unless the older members second their labors by a steady and uniform practice of good examples.

The great object of establishing and maintaining schools in the Society, is to promote the improvement of the children; not only to give them literary instruction, but to teach them good moral principles, and train them up in virtuous habits, by directing their opening faculties into proper channels for future usefulness. We may often observe in the rising faculties of children a great display of sprightliness & activity, and these active faculties will always find some place or channel for active operation; and if left to chance or accident, or directed by improper objects, or unsuitable & bad examples, they are eminently exposed to take a wrong turn, & in such cases their ruin is often sealed before their friends are aware of it.

We do not expect nor wish to make great scholars of our children. Our desire is to give them as much letter learning as may be put to proper use, and fit them for business in the Society of Believers. But a more important object is, to give proper exercise to their mental faculties, and turn those faculties into the proper channel of usefulness for their own benefit and the benefit of their Brethren & Sisters, to plant and cultivate virtuous principles and habits; and this may easily be done by seasonable & proper attention. Therefore every one should lend an encouraging & helping hand; and no one aught ever to drop a word of discouragement in presence of the children about their improvement; nor speak diminutively or lightly of their school instructions in any way or manner whatever; for this will have a direct tendency to frustrate the object of school instruction & destroy all its benefits. But let every one, as occasion offers, encourage the children to improve their time faithfully, and gain all they can while they are young and have a privilege to go to school; for they will soon be too old to go; and if they do not improve their time while young, they will have cause to lament their negligence and misimprovement of time when it is too late.

Such conversation as this, coming occasionally from the Brethren and Sisters, will many times make a greater impression and have more effect upon their young minds than the counsels & admonitions of their Teachers which they are in the habit of hearing daily repeated.

It is also a matter of importance that those who have the immediate care of the children at home, should see that they are regular in their attendance to the school, and not let them be absent a single day when they are able to go: for every day's absence from their class, is not only so much time lost to the scholars, but it makes difficulty for the teacher, by interrupting the regular course of their studies, especially where they are classed with other children in the pursuit of any particular branch of study. They should also see that the children are clean, that their hands and faces are washed, & their hair combed, that their garments are whole, and their shoes in good order; they should also be cautioned to go directly to school, in proper order, and not stop to play by the way.

There is another matter to which I would recommend & urge particular attention; namely, frequent visits to the school. School visitations have been found by experience to be attended with excellent effects. They tend to excite the ambition of children, & keep their attention alive to their studies, and serve as one of the best means of encouraging the school and adding strength and assistance to the Teacher's labors. And these visitations should not be left entirely for the Elders & Deacons to perform; but every member who is interested in the improvement of the children, should take suitable opportunities to visit the school; and when there, should take pains, in union with the Teacher, to notice the improvement of the children, & encourage them to persevere; being careful in the mean time not to interrupt the order & regulations of the school.

If these things are properly attended to, and every member of the family is careful to unite in the gift of encouraging the school and promoting the improvement of the children, in the manner herein recommended, every good Believer will soon be sensible of the benefits resulting from the school & feel an interest in its prosperity; and the children will then be in a fair way to be brought up under a blessing, & to become useful and profitable members of the Society.

Seth Y. Wells.
Watervliet, Jan.y. 26th. 1832

At a meeting of the Trustees of School District No 14, at the Trustees Office in Watervliet, January 27th 1832, the foregoing Address was read and approved, & ordered to be put on the school Record.

FORTY-ONE

A Shaker Hymn

Source: "Christ Second Appearing," verse and music (letter), Joseph P[arker], Father William and Father James to various instruments, Union Village, Whitewater, Harvard, Hancock, Canterbury, and Watervliet, New York, 1840–1852, pp. 29–30. Western Reserve Historical Society, Shaker Communities, Shaker Manuscripts, 1723–1952, reel 89, box 268, vol. SM 12.

Music was an essential tool for Shaker evangelism. Shaker missionaries taught the doctrines of their faith through hymns like this one, which reads like a catechism. The opening verse asks "How has Christ to us appeared? How to us is he made known?" The remaining verses explain to newcomers—and affirm for the faithful—that Mother Ann Lee and her followers are "the channel" through which the Spirit of God appears to mankind. The verses of the hymn are presented here without the accompanying musical notation.

⁕ ⁕ ⁕

Christ's Second Appearing

1. How has Christ to us appeared
How to us is he made known?
By what tie is he endeared

Thro' what chanel does he come?
In what City or what tower
To what place does he incline?
On what summit in what bower,
Where may he be said to shine?
2.   In what *pure* and holy places,
Can we see his heavenly mien?
Where the bright Angelic graces,
Where O where can they be seen?
Has he sent his gospel to us,
Do we yet the truth believe,
Does his spirit still pursue us
Do we still his word receive?
3.   First in our beloved Mother,
In her follower's next, he's found,
Who did learn to love each other,
And to keep all evil down.
By the tie of true affection,
He to them to us is dear,
By his counsel and protection,
We are made to persevere.
4.   Thro' this chanel we received him,
In this line did he appear,
By their teaching we believed him,
In his loving subjects here.
Zion is the holy temple
Where our savior does repose,
Each that follows his example,
In his spirit daily grows.
5.   On the point of self denial subjection,
In the bower of love we see,
Here is Christ the resurrection,
Here he shines eternally.
In his children who obey him,
Here it is we get the sight,
In his actions do portray him.
This indeed is heavenly light.
6.   In the messengers of heaven,
They who did the tidings bear,

They to whom the keys are given,
Lo the graces do appear.
Here the tree of life is growing,
Here the hungry soul is fed,
Here the heavenly juice is flowing,
Freely from the fountain head.

FORTY-TWO

Complex Marriage

Source: *First Annual Report of the Oneida Association; Exhibiting Its History, Principles, and Transactions to Jan. 1, 1849* (Oneida Reserve, NY: Leonard and Co., 1849), 54–58. The copy of this report used to make this transcription is housed in the Oneida Collection, Department of Special Collections, Syracuse University Library.

The Oneida Association's practice of "complex marriage" frequently elicited curiosity and criticism. In the practice, all adult members of the community were considered married to each other and abandoned monogamy for a system of free love that permitted sexual intercourse between consenting individuals. When the Oneida Association published its first annual report in 1848, it included a nearly twenty-page exposition of the biblical justifications for this system titled "Bible Argument."[1] The report also included several testimonials of community members who celebrated different benefits of the practice. A sampling of those testimonials is featured here.

✺ ✺ ✺

[. . .]

---

1. *First Annual Report of the Oneida Association*, 23–42.

QUESTION III.—What has been the effect of the Social Theory of this Association, upon your character?

ANSWERS

JOHN ABBOTT

The doctrine of free love as advocated by Mr. Noyes, is a subject that my mind has dwelt upon and investigated for a number of years. I had become fully satisfied before I joined this Association, that the time would Come when the institutions of the world would give place to the direct government of God;—when exclusiveness and selfishness in respect to marriage would not exist. The conclusions I have come to on that subject, have done much to break up the spirit of legality and selfishness in me, and to turn my thoughts to an acquaintance with the laws of God, not only on that subject but on all others. I am sure that the free-love theory has had a great effect in bringing me into love and union with God, and all, the family of God, and to cause me to seek to improve my character and make myself attractive. I think our social theory is the cross of Christ, to separate us from the world and from all false fellowships.

LAURA A. ABBOTT

The effect of our social theory upon my character, has been to enlarge my heart towards God and his children, and to root out selfishness. I feel that it has given me that love which seeketh not her own; and that it is fast restoring me to the vigor of youth.

JONATHAN BURT

The effect upon my character, of our social theory, as taught by Mr. Noyes in his Bible Argument, has been—1st, to bring to light deep-rooted and subtle traits of selfishness, previously unthought of by my-self. 2d, It has brought to light an unsanctified state of my amative passions, discovering to me the true nature of the spirit of lust which worketh to envy, and is ungovernable and restless in its character. 3d. It has revived in my spirit a new and energetic feeling of loathing toward the spirit of selfishness in all its forms. 4th. It has proved to me more effectually than I ever realized before, the impotency of human energy to overcome the above evils. 5th. It has led me to seek and expect the inspiration of God to control the action of the passions and members of my body. 6th. Facts have proved to be in harmony with my faith Christ has in an enlarged sense manifested himself my life, wisdom, righteousness and strength.

SARAH A. BRADLEY

If I had no evidence of the truth of the doctrines presented in the Bible Argument, but the change they have produced in my character, I should know they were of God. 'A corrupt tree cannot bring forth good fruit.' Previous to my knowledge of these doctrines, false modesty found a faithful representative in me; but I have turned traitor and mean to do all in my power to annihilate it, and have true modesty take its place. I used to make a distinction between brotherly love and the love which I had for my husband; but I was brought to see that there was but one kind of love in the kingdom of God. I have found that true love is a great stimulus to improvement. Free love has brought to light defects in my spiritual character which nothing else could—idolatry, exclusiveness, and various other evils. Although the process of destroying selfishness has been an extremely painful one, I am very thankful for the experience I have had. It has brought me very near to God, and I now feel an interest in the happiness of all. I have learned that love is the gift of God.

HENRY W. BURNHAM

The theory of sexual morality adopted by this Association, while it allows liberty which in the world would lead to licentiousness degrading to both soul and body, here produces the opposite effects; i.e. it invigorates with *life*, soul and body, and refines and exalts the character generally. It is calculated to abolish selfishness in its most subtle and deep-rooted forms, and practically adapted to fulfil the prayer of Christ in respect to the unity of the church, and thus introduce her gradually into the glories of the resurrection. My chief reason for believing this is because its development is invariably attended by the manifest judgment of God.

ABBY S. BURNHAM

The effect that free love has had upon my character, has been to raise me from a state of exclusiveness and idolatry, to a greater enlargement of heart, and freedom of communication with God and this body.

Selfishness is being purged out, and its place supplied with the pure love of God. I feel that I am not my own, but am bought with a price, therefore I am to glorify God with my body and spirit which are his. I see more clearly than ever before the beauty of Christ's prayer, that we all may be *one*, even as he and the Father are one.

SARAH A. BURNHAM

The social theory, as advocated by Mr. Noyes and this Association, and sustained by the Bible, has had a tendency to enlighten my understanding, and to try, enlarge and purify my heart.

GEORGE CRAGIN

The social theory of this community is, and has been from the first, associated in my mind with the end of this world, and the beginning of the kingdom of heaven upon earth. The evidence of its truth is as *firmly rooted* and *grounded* in my heart and mind as the gospel of salvation from sin; and my confidence therefore cannot be destroyed in one, without destroying it in the other. Of its effects upon my character I could say much. But in brief, I can say it has greatly enlarged my heart by purging it from exclusiveness—it has tamed and civilized my feelings, purified my thoughts, and elevated into the presence of God and heaven the strongest passion in the social department of my nature. I regard the 'Bible Argument,' so called, as the *social gospel*, second only to the gospel of salvation from sin, and destined to repair the second breach in the fall.

MARY E. CRAGIN

I think the development of the social theory most favorable to the formation of character. It brings out the hidden things of the heart as nothing else could, by exciting the stronger passions of our nature, and bringing them out where they can be purified. Love without law, yet under the control of the Spirit of God, is a great beautifier of character in every respect, and puts the gilding on life. It is the manifestation of the resurrection power—revivifying soul and body. The best result in my own experience has been, that it has brought me into fellowship and acquaintance with the Father and the Son, more than any thing else ever did—and thereby I know that the doctrine is of God. [. . .]

FORTY-THREE

John Humphrey Noyes's Home Talks

Source: John Humphrey Noyes, *Home-Talks*, ed. Alfred Barron and George Noyes Miller (Oneida, NY: Oneida Community, 1875), 282–84, 333–35.

John Humphrey Noyes frequently spoke informally to Oneida residents about spiritual and social matters. The community eventually dubbed these teachings "home talks" and published many of them in a book based on notes taken by residents on these talks that Noyes reviewed for accuracy.[1] Two of these published home talks are featured here as examples of the type of teachings community members heard from their leader. In one, Noyes philosophized on the organization and function of families and the binding role of love in what he termed "family communism." In the other, Noyes discussed the need of individuals to identify their personal faults in order to correct them.

❧ ❧ ❧

[. . .]

---

1. Noyes, *Home-Talks*, 1.

Family Communism

COMMUNISM, dreadful bugbear as it is on a large scale, is the fundamental principle of every family. The man keeps no account with his
wife, but cares for her as for himself. Man and wife keep no account for
their children, but regard them as their own flesh. This is the theory at
least of the family compact. Thus all children are born in Communism,
and for the sweetest part of their lives are nourished and brought up
in Communism. They come in contact with the opposite principle of
trading selfishness, only when they begin to leave the family circle and
mingle with the world.

Communism is really the very essence of Home. The man who turns
his back in imagination from the desert of common life to the oasis of
his childhood, and sings *"Home, sweet, sweet Home,"* is unconsciously
thinking of Communism, and longing to return to it.

The Communism which begins with marriage, does not stop at the
first generation, but reaches the grandchildren, and like a light shin-
ing in a dark place, is reflected back to parents and grandparents, and
glances far and wide among uncles and aunts and cousins, till it is lost
in distance.

And we must not imagine that this family-feeling which thus radiates
unity in little circles all over the world, has its seat and cause exclusively
or even chiefly in consanguinity. On the contrary its very beginning
is in the love that arises between man and woman as such, without
blood relationship. Husbands and wives are related to each other only
as members of the human race; and yet their love is the source of the
love between brothers and sisters and cousins and all kindred. They
are the real founders of the family Community. So, if the old saying is
true that "blood is stronger than water," we must add to it that "love is
stronger than blood."

Thus it appears not only that we are all born and brought up in
Communism, but that one of our very strongest natural proclivities in
adult life is for *Communism with non-relatives*, and the founding of small
Communities. With such germs in our nature and education, it can
not be so difficult as many imagine, for us to fall in with the spirit
of progress (which is really the spirit of Pentecost) and allow science
and inspiration to organize family-Communism on the grandest scale.
It will be but returning home; only we have to give up the old one-
horse wagon for two, and go by the great railroad train that carries a
meeting-house-full. [. . .]

FIGURE 15. Oneida Association members, 1867. This photograph of a group of men, women, and children of the Oneida Association was taken during a break from their work raking and hoeing a field. (Courtesy of the Oneida Community Mansion House)

Self-Surgery

THE difficulty in regard to judging evil in ourselves is, that it is too near us. We can not see things that are in our very eyes. They must be a little distance off, that we may get a clear view of them. It is comparatively easy for us to see other folk's faults. We can criticise others, when we cannot criticise ourselves; and it is one good feature of our system of criticism, that it exercises us in sincerity and sharp-sightedness in judging character at some distance from us. But thorough self-judgement is possible and necessary, and sooner or later we shall have to inspect ourselves just as we inspect others.

Besides the mechanical difficulty of seeing things in our own eyes, there is a difficulty in our sensibilities; they gather around to confuse and hinder when we undertake to judge ourselves. To deal truthfully with our faults in the midst of our sensibilities is almost impossible. But that is just what we must learn to do. We must learn to fight manfully in a battle with an enemy who has got nearer than our household, and nearer than our dearest friend, nearer than hand-grips or throat-grips, an enemy in the very presence of our inmost life.

We all know how hard it is to be thoroughly sincere with a friend; but it is infinitely harder to be thoroughly sincere with ourselves. God can enable us to do it, and that is what we must pray for. God stands far enough off and is clear enough from the confusing sensibilities of the case, to be able to see us clearly and judge us truthfully; and if we submit ourselves to him, he can put our perceptions and his power and will into us, and so enable us to fight the closest of all battles—self-judgement. "The word of the God is quick and powerful, sharper than a two-edged sword, piercing even to the dividing asunder of soul and spirit. All things are open to his eyes." That is our hope. It ought to give us hope, that there is one who can look our enemy right in the eye. Even if we could see our enemy we should not dare strike, for fear of hurting ourselves. Here comes God to help us. He can see our enemy and just where to strike him, and he is not afraid to do it. Let us put ourselves into his hands.

The enemy I am talking of is what Paul calls the "old man." "Put ye off the old man," he says. What is the "old man?" It is yourself, it is your life. And how are you going to put it off? That is a harder problem than that of the butterfly breaking out of its chrysalis, or the snake shaking off its skin. It is a sharp dissection, and we shall want sharp eyes and sharp knives to do it with. Let us invite the surgery of God. [. . .]

FORTY-FOUR

A Rebuttal of Noyes and Perfectionism

Source: Hubbard Eastman, *Noyesism Unveiled: A History of the Sect Self-Styled Perfectionists; with a Summary View of Their Leading Doctrines* (Battleboro, VT: Hubbard Eastman, 1849), 85–90.

In 1849, Rev. Hubbard Eastman published *Noyesism Unveiled: A History of the Sect Self-Styled Perfectionists,* a book that claimed to expose the truth behind the Oneida Association. The book was critical of nearly every aspect of Noyes's teachings. In the excerpt of that book featured here, Eastman argued that Noyes's teachings on complex marriage were merely a façade that he designed to justify licentiousness.

❧ ❧ ❧

[. . .]

Chapter X

Principles taught by Noyes

In addition to the facts already presented, so strikingly illustrative of the character of Noyesism, we shall now proceed to notice some of the principles taught by Mr. N., and considered as essential parts of the system. It will be seen on examination that the principles and practices of Noyes and his followers go hand in hand, and are in perfect keeping the one with the other.

But we would frankly acknowledge that we continue the investigation of the subject with extreme reluctance; and no consideration whatever, but a settled conviction of the necessity of so doing, in order to apprize the public, and especially the young, of the danger to which they are exposed, would induce us to proceed in the work. Much perplexity arises from the fact that Mr. Noyes, in speaking of some points, has descended so low, and unblushingly published sentiments so sensual and debasing in their character and tendency, and in some instances used language so very obscene and vulgar, that it is extremely difficult and almost impossible to present the subject in a just light, without transgressing the common rules of propriety. But we will endeavor to avoid corrupting the mind of the reader while we seek to remedy the existing evil.

The utter impiety and solemn mockery to which Mr. Noyes descends in trying to couple his gross licentiousness with the sublime mysteries of Christianity, can but shock the sensibilities of every virtuous mind, and is an utter outrage upon the moral sense of a Christian community! *Never* was the grace of God more completely turned into lasciviousness!—*Never* was the demon of darkness more effectually transformed into an angel of light, than in the instance before us! The characters spoken of in scripture as—"Having eyes full of adultery, and that cannot cease from sin," come up before us in all their native corruption under the cover of Noyesism!

In investigating the subject, we shall quote somewhat largely from the writings of Mr. Noyes, thereby presenting his principles to public view in their native dress. We shall however withhold some portions of his language which he has unblushingly blazoned abroad through the medium of his official organ. Though it may have been read with pleasure by the Noyesites, who have cast out all the bond-woman's children not excepting *"decency"*—yet it is utterly unfit for the public eye. In the letter addressed to Mr. Hollister, and which has already been alluded to, Mr. N. writes as follows:—

"About three months from the time when I received Christ as a whole Savior, my mind was led into long and deep meditation on the subject which principally interests Shakers—the relation of the sexes. I then came to the conclusions in which I have since *stood*, viz. that the outward act of sexual connection is as innocent and comely as any other act, or rather, if there is any difference in the character of outward acts, that is the most noble and comely of all. This sentiment, covered with any covering but that of the Spirit, is licentiousness. The same is true of *every* principle of human action. 'Whatsoever is not of faith is sin;' and to him that believeth, '*all* things are lawful.' God tells me that He does not care so much *what* I do, as *how* I do it, and by this word I walk in all things. I never inquire whether it is *right* to do this, or *wrong* to do that, but whether God *leads* me to do it or not. I look not at the *thing* to be done, but at the *influence* by which it is done. These principles I apply to the use of women, ardent spirits, money, carnal weapons, &c. So I have testified for the past five years; and every day sinks me deeper and deeper in the certainty that these are the principles of God, and his heavenly hosts."

The above are the settled principles of Mr. Noyes, and they throw a flood of light upon the whole system which he has laid down. And they have been the rule by which he has walked from 1834 up to the present time.

Now, if sentiments of like character, or equally licentious in their tendency, should come out from those hot-beds of iniquity, city brothels, it would not be very surprising; but coming as they do from a man claiming to be a *Christian*, and setting himself up as the founder of a sect which is called *religious*, it surpasses any thing which has ever existed either in ancient or modern times. Verily this *is* a "master stroke of Satanic policy—a refinement of wickedness which puts papacy to the blush," and is the "very *incarnation* of impurity." As a kind of screen for his wickedness, Mr. N. impiously and hypocritically pretends to throw the "covering of the Spirit" over all his acts, of whatever character! To him *all* things are lawful! This is throwing off all legal restraint, and stepping out upon the platform of universal freedom. If this is not unrestricted *license*, then we know not what is. Under such principles a man might carry out whatever notions might chance to come into his head, and if his course was questioned at all, he might reply—"*I am led by the Spirit.*" This reply would answer all questions!

But to return—Let the reader bear in mind that the long and deep meditations of Mr. N. upon this subject commenced about three months after he came out a staunch Perfectionist, which was in Feb. 1834. Now he asserts that he had since "*stood*" in the conclusions to which he then came, which conclusions are contained in the extracts already given—that he had walked by the rule there laid down *"in all things"*—and says—*"These principles I apply to the use of women, ardent spirits, & c."*—And that he had testified the same from 1834 up to 1839.

How do these statements agree with the assertion that there had been nothing immoral among the "believers" in Putney up to Feb. 1842? However it might have been with his followers, we venture to say that the reader will find it difficult to believe that Mr. N. had been guiltless all the while, his protestations of innocence to the contrary notwithstanding.

But let us hear him again.—In the Spiritual Moralist of June 13, 1842, he writes as follows:—

"In the winter of 1834, I abandoned the popular religious system in which I had been educated, and became a perfectionist. The change in my views at that time, was not confined to the subject of holiness, but extended to every department of theology and morals. Finding gross error in the *foundation* of my previous faith, I suspected error in every part of the *superstructure*. I therefore gave it up altogether, and commenced a new course of investigation, trusting myself more exclusively than I had before done, to the guidance of the Bible and the Spirit of truth. The subject of *sexual morality* was early forced upon my attention, by its close connection with those peculiar views of the *law*, of the *leadings* of the Spirit, and of the *resurrection*, which are among the principal elements of my testimony in the Perfectionist and in the Witness. Personal circumstances of an interesting character, the startling and in some instances the corrupt suggestions of men with whom I was then connected, and a variety of scandalous reports concerning the licentious doctrines and practices of certain Perfectionists, conspired to urge me to a thorough examination of the matter. On the one hand my *practical* propensities, trained as they had been in the school of New England sobriety, and confirmed by the deep interest which I had taken in the Moral Reform enterprise, strongly attached me to the ordinary maxims of sexual virtue. On the other hand, I cared nothing for reputation, for I had none to lose, and was therefore free to adopt any *theory*, however 'heretical' and offensive, which the gospel of the resurrection might require. Under these circumstances, I meditated on the subject much of the time for two years. My mind was particularly exercised in relation to it during several long seasons of spiritual trial. In the winter of 1836-7 my views assumed a definite and satisfactory form."

What the *"definite and satisfactory form"* was, which the views of Mr. Noyes assumed in the winter of 1836–7, we gather from what is familiarly called and generally known as the "Battle Axe Letter." This letter bears date, Jan. 15, 1837, and on account of the peculiar doctrines which it contains has acquired considerable notoriety, and exhibits the views of Mr. N. in a—to him—"definite and satisfactory form." [. . .]

Part VII

Religion and New York Politics

While previous sections have highlighted how economic and demographic developments shaped Christian evangelism, this section looks more closely at the relationship between politics and religion in early nineteenth-century New York. As religion helped shape—and was shaped by—a more democratic society in New York, lawmakers created an increasingly democratic political culture in the state. The two developments worked together to position the Burned-over District and its residents for a leading role in the various reform movements taking shape in the United States in the nineteenth century.

In 1777, New York drafted its first constitution, a conspicuously undemocratic document when compared with the wartime constitutions of neighboring Pennsylvania and Massachusetts. It concentrated political power in the offices of the governor, the Senate, and the judiciary at the expense of the more popularly elected Assembly. It instituted a stratified voting system, setting significantly higher property requirements for the election of the powerful governor and senators. The constitution acknowledged "the free exercise and enjoyment of religious profession and worship, without discrimination or preferences" but also asserted that religious freedom did not "justify practices inconsistent with the peace and safety of this State."[1] In Albany County, patriot authorities acted on this last proviso to detain and question the pacifist Shakers during the Revolutionary War.

In 1821 New York adopted a new constitution that reflected the developing democratic spirit of the era. It eliminated property qualifications for white male voters and converted executive appointed offices into elected offices. It created new legislative districts in central and western New York, thereby shifting political power from merchants and manor lords in the east to small farmers and mechanics in the west. The new constitution codified a state Bill of Rights, and perhaps most important, it established an electoral procedure for amending the constitution. The result was a steady devolution of state power to local governments and the broadening of the electorate to include more white males, although not women or Black men. Thereafter, New York experienced a decisive uptick in political activism, civic engagement, and electoral politics.

All the documents in this section illustrate this trend toward democracy and its effect on how New Yorkers perceived of, and interacted with, their government. The selections from the 1821 and 1846 constitutions illustrate the process of democratization in New York State. Four other documents showcase the diversity of interests and causes championed by New Yorkers. Collectively, these documents show the varying degree of Christian influence on popular political participation and political rhetoric. The opening and closing documents are excerpts from the same source, the memoir of a New York State legislator who emphatically supported the spirit of democratization that swept across New York, but also expressed some doubts about the social benefit of certain democratic reforms.

---

1. Constitution of New York (1777), Article XXXVIII.

FORTY-FIVE

Abijah Beckwith's Reflections on a Political Career

Source: Abijah Beckwith Papers, #2513, Division of Rare and Manuscript Collections, Cornell University Library, n.d.

Abijah Beckwith represented Herkimer County as a member of the New York State Assembly (1816-1817, 1823, and 1847) and the New York State Senate (1835-1838). In 1847, he reflected on his political career in a letter addressed to his grandson. In this selection from that account, Beckwith proudly related his experiences as a public servant and explained his votes on key issues and the electoral consequences. His political career exemplifies how democratization opened political doors for men with little formal education or personal wealth.

❧ ❧ ❧

[. . .]

In Eighteen hundred and sixteen I was Elected a member of the Assembly and took <my seat> the first January 1817. Among the important laws passed was one for the construction of <the> Erie and Champlain Canals, with a sistem of finance to secure the debt for their construction. For this law I voted, and was censured by my constituents for it. It was the practice of the Democratic party of the County and to which I belonged, when they Elected a young man for the first time, to Elect him the next year. But owing to <the> vote on the canal bill I had to wait until the propriety of the vote was tested by actual experience. It was during this Session that Governor Tompkins recommended the abolition of slavery in this State, And a bill was passed for its gradual abolition, for which bill I voted. And of these two votes I have always been well satisfied. But at the time both looked somewhat different from what they now do. We had then no experience in Canal making then, and it looked like a monstrous undertaking. And the contracting of a frightful debt, I never felt so great responsibility resting upon me, for any vote I ever gave, and believe that was the case generally with those who voted with me. The slave question had not been discussed then, as it has since and appeared different from what it now would.

In 1820 I was appointed Deputy Marshal to take the United States Census for the County of Herkimer. But by an arraingement in which I concurred Abijah Mann Jr was afterwards appointed for the northern section of the county. And I took the Southern, As I was indebt at the time and it being soon after the war all the products of the products of the farm was very low, this was under the circumstances of the case the best Office in a pecuniary point of view I ever had.

I was a member of the Legislature in 1823. This was the first session after the adoption of what was called the new Constitution. And was of course an important session, as it tended to give legislative construction to that instrument.

The next Office was that of Clerk of the County do not recollect the year I was Elected, The term was for three years, At the expiration of which I was again Elected and served three years longer making six years, During all this time my family lived at home on the farm, I usually went from home to the Office on monday mornings, a distance of some ten miles and back Saturday Evenings, Staying with my family over sunday, Usually worked hard while at the Office,

In 1834 was Elected to the Senate of this State took my seat Jany 1.1835, served the term of four years, acted my part as well as I could made some speeches &c. Was a member of this legislature in 1847 It being the first session after the then new Constitution, was considered a very important one, And we were in session an unusual length of time

In both instances of the alterations of the Constitution I was a strong advocate for the reforms contemplated, and for the calls of the Conventions, And in both instances advocated the reforms presented to the people by the new Constitutions, and voted for them, which probably was one of the reasons why I was in both instances returned to the first legislature after their adoption by the people.

In addition to what has been stated, was frequently Supervisor of the Town, served often as *Arbitrator*, Referee, Executor &c. Was very often a Delegate to Conventions for the nomination of Candidates to Office, both in the county, Senatorial District, and the State.

From the foregoing, it will readily be perceived, that I too a great extent made politics a study. And the many and frequent Offices I have held shows that, Considering my Occupation, and limited Education, I have succeeded tolerably well, But whether I have enjoyed life the better for it, is a matter of doubt; and whether my Family is as well off, is also very doubtful, Have received a large amount of money for public services But a considerable portion of it has been swollowed up in expences, and altho' I have always returned to my farm, when each term of Office expired and went to work, Still my attention has not been as much devoted to money making as it probably would have been, had it not been so much taken up with political matters, And in a pecuniary point of view it would probably have been better for myself and family if I had never held any Office, Still there is some things about it, that are pleasant, I have formed an extensive acquaintance, And have many personal friends, among those who are considered the better class of people, and particularly among those who are of <the> same political party with myself.

The last election to the assembly has been gratifying in this, That thirty years from the time I was first Elected, The people of the same Country, which whom I had associated during the whole time, And who had so often expressed their *partiality* to me, should have given this last expression of their confidence. ~~in me~~. [. . .]

FORTY-SIX

Selections from New York's 1821 Constitution

Source: New York [State] et al., *The Constitution of the State of New York: With Notes, References and Annotations, together with the Articles of Confederation, Constitution of the United States, New York State Constitutions of 1777, 1821, 1846, Unamended and as Amended and in Force in 1894, with an Index of the Revised Constitution and the Constitution of the United States* (Albany: J. B. Lyon, 1894), 58–71.

Articles 7 and 8 of New York's 1821 constitution laid a foundation for popular political activism and especially religious activism in New York State. The first article protected religious freedom and freedom of expression. The second established new procedures for amending the state constitution. Reformers of all stripes would act on these rights, advocating for numerous causes with the hope of achieving lasting change.

❦ ❦ ❦

WE, the people of the state of New York, acknowledging with gratitude the grace and beneficence of God, in permitting us to make choice of our form of government, do establish this constitution.
[. . .]

Article VII

[. . .]

§ 3. The free exercise and enjoyment of religious profession and worship, without discrimination or preference, shall forever be allowed in this state, to all mankind; but the liberty of conscience hereby secured, shall not be so construed as to excuse acts of licentiousness, or justify practices inconsistent with the peace, or safety of this state.

§ 4. AND WHEREAS, The ministers of the gospel are, by their profession, dedicated to the service of God, and the cure of souls, and ought not to be diverted from the great duties of their functions; therefore, no minister of the gospel, or priest of any denomination whatsoever, shall at any time hereafter, under any pretense or description whatever, be eligible to, or capable of holding, any civil military office, or place within this state. [. . .]

§ 8. Every citizen may freely speak, write, and publish his sentiments, on all subjects, being responsible for the abuse of that right; and no law shall be passed, to restrain, or abridge the liberty of speech, or of the press. In all prosecutions or indictments for libels, the truth may be given in evidence, to the jury; and if it shall appear to the jury, that the matter charged as libellous, is true, and was published with good motives, and for justifiable ends, the party shall be acquitted; and the jury shall have the right to determine the law and the fact. [. . .]

Article VIII

Section 1. Any amendment or amendments to this constitution, may be proposed in the senate or assembly, and if the same shall be agreed to by a majority of the members elected to each of the two houses, such proposed amendment or amendments, shall be entered on their journals, with the yeas and nays taken thereon, and referred to the legislature then next to be chosen; and shall be published, for three months previous to the time of making such choice; and, if in the legislature next chosen as aforesaid, such proposed amendment, or amendments, shall be agreed to, by two-thirds of all the members elected to each house; then it shall be the duty of the legislature to submit such proposed amendment, or amendments, to the people, in such manner, and at such time, as the legislature shall prescribe; and if the people shall approve and ratify such amendment, or amendments, by a majority of the electors qualified to vote for members of the legislature, voting thereon, such amendment, or amendments, shall become part of the constitution.

FORTY-SEVEN

An Anti-Masonic Declaration of Independence

Source: Solomon Southwick, *Speech of Solomon Southwick, at the Opening of the New-York Anti-Masonic State Convention: At the Capitol, in Albany, February 19th, 1829; Containing, 1. A Concise Statement of Every Important Fact, Relating to the Masonic Outrages on William Morgan and David C. Miller; 2. A Concise Statement of Every Important Fact, Amounting to a Presumptive Proof of the Murder of William Morgan at or near Fort Niagara* (Albany, NY: Printed by B. D. Packard, 1829), 14–15.

The Burned-over District gave rise to new religions and new political parties. Of the latter, one of the most successful was the Anti-Masonic Party, a single-issue party that traced its origins to the disappearance of William Morgan. Morgan was a disgruntled Freemason who, in 1826, announced plans to publish a tell-all account of the secrets of the fraternal order. Morgan disappeared, however, before the book appeared in print. Friends and neighbors in Batavia, New York, organized search parties and sought state assistance in Morgan's recovery, but he was never seen again. People concluded—without evidence—that vengeful Freemasons had murdered Morgan to prevent the book's publication and that politicians and business leaders with ties to the Masons had conspired to conceal the truth about Morgan's disappearance.

"The Morgan Affair," as it became known, fueled a moral crusade against Freemasonry in central and western New York and the formation of the Anti-Mason Party. Solomon Southwick, the Anti-Mason Party candidate for governor in 1828, garnered 12 percent of the popular vote. More than a dozen Anti-Masonic candidates were elected to the House of Representatives from New York between 1827 and 1833. "The Anti-Masonic Declaration of Independence," excerpted below, articulates the Christian and political values of the anti-Mason activists.

❧ ❧ ❧

Anti-Masonic

Declaration of Independence

At an adjourned meeting of the Convention of Seceding Masons held at Le Roy

July 4th, 1828, SOLOMON SOUTHWICK, *President*, and Rev. David Bernard, *Clerk*.

AUGUSTUS P. HASCALL, Chairman of the Committee appointed to draft a Declaration of Independence, from the Masonic Institution, reported the following, which was accepted and signed.

When men attempt to dissolve a system which has influenced and governed a part of community, and by its pretensions to antiquity, usefulness and virtue would demand the respect of all, it is proper to submit to the consideration of a candid and impartial world the causes which impel them to such a course. We seceders from the masonic institution, availing ourselves of our natural and unalienable rights, and the privileges guaranteed to us by our constitution, freely to discuss the principles of our government and laws, and to expose whatever may endanger the one, or impede the due administration of the other, do offer the following reasons for endeavoring to abolish the order of Freemasonry, and destroy its influence in our government. [. . .]

That it is opposed to the genius and design of this government, the spirit and precepts of our holy religion, and the welfare of society, generally, will appear from the following considerations.

It exercises jurisdiction over the persons and lives of citizens of the republic.

It arrogates to itself the right of punishing its members for offences unknown to the laws of this or any other nation.

It requires the concealment of crime and protects the guilty from punishment.

It encourages the commission of crime by affording the guilty facilities of escape.

It affords opportunities for the corrupt and designing to form plans against the government and the lives and characters of individuals.

It assumes titles and dignities incompatible with a republican government, and enjoins an obedience to them derogatory to republican principles.

It destroys all principles of equality by bestowing its favor on its own members, to the exclusion of others, equally meritorious and deserving.

It creates odious aristocracies by its obligations to support the interest of its members in preference to others of equal qualifications.

It blasphemes the name and attempts the personification of the Great Jehovah.

It prostitutes the sacred scriptures to unholy purposes to subserve its own secular and trifling concerns.

It weakens the sanctions of morality and religion by the multiplication of profane oaths and immoral familiarity with religious forms and ceremonies.

It discovers in its ceremonies an unholy commingling of divine truth with imperious human inventions.

It destroys a veneration for religion and religious ordinances, by the profane use of religious forms.

It substitutes the self righteousness and ceremonies of masonry for vital religion and the ordinances of the gospel.

It promotes habits of idleness and intemperance, by its members neglecting their business to attend meeting and drink its libation.

It accumulates funds at the expense of indigent persons, and to the distress of their families, too often to be dissipated in rioting and pleasure, and its senseless ceremonies and exhibitions.

It contracts the sympathies of the human heart for all the unfortunate, by confining its charities to its own members; and promotes the interest of the few at the expense of the many.

An institution, fraught with so many great evils, is dangerous to our government, and the safety of our citizens and is unfit to exist among free people. We, therefore, believing it the duty we owe to God, our country and our posterity, resolve to expose this mystery, wickedness, and tendency, to public view, and we exhort all citizens who have a love of country and a veneration for its laws, a spirit of our holy religion and a regard for the welfare of mankind, to aid us in the cause which we have espoused—and appealing to Almighty God for the rectitude of our motives we solemnly absolve ourselves from all allegiance to the masonic institution and declare ourselves free and independent. And in support of these resolutions, our government and laws, and the safety of individuals against the usurpations of all secret societies, and open force, and against the "vengeance" of the masonic institution, "with our firm reliance on the protection of divine providence, we mutually pledge to each other, our lives, our fortunes and our sacred honor."

July 4, 1828.

FORTY-EIGHT

Report of the Cayuga County Temperance Society

Source: "Second Annual Meeting of the Cayuga County Temperance Society," *Auburn (NY) Free Press*, March 20, 1833.

Temperance societies sprang up throughout the United States in the first half of the nineteenth century, but New York outpaced all other states in both the number of societies and overall membership. Of the approximately 3,000 temperance societies in the United States by 1831, New York was home to 727 of them, more than three times the number in any other state.[1]

In 1833, the Cayuga County Temperance Society published its second annual report. The report celebrated the proliferation of temperance societies and the steady rise of membership in the county. In total, the county boasted thirty-two temperance societies, although some were not affiliated with the county society. Furthermore, some towns supported as many as five such societies. Despite the growth of the temperance movement, the report lamented the limited influence of their moral suasion campaign within Cayuga County. As a consequence, the report urged more widespread dissemination of temperance literature

---

1. "Temperance Societies," the *Gem* (Rochester, NY), May 21, 1831.

and greater attendance at public meetings where temperance was preached.

* * *

Report

Your committee, in presenting their second annual Report, have but few facts to relate, with respect to temperance measures pursued through-out the County during the past year. From the best information which they have been able to obtain, and from personal observation, they are led to the painful conclusion that this subject does not retain that deep hold upon the affections, and benevolent feelings of community that its importance imperiously demands. They are brought to this conclusion from the fact that little appears to have been done in this work of moral reform, amongst us, and by us throughout the County, in comparison to what might and ought to have been done. From a remissness on the part of the officers of the different town societies in sending in their an-nual reports to the Executive committee of the County Society, we have been deprived of the legitimate, and in a great measure the only source of information as to the Temperance movements in different parts of the county. In consequence of this omission, your committee have failed doubtless in getting possession of many facts and incidents in relation to this subject which would be cheering, and would cast a ray of sun-shine over the dark picture before us.

A request has been made, that the secretary of each of the different auxiliary town societies would send to the Secretary of the County So-ciety, copies of their respective annual reports. This request was made with a view of embodying as usual in this report a concise history of be-nevolent operation during the past year, with the expectation that from that statement, the plan for future operation might be more judiciously devised, and more vigorously executed. But in very few instances has it been complied with.

Yet, after all, your committee are happy in being able to state, from their own observation, their belief that the cause of Temperance has yet among us, many warm and ardent friends; that this cause, the bare mention of which a few years ago excited a smile of incredulity upon the countenance of the man of real benevolence, and a sneer of contempt, and a biting sarcasm from the man who prized higher the profits de-rived from the traffic in ardent spirits, than the temporal and eternal well-being of his friends and neighbors, now finds a *friend* if not an advocate in almost every benevolent bosom. But friendship alone, without corresponding exertion, will never bring about that state of things so ardently and anxiously *sought* for, and *labored* for by our most active pioneers in this field of philanthropy and virtue.

Soon after the last annual meeting the plan of holding adjourned meetings of the County Society in the different towns was adopted. In pursuance of said plan a meeting was held at Cayuga in the month of February last; and another about the twentieth of the same month in the town of Sennett, neither of which were so fully attended as was expected. In adopting this measure it was anticipated that said meetings would be attended by delegates from each of the auxiliary societies; and that from a mutual and free interchange of views and feelings upon the subject for which they had assembled, each member would return to his home, with fresh courage, resolved to engage in the work with renewed and redoubled energy.

This they might reasonably expect, for the fact cannot be doubted that before any benevolent project whatever can gain the assent and support of community it must be understood, and its claims upon them canvassed and closely scrutinized, and in order that it be understood it must be talked about—and the public mind embued with the subject of its claims to favourable notice—then, and not before, the people will take sides, either approve or disapprove of it—and when they do so, will feel, that upon themselves must rest the responsibility whichever course they may take.

Had these meetings been thus fully attended, your committee think there is little doubt, that in the benefits resulting from them, their fondest anticipations would have been realized.

As before remarked, we feel that nothing is wanting upon this subject, but information, to be widely disseminated throughout the community. This information should go not only into the drawing room of the rich and influential—and the polite and fashionable circle—but it should find its way into every hamlet, into every farm house, and every hovel in the land. These are the places where the ruinous effects of intemperance are most deeply felt, and here it is that the dealer in ardent spirits, the arch enemy of the happiness and prosperity of his fellow mortal, holds almost undisputed sway.

It is a well known fact, that no sooner was the temperance effort commenced, and it was known that good results were flowing from the effort, than the rum maker, the rum vender, and the rum drinker,

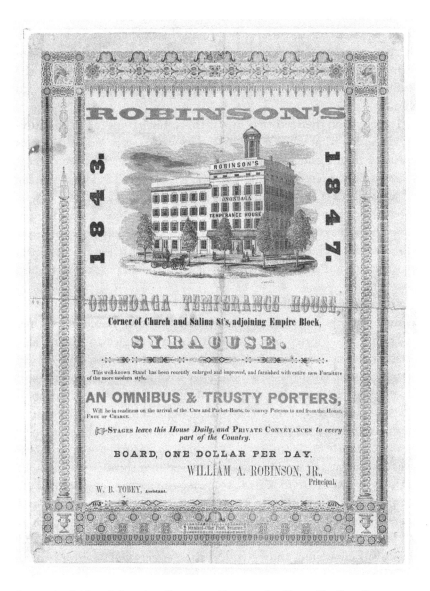

FIGURE 16. Robinson's Onondaga Temperance House, c. 1847. The proliferation of temperance societies in the Burned-over District encouraged entrepreneurs to organize alcohol-free establishments. In Syracuse, New York, teetotalers gathered in temperance meeting halls, shopped in temperance grocery stores, and boarded at temperance hotels like this one. (Library of Congress)

raised with one accord, their cry, long and loud against it. Here the tongue of hatred assails it, ascribing to it objects and ends of which its advocates never dreamed or thought. There the voice of derision and satire marches to the attack with all their bitterness and rancour. By this means the public mind, more particularly among the less informed classes of society, became embued with prejudices against the temperance measures, which nothing but correct information can eradicate.

The question then returns—how is this information to be communicated? And in what manner is it to find its way to every individual, so as to elicit a candid and impartial examination? It *is not*, let it be remarked, *it cannot* be expected that the plan of delivering addresses upon the subject will effect the desired object. This plan has had, and still has, its good effects; but it is well known that very few of those opposed to the temperance measures go to hear addresses, when delivered. Some are kept away by prejudice, whilst an increasing appetite for ardent spirits in others admonishes them, that it will disturb their peace of mind and conscience.

When they reflect, that by constant indulgence they have succeeded in hushing the voice of conscience, that this ever watchful centinel upon the moral watch tower in their bosom is lulled to silence, and ceases to warn, they feel comparatively easy, and shrink from a candid examination of their real situation. They wish not to be disturbed; and say by their conduct, that they are safe and contented to sleep upon the crumbling verge of the volcano, although liable at every moment to break and precipitate them to the depths below—simply because their eyes are shut. It has been justly said that the press is the great moral lever that moves the world—and it is believed that through the medium of the press, we are to look in a great measure for the accomplishment of our wishes in this respect. Let information, such as anecdotes, and plain matters of fact, illustrative of the dire evils of intemperance in the form of pamphlets, tracts, circulars and news papers be freely and extensively circulated, and we believe their effects will be most benign and salutary.

In this way information will seek out (if we so speak,) the individual, however unwilling he may be to meet it, and commune with it.—Yes, it will seek him out, and reason with him—tell him of the evils of intemperance—of what is doing in other places to avert or counteract the evil, and address a warning admonition to his understanding and conscience. He may at first determine that he will read nothing upon the subject, but let the paper lie by him and around him, and meet his eye at every turn, and he is a strange being, that will long hold out and learn nothing of its contents.

Whilst upon the subject the committee feel a peculiar pleasure in recommending to the favourable notice of every one, the Temperance Recorder, a paper issued monthly, and published under the patronage and immediate direction of the State Temperance Society. This publication, from the low terms upon which it is offered to subscribers, from the extent of its circulation and character of the matter contained in its columns, brings, it is believed the desired information within the reach of every individual. The terms are, one copy fifty cents per annum. Societies or individuals enclosing $5, postage paid, can receive 20 copies. $10, 40 copies,—and 100 copies for $25. What society, we ask, is there within the bounds of our county that cannot raise the sum of $5 or even $10 for an object like this?

Your committee can devise no better plan for the universal dissemination of the desired information than, that the executive committee of each auxiliary society, or individuals within their bounds raise by subscription or otherwise, all the funds possible for the purpose, and when the same is forwarded, let the names of individuals in each school district within the bounds of the society be designated to whom the publication may be directed, and whose duty it shall be, whenever a number comes to hand, after having read it, to hand it to his neighbor with a request that he would read it and put it in circulation and keep it circulating until every individual within the School district shall have an opportunity of learning its contents. But this is a mere suggestion, and as such only is communicated. Each town society can doubtless devise the best manner in which the circulation can be made.

This publication comes to us under the patronage and sanction of names, the bare mention of which, is sufficient to silence every objection as to the motive of those who established, and now conduct it. At the head of its patrons stands the chancellor of our State, the enlightened statesman, the able jurist and the friend of philanthropy and virtue.

There are many other papers in the State which are doing vast good in the Cause of Temperance, and highly deserve the patronage of every one.

Your Committee have learned with pleasure from the Col. of the squadron of Light Dragoons in our county, that their last general review was performed with perfect order, cheerfulness, and good feelings, both by officers and soldiers, without the aid of any stimulus than patriotism, and that sense of duty to themselves and their country which ought to actuate every freeman, and that not a drop of any other kind of spirits was brought upon the ground. We have heard the same of other military corps, within the County, but have had no *authentic* information upon the subject.

Your Committee think they can present the subject in no clearer or more favourable light, than by referring to the several town reports that have been received, and making short extracts from the most interesting parts of them. They shall also notice the societies from which no reports have been received, by advertising to the last annual report of this society. This will be done in a great measure for the purpose of giving to the State Society the "Post Office address" of each town society, as far as practicable, that each may have the benefit of the gratuitous distribution of publications from the State Society.

They therefore commence with the town of Auburn.

In this town there are four Societies.

1. "Auburn Temperance Society" was organized in July, 1831, and now numbers about 866 members.
    'There are in the village, it is believed, nineteen groceries, at fourteen of which ardent spirits are daily sold to be drank within the establishment, in open and direct violation of the law of the land, and in violation of the bonds given by some of their owners at the time of receiving their license. Your committee are credibly informed that at some of these groceries the proprietors are in the habit of keeping an open house and selling ardent spirits on the Sabbath, in violation, not only of every principle of religion and morality, but of the statute law of the state in which we live.—Your committee in reference to this subject would only ask why justice, and the law of the land are suffered to sleep when their principles are violated? Why is it not the penalty enforced against the offender?' Post office address, Auburn, N.Y.

2. "The Young men's Temperance Society" was organized Sept. 25th, 1830—118 members in 1831.*

3. The "Temperance Society of Auburn Theological Seminary" was formed June 26th, 1828. This society is not Auxillary [Auxiliary].*

4. The "Auburn States Prison Temperance Society" was organized August, 1831. Not auxiliary.* "Post office address, Auburn N.Y."

Aurelius has three Societies.

1. "Aurelius Temperance Society" was formed in May, 1830—Post office address "East Cayuga, N.Y."*
2. The "Clarksville Temperance Society" was formed July, 1831— Post office address, "Auburn, N.Y."*
3. The "Fosterville Temperance Society" was organized, as the committee are informed during the past year. Post office address, "Fosterville, N.Y."*

The "Brutus Temperance Society" was formed October 29th, 1831. Present number of members about 100. Post office address, "Weeds Port, N.Y."

The "Conquest Temperance Society" was organized Dec. 8th, 1831. Post Office address, "Conquest, N.Y."

The 'Fleming Temperance Society' was formed Aug. 5th, 1831. Number of members about 60. P.O. address, 'Fleming, N.Y.' The Report says "There are in this town four Inns which retail ardent spirits—there are two stores in town, one of which discontinued the sale of ardent spirits last year, and the other this year," &c.

Genoa has three Societies

1. The "Genoa Society for the promotion of Temperance" (at Northville,) was organized Aug. 18, 1828. Present number of members 184, having an increase of 94 since last Report. Post Office address, "Kings Ferry, N.Y."

From the Report we learn, "The Temperance Reformation has strongly altered the aspect of affairs in this section since 1828. Then in Northville, there were three stores and one Tavern, all of which sold spirits by small measure; now no spirits are to be had except at the Tavern, and there the sales have depreciated one half; then it was no disgrace for a man to get drunk,—even the confirmed drunkard who is but a wreck of those times still floating on the subsiding wave—steals away silently and alone, ashamed to be seen in his degraded infamy. Then a young man could scarcely hope to become a favorite with his comrades and in society without sustaining the character of a "good fellow for a scrape," now it has become a title which few are found to covet; then our farmers, without an exception made use of spirits in their harvest fields, and kept it in their houses; and indeed they could scarcely do otherwise, for without it they could not procure laborers; now not one, even the drunkard himself dares carry it into the field or offer it to his hands. Then intemperance could claim a victim in almost every house, and death almost every month,—now prosperity at every door proclaims with clarion voice,—Temperance, temperance is here."

2. The "East Genoa Temperance Society" was organized Jan. 25, 1833. Number of members 46. It held a Temperance meeting on the 26th Feb. Last, when as the report says, "a goodly number *eased* their minds by giving their name to the Temperance cause." Doct. D. Barber of Genoa, Merchant, has discontinued the traffic in ardent spirits. Post Office Address, "East Genoa N.Y."

3. The "East Genoa Youths' Temperance Society" was formed Aug. 30, 1831. Number of members 121—when first formed it had but 8 members.

The Ira & Cato Temperance Society; has lately divided into two, one of which is called "The Ira Temperance Society" Post Office address, "Ira, N.Y."

The other is called "The Temperance Society of the town of Cato." It was formed Feb. 22, 1833. Post Office address, "Cato 4 Corners, N.Y." The numbers of members in both Societies, are 529 who live up to their pledge; Increase since last May, 100. Number of school districts, 6. No distilleries discontinued out of principle,—one burned—none in operation. Three stores that do not sell ardent spirits, and three that do sell; one Temperance Inn kept by Mr. Jonas H. Titus of Ira—and 8 in which ardent spirits are sold. In these societies the 26th Feb. Last was observed.

The Ledyard Society for the promotion of Temperance, was formed Sept. 15th, 1831—present number of members 138, an increase of 28 since Nov. 20th, 1832. No school district societies in the town of Ledyard. One distillery in operation for the manufacture of Cider Brandy. Three Stores which do not sell ardent Spirits, kept by Messrs. Wood and Brownell, C.E. and J. Shepherd, and Geo. H. Hamm. Ardent Spirits are sold in all the Inns. The 26th Feb. Was observed by this society, and the meeting attended by between 3 and 400 persons. The Report further says;—"There are three Tavern keepers in the town of Ledyard at the present time, all of whom sell ardent spirits. The number of persons who have been Inn keepers in the town is not known to us, but the proportion who have been successful is very small, in our opinion."

Locke has two Societies.

1. The Locke Temperance Society (at Summer Hill) was formed July 15th, 1830. This society was formed before the division of the town of Locke, and is now mostly in the town of Summer Hill, but yet retains its old name. Number of members 245. Post Office address, "Summer Hill, N.Y."
2. The Milan Temperance Society was organized January, 1832, with 14 members amidst great opposition. It now numbers 103 members—increase 89. In this town there is one distillery in operation. Two stores, neither of which sell ardent spirits. "On the 26th Feb. last, an address was delivered to the Society, at which meeting there were probably 300 persons attended." At the late annual meeting, measures were taken for having an address delivered in each of the School districts in this town, which is being accomplished with much apparent good." Post Office address, "Locke, N.Y."

Mentz has three Societies.

1. The Mentz Temperance Society (at Port Byron) was organized Nov. 1831. Post Office address, "Port Byron, N.Y."*
2. A Society at "Centre Port."*
3. "the Throopsville Temperance Society" was organized Nov. 15th, 1831. Number of members 160—the report says "We have within the limits of our society, one tavern, and one distillery, lately erected and one discontinued and converted into a tannery." Post Office address, 'Throopsville, N.Y.'

"The Oswasco Temperance Society" was organized May 14th, 1831. Post Office address, "Oswasco, N.Y."*

Sennett has two Societies.

1. "The Senate Temperance Society" was formed Nov. 15th, 1831. Post Office address, "Brutus, N.Y."*
2. The young people's Temperance Society of Sennett and Brutus, was formed Feb. 25th, 1832, with 25 members—it now numbers 93 members. Post Office Address, "Brutus, N.Y."

The Scipio Temperance Society was organized Sept. 24th, 1831. Present number of members 175—increase since last report 75. The Society also reports one School district society in this town, numbering upwards of 100 members. Post Office address, "The Square, N.Y."
Sempronius has five Societies.

1. "The Moravia Temperance Society" was formed July, 1830. Present number of members 140. Post Office address, "Sempronius, N.Y."
2. The Sempronious Young People's Temperance Society was formed Sept. 1831. Present number of members 150. Post Office address, "Sempronius, N.Y."
3. The East Sempronius Temperance Society has 60 members. Post Office address, "East Sempronius, N.Y."
4. The "Kelloggs Ville Temperance Society" has 82 members. Post Office address, "Kellogg's Ville, N.Y."
5. The West Hill Temperance Society has 100 members. The report says, "There are four stores kept, in which ardent spirits are not sold, and six stores that sell spirits. There are nine public houses in town, all of which sell ardent spirits."

Sterling has two societies.

1. The "Sterling Temperance Society" was organized August 24th, 1829. Post Office address, "Sterling, N.Y."*
2. The "Sterling Young People's Society" was formed August 10th, 1831. Post Office Address, "Sterling, N.Y."*

Victory has two Societies.

1. The "Victory Union Temperance Society" was organized July, 1830—not auxiliary. Post Office address, "Victory, N.Y."

2.   "The Victory Young People's Society" was formed Nov. 1830. Present number of members 177. This society has lately become auxiliary to the County Society. This society reports a tavern kept by a man of "better principles," who fain would turn the monster Intemperance out of doors, had he not "A family to support"—and also two Temperance Stores.

All which is submitted.
J.H. BEACH, *President.*
A. GOULD, *Sec'y.*
*No report since last year.

FORTY-NINE

A Sabbatarian Convention

Source: "Sabbath Convention at Geneva," *Geneva (NY) Gazette*, December 28, 1836.

Early Americans believed that the health and well-being of the American republic rested on a virtuous population. Accordingly, the same Christians who celebrated revivalism also fretted over spotty attendance at Sunday worship services. Where else but in church would Americans receive the moral instruction necessary for good republican governance?

The following report from the 1836 "Sabbath Convention" articulated key tenets of Sabbatarianism, the Christian practice of observing Sunday as a day for worship and rest. The report explained the meaning and purpose of the Sabbath as well as the convention participants' growing concern that the "business habits of our countrymen" discouraged Sabbath observance. Like their counterparts in the temperance movement, these Sabbatarians grappled with how to address this problem of Sabbath neglect. Moral suasion? Public education? Political action? What was the right way—the Christian way—to promote social change?

✷ ✷ ✷

Sabbath Convention at Geneva

At the hour to which the Convention had been called, a highly respectable body of gentlemen appeared from this and the adjoining counties, and a large congregation from the village and neighborhood. The Hon. Jacob Sutherland, of Geneva was chosen President, and Walter Hubbell, Esq. of Canandaigua, Secretary.

The meeting was opened with prayer, by Rev. E. Johns, of Canandaigua.

Mr. Dwight, of Geneva, one of the gentlemen calling the Convention, stated that its object was to promote a better observance of the Sabbath in the community generally; that our weapons thereto were moral influence, thro' example and instruction—that much had already been accomplished—that respectable men were seldom seen travelling on the Sabbath—that the conscience of the church needs to be quickened—the public mind to be enlightened in respect to what the Sabbath does for man, and especially in respect to the subject of investing property where it will be used in violating of the Sabbath. He said that to expedite the proceedings of the Convention, a series of resolutions had been prepared, which would be read by Rev. M. P. Squier, and that in the evening an additional series of resolutions would be presented by Hon. S.M. Hopkins.

Mr. Squier, then read the resolutions, as follows:

Resolved, That this Convention regard the Sabbath as a divine institution, mercifully appointed of God, for the benefit of man, and that the faithful, religious observance of it is commended by our sense of the authority of God, and of his goodness towards us.

Resolved, That independently of the value of the Sabbath to the purposes of religion, to which it is unquestionably indispensable, we regard the rest which it provides as needful for both man and beast, and recognise the constitution of nature, and the arrangements of Providence, as coinciding with the revealed injunction—"Remember the Sabbath day to keep it holy."

Resolved, That we regard the Sabbath, viewed as a day devoted to moral and religious instruction, reading, reflection and prayer, to be of incalculable importance to community at large, and to every interest of the social state of man.

Resolved, That we see no real good promoted, public or private, by infringing upon the Sabbath in the intercourse, business and pursuits of this world, but on the other hand, are fully confident, that much is gained every way, by confining them to the "six days" of the week, which by divine appointment are allotted to them: that society at large, without disparagement, may enjoy the rest of the Sabbath day, and that all would hereby be better prepared to fulfill the duties, owed from man to man, and to sustain in common all the relations of this world.

Resolved, That we contemplate with deep regret and anxiety, the tendencies to increased desecration of the Sabbath, in our own country at the present day; and we feel constrained to entreat all who regard the virtue and happiness of their fellow men, to give attention to this subject—to look to the moral degradation of those countries, where the Sabbath has lost its hold on the public mind, or where its light has never shone; and to give their personal influence, and their united efforts, in every consistent and proper way, in behalf of the more uniform regard of that sacred day.

Resolved, That we feel obliged to enumerate, as among the more common and open violations of the Sabbath—travelling, journeying in public or private conveyances on that day; the transporting and opening of the mails, and the conveyance and discharge of goods and merchandise upon the great thoroughfares of the State. And we do much deprecate the continuance of these things, and implore of all who may be concerned in them or in other forms of the violation of the Sabbath, to reflect on the injury to which they may be accessory to the public morals of the community, and to all the objects for which the benevolence of God has consecrated the Sabbath day.

Resolved, That we highly approve of the decision of those rail road companies, who have determined that their property shall not be used in violation of the Sabbath; and that we do, with much interest in the subject, recommend it to the Directors of other rail roads, formed or in contemplation, to follow this laudable example.

Resolved, That we invite the serious attention of men of business, and our fellow-citizens generally, to the importance of the preservation and the due observance of the Sabbath, to all the *civil* and *social* institutions of our country.

On motion of Henry Bradley, Esq., of Penn-Yan, seconded by D.W. Forman, of Seneca Falls, these resolutions were taken up article by article. When by a separate vote on each, they were all carried without dissent as the unanimous voice of the convention.

The passing of the above resolutions, which occupied the afternoon and a part of the evening, called forth much interesting and instructive expression of sentiment and comparison of views, well calculated to promote the design of the meeting, and fix in all present, a deep conviction of the unyielding claims and importance of the Sabbath day. The following gentlemen favored the meeting with addresses, during the passage of the above resolutions: Henry Wells and Henry Bradly, Esqrs., of Penn-Yan; Rev. E. Johns, of Canandaigua; Rev. Mr. Griswold, of Prattsburgh, Steuben county, and Samuel M. Hopkins, Esq., and Rev. Messrs. McLaren and Squier, of Geneva.

Mr. Hopkins rose to offer some further resolutions, which, as they did not chiefly regard the Sabbath in its most sacred and elevated character, he was desirous to introduce some explanations.

There are two ways of conducting these discussions and two classes of persons to whom we may address ourselves. We may collect an assembly of christians, like the present, who love the day as a joy and blessing, and reverence it as a divine institution: these we may address upon its divine and sanctifying influences on the heart of the christian; all this they believe and have felt before; they will go away as they came, believing it still, and as to any general effect upon the community, we shall remain as we were.

Yet it had been well remarked by the gentleman who opened the debate (Mr. Dwight) that we are a small minority who thus believe. The immense majority are not with us. And yet it depends on that majority whether the Sabbath shall be publicly observed or obliterated from all public observance. Mr. Hopkins said it was his solemn conviction, that we were now arrived at a crisis in the state of public manners which must soon determine that point.

There is, he said, another and much larger class of persons to whom we may appeal on every point of right, and duty, and benevolence and public spirit, which regards the life that now is. They do justice among men; and their fault is that they walk not humbly towards God. To such he apprehended we should do right to appeal; and to appeal to them on the motives by which they may be influenced: on motives derived from humanity, worldly morals, education, public improvement, and especially political liberty. He conceived that we had the express authority of the gospel, and the constant usage of the christian ministry for enforcing the benefits of our religious institutions, as well in respect to the "life that now is," as to that which "is to come."

But he thought it a matter of high duty on the part of christians, neither to let down the claims of the day to secular interests chiefly, *nor to appear to do so*. Christians must uphold it as divine. But in that same sense none but the church will sympathise with them. If we were to save the day from public desecration and neglect, that must be done, to all present appearance, by appeals to the consciences of others. He believed that such an appeal could be made in a manner which ought to be convincing. And the resolutions he would now offer, embraced a system of ideas, which he had some feeble hope would tend to that result.

1. *Resolved*, That as the Sabbath was made for man, so the greatest benefits of it, are those which regard the highest interests of man, that is his eternal interests; that the sanctions of the Sabbath is the express and revealed command of God: that its uses are mainly and chiefly the improvement of man in his spiritual preparation: that to those who regard the day, it is not a burden but a blessing, and the foretaste of a better rest; and that those who entertain these views of it, can never compromise them by placing the sanction of the day on lower authority, nor by treating it as chiefly an institution for temporal benefit. Nevertheless—

2. *Resolved*, That the Sabbath was also made for man in all his interests and relations: not only for bodily and mental rest, and for mercy to all that labor, but also as essential to the security of social and political blessings. And as unhappily there are large and influential portions of our fellow citizens who do not practically reverence the institution as divine, it is right and proper to present a universal appeal to such, upon the influence of the Sabbath on the intellectual condition of man and on worldly morals, on civilization, on social happiness, and on political liberty. In those points of view this Convention respectfully submit to the candor of their fellow-citizens of all creeds and sections the following

Propositions

1. That in all past experience, mankind have been held under the necessary restraints of government, chiefly by three means— 1st. Absolute force: 2d. Superstitious terrors: and 3d. A sense of moral obligation. The first produces despotism; the second,

idolatry and priestcraft; and the third depends on notions, more or less clear, of right and wrong, and constantly tends towards liberty, civil, religious and political.

2. That a general sense of moral obligation has never been long preserved among any people, without assiduous moral inculcation; nor has *that* been effectual, except where the principles of morals had a sanction in the general belief of the government of a just Supreme Power. And where moral duties have not been so taught and sanctioned, mankind have been sunk in barbarism or in slavish subjection; the female sex have been grossly degraded; the domestic affections little known, and fraud, pollution, perjury, oppression and cruelty, little restrained.

3. That neither the art of printing, nor the great and early discoveries in science, nor immense population, wealth and resources, nor the highest national stability from early ages, nor all combined, have been able to save nations from the lowest degradation of vice and slavery, where morals were wanting.

4. That there is not, at present, any example known, of improvement in the condition of any people, without the influence of the Sabbath and its kindred institutions. And the general present tendency of nations, which are without this influence, is retrograde; the savage growing more savage, and the partly civilized, more corrupt.

5. That if knowledge, without virtue, is power, it is chiefly so for purposes of evil.

6. That since the publication of Christianity, there has been no political liberty, except within its pale; and since the reformation, almost no free institutions, except among Protestants. And that at the present moment, the influence of liberty throughout the world, is in exact proportion to the light of Christianity in its true and genuine meaning.

7. That to any substantial purpose there is not now in the world, any arrangement for the general teaching of moral duties, except through the Sabbath; and with very slight exceptions, no morals taught except those of Christianity. And this Convention appeal to the candor of all men, whether in the present state of mankind, there is any prospect of any new system of morals, or better plan of teaching; and whether any

such new system can be expected to have a better influence upon mankind, than the Gospel is adapted to exercise.

8. The experience of the world, therefore, shows that public liberty and national improvement cannot be without public morals; nor morals without a sanction. Moral duties cannot be competently taught, except at stated, general and public assemblies of the people; nor can such assemblies be sufficiently universal, unless business is generally suspended; and in these different circumstances together appears, *in part*, the philosophy of the Sabbath. And if no Sabbath had been previously known, and it were now first given, the command would be more important to the temporal interests of man, than all human improvements collectively.

9. That the active and business habits of our countrymen are, at present, drawing vast numbers of the youth, and of the laboring population into employments which allow no day of rest; which cut them off from the improvement, and which bring them into associations where they mutually corrupt and are corrupted. Men of business are also drawn into violations of the Sabbath by the seeming necessities of business. Pious men who will not yield to this, are more and more driven from the pursuits of commerce and all public occupations; and all these occupations are now rapidly tending to deprive great and increasing numbers of our citizens of the benefit of this institution.

10. That as man needs the elaborate training of education, for every pursuit, whether of science or activity, so he needs it especially for infixing those moral principles which guard him against the illusions of interest, passion and appetite. But men, who, by their votes, have in their hands the destiny of nations and the hopes of free governments, more especially need intelligence and honesty. And if increasing numbers of our youth are to grow up, as they now begin to do, without any competent sense of moral duties and in great ignorance: and if our vast and populous nation is soon to be governed by *such* a democracy, then this Convention would solemnly ask what hope we can have to escape from scenes of calamity and desolation, of prostration and ruin—final degradation and slavery, such as the world has seldom witnessed. Therefore,

3. *Resolved,* That fully believing the truth of these propositions, this Convention submit them to the candor of their countrymen. And if the opinions here expressed are substantially true, this Convention earnestly appeal to all men of all creeds—to patriots, philanthropists, and men of business—to all who love our common country, or feel an interest in the dignity and improvement of human nature and the prospects of posterity—to join in one great effort to save our country and her liberty, civilization and improvements, from ruin that must follow the general prostration of morals.

These resolutions, after appropriate addresses from Messrs. Hopkins, Johns, Griswold, McLaren and Hubbell, were unanimously adopted.

On motion of Henry Bradley, Esq., seconded by Rev. M.L.R.P. Thompson, of Canandaigua,

Resolved, As the sense of this Convention, that the taking of papers and letters from the post-office on the Sabbath, is a violation of the fourth commandment, very much to be deplored.

On motion of H. Dwight:

Resolved, That editors of newspapers be requested to publish the doings of this Convention, and that this request be extended to clergymen, to read the same from their pulpits, on some convenient Sabbath, and that a copy be furnished for this purpose, signed by the President and Secretary.

The meeting was closed with prayer, by the Rev. John F. McLaren, of Geneva.

JACOB SUTHERLAND, *Pres't.*

FIFTY

The Anti-Rent Wars

Source: "Equal Rights," *Albany Freeholder*, August 6, 1845.

While pioneers poured into central and western New York to purchase land for farming, thousands of farmers in the Hudson River Valley continued to rent the land they worked. Some of these tenant farmers had worked the same land for generations, paying rents to land barons who had secured their titles from the Dutch West India Company or the English crown in the seventeenth century. These tenants were not necessarily poor, but they were economic dependents, reliant on their landlords for access to acreage, firewood, water rights, and housing. Hudson Valley tenant farmers shared with the New England pioneers a dream of owning the ground they worked.

On July 4, 1839, the tenants of the estate of Stephen Van Rensselaer IV drafted a petition demanding lower rents, debt relief, and a path to landownership. When Van Rensselaer rejected their demands, the petitioners became protesters. They assembled militias to defend themselves against forced eviction and organized politically to advance their cause with the New York State government. Although the Anti-Rent War (1839–1845) started in the Hudson River Valley, the tenants gained support with working people across the state. They popularized their cause in newspapers and joined with other landless workers to endorse political candidates who championed their call for economic fairness. In the following poem, "Equal Rights," published in the anti-rent newspaper the *Albany Freeholder* in 1846, the anti-renters made an explicitly Christian argument for land reform in New York.

❧ ❧ ❧

(*For the Freeholder.*)
EQUAL RIGHTS

We know and feel that we are men
Of Heavenly mould, high-born and free;
A part of all, that e'er has been,
A part of all, that e'er shall be;
Tho' fettered to this earthly clod,
We know we are the sons of God.
All sons of God-alike we bear,
The image of our common sin.
All sons of God? We then should share
Alike his bounty, and acquire
An equal right to all that's given,
By the impartial hand of Heaven.
Then holy is our cause, and just,
While equal freedom we proclaim;
We know it will prevail, it *must,*
Or justice be an empty name.
Then on! Press on for equal laws;
The God of Justice owns our cause.
Ye proud oppressors! calm your rage;
Your spell is broke, your hope is vain
To "Lord it o'er God's heritage."
Shall sons of God be slaves of men?
Our God Forbid! We *will* be free,
Or die in the cause of liberty.

FIFTY-ONE

Selections from New York's 1846 Constitution

Source: New York [State] et al., *The Constitution of the State of New York: With Notes, References and Annotations, together with the Articles of Confederation, Constitution of the United States, New York State Constitutions of 1777, 1821, 1846, Unamended and as Amended and in Force in 1894, with an Index of the Revised Constitution and the Constitution of the United States* (Albany: J. B. Lyon, 1894),103–26.

New York's 1846 constitution embodied the democratizing impulse of the era. For example, Article XIII normalized constitutional referendums and established procedures for vicennial constitutional review and reform—a practice that continues today. It affirmed the people's rights to assemble and petition, and thereby endorsed the grassroots activism of working people, temperance and Sabbatarian advocates, and other reformers and activists. It addressed the anti-rent agrarian insurrection by formally abolishing "feudal tenures." Finally, this constitution took additional steps to broaden the white electorate, but also affirmed the property-holding qualifications for the Black electorate.

In a speech on the convention floor, delegate Churchill Cambrelling, a farmer from Long Island, called the new constitution "the first constitution ever formed that rested, not nominally, but in fact, on a popular foundation—which made your legislative, judicial and executive departments, distinct in reality as well as in name, and all of them springing directly from the people."[1] The excerpt featured here showcases many of the democratic reforms that the 1846 constitution enshrined as state law.

✻ ✻ ✻

The Constitution of the State of New-York

WE THE PEOPLE of the State of New-York, grateful to Almighty God for our freedom: in order to secure its blessings, DO ESTABLISH this Constitution

Article 1

[. . .]

Section 7. When private property shall be taken for any public use, the compensation to be made therefor, when such compensation is not made by the State, shall be ascertained by a jury, or by not less than three commissioners appointed by a court of record, as shall be prescribed by law. Private roads may be opened in the manner to be prescribed by law; but in every case the necessity of the road, and the amount of all damage to be sustained by the opening thereof, shall be first determined by a jury of freeholders, and such amount, together with the expenses of the proceeding, shall be paid by the person to be benefitted.

Section 8. Every citizen may freely speak, write, and publish his sentiments on all subjects, being responsible for the abuse of that right; and no law shall be passed to restrain or abridge the liberty of speech, or of the press. In all criminal prosecutions or indictments for libels, the truth may be given in evidence to the jury; and if it shall appear to the jury, that the matter charged as libellous is true, and was published with good motives, and for justifiable ends, the party shall be acquitted; and the jury shall have the right to determine the law and the fact.

Section 9. The assent of two-thirds of the members elected to each branch of the Legislature, shall be requisite to every bill appropriating the public moneys or property for local or private purposes.

Section 10. No law shall be passed, abridging the right of the people peaceably to assemble and to petition the government, or any

---

1. *Report of the Debates and Proceedings of the Convention for the Revision of the Constitution of the State of New York: 1846* (Albany: Printed at the office of the Evening Atlas, 1846), 110.

department thereof, nor shall any divorce be granted, otherwise than by due judicial proceedings, nor shall any lottery hereafter be authorized or any sale of lottery tickets allowed within this State.

Section 11. The People of this State, in their right of sovereignty, are deemed to possess the original and ultimate property in and to all lands within the jurisdiction of the State; and all lands the title to which shall fail, from a defect of heirs, shall revert, or escheat to the people.

Section 12. All feudal tenures of every description, with all their incidents, are declared to be abolished, saving however, all rents and services certain which at any time heretofore have been lawfully created or reserved.

Section 13. All lands within this State are declared to be allodial, so that, subject only to the liability to escheat, the entire and absolute property is vested in the owners according to the nature of their respective estates.

Section 14. No lease or grant of agricultural land, for a longer period than twelve years, hereafter, made in which shall be reserved any rent or service of any kind, shall be valid. [. . .]

Article II

SECTION 1. Every male citizen of the age of twenty-one years, who shall have been a citizen for ten days, and an inhabitant of this State one year next preceding any election, and for the last four months a resident of the county where he may offer his vote, shall be entitled to vote at such election in the election district of which he shall at the time be a resident, and not elsewhere, for all officers that now are or hereafter may be elective by the people; but such citizen shall have been for thirty days next preceding the election, a resident of the district from which the officer is to be chosen for whom he offers his vote. But no man of color, unless he shall have been for three years a citizen of this State, and for one year next preceding any election shall have been seized and possessed of a freehold estate of the value of two hundred and fifty dollars, over and above all debts and incumbrances charged thereon, and shall have been actually rated and paid a tax thereon, shall be entitled to vote at such election. And no person of color shall be subject to direct taxation unless he shall be seized and possessed of such real estate as aforesaid [. . .]

Section 3. For the purpose of voting, no person shall be deemed to have gained or lost a residence, by reason of his presence or absence, while employed in the service of the United States; nor while engaged in the navigation of the waters of this State, or of the United States, or of the high seas; nor while a student of any seminary of learning; nor while kept at any alms house, or other asylum, at public expense; nor while confined in any public prison.

Section 4. Laws shall be made for ascertaining by proper proofs the citizens who shall be entitled to the right of suffrage hereby established.

Section 5. All elections by the citizens shall be by ballot, except for such town officers as may by law be directed to be otherwise chosen. [. . .]

FIFTY-TWO

Abijah Beckwith's Consideration of Civil Rights for Women

Source: Abijah Beckwith Papers, #2513, Division of Rare and Manuscript Collections, Cornell University Library.

As an elected official, Abijah Beckwith championed some of the more "progressive" causes of the antebellum era: the Erie Canal, religious liberty, and the expansion of the franchise. He also fiercely opposed slavery. He predicted in 1846 that if enslaved people in the South "make a bold strike for freedom," then "the north will not readily take sides with the masters to restrain them in their Tyranny and oppression." When the New York State Democratic Party did not, in fact, stand up to the Southern slavocracy, Beckwith renounced his party and affiliated with the Free Soil Party.

Beckwith believed his philosophy of government aligned perfectly with the Revolutionary era's principles of democracy and liberty, but he was conflicted about how to apply these same principles to the political status of women. In this 1851 letter to his daughter, Beckwith wrestled with the question of women's civil rights. His candor serves as a reminder of the limits of democratic reform in otherwise progressive New York State.

𝕤 𝕤 𝕤

As to the question of Womens rights, which has of late been much discussed, considering it as an abstract question of mere right, I have no
doubt but they are entitled to all the civil and political rights, equally
with the men, and <as> a general rule, when we admit a thing as right
in principal, it is verry difficult to show that its application would be
wrong. Still this may be an exception to the general rule. It has been
often said that a majority of our women do not wish to have the right
of voting at our Elections extended to them; but this is no proof that
those who wish wish to vote should be deprived of the right, as it would
not be compulsive on those who did not wish to exercise it, The great
question seems to me, to be would the right of voting, and holding political offices equally with the men, improve their condition and add to
their comfort and happiness? Would the condition of society and our
social relations be improved by it? Would family friendships and the
close ties of consanguinity, so Essential to the happiness of all civilized
communities be improved by it? These questions I have not examined
with sufficient care to have made up my mind deffinitely, But am en-
clined to think that we are better off as we now are, than we should be if
our women enjoyed and exercised all the rights th equally with the men
and held their share of the offices, I readily admit that our women are
capable, and in this respect are equal with the men, and if they should
make politicks a studdy we should find as good politicians among our
women as we do among our men. But if they should turn their attention to the studdy of politicks they would be more likely to neglect the
important duty of training our children, and when they are neglected
we shall commence to retrograde, Our men pay but little attention to
training the minds of boys until they are some twelve years old, and
then their object usually is to prepare them to make active thorough
business men, or in other words to make money, The girls are usually
wholly under the care of our women, It is from our women that our
children of both sexes, learn those fine feeling of sympathy and friendship, of modesty and self respect, and pride of character acquired by virtuous action, in short to "do as they would wish to be done by" which
is the *essence* of Morality and the best rule of politeness, If our women
were to turn politicians would they not teach politicks instead of what
they now teach, again in all our gathering where we are associated together, the presence of women make the company social pleasant and
agreeable The subject of politicks is seldom mentioned, and the savage
temper of our men is softened, would it be so if our women took the

same interest in politicks that our men do,? There is no subject which rouses the savage propensity of our men like that <of> politicks it has been the cause of most <many> of the duells which have been fought, Would it not have the same affect on our women, if they were to vote and hold office? Would it not be likely to change their habits of thinking, and to change their fine modest and amiable dispo and femenine dispositions, to that of the more savage and masculine, Again, in exciting political contests if the Husband took one side of the question and was about to vote one way and the wife the other, would it not disturb that unity and close friendship which ought to exist between husband and wife, <and> which is so essential to good society and our well being? All experience has shown that whenever our women enter with warmth into any controversity, that they have the use of that unruly member, the tounge [tongue], at least to as great an Extent as our men, and a controversity of this nature between husband and wife would not be likely to add to their happiness, or to the good of their family, and these social relations by at the are the foundation of good society, let them be disturbed and you sap the foundation of civilized government.

When I commenced I had no idea of writing this long story about children and women, and know not why I have gone into it, unless it be is because I am writing to a woman. I have not studdied this, have wrote rappidly such ideas as came into my mind without any studdy or effort, not expecting they will be read except by yourself and perhaps some particular friends—

Columbia Nov—7–1851.

Your Father
ABeckwith

The same subject continued

I wrote the previous article yesterday, and thinking of your Mother and of Mothers and women generally, and of their influence in society naturally led me to consider their rights, and when I concluded I supposed I had said all I had to say on the subject, But I last night received a paper Edited by a Missis [Jane] Swisshelm, a german lady I believe, containing the proceedings of a Woman's Rights convention held at Worcester, lately, at which letters were read from distinguished persons of both sexes, of our own country, and one from Miss Martineau dated in England, from which it appears the subject is discussed there as well as here, It probably will be more or less discussed during your life and may become a subject of general agitation, I give you my views from a hasty Examination of the subject, but without <a> wish to dictate, or prejudice your mind one way or the other,

If women were allowed to vote at the Elections and to hold Office the same as men do, it would put them on Equal footing, as all other rights would follow as a matter of course, I have already admitted that considering it as an abstract right, ther can be no doubt but ~~our women~~ <they> ought to enjoy each and all the rights Equally with the men, And because they have not ~~heretofore~~ in any community heretofore enjoyed these rights, it is no argument with me that they should not now enjoy them, I have ever been a reformer, and am not afraid of changes. The question with me is not what has been done, but what ought to be done.

It is a well settled principal with us, That the government derives all its just powers from the governed, And that all those who are to be governed by the laws, and are compelled to pay their portion of the expences, should be allowed to vote for all the Officers who constitute and administer the government, And that equal benefits & equal burthens <ought to> Extend to all, And this seems to be a plain commonsence rule of justice. Still our women are subject to all our laws, (Except such as confer special privileges on ~~on~~ our men) <And> to the pains and penelties of our criminal code, and are compelled to pay there full share of taxes on all the property they possess, without having a right to vote for the Officers who constitute ~~ou~~ <and> administer the Government, This seems wrong, and at war with ~~the one~~ the fundamental principals of our government and institutions, and to plain common sence,

Still it is well to consider what would be the affect of the proposed change in its practical opperation, and the consequences likely to grow out <of> it, Nature has so ordered it, That some twenty years of the best portion of the lives <of most of> our women are spent in bringing forth and bringing up a family of children, True the mother might perhaps employ some other ~~person~~ <woman> to take charge of her child, but this would be a perversion of a plain natural principal, and if all mothers wished to take this course and abandon their children, to the care of others they could not find a number sufficient. (I have ~~Insisting~~ <already> alluded to the importans of the mothers training her own children,) It is the better part of wisdom to conform to natural principals, which we cannot alter and are in no way responsible for. Would not the holding of public Offices by our women, divert a portion of them, at least from a plain natural duty?

Again if women were allowed, in all respects, Equal rights with men, would not our <married> women claim an Equal right with their husbands in the controll and management of their joint property? a right to buy and sell, &c, and would not this lead to serious difficulty? It may be said that this would be regulated by marraige contracts, and by public opinion, still is <it> not reasonable to suppose that this matter would have to <be> regulated by law? And do we not know that people are very sensitive in all matters which relate to property? And if the question should come up in a legislature composed of both sexes should we not see the the men arraigned on one side trying to secure to the husband as the control of as large a portion of the property as possible, which on the other hand the women would <be> likely to be very anxious that the wife should be allowed to have the controll of at least the half, This would be at best an unpleasant controversy, But suppose it should be compromised allowing each to control the one half, Would not this lead to trouble and littigation between husband and wife?

Would not this question of the rights of husband + wife, in relation to property + other matters, enter into our Elections? And should we <not> see the men anxious to nominate and elect members to the legislature who would favor their side of the question? While on the other, <hand> the women would be striving to procure the nomination and Election of candidate who would favour their interests, This would be an unpleasant controversy and would unsettle and destroy all good society,

From the partial examination I have been able to give this question, since I commenced writing yestarday, (and I had not Examined it before) I consider it a troublesome question, and am not prepared to give an opinion,

Nov 8-1851   ABeckwith

PART VIII

Abolitionism and Ultraism in the Burned-over District

At the beginning of the nineteenth century, New York's abolition movement included men and women who represented diverse Christian denominations, social classes, and political ideologies. Some members of the movement were nationally prominent figures, such as Frederick Douglass, the Grimké sisters, and Gerrit Smith. Most were average members of their communities. Some joined the movement because they viewed slavery as a sin against God. Others did so because they resented federal policies that favored the South's slave economy over the North's free labor economy. All agreed that the United States would be stronger without slavery, but they disagreed—often publicly—about how to achieve this goal.[1]

Most white Americans preferred an abolition strategy that would not disrupt the country's economic, social, or political systems, and in the 1820s, many reformers believed the American Colonization Society offered such a peaceable solution. The Colonization Society raised funds to pay slaveholders to emancipate slaves who then agreed to resettle to West Africa, the Republic of Haiti, or another destination outside the United States. But by the 1830s, all Black abolitionists and a growing

---

1. Manisha Sinha, *The Slave's Cause: A History of Abolition* (New Haven, CT: Yale University Press, 2016), 195-96.

number of white abolitionists rejected this gradual, partial, and compensated approach. Instead, they demanded the immediate, total, and unconditional liberation of enslaved Black Americans. Equally important, the ultraists within the abolitionist movement adopted more confrontational tactics to put more pressure on the federal government to take a stand against the economic and political interests of slaveholders, derisively referred to as the Slave Power or slavocracy.² While religious revivalism in the state had grown church membership and fueled social reform, these reform movements in turn caused schisms within religious societies.

While the documents in part 7 explained the dual influence of Christian revivalism and democratization on New York politics, this final section focuses on the antebellum political and social context that led many antislavery activists to ultraism. In the opening document, an ordained minister in the African Methodist Episcopal Church, Thomas James, described his early antislavery activities. He also depicted the camaraderie he found with other antislavery activists (white and Black) as well as the violence he experienced at the hands of antiabolitionist mobs. The 1836 address by New York's Governor W. L. Marcy and the resolutions adopted by the New York Annual Conference of the Methodist Episcopal Church present arguments against abolitionism. They articulated the concerns of secular and religious leaders who feared the influence of ultraism within their respective spheres. In the prospectus of the abolitionist journal *The Friend of Man*, the editors responded to these rebukes and foreshadowed the future fracturing of political and denominational alliances.

Gerrit Smith features prominently in this part. His sincere and intense Presbyterian faith informed a lifetime of social activism and philanthropy. He championed abolition, temperance, the anti-Mason movement, civil rights for women, education access for Black Americans, and numerous other social, political, and religious causes. Smith moved slowly from the reformist wing to the ultra wing of the abolition movement, but once there, he worked feverishly to advance the cause. He presided over the 1835 and 1836 meetings of the New York State Anti-Slavery Society and organized petition drives. He denounced American churches for capitulating to the slavocracy, a view shared by Frederick Douglass, who would publish his own scathing critique of

2. Sinha, 461–68; Cross, *Burned-Over District*, 217–26.

the church the following year. Smith also expedited a religious schism within the Presbyterian Church with his financial and personal support of abolitionist churches.

This part concludes with the Reverend Samuel Ringgold Ward's account of the Jerry Rescue in 1851. William "Jerry" Henry was a fugitive slave who had lived securely in Syracuse for almost a decade when he was seized by federal marshals who came to the Burned-over District to enforce the newly enacted Fugitive Slave Act. Henry attempted to escape their grasp, but the marshals brutally subdued him in full view of a crowd that included members of the abolitionist Liberty Party. The arrest enraged party members and many other Syracuse citizens. It also affirmed the abolitionists' view that the federal government was a tool of the Slave Power.[3]

The Syracuse Vigilance Committee, an organization of volunteers charged with protecting free Blacks and fugitive slaves from forced deportation, acted quickly to develop a plan to rescue Henry. They led a mob to the jail, broke down the door with a battering ram, secured Henry, and kept him hidden in the city for several days before transporting him by wagon to Canada. This direct action energized and emboldened abolitionists across America. Years after the event, abolitionists would gather to celebrate "Jerry Rescue Day" on October 1 as a historical event that affirmed the righteousness of ultraism and justified direct action in the fight against slavery.[4]

3. Angela F. Murphy, *The Jerry Rescue: The Fugitive Slave Law, Northern Rights, and the American Sectional Crisis* (Oxford: Oxford University Press, 2016).

4. Murphy, *Jerry Rescue*.

FIFTY-THREE

Rev. Thomas James on Antislavery Activism

Source: Thomas James, *Life of Rev. Thomas James* (Rochester, NY: Post-Express Printing Co., 1886), 7–8, New-York Historical Society.

Thomas James escaped from a life of slavery in Canajoharie, New York, by fleeing to Canada for three months in 1821. Upon his return to the United States, he settled in Rochester, where he accepted work on the Erie Canal, learned to read and write, and then joined the African Methodist Episcopal Church. In 1827, the same year New York formally abolished slavery, James organized the AME Zion Church in Rochester. Six years later he was ordained to the ministry by Bishop Christopher Rush.

In 1831, James discovered the antislavery writings of Arthur Tappan, a Manhattan-based businessman and philanthropist who, with William Lloyd Garrison, founded the American Anti-Slavery Society. This discovery changed the trajectory of his life, prompting him to dedicate himself completely to abolition and civil rights. He vowed to never quit "until the colored man became the equal of the white in the eye of the law, if not in the sight of his neighbor of another race."

In this excerpt from his 1886 memoir, James looks back on his earliest antislavery activities in central New York. His account serves as a reminder that although New York was a "free state," its citizens did not universally embrace the abolitionist cause.

❧ ❧ ❧

[. . .]

In the early summer of 1833 we held the first of a series of anti-slavery meetings in the court house. The leading promoters of that meeting were William Bloss, Dr. Reid—whose widow now in the 86th year of her age still lives in Rochester—and Dr. W. Smith. There was a great crowd in attendance on the first night, but its leading motive was curiosity and it listened without interfering with the proceedings. The second night we were plied with questions, and on the third they drowned with their noise the voices of the speakers and finally turned out the lights. Not to be baulked of his purpose, Mr. Bloss, who was not a man to be cowed by opposition, engaged the session room of the Third Presbyterian church, but even there we were forced to lock the doors before we could hold our abolition meeting in peace. There we organized our anti-slavery society, and when the journals of the day refused to publish our constitution and by-laws, we bought a press for a paper of our own and appointed the three leaders already named to conduct it. It was printed fortnightly and was called *The Rights of Man*. I was sent out to make a tour of the county in its interest, obtaining subscriptions for the paper and lecturing against slavery. At Le Roy I was mobbed, my meeting was broken up and I was saved from worse treatment only by the active efforts of Mr. Henry Brewster, who secreted me in his own house. At the village I next visited, Warsaw, I was aided by Seth M. Gates and others, and I was also well received at Perry. At Pike, however, I was arrested and subjected to a mock trial, with the object of scaring me into flight from the place. At Palmyra I found no hall or church in which I could speak. Indeed, the place was then a mere hamlet and could boast of but half a dozen dwellings. My tour embraced nearly every village in this and adjoining counties, and the treatment given me varied with the kind of people I happened to find in the budding settlements of the time. In the same fall I attended the first Anti-Slavery State Convention at Utica.

In 1835 I left Rochester to form a colored church at Syracuse. Of course I joined anti-slavery work to the labor which fell upon me as a pastor. In the city last named the opponents of the movement laid a trap for me, by proposing a public discussion of the leading questions at issue. I was a little afraid of my ability to cope with them alone, and, therefore, quietly wrote to Gerrett Smith, Beriah Green and Alvin Steward for help. When the public discussion took place, and these practiced speakers met and answered the arguments of our opponents, the representatives of the latter—the leading editor and the foremost lawyer of the place—left the church in disgust, pleading that they had a good case, but did not expect to face men so well able to handle any question as the friends of mine I had invited. After their retreat from the hall, the two champions of slavery stirred up the salt boilers to mob us, but we adjourned before night, and when the crowd arrived at the edifice they found only a prayer meeting of the church people in progress, and slunk away ashamed. [. . .]

FIFTY-FOUR

New York Governor William L. Marcy Denounces Abolitionism

Source: William L. Marcy, "Annual Message, 1836," in *State of New York: Messages from the Governors*, ed. Charles Z. Lincoln, vol. 3 (Albany: J. B. Lyon, 1909), 570–84.

In his five-year tenure as governor of New York, William L. Marcy championed several popular democratic reforms, including public funding for common schools, banking regulation, and enlargement of the New York canal system. But he also opposed abolitionism. His objections likely stemmed from his political experience first as New York State comptroller (1829–1831) and as a United States senator (1831–1832). As comptroller, he recognized that Northern hostility to the slave economy undermined an otherwise profitable economic relationship between New York bankers, merchants, and industrialists and Southern plantation owners. As a United States senator, Marcy had been an eyewitness to the 1832 Nullification Crisis, and that experience taught him the lengths to which Southern leaders would go to protect their constitutional rights in regard to slavery.

In the excerpts of Governor Marcy's 1836 address to the New York State legislature featured here, Marcy denounced New York abolitionists as a threat to state and national security. More troubling, he suggested that those who shared his views should assist in regulating the radicalism of their abolitionist neighbors. Readers will recognize the connection between Marcy's remedy for abolitionism and the vigilantism that Rev. Thomas James described in his memoir.[1]

❧ ❧ ❧

Message from the Governor

To The Senate and Assembly

[. . .]

Having concluded my remarks on the subjects in which our constituents have an immediate and exclusive interest, my sense of duty will not permit me to abstain from presenting to you, at this time, some considerations arising from our federal relations.

This State is a member of a community of Republics, subject in many things to one general government, and bound together by political ties that must not be sundered. This relation gives us rights essential to our well-being, and imposes on us duties equally essential to the well-being of our sister States. As we value the immense advantages that spring from this Union, so we should cultivate the feelings and interests that give it strength, and abstain from all practices that tend to its dissolution. A few individuals in the middle and eastern States, acting on mistaken motives of moral and religious duty, or some less justifiable principle, and disregarding the obligations which they owe their respective governments, have embarked in an enterprise for abolishing domestic slavery in the southern and southwestern States. Their proceedings have caused much mischief in those States, and have not been entirely harmless in their own. They have acquired too much importance, by the evils which have already resulted from them, and by the magnitude and number of those which are likely to follow if they are further persisted in, to justify me in passing them without notice. These proceedings have not only found no favor with a vast majority of our constituents, but they have been generally reprobated. The public indignation which they have awakened, has broken over the restraints of law, and led to dangerous tumults and commotions, which, I regret to say, were not in all instances suppressed without the interposition of the military power. If we consider the excitement which already exists among our fellow-citizens on this subject, and their increasing repugnance to the

---

1. See "Rev. Thomas James on Antislavery Activism," chapter 53 herein.

abolition cause, we have great reason to fear that further efforts to sustain it will be attended, even in our own State, with still more dangerous disturbances of the public peace.

In our commercial metropolis, the abolitionists have established one of their principal magazines, from which they have sent their missiles of annoyance into the slaveholding States. The impression produced in those States, that this proceeding was encouraged by a portion of the business men of the city of New-York, or at least was not sufficiently discountenanced by them, threatened injurious consequences to our commerce. A proposition was made for an extensive voluntary association in the South, to suspend business intercourse with our citizens. A regard for the character of our State, for the public interest, for the preservation of peace among our citizens, as well as a due respect for the obligations created by our political institutions and relations, calls upon us to do what may be done, consistently with the great principles of civil liberty, to put an end to the evils which the abolitionists are bringing upon us and the whole country. With whatever disfavor we may view the institution of domestic slavery, we ought not to overlook the very formidable difficulties of abolishing it, or give countenance to any scheme for accomplishing this object, in violation of the solemn guarantees we are under not to interfere with the institution as it exists in other States. [. . .]

If we view the labors of the abolitionists in the calm light of reason, undisturbed by any morbid sympathy and uninfluenced by the spirit of fanaticism—if we look at their object, connected as it must be with the means they are using to attain it—if we regard the utter improbability of their ever reaching the end by the use of these means, and the certain consequences which must result from pushing forward their efforts in the present direction, we must, I think, characterize their schemes as visionary and pernicious.

Their avowed object is to abolish slavery in the southern and southwestern States; and their means thus far have been confined to the organization of societies among us and to publications of various kinds on the subject of slavery, which are regarded throughout these States as libels on their citizens, and provocatives to insurrection among their slaves. So far as their proceedings are designed to operate upon this State, we may inquire what end or object they have in view. It cannot be to abolish slavery here, for it does not exist among us. Is it to convince the people of this State that slavery is evil? Such is now the universal sentiment, and no man can be found among us who entertains a thought of returning to our former condition in this respect. If the abolitionists design to enlist our passions in their cause, such a course would be worse than useless, unless it had reference to some subsequent action. If it is expected in this manner to influence the action of Congress, then they are aiming at a usurpation of power. Legislation by Congress would be a violation of the Constitution by which that body exists, and to support which every member of it is bound by the solemn sanction of an oath. The powers of Congress cannot be enlarged so as to bring the subject of slavery within its cognizance, without the consent of the slaveholding States. The proceedings of the abolitionists have rendered their object in this respect absolutely unattainable. They have already excited such a feeling in all those States, that a proposition so to enlarge the powers of Congress, would be instantly rejected by each with indignation. If their operations here are to inflame the fanatical zeal of emissaries, and instigate them to go on missions to the slave-holding States, there to distribute abolition publications and promulgate abolition doctrine, their success in this enterprise is foretold by the fate of the deluded men who have preceded them. The moment they pass the borders of those States, and begin their labors, they violate the laws of the jurisdiction they have invaded, and incur the penalty of death or other ignominious punishment. I can conceive no other object that the abolitionists can have in view, so far as they propose to operate here, but to embark the people of this State, under the sanction of the civil authority, or with its connivance, in a crusade against the slave-holding States, for the purpose of forcing abolition upon them by violence and bloodshed. If such a mad project as this could be contemplated for a single moment as a possible thing, every one must see that the first step towards its accomplishment, would be the end of our confederacy, and the beginning of a civil war.

So far, therefore, as it respects the people of this State, or any action that can emanate from them, I can discover no one good that has resulted, or can be reasonably expected to result, from the proceedings of abolitionists; but the train of evils which must necessarily attend their onward movements, is in number and magnitude most appalling. [. . .]

If this State could be brought to think that the advantages it derives from the federal constitution, are not a sufficient compensation for the restraints imposed by that instrument; if, for the sake of displaying a morbid and fanatical spirit of false philanthropy, even at the risk of encountering the danger and incurring the responsibility of an attempt to reform the institutions of other States, it should be willing to give up these advantages, honor and duty would require it, before entering on such an experiment, to call upon the other States to release it from the solemn engagements it contracted in becoming a member of the Union; but so long as the peoples of this State cling to the advantages which this compact secures to them; so long as they profess to regard it as the source of their highest earthly good, and the object of their most cherished aspirations, they will, I trust, ever regard it as due alike to duty, to consistency, and to honor, to fulfill in its spirit every injunction it imposes, and to respect and observe with the utmost fidelity, all the great principles on which it is founded. [. . .]

When the very small number that still adhere to this cause, see that the immense majority of the people of this State, including certainly a proportionate amount of intelligence and worth, and embracing men of all sects in religion, and of all parties in politics, are utterly and irreconcilably opposed to them; and that their measures are regarded with the deepest repugnance by all who affectionately cherish the Union and harmony of the States; including among them philanthropists at least as enlightened and sincere as any of themselves; they will, it is confidently hoped, be induced to pause in their career, and to sacrifice on the altar of their common country, the opinions and motives which have hitherto prompted them to exertions regarded with so much abhorrence by so great a majority of their fellow-citizens.

When, to the just influence which may reasonably be anticipated from the sentiments of the people, so unitedly and powerfully expressed, and rendered still more efficacious, as I think they might and should be, by the opinions and views of their assembled representatives, is added the overwhelming weight of the arguments addressed to the reason and the consciences of those who yet adhere to the abolition cause, it would be imputing to them a deplorable degree of mental blindness and fanatical delusion, not to expect a general abandonment of their wild schemes. All but those who are confirmed in fanaticism or reckless of consequences, it is believed, will be constrained by the decided and constantly increasing force of public opinion, to give up their dangerous attempts to act on the institutions of other States. Those who may not be thus reclaimed or controlled, will be too few in number and in influence, I am persuaded, to excite apprehension.

Relying on the influence of a sound and enlightened public opinion to restrain and control the misconduct of the citizens of a free government, especially when directed, as it has been in this case, with unexampled energy and unanimity to the particular evils under consideration, and perceiving that its operations have been thus far salutary, I entertain the best hopes that this remedy, of itself, will entirely remove these evils, or render them comparatively harmless. But if these reasonable expectations should, unhappily, be disappointed; if, in the face of numerous and striking exhibitions of public reprobation, elicited from our constituents by a just fear of the fatal issues in which the uncurbed efforts of the abolitionists may ultimately end, any considerable portion of these misguided men shall persist in pushing them forward to disastrous consequences, then a question, new to our confederacy, will necessarily arise, and must be met. It must then be determined how far the several States can provide, within the proper exercise of their constitutional powers, and how far in fulfillment of the obligations resulting from their federal relations, they ought to provide, by their own laws, for the trial and punishment by their own judicatories, of residents within their limits, guilty of acts therein, which are calculated and intended to excite insurrection and rebellion in a sister state. Without the power to pass such laws, the States would not possess all the necessary means for preserving their external relations of peace among themselves, and would be without the ability to fulfil in all instances, the sacred obligations which they owe to each other as members of the Federal Union. Such a power is the acknowledged attribute of sovereignty, and the exercise of it is often necessary to prevent the embroiling of neighborhood nations. The general government is at this time exercising that power to suppress such acts of the citizens of the United States, done within its jurisdiction, in relation to the belligerent authorities of Mexico and Texas, as are inconsistent with the relations of peace and amity we sustain towards those States. Such a power, therefore, belonged to the sovereignty of each of the States, before the formation of the Union, and as far as regards their relation to each other, it was not delegated to the general government. It still remains unimpaired, and the obligations to exercise it have acquired additional force from the nature and objects of the federal compact. I cannot doubt that the Legislature possesses the power to pass such penal laws as will have the effect of preventing the citizens of this State and residents within it, from availing themselves, with impunity, of the protection of its sovereignty and laws, while they are actually employed in exciting insurrection and sedition in a sister State, or engaged in treasonable enterprises, intended to be executed therein. [. . .]

In discharging the various and responsible duties, devolved on you as legislative guardians of this State, I shall give you my cheerful co-operation, in the confident hope that your labors will subserve the best interests and advance the general welfare of our constituents.

W. L. Marcy.

Albany, January 5, 1836

FIFTY-FIVE

New York Methodists on Abolitionism

Source: Lucius C. Matlack, *History of American Slavery and Methodism, from 1780 to 1849: And History of the Wesleyan Methodist Connection of America* (New York, 1849), 67–68.

In 1836 the General Conference of the Methodist Episcopal Church issued a pastoral letter urging their clergy and parishioners to "refrain from the agitating subject" of abolitionism for the sake of denominational fellowship. The letter garnered a mixed reaction among New York Methodists. Many laypeople and clergy challenged the substance of the letter and the General Conference's authority to issue such a directive. But the clergy who exercised control over the New York Annual Conference accepted the pastoral letter as authoritative and binding. In 1836 the conference adopted its own resolutions of censure against ministers and church leaders who engaged in antislavery activism or solicited the antislavery newspaper *Zion's Watchman.*

Lucius C. Matlack printed the following excerpt of the 1836 New York Annual Conference resolutions in *The History of American Slavery and Methodism, from 1780 to 1849.* He identified these resolutions— and similar motions adopted by other conferences—as precipitating factors in the eventual splintering of the Methodist Episcopal Church.

❧ ❧ ❧

[...]

The same year, the New York Conference came up to the work, and adopted the following Report, which was prepared and read by Dr. Bangs.

"The Committee to whom was referred the subject of abolitionism, beg leave to Report:—

"That having deliberated together on this subject, they are of the opinion that it is the duty of the members of this Conference, wholly to refrain from all abolition measures and movements, as being incompatible with their duty as ministers of the Lord Jesus Christ, and as promoters of the peace and welfare of the Church to which they belong. They, therefore, recommend to the Conference the adoption of the following Resolutions:—

"*Resolved*, That this Conference fully concur in the advice of the late General Conference, as expressed in their pastoral address in the following words:—

"(The part of the Pastoral Address here referred to is on page 43. This resolution binds the members of the Conference, in the language of the Address, 'WHOLLY to *refrain* from this agitating subject.')

"*Resolved*, That we disapprove of the members of this Conference patronizing, or in any way giving countenance to a paper called 'Zions Watchman,' because, in our opinion, it tends to disturb the peace and harmony of the body, by sowing dissensions in the Church.

"*Resolved*, That although we would not condemn any man, or withhold our suffrages from him on account of his *opinions*, merely, in reference to the subject of abolitionism, yet we are decidedly of the opinion that *none ought to be elected to the office of a deacon or elder in our Church*, UNLESS *he give* A PLEDGE to the Conference that he will *refrain from agitating* the Church with discussions on this subject, and the more especially as the one promises 'reverently to obey them to whom the charge and government over him is committed, following with a glad mind and will their godly admonitions,' and the other, with equal solemnity, promises to 'maintain and set forward, as much as lieth in him, quietness, peace, and love among all Christian people, and especially among them that are or shall be committed to their charge.' All which is respectfully submitted.

"D. Ostrander, Chairman."

At a subsequent session of the same Conference, they resolved,

"That in the judgment of this Conference, it is incompatible with the duty which its members owe to the Church, as its ministers, for them to be engaged in attending anti-slavery societies, either in or out of the Church, or in any way agitating the subject so as to disturb the peace and harmony of the Church, and that they be, and hereby are affectionately advised and admonished to refrain from all these things."

FIFTY-SIX

Establishing an Antislavery Newspaper

Source: "Prospectus of the Friend of Man," *Friend of Man* (Utica, NY), June 23, 1836, microfilm, Cornell University Library.

The heavy-handed response of church leadership to the abolitionist movement had the effect of forcing Christian abolitionists to choose between their convictions and their denominational affiliations. So many Methodists chose abolitionism that in 1843 the breakaway Methodists convened in Utica to organize the Wesleyan Methodist Connection, a proabolition conference of Methodists. The "Prospectus" of the inaugural edition of the abolitionist journal the *Friend of Man* captured the mentality of antebellum Christian ultraists. It articulated the angst and anger felt by many New York Methodists and others who feared the church had lost its moral compass.

§ § §

Prospectus of the Friend of Man

"THIS COMMANDMENT HAVE WE FROM HIM, THAT HE
THAT LOVETH GOD LOVE HIS BROTHER ALSO."

I John, iv. 21.

Ever since God created man in his own image, his fundamental law has required every man to regard every other man as his equal, and love him as he loves his own soul. And ever since Cain sought the favor of his Maker by a pretended worship, without love to his brother, the progeny of Cain have dreamed themselves religious, while saying in their hearts, "Am I my brother's keeper?"

The second table engraved by the finger of God on Sinai, contained a solemn re-enactment of that original law; a decisive testimony against such selfish and spurious religion. Century after century holy men were inspired to tune the harp of melody and sweep the lyre of prophecy, in unison with the statues of righteousness. Of their testimony, the fiftieth Psalm; with the first and fifty eighth chapters of Isaiah, may be adduced as incidental, yet glowing specimens. But the religion of Cain had corrupted and well nigh displaced the religion of the law and the prophets, when Jesus Christ himself appeared among men to "magnify and make honorable" its requirements. For this cause his Sermon on the Mount unfolded its long forgotten principles, and vindicated from perversion its oft misconstrued enactments. For this cause he "went about doing good" to the bodies as well as the souls of men, that his followers might imitate his example. For this cause he put forth the parable of the good Samaritan which teaches us to be neighbor to him who is fallen among thieves. For this cause he tested the religion of the rich young man, who imagined he had "kept" the law "from his youth up" by a requirement which sent him "away sorrowful." For this cause he drove the extortioners, as thieves, with a scourge of cords, from the house of prayer. For this cause he denounced woes upon the orthodox and high professing Scribes and Pharisees, whose hypocrisy was attested by their oppressions. For this cause he announced his fixed determination to distribute the awards of the last Judgment upon the principle of considering the good or ill treatment of one of the least of his earthly brethren to be virtually the treatment of his own person.

Christianity, while it remained such, was emphatically the *Friend of Man*. It could only become otherwise by a corruption which should extinguish its vital principle of equality and impartial love. The mystery of Iniquity began early to work. The Apostles themselves were "in perils among false brethren," who "loved to have the preemence [preeminence]," and "lord it over God's heritage." In this spirit was revealed the *Man of Sin* who exalted himself above all that is called God. Christianity degraded became the ally of despotism. Tyranny dreaded the light that shone upon its own deformity, and deemed it unsafe to entrust to the injured poor the privilege of reading the Bible that condemned their own grievous wrongs!

This was the slumber of "the dark ages." Luther illumined its dungeon with a few gleams of day light. But we live in an age in which Protestants—so called—are redoubling its horrors, and becoming clamorous for the perpetuity of its darkness. In our own country, (so boastful of its liberties) they not only withhold the Bible from their brethren, but claim, and hold, and buy, and sell their souls and bodies as goods and "chattels personal." They "forbid to marry," and put asunder whom God hath joined together. They expunge, not the second merely, but every command of the Decalogue, particularly the first, the fifth, the seventh, and the eighth. They effectually say to their brother, "thou shalt have no other God before thy earthly Master.* They annul the law of obedience to the parent and of instruction to the child. They declare the wife and husband, "not entitled to the conditions of matrimony." They sanctify and legalize "the highest kind of theft," i.e. robbery of the labor of a whole life—the person of the laborer himself. They extort, not the unwilling tithe of the reaper's toil, but the hire itself, and the reaper with his hire! They "use their neighbor's service without wages, and give him not for his work." They judge not the cause of the widow, neither doth the cry of the needy come before them.

Such to an alarming extent, is the religion of the nineteenth century, in America—a religion which claims to be the religion of Protestants, and of the Bible! It prates of the horrors of the inquisition, and erects gibbets for the defenders of the truth—the advocates of the poor! It builds the tombs of the reformers, and accounts it insanity and treason to ask for the oppressed American the occupancy of so elevated a condition as that *from* whose degradation it was the labor of the Reformers to redeem the benighted peasantry of Europe!

A remonstrance has been raised against these accumulated wrongs; a rebuke has been uttered against these unparalleled sins. Satan is roused from his seat, and wages war against the throne of God and of the Lamb.— Lawless violence has been wielded by the boasted guardians of the law. The National Constitution has been trampled in the dust, under the plea of preserving the Constitution. The bands of society have been severed under the pretext of preventing disunion. The contemners of law have been clamorous for despotic legislation. A corrupted christianity looks complacently on, and cautions the transgressor, not against his sin, but against its *too sudden abandonment*! Its anathemas, so charitably withheld from *iniquity*, are thundered fiercely upon the heads of its reprovers. Instead of calling to her children in the confines of Babylon,—"Come out of her, my people, that ye partake not her sins, and that ye receive not her plagues,"—she is heard proclaiming that all who 'in any way impair her powers,' are justly liable to the highest civil penalties and ecclesiastical censures."+

Such is the crisis in which it is proposed to publish, in the heart of our "empire state" a weekly paper to be called "THE FRIEND OF MAN." Its object will be to maintain the equality and inalienable rights of all men:—To plead for the down trodden slave:—To support republican freedom: —To assert and exercise the right of free discussion—the right to investigate *truth*,—to proclaim and practice *duty*. In doing this it will seek to restore and promote *the religion of the Bible*—the religion of supreme love to God, the Father of all men, and of equal and impartial love to all his offspring, without respect of persons.

The promotion of "pure and undefiled religion," as defined by the apostle James, we propose as the beginning and the ending, the means and the object of our labors. Men will never "walk humbly with God" while they walk arrogantly towards man. "If a man love not his brother whom he hath seen, how can he love God whom he hath not seen?" When the solemnity of man's inalienable rights are duly appreciated, then, and not until then, will men begin to conceive the nature and magnitude of HIS claims, in whose sight the nations of the earth are as the small dust of the balance.

Our labors, therefore, will not be confined by the subject of SLAVERY. INTEMPERANCE, GAMING AND WAR are giant enemies of our race, closely allied to slavery, and demanding the ceaseless opposition of the *Friend of Man.*—Violence will oppress men, so long as men avenge themselves by violence. The dishonesty that covets wealth without earning it, and seeks gain without an equivalent, is the same principle that fattens upon the unrequited labor of the slave. And so long as our rulers "drink wine, and our princes strong drink," so long will they "forget the law, and prevent the judgment of the afflicted." There is no escape from slavery, but the freedom of virtue—no charter of human liberty, but the law of the Creator.

"THE FRIEND OF MAN," by seeking to cultivate and extend the religion of holy love and of the Bible, may hope, in some good measure, to escape the trammels of narrow bigotry; avoiding at the same time, the spurious liberality that deems it heavenly charity to shake hands with sin. By supporting the principles of liberty and the practices of righteousness—by rebuking lordly iniquity in high places—by thwarting the selfish purposes of partizan rivals of every name, we may hope to escape the polluting infection of party politics, and (while seeking to secure the liberties of the people) afford some guarantee that we will not become the tools of demagogues or of men in power.

Our departments of religious and secular intelligence, and miscellaneous reading selections, will receive constant attention, and vary in extent, from time to time, according to the amount of interesting matter afloat, and according to the wants and exigencies of the great cause in which we chiefly labor.

* "The slave is *entirely* subject to the will of his master to whom he belongs."—*Slave Code*
+ Literary and Theological Review

FIFTY-SEVEN

Resolutions of the New York State Anti-Slavery Society

Source: *Proceedings of the First Annual Meeting of the New-York State Anti-Slavery Society: Convened at Utica, October 19, 1836* (Utica, NY: New York State Anti-Slavery Society, 1836), 9-12.

In 1835, New York abolitionists proposed to convene in Utica to establish the New York State Anti-Slavery Society. A hostile mob disrupted the convention and drove its participants from the city. The undaunted conventioneers reconvened at the home of Gerrit Smith to complete their work. The following year the representatives returned to Utica for the first annual meeting of the society and adopted a set of resolutions. The resolutions, featured here, underscore the dual influence of Christianity and democracy on the abolitionist movement in New York. Just as Christianity justified the abolitionists' mission, so democratic values defined their strategies for achieving their goal.

✻ ✻ ✻

Resolutions

The following Resolutions were adopted during the Meeting:—
1. Resolved, That we regard that device of American Legislation which reduces man, made in the image of God, to the

condition of a mere chattel, as annihilating all moral attributes and relations, and as necessarily involving the highest crime that can be committed on *moral being*; and consequently that whoever claims the right of property in man by virtue of a title founded in such legislation, makes himself a sinner of the first magnitude.

2. Resolved, That since Slavery is a rude and presumptuous invasion of the prerogatives of Jehovah who has expressly declared "All souls are mine," its abolition demands the moral energies of the Christian World.

3. Resolved, That we should prove ourselves unworthy of every claim to the character of philanthropists, of Christians, of patriots, and of the friends of liberty; if, with our views of American Slavery, we should terminate or remit our efforts in the cause of immediate emancipation.

4. Resolved, That agents of this, or of the Parents Society, or both, ought to be employed, without unnecessary delay, in every county of this state, to visit every township and school district in regular succession, to circulate our publications—to converse with individuals—to lecture as opportunity offers—to circulate petitions—to organize auxiliaries—and thus carry the knowledge of our principles and the adoption of our measures into every portion of the state, and that, with the blessing of God, we will sustain the State Society in the prosecution of this work, until it shall be fully accomplished.

5. Resolved, That, in the opinion of this Meeting, *Ten Thousand Dollars* should be raised for the use of the Society, for the coming year, and that the members of this Meeting be now invited to give their pledges as individuals or for their respective local societies for this purpose.

6. Resolved, That we welcome as most important and powerful coadjutors in the glorious cause of Emancipation, the females of our country.

7. Resolved, That the prejudice peculiar to our country, which subjects our colored brethren to a degrading distinction in our worship assemblies and schools, which withholds from them that kind and courteous treatment to which, as well as other citizens, they have a right, at public houses, on board steamboats, in stages, and in places of public concourse, is the

very spirit of slavery, is nefarious and wicked, and should be
practically reprobated and discountenanced.

8. Resolved, That the friends of the colored people deem it their
duty to use their influence to procure places, and encourage
colored youth to learn trades, and help them into honorable
employments.

9. Resolved, That the prejudice which excludes *colored
youth* from the advantages of our Colleges and Literary
Institutions, is *unchristian, inhuman*, and *cruel*; and demands
the unqualified reprehension of every friend of education
and philanthropist.

10. Resolved, That while as abolitionists, we disavow all connection
with party politics; yet, feeling it our duty to exercise the
elective franchise, we deeply regret the disposition of our fellow
citizens to elevate to office men who openly sacrifice the rights
of northern freemen to SOUTHERN SLAVERY.

11. Resolved, That we most cordially sympathize with our
brethren, [James G.] Birney, [David] Nelson, [Elijah] Lovejoy,
and others, who have been called to learn by experience, how
to feel for "them that are in bonds as bound with them;" and
we would offer sincere thanks to our great Protector, that
though cast down they are not destroyed.

12. Resolved, That it may be recommended to religious
communities to memorialize their Southern brethren who
hold their fellow men in bondage, remonstrating with them
in the spirit of Christian love, and urging them to the duty of
letting the oppressed go free.

13. Resolved, That we detest and abhor as the most nefarious
of trafficks, the internal slave trade, which is now carried
on between the states, attended as it is with most of the
cruelties of the African slave trade, by which, more than ONE
HUNDRED AND TWENTY THOUSAND annually, are torn
from their homes, and driven like beasts to a Southern market;
and, that it is the duty of every freeman in this nation, to
lift his voice against it, and cease not to petition Congress to
put forth the same arm to stop this nefarious traffick, which
crushed the African slave trade.

14. Resolved, That, as a member of His family, who is the Father
of us all, every sufferer, and most of all the slave, has a strong

claim on every man, for his warm sympathies, and prompt and strenuous aid.

15. Resolved, That the doctrine so often advanced in justification of slavery, that what is abstractly wrong is practically right, involves violence to human nature, contradiction to God, and the subversion of the standard and disruption of the bonds of a pure morality.

16. Whereas, it was principally by the influence of Christianity, that the slave trade both in England and America, and recently slavery itself in the British West Indies, were abolished, and as it is by the same influence, that we can reasonably hope for its abolition in this country, therefore, Resolved, That the high and decided stand which the Christians of Great Britain have taken on this subject, and the disinterested and persevering efforts, which they are using for the abolition of slavery throughout the world, are very grateful to our feelings, and should meet a hearty response in the bosom of every Christian in the United States.

17. Resolved, That the females of our country are especially responsible for the prevalence and continuance of the cord of caste, which is fearfully withering and destructive and its bearing on our colored brethren.

18. Resolved, That the sophistry, threatenings and violence, which have been employed to intimidate and crush the abolitionists, afford appropriate and ample confirmation of the soundness of their doctrines, and the wisdom of their measures.

19. Resolved, That the friends of human nature have a right confidently to expect from the christian pulpit, a hearty and earnest advocacy of universal and immediate emancipation.

20. Resolved, That the present pressing crisis of the anti-slavery cause in this country, calls *loudly* for a more extensive circulation of anti-slavery publications, and that it is therefore the duty of abolitionists *personally*, to make immediate and vigorous efforts to get at least one anti-slavery periodical into every family in the land.

21. Resolved, That our hope for the speedy and bloodless abolition of slavery is in God alone, who can enlighten and sanctify the hearts of men—and that it is our duty in our

closets, families, and social prayers to make this a subject of fervent supplication.

22. Resolved, That while we have a heart to pray, and a tongue to plead, and a hand to toil, we will, by the help of God, subserve without ceasing the cause of holy freedom.

23. Resolved, That the people of this State ought to petition their next Legislature to memorialize the national Congress in its legislative capacity, to abolish slavery in the District of Columbia and the internal slave trade now carried on in the District and between the several states.

24. Resolved, That the system of American Slavery, which reduces men, made in the image of God, and redeemed by the blood of Christ, to the condition of beasts, calls loudly for the reprobation of the church; and that northern Christians especially, are called upon to bear a steady and faithful testimony against any branch of the church that in any way sanctions or upholds the slavery of this land; and if that testimony is still disregarded, it is the duty of the churches which are pure from this "shocking abomination" solemnly to withdraw fellowship from those professing Christians and churches who disregard their admonitions.

25. Resolved, That every county, town, and district, be earnestly entreated to listen to the cry of 2,500,000 American citizens, robbed of all their rights, and without delay, to obtain as far as possible signatures to petition to Congress, to abolish slavery in the District of Columbia, and the territories, to put a stop to the internal slave trade, and prohibit the exportation of slaves to Texas.

26. Whereas—His Excellency, the Governor of this State, in his last annual message to the legislature of the same, thought proper to repeat the commonplace accusations of our opponents of that period, accusing Abolitionists of seditious and insurrectionary conduct, and whereas, the Hon. the Senate and House of Assembly in a preamble and resolutions adopted by them, saw fit fully to sanction the sentiments and statements of said message:

And whereas, in his said Message, His Excellency the Governor asserted it to be within the rightful and constitutional prerogatives of the Legislature of this State, to enact penal laws prohibiting the circulation and publication of Anti-Slavery writings, and suppressing Anti-Slavery efforts, declaring that *"without the power to pass such laws, the states would not possess all the necessary means for preserving their external relations of peace among themselves,"* and only refrained from recommending their enactment, because it was alleged that abolitionism was on the decline:

And whereas, the said Senate and House of Assembly, in said preamble and resolutions have fully sanctioned and adopted the sentiment: Therefore,

Resolved, (1.) That since Abolitionism is *not* on the decline but on the advance in this State, it becomes the duty of Abolitionists, as well as the people at large, to examine the subject, and meet the crisis it presents.

Resolved, (2.) That Abolitionists, not only as citizens as innocent men, but as persons accused of crime, whether innocent or guilty, are entitled to be heard in self defense, before the Legislature of this State, and be held innocent until their guilt can be made to appear.

Resolved, (3.) That it is the duty of Abolitionists, and of all the friends of freedom and equal rights in the State, to petition the State Legislature to give the Abolitionists a full hearing in the premises, and extend to them such redress as truth and justice may be found to demand.

Resolved, (4.) That justice to the rights of a slandered and innocent class of citizens, a regard to the fundamental principles of human rights, a prudent regard for the public welfare, and for the freedom and independence of the non-slaveholding states, unitedly forbid the existence of any species of legislative action against Abolitionists.

Resolved, (5.) That we regard the legislative resolutions of the Hon. Senate and House of Assembly of this State, against Abolitionists, as an unconstitutional assumption of judicial power, yet exercised in a manner contrary to, and subversive of, all regular judicial proceedings, possessing all the essential features of an *ex post facto* law, substituting the unlimited infliction of public odium and proscription upon persons unconvicted of crime, for the definite and limited punishment awarded by law and executed by the public officers, and therefore, far more injurious to their victims and dangerous to the liberties of the people, than any penal enactments however unjust and despotic.

FIFTY-EIGHT

Creating Antislavery Petitions

Source: "Petitions! Petitions!! Petitions!!!," *Friend of Man* (Utica, NY), August 2, 1837, Cornell University Library.

Abolitionists across the United States agreed that consciousness raising was a necessary first step in the goal of ending slavery. They purchased or established printing presses to publish abolitionist newspapers and the testimonials of former slaves. They also organized governmental petition drives of unprecedented scope, flooding Congress with petitions calling for the end of slavery in the United States.

Abolitionist newspapers played a critical role in coordinating such political action. As an example, in August 1837 the *Friend of Man* published templates for eleven different petitions with instructions for readers to cut the text from the paper, fill in the blank spaces left in the text, paste the extract to another sheet of paper, and then to gather signatures. The templates reprinted here call on Congress to act on several abolitionist priorities.

🟊 🟊 🟊

Petitions! Petitions!! Petitions!!!

Reader: Examine the following petitions, and if you wish to live in a country where the people *enjoy the right* of petition, then EXERCISE

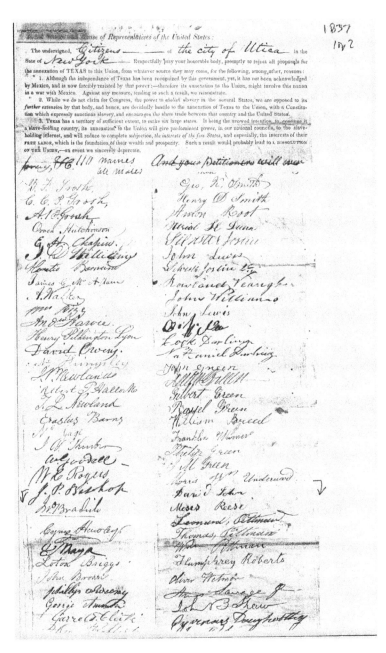

FIGURE 17. Utica antislavery petition, 1837. In 1837 the *Friend of Man*, a newspaper published by the New York State Anti-Slavery Society, printed for public use the language of petitions to various governing bodies. All that antislavery advocates had to do was to cut the language from the newspaper, paste it to the top of a blank sheet of paper, and then gather signatures. Pictured here is one such petition completed by antislavery advocates in Utica, New York. (National Archives; image courtesy of New York Heritage Digital Collections)

that right in such a manner as to prevent it from being taken away.—
And ASK YOUR NEIGHBORS to join with you in this work. *Cut the petitions
apart,* and paste them on separate half sheets of white paper, for signatures. Then sign your own name, and go among your neighbors for
their names. The petitions respecting TEXAS should be in Washington
by the first of September. For further directions, see the first page.

1. *To the Senate and House of Representatives of the United States:*
   The undersigned, [blank] of [blank] in the State of [blank]
   Respectfully pray your honorable body immediately abolish
   SLAVERY and the SLAVETRADE in the DISTRICT OF COLUMBIA.
2. *To the Senate and House of Representatives of the United States:*
   The undersigned, [blank] of [blank] in the State of [blank]
   Respectfully pray your honorable body, immediately to abolish
   SLAVERY and the SLAVE TRADE in those TERRITORIES of the
   United States where they exist.
3. *To the Senate and House of Representatives of the United States:*
   The undersigned, [blank] of [blank] in the State of [blank]
   Respectfully pray your honorable body, so to exercise the
   Constitutional power vested in you to "regulate COMMERCE
   AMONG THE SEVERAL STATES," as entirely to prohibit the
   Domestic Slave Trade.
4. *To the Senate and House of Representatives of the United States:*
   The undersigned, [blank] of [blank] in the State of [blank]
   Respectfully pray your honorable body, not to admit any NEW STATE
   to this Union, whose Constitution tolerates DOMESTIC SLAVERY.
5. *To the Senate and House of Representatives of the United States:*
   The undersigned, [blank] of [blank] in the State of [blank]
   Respectfully pray your honorable body promptly reject all
   proposals for the annexation of TEXAS to this Union, from
   whatever source they may come for the following, among other
   reasons:

1. Although the independence of Texas has been recognised by
   this government, yet, it has not been acknowledged by Mexico,
   and is now forcibly resisted by that power:—therefore its
   annexation to the Union, might involve this nation in a war
   with Mexico. Against any measure, tending to such a result, we
   remonstrate.

2. While we do not claim for Congress the power to *abolish slavery* in the several states, we are opposed to its *further extension* by that body, and hence are decidedly hostile to the annexation of Texas to the Union, with a Constitution which expressly sanctions slavery, and encourages the slave trade between that country and the United States.

3. Texas has a territory of sufficient extent, to make six large states. It being the avowed intention to continue it a slaveholding country, as annexation to the Union will give predominant power, in our national councils, to the slaveholding interest, and will reduce to complete subjection, *the interests of the free states*, and especially the interests of their FREE LABOR, which is the foundation of their wealth and prosperity. Such a result would probably lead to a DISSOLUTION of the UNION,—an event we sincerely deprecate.

6. *To the Senate and House of Representatives of the United States*:
The undersigned, [*blank*] of [*blank*] in the State of [*blank*] Respectfully pray your honorable body, promptly to reject all proposals for the annexation of TEXAS to this Union, from whatever source they may come.

7. *To the Honorable, the Legislature of the State of* [*blank*]:
The undersigned, [*blank*] of [*blank*] in the County of [*blank*] Respectfully pray your honorable body, to adopt resolutions, declaring:

1. That Congress has the constitutional power to abolish slavery, and the slavetrade, in the District of Columbia.
2. That it has the constitutional power to abolish it in the several Territories of the Union, where they exist.
3. That it has the constitutional power to prohibit the slavetrade between the several States of the Union.
4. That, in regard to these particulars, Congress ought immediately to exercise that power.

We also pray your honorable body, to send a copy of said resolutions to each of the Senators and Representatives, of this State, in Congress, to be by them laid before that body.—To the Governors of the several States, to be by them laid before their respective legislatures; and to the President of the United States.

We also pray you, to instruct the Senators, and request the Representatives of this State, in Congress, to use their utmost influence for the immediate abolition of slavery and the slave trade in the District of Columbia; and in those Territories of the Union where they exist;—and also for the immediate prohibition of the slavetrade between the several States.

8. *To the Honorable, the Legislature of the State of [blank]:*
   The undersigned, [blank] of [blank] in the County of [blank] Respectfully pray your honorable body, immediately to repeal all laws in this State, which make any distinction among its inhabitants, on account of COLOR.

9. *To the Honorable, the Legislature of the State of [blank]:*
   The undersigned, [blank] of [blank] in the County of [blank] Respectfully pray your honorable body, immediately to pass a law, securing to every human being in this State, a TRIAL BY JURY, in all cases where his or her liberty is in question.

10. *To the Honorable, the Legislature of the State of [blank]:*
    The undersigned, [blank] of [blank] in the County of [blank] Respectfully pray your honorable body, to protest against the admission of any new state to the Union, whose Constitution tolerates domestic slavery;—and to forward a copy of said protest to each of the Senators and Representatives, of this State, in Congress, to be by them laid before that body.—to the Governor of the several States, to be by them laid before their respective legislatures; and to the President of the United States.

We also pray you, to instruct the Senators, and request the Representatives of this State, in Congress, to use their utmost influence to prevent the admission of any new State to the Union, whose Constitution tolerates domestic slavery.

11. *To the Honorable, the Legislature of the State of [blank]:*
    The undersigned, [blank] of [blank] in the County of [blank] Respectfully pray your honorable body, to protest without delay against the annexation of Texas to this Union;—and to

forward a copy of said protest to each of the Senators and Representatives, of this State, in Congress, to be by them laid before that body.—to the Governor of the several States, to be by them laid before their respective legislatures; and to the President of the United States.

We also pray you to instruct the Senators, and request the Representatives, of this State, in Congress, to use their utmost influence to prevent the annexation of Texas to this Union.

FIFTY-NINE

How to Be an Abolitionist

Source: "Some of the Duties of an Abolitionist; (and Every Whole Man Is an Abolitionist.)," August 27, 1841, Gerrit Smith Pamphlets and Broadsides, Special Collections Research Center, Syracuse University.

Although many New Yorkers opposed slavery and supported its end, they remained wary of ultraism. The following broadside published by prominent reformer Gerrit Smith in Peterboro, New York, likely affirmed the popular perception of abolitionists as uncompromising and perhaps even unreasonable.

❧ ❧ ❧

Some of the Duties of An Abolitionist; (*And Every Whole Man Is An Abolitionist*)

1. He must pray and labor heartily for the welfare of the slaveholder and slave. He must pity the former, and sympathize with the latter: and all that he does for either, he should do in the name and for the sake of his God and his Savior Jesus Christ.
2. God "is no respecter of persons;" "nor regardeth he the rich more than the poor, for they are all the work of his

hands:"—therefore the Abolitionist must refuse to attend worship in those Churches, where a colored skin is made a badge of inferiority, and a justification for contempt and hatred.

3. He must not countenance the preacher, who refuses to plead and pray for the slave.

4. He must never vote to make a legislator of a man, who approves of, or who can tolerate laws in favor of slavery. The foundation of doctrine of a Republic is that "all men are created equal."

5. He must believe, that God "hates robbery for burnt offering;" and must therefore refuse to patronize those Associations, that solicit the contributions of slaveholders.

6. He must, if he would keep himself untainted with, and would most effectually protect against, the most horrid form of robbery, (for such is slavery,) refuse to consume the production of slave labor.

7. He must disconnect himself from all National parties in the United States, whether political or ecclesiastical, for the reason, that all such parties, whilst slavery exists in the United States, must, from the very nature of the case, be pro-slavery.

Let ten thousand men and women in the United States solemnly pledge themselves in the year 1841 to the conscientious discharge of the foregoing duties; and such will be the power of this uncompromising and self-denying testimony against slavery, that ere the year 1850 shall have arrived, the United States will be a land of impartial and universal liberty.

PETERBORO', August 27, 1841.

SIXTY

Gerrit Smith's Critique of the Clergy on Abolitionism

Source: "Gerrit Smith's Opinion of the Clergy," *Practical Christian* (Mendon, MA), May 11, 1844.

At about the same time that Gerrit Smith committed himself to the abolition of slavery, he joined the Union Church movement, also known as the Free Church movement. Christian Unionists argued that sectarianism undercut evangelism, and more particularly the effectiveness of the Christian mission to end slavery in the United States. Smith agreed with that premise, having seen for himself how his own Presbyterian sect had moderated their antislavery views for the sake of unity within the denomination.[1]

Smith was loosely affiliated with the Union Church movement until 1843 when, after much deliberation, he formally separated from the Presbyterian Church to establish the Church of Peterboro, a Union Church. This broadside was published the following year and can be read as both a critique of sectarian religion and a subtle endorsement of the Union Church movement.

❧ ❧ ❧

---

1. Ralph Volney Harlow, *Gerrit Smith, Philanthropist and Reformer* (New York: Henry Holt, 1939).

Gerrit Smith's Opinion of the Clergy

This devoted philanthropist, in an address 'to the friends of the slave in the town of Smithfield,' published in the Utica Liberty Press, thus speaks of the American Clergy:

Pardon me for again warning you against the most guilty and corrupting body of men in the land. I mean the clergy. With comparatively few exceptions, they are unworthy and dangerous spiritual guides. It is not too much to say, that the minister who does not plead for God's poor, is a minister of Satan, not of Jesus Christ. Abolitionists, how long will you be guilty of yielding to your sectarian predilections, and of hearing a pro-slavery preacher, because, like yourselves, he is a Universalist, or Presbyterian, or Baptist, or Methodist? How long before you shall feel that you owe more to the slave and to truth than to sect? Who of you would attend on the ministry of the most admired preacher of your sect, were your own child in slavery, and the preacher refused to plead for it?

One of the most recent instances of atrocious clerical wickedness on a somewhat large scale, is to be seen in the proceedings of a Convention of ministers in Lennox, Mass. They pass resolutions which chime in with the popular feelings of the North against slavery; and then declare that a part of their plan of operating against slavery is, 'to leave all the political party arrangements of the country wholly untouched, and to interfere with no man's exercise of the elective franchise, so that men of all parties are invited to act with us, and no man, in order to become a member of this Association, is required to abandon his political connexions.' These ministers would be consistent with themselves, were they to contrive a plan of promoting temperance, which shall 'interfere with no man's exercise of the' rum-drinking privilege, but which shall leave every man free to get drunk. They would be consistent with themselves, were they to inform habitual liars, thieves and adulterers, that they had discovered a way for getting them to Heaven without disturbing their wicked habits. What greater absurdity could these ministers utter, than that men can help overthrow slavery, whilst they cling to parties which are the very pillars of slavery?

Why are these clergymen so much opposed to the breaking up of the great pro-slavery political parties? The ready answer is, because they forsee that the breaking up of these parties and the breaking up of these pro-slavery churches must accompany each other; and that, when the pro-slavery churches are broken up, the occupation of the pro-slavery ministers will be gone.

Your friend,

GERRIT SMITH

Peterboro', March 12, 1844.

SIXTY-ONE

The Jerry Rescue

Source: Samuel Ringgold Ward, *Autobiography of a Fugitive Negro: His Anti-slavery Labours in the United States, Canada, & England* (London: J. Snow, 1855), 117–28.

In October 1851, antislavery advocates in Syracuse, New York, rescued William Henry, a fugitive slave also known as Jerry, from a jail cell where he awaited his extradition to the South. Rev. Samuel Ringgold Ward participated in the liberation campaign, later dubbed the "Jerry Rescue." Ward's description of the rescue should be read as both evidence and allegory. His account qualifies as eyewitness testimony, but he was not an impartial observer. In this excerpt from his autobiography, Ward related the details of the incident and indicated what lessons abolitionists should take from it.

❧ ❧ ❧

[...]

Residing then at Syracuse, we went home, arriving on Wednesday, the first day of October. We found the whole town in commotion and excitement. We soon learned the cause. A poor Mulatto man, named Jerry, at the suit of his own father had been arrested under the Fugitive Law, had been before the Negro-catcher's court, had escaped,

FIGURE 18. Samuel Ringgold Ward, 1817–c. 1866. A licensed Congregational minister, author, abolitionist, and advocate for fugitive slaves seeking refuge in New York, Samuel Ringgold Ward served as the pastor of an all-white congregation in Wayne County between 1841 and 1843. (Schomburg Center for Research in Black Culture, Jean Blackwell Hutson Research and Reference Division, New York Public Library)

had been pursued and retaken, and was now being conveyed to prison. I went to the prison, and, in company with that true sterling friend of the slave, the Reverend Samuel J. May, was permitted to go in and see the man. He had fetters on his ankles, and manacles on his wrists.

I had never before, since my recollection, seen a chained slave. He was a short, thick-set, strongly built man, half white though slave born. His temperament was ardent, and he was most wonderfully excited. Though chained, he could not stand still; and in that narrow room, motioning as well as he could with his chained, manacled hands, and pacing up and down as well as his fetters would allow, fevered and almost frenzied with excitement, he implored us who were looking on, in such strains of fervid eloquence as I never heard before nor since from the lips of man, to break his chains, and give him that liberty which the Declaration of Independence assumed to be the birthright of every man, and which, according to the law of love, was our duty towards a suffering brother.

I cannot recall the *ipsissima verba* of his eloquent pleading. As far as I can revive his sentences in my memory, he exclaimed— "Gentlemen, behold me, and these chains! Why am I bound thus, in a free country? Am I not a man like yourselves? Do you not suppose I feel as other men feel? Oh, gentlemen, what have I done to deserve this cruel treatment? I was at my work, like an honest industrious man. I was trying to act the part of a good citizen; but they came upon me, and accused me of crime. I knew I was innocent; but I felt it my duty to go before the court, to declare and to prove my innocence. For that reason I let that little Marshal, I think you call him, put handcuffs on me. You know, gentlemen, handcuffs don't hurt an innocent man! But after they put the irons on me, they told me they were taking me as a runaway slave! Didn't I tell you I was innocent? They confessed I was. If I had known what they were about, do you think I should have *let that little ordinary man put irons on me?* No, indeed! I have told you how deceitfully they took me. When I saw a good chance, I thought it was not wrong to break away from them. I watched my opportunity: I dashed out of the door; I ran like a man running for his freedom; but they overtook me, and brought me back, and here I am like a wild beast, chained and caged.

"Gentlemen, is this a free country? Why did my fathers fight the British, if one of their poor sons is to be treated in this way? I beseech you, gentlemen, as you love your own liberty, break these chains of mine; yes, and break the chains that bind my brethren in the South, too. Does not the Bible say, 'Break every yoke, and let the oppressed go free'? Don't you believe the Bible? I can't read it as some of you can, but I believe what it says, and I ask you, gentlemen, to do for me what that book commands. Suppose that any one of you were in my position. What would you wish me to do? I beg of you, gentlemen, to do for me what you would wish, were you where I am. Are not all men born free and equal? How is it, then, that I must wear these chains? Give me, O give me, gentlemen, that freedom which you say belongs to all men, and it is all I ask. Will you who are fathers, and brothers, see a man dragged in chains to the slavery of Tennessee, which I know is worse than death itself? In the name of our common nature—in the name of the Declaration of Independence—in the name of that law in the Bible which says, "do as you would be done by"—in the name of God, our common Father—do break these chains, and give me the freedom which is mine because I am a man, and an American."

What a sight! and what sounds! A slave, in a free Northern city chained as no felon would be chained, with the blood of Anglo-Saxons in his veins. Still, a slave; the son of a wealthy planter in Tennessee, and still a slave; arrested by a United States officer and several assistants, who were sworn to support the glorious Federal Constitution, serving under the freest government under the sun, the land of liberty, the refuge for the oppressed of all the world! And for what was he arrested? What was his crime? A love of that liberty which we all declared to be every man's inalienable right! And this slave was quoting the Declaration of Independence in chains! He was not the subject of some Czar, some

"Turbaned Turk or fiery Russ:"

no, he was an American by birth, and a slave as well; so said the chains upon him: and on his lips were liberty's and religion's great watchwords! I never saw extremes so meet. I never saw how hollow a mockery was our talk about liberty, and our professions of Christianity. I never felt how really we were all subject to the slave power; I never felt before the depth of degradation there is in being a professed freeman of the Northern States. Daniel Webster had, a few months before, predicted the execution of the Fugitive Law in that very town. The people laughed him to scorn. We now felt, however, how much better he knew the depths to which Northern men can sink than we did. While these thoughts were galloping through our brains, this manacled son of a white man proceeded with his oration in his chains, and we felt dumb and powerless. A great crowd gathered about the door; and after looking on and drinking in as much of the scene as my excitable nature would allow, I turned to go away, and at that moment the crowd demanded a speech of me. I spoke. I ceased; but I never felt the littleness of my always little speeches, as I did at that moment. Jerry had made *the* speech of the occasion, and all I could say was but tame and spiritless in comparison with his

"Words that breathed and thoughts that burned."

The substance of what I said is as follows:— "Fellow citizens! we are here in most extraordinary circumstances. We are witnessing such a sight as, I pray, we may never look upon again. A man in chains, in Syracuse! Not a felon, yet in chains! On trial, is this man, not for life, but for liberty. He is arrested and held under a law made by 'Us the People'— pursuant, we pretend, to a clause in the constitution. That constitution was made 'to secure the blessings of liberty to ourselves and our posterity.' Here is a man one of 'ourselves'; and the colour he bears shows that he belongs not altogether to my race, but that he is one of the 'posterity' of those who framed and adopted our Federal Constitution. So far are we from 'securing' to him the 'blessings of liberty,' that we have arrested him, confined him, and chained him, on purpose to inflict upon him the curses of slavery.

"They say he is a slave. What a term to apply to an American! How does this sound beneath the pole of liberty and the flag of freedom? What a contradiction to our 'Declaration of Independence'! But suppose he be a slave: is New York the State to recognize and treat him as such? Is Syracuse the city of the Empire State in which the deeds which make this a day unfortunately memorable, should be perpetuated? If he be not a slave, then, he is the most outraged man we ever saw.

"What did our fathers gain by the seven years' struggle with Great Britain, if, in what are called Free States, we have our fellow citizens, our useful mechanics and skilful artisans, chained and enslaved? How do foreign nations regard us, when knowing that it is not yet three short months since we were celebrating the Declaration of Independence, and to-day we are giving the most palpable denial to every word therein declared?

"But I am told that this is a legal transaction. That it is wrong and unwise to speak against a judicial proceeding, not yet completed: I admit it all. I make no pretensions to speak wisely. I have heard a speech from Jerry. I feel for him, as for a brother; and under that feeling, I may not speak quite so soberly as I ought. 'Oppression maketh a wise man mad.' I feel oppressed in a twofold sense. Yonder is my brother, in chains. Those chains press upon my limbs. I feel his sufferings, and participate his anguish. I feel, and we may all feel, oppressed in another sense. Here are certainly five-and-twenty hundred of us, wild with excitement in behalf of our chained brother, before our eyes, and we are utterly powerless to help him! We hear his strong, thrilling appeals, until our hearts sicken and our heads ache; but there is none among us that has the legal power to lift a hand in his defence, or for his deliverance. Of what advantage is it that we are free? What value is there in our freedom, while our hands are thus tied?

"Fellow citizens, whatever may be the result of these proceedings—whether our brother leaves the court, a declared freeman or a chained slave—upon us, the voters of New York State, to a very great extent, rests the responsibility of this Fugitive Slave Law. It is for us to say whether this enactment shall continue to stain our statute books, or be swept away into merited oblivion. It is for us to say whether the men who made it, and those who execute it before our faces, shall receive our votes, or shall by those votes be indignantly rebuked. Tell me, ye sturdy working men of Onondago, shall your votes be consecrated to the latter, or prostituted to the former? Do you swear fealty to freedom this day? Do you promise, so help you God! so to vote, as that your sanction never more shall be given to laws which empower persons to hunt, chain, and cage, MEN, in our midst? (cries of 'yes, yes.') Thank you, fellow citizens, in the name of our brother in prison! thank you for your bold, manly promise! May we all abide by it, until deeds of darkness like the one we now lament shall no longer mar our institutions and blacken our history."

But the crowd felt rightly. They saw Gerrit Smith and me go off arm in arm to hold a consultation, and, two and two, they followed us. Glorious mob! unlike that of 1834, they felt for the poor slave, and they wished his freedom. Accordingly, at nine o'clock that evening, while the court was in session trying Jerry for more than his life, for his liberty, the mob without threw stones into the window, one of which came so near to the judge that, in undignified haste, he suddenly rose and adjourned the courts. In an hour from that time, the mob, through certain stalwart fellows whom the Government have never had the pleasure of catching, broke open the door and the side of the building where Jerry was, put out the lights, took him out in triumph, and bore him away where the slave-catchers never after saw him.

The Marshal of the United States, who had him in custody, was so frightened that he fled in female attire: brave man! According to the

Fugitive Law, he had to pay Jerry's master one thousand dollars; for so
the law expressly ordains.

An assistant Marshal, who was aiding this one, fired a pistol when *en-
trée* was first made. He injured no one, but a stout stick struck his arm
and broke it. Escaping out of a window soon after, he broke the same
arm again, poor man! These two were not like a Marshal in Troy, in the
same State, who, rather than capture a slave, resigned his office.

The papers in the interest of the Government, in publishing an account of this affair, connected my name with it in a most prominent
manner. The Marshal with broken arm was especially commended to
my tender regard. The Government, under the advice of Daniel Webster
(whose Christianity, I find, is highly lauded in this country; it was always a *res non* in his own), ordered all the parties, directly or indirectly
engaged in the rescuing of Jerry, to be put on trial for *treason*! For it
was the doctrine of Mr. Webster and Mr. Fillmore, that opposition to
the Slave Law was "treason, and drew after it all the consequences of
treason." I knew enough to understand that *one* of the "consequences
drawn after treason" is a *hempen rope*. I had already become hopeless
of doing more in my native country; I had already determined to go
to Canada. Now, however, matters became *urgent*. I could die; but was
it duty? I could not remain in that country without repeating my connection with or participating in such an affair as I was then *guilty* of. If
I did my duty by my fellow men, in that country, I must go to prison,
perhaps; certainly, if the Government had their way, to the gallows. If
I did not, I must go to perdition. Betwixt the two, my election was made.
But then, what must become of my family, both as to their bread in my
then circumstances, and as to their liberty in *such* a country? Recollect-
ing that I had already my wife's consent (without which I could not
take any important step of the sort) to go to Canada, I concluded that
I must go immediately. I went; and a month or two after, my family followed: since which time we have each and severally been, *con amore*, the
most loyal and grateful of British subjects.

Jerry lived at Kingston, Canada, until the latter part of 1853, when he
died, a free man, by virtue of living in British soil. The courts would not
entertain the charge of treason against those accused in this case, from
its manifest absurdity. They did hold, however, that they had broken the
Fugitive Law, and must be tried for that. Luckily, but one person who was
accused was ever convicted. He died before the court, in its mercilessness,
could wreak its full vengeance upon him. He was innocent, I know.

When the accused were summoned to Auburn, twenty-six miles from Syracuse, to attend trial, the Railway Company provided carriages for the accused and their wives, *gratis*. Returning from Auburn, several of those ladies were in the large carriage into which the Government prosecutor entered. They unanimously requested his departure. They afterwards made up a purse of *thirty* pieces of silver, of the smallest coin of the country, and presented to him—wages of iniquity and treachery. The chains (which I helped to file off) of Jerry were packed in a neat mahogany box, and sent to President Fillmore. The Hon. W. Seward voluntarily became bail for the accused. He has been Governor of his native State. He is now one of its senators. This, however, is his highest honour. So he esteems it. [. . .]

Conclusion
The Legacy of the Burned-over District

The flames of religious revivals in central and western New York petered out in the mid-nineteenth century, and the intensity of the corresponding ultraism eventually diminished as well. But they never disappeared entirely.

Just as demographic shifts had contributed to the rise of the Burned-over District, they facilitated its end as well. Newborn settlements that had once teemed with migrants willing to forsake the religious traditions of their families back in New England had matured. By the 1860s many had become well-established towns and cities with new religious traditions firmly in place. The region had challenged the religious status quo only to establish a new one in its stead.

Furthermore, for many of the millions of Americans who poured into central and western New York in the early 1800s, the region turned out to be only a temporary stop on their way farther west. One historian has portrayed Albany as America's first gateway to the west because, as the nineteenth century advanced, hundreds of thousands of Americans eventually left New York for the states and territories of the Old Northwest. Others went even farther, settling in places such as Missouri and Iowa.[1]

---

1. Elizabeth E. Covart, "Collision on the Hudson: Identity, Migration, and Improvement of Albany, New York, 1750-1830" (PhD diss., University of California, Davis, 2011), 160-224.

Some of the Burned-over District's most prominent figures were a part of this trend. By 1835 Charles Finney had moved to Ohio to join the faculty of Oberlin College, an institution of higher education considered radical for its time because it admitted women and people of color as students. Finney eventually presided over the college and advanced its mission as a bastion of reform-minded student activism.[2] Many of Finney's supporters and friends, such as Theodore Weld, also remained active in reform movements, as did the Grimké sisters. In 1838, despite some of their disagreements on the prioritization of certain reforms, Weld and Angelina Grimké married.[3]

Joseph Smith and the majority of his followers left New York. By 1831, the church was headquartered in Kirtland, Ohio. Persecution eventually forced the church to move to Missouri and Illinois before fleeing to the Great Salt Lake Valley in 1847. Nevertheless, the church maintained congregations in New York and eventually purchased many of the significant places from its founding era, including the Smith family farm where Joseph Smith said that his first vision of deity occurred and the hill where he claimed to have uncovered the gold plates. Today, hundreds of thousands of visitors flock to these sites, including Latter-day Saints who view their trip as a historic pilgrimage of sorts.[4]

The number of believers in the biblical calculations of New York resident William Miller dwindled in the immediate aftermath of Miller's failed millennial predictions remembered as "the Great Disappointments." But the movement did not die. Several of its members continued to believe that the Second Coming of Jesus was imminent but ceased trying to predict his advent. The largest church to grow out of Millerism was the Seventh-day Adventist Church, which former Millerites established in Michigan in 1863.[5]

The Shakers remained in New York and New England while expanding geographically to Ohio, Kentucky, and Indiana and short-lived communities in Florida and Georgia. The Shakers routinely received guests and long-term visitors to their communities, but by the 1840s the communitarianism they had pioneered in the 1780s was no longer novel. Communalism enjoyed a surge in the 1840s, offering the curious

---

2. Finney, *Memoirs of Rev. Charles G. Finney*, 336–51.
3. Lerner, *Grimké Sisters from South Carolina*, 176–82.
4. Bushman, *Joseph Smith, Rough Stone Rolling*, 122–26; Spencer W. McBride, "Pilgrimage to History," *New York Archives* 15, no. 1 (Summer 2015): 16–19.
5. Rowe, *God's Strange Work*, 230–32.

and the disillusioned a buffet of choices in alternative models for governance, domestic life, and economy. Even the gender equity practiced by the Shakers was now more broadly available to American women, who engaged in public life by participating in reform movements such as abolition, temperance, education reform, and civil rights. At the start of the twenty-first century there was only one active Shaker village—at Sabbathday Lake, Maine.[6]

The Oneida perfectionists also maintained a presence in New York for several decades. However, the community started to fracture in the 1870s when John Humphrey Noyes attempted to have his son, Theodore, succeed him. Theodore Noyes did not share his father's religious beliefs, and many who wished to maintain that aspect of the community left New York for Southern California, where they helped settle Orange County.[7] Facing immense criticism from outside the community, John Humphrey Noyes fled to Canada in June 1889, and soon thereafter the Oneida perfectionists abandoned complex marriage. Two years later, the Oneida Association dissolved, but the commercial aspects of the community continued, and the resulting company, Oneida Limited, became one of the premier makers of silverware in the United States.[8]

The Latter-day Saints, Millerites, Shakers, and Oneida perfectionists were four of the most prominent new religious movements associated with the Burned-over District, but they were not alone. The region remained fertile ground for new groups and communities that challenged the religious and social status quo. Indeed, New York was the site of dozens of so-called utopian communities. Some only lasted in the state for a short period of time, while others endure to the present. One example of the former, the Community of True Inspiration, founded the Ebenezer Colonies southeast of Buffalo in 1843, where they prepared for the end of the world; the community moved to Iowa in 1855.[9] In 1853 John Murray Spear founded the spiritualist community of Harmonia, also known as "the Domain," in Chautauqua County; Spear designed the community as a place where he and his followers could

6. Katherine Lucky, "The Last Shakers?," *Commonweal* 146, no. 17 (December 2019): 32–38.

7. Spencer C. Olin Jr., "Bible Communism and the Origins of Orange County," *California History* 58, no. 3 (Fall 1979): 220–33.

8. Spencer C. Olin Jr., "The Oneida Community and the Instability of Charismatic Authority," *Journal of American History* 67, no. 2 (September 1980): 285–300.

9. Donald F. Durnbaugh, "Work and Hope: The Spirituality of the Radical Pietist Communitarians," *Church History* 39, no. 1 (March 1970): 83–85.

commune with the spirits of deceased people while also working toward women's equality and the abolition of slavery.[10]

Perhaps the most notable and enduring of these intentional religious communities in western New York came as a result of the popularization of spiritualism by the Fox sisters. In Wayne County during the late 1840s, Margaretta and Catherine Fox stated that they communicated with spirits via knocks, or rappings, on wood floors or walls. Eventually, their older sister, Leah, managed them as they traveled the state holding public séances and, by extension, evangelizing for the spiritualist movement. Later in her life, Margaretta confessed that it had all been a hoax, a confession she recanted several years later. Nevertheless, spiritualism attracted many men and women to western New York, and in 1878 spiritualists founded the Lily Dale community on the shores of Cassadaga Lake, a place that remains the center of organized spiritualism in the United States.[11]

Mainline Protestant denominations continued to flourish in central and western New York, and many of those churches persisted in advocating for reform. Perhaps the epitome of this continuing connection between religion and reform that was once so concentrated in the region is the establishment of the Chautauqua Lake Sunday School Assembly. Founded in 1874, the Chautauqua assembly served as a training ground for Methodist Sunday school teachers but quickly moved beyond religious instruction to focus on a broad range of subjects. The assembly, now called the Chautauqua Institution, became a model for making general education accessible to average Americans, and hundreds of "chautauquas" sprouted up throughout the country as tent meetings that brought the latest discoveries in the arts and sciences to people living in rural areas.[12]

The legacy of the Burned-over District is deeply entwined with the legacy of the state of New York in the early nineteenth century. Religious revivalism was a national phenomenon at that time. Demographic

---

10. Russell Duino, "Utopian Theme with Variations: John Murray Spear and His Kiantone Domain," *Pennsylvania History: A Journal of Mid-Atlantic Studies* 29, no. 2 (April 1962): 140–50.

11. David Chapin, "The Fox Sisters and the Performance of Mystery," *New York History* 81, no. 2 (April 2000): 157–88; Barbara Weisberg, *Talking to the Dead: Kate and Maggie Fox and the Rise of Spiritualism* (New York: HarperCollins, 2004).

12. R. B. Tozier, "A Short Life-History of the Chautauqua," *American Journal of Sociology* 40, no. 1 (July 1834): 69–73; John C. Scott, "The Chautauqua Movement: Revolution in Popular Education," *Journal of Higher Education* 70, no. 4 (July–August 1999): 389–412.

trends unique to central and western New York led to the area's high concentration of revivalism and the corresponding impulse for political and social reform at a time when New York was the most populous and, politically, the most influential state in the country. But that influence extended beyond politics. As the nineteenth century marched on and the state's population dispersed farther west, these former New Yorkers took their new ideas about religion and the ordering of society with them. The Burned-over District served as both the epitome of many national trends in religion and social reform and then as a catalyst to those trends elsewhere.

Acknowledgments

This book was inspired by our experience leading two National Endowment for the Humanities Landmark of American History and Culture Workshops on the history of revivalism and reform in early nineteenth-century America (2013 and 2016). A total of 160 K–12 teachers, librarians, and administrators participated in those workshops. The questions they asked—and the presuppositions they challenged—provided the original impetus for this book. We thank those NEH Summer Scholars for the "aha moments" that spurred this documentary history.

We have benefited from immense support in researching and writing this book. Working with Michael McGandy and the rest of the capable team at Cornell University Press was a pleasure. Michael believed in this project from its earliest stage, and his editorial acumen helped shape it for the better. Special thanks to our cheerful research assistants Rosie Hren, who visited repositories and transcribed some challenging handwriting, and Madison Porter, who transcribed several manuscript documents, including some that did not ultimately make it into the finished book. Throughout the processes of researching, writing, and revising this book, we received useful feedback and advice from several of our fellow scholars and friends. We appreciate the scholarship and collegiality of Carol Medlicott, Glendyne Wergland, Robert P. Emlen, and Jerry Grant, fellow members of the NEH Landmark Workshops instructional team. More recently, we have leaned into the expertise and friendship of Mason Allred, Christopher Blythe, Rachel Cope, Liz Covart, Brian Franklin, Matthew Godfrey, David Golding, Christopher Jones, Adam Jortner, Matthew McBride, Michael Leroy Oberg, Brent Rogers, and Jordan Watkins.

A documentary history is dependent on archives and libraries and the men and women who build, maintain, and make them accessible to researchers. The global COVID-19 pandemic complicated our access to many repositories, but library professionals remained dedicated to supporting patrons such as us. We are especially grateful to Vicki Weiss, senior manuscripts librarian, Manuscripts and Special Collections, at

the New York State Library, and Sarah C. Symans at the J. Spencer &
Patricia Standish Library, Siena College, both in Albany, New York.
Librarians and staff at the following institutions also greatly facilitated
our research: Special Collections at Hamilton College; the Church History Library in Salt Lake City; the Special Collections Research Center at Syracuse University; and the Division of Rare and Manuscript
Collections at the Cornell University Library. Funding for some of the
travel and research for this book was provided by our respective home
institutions, Siena College, the Joseph Smith Papers, and the Church
History Department of the Church of Jesus Christ of Latter-day Saints.
In acknowledging that these people and institutions helped improve
this book, we note that we are ultimately responsible for its contents.

We acknowledge the vital support of our friends and family to our
work as historians. Jennifer thanks her husband, George, whose love
and cuisine nurtures everything she does, and her children, Josephine
and Casey, who have supported their "working mom" by keeping her
company at the NEH workshops and related research expeditions.
Spencer thanks his wife, Lindsay, and his children, Erik, Laney, Joshua,
and Thomas, for their love, their deep reserves of patience, and their
unwavering encouragement.

Selected Bibliography

In this selected bibliography we include all of the sources in which are found the documents featured in this book. In addition, we include secondary sources that were particularly useful to us in contextualizing the featured documents or that serve as especially relevant reading for those who desire to dive deeper into certain topics.

Ahlstrom, Sydney E. *A Religious History of the American People*. 2nd ed. New Haven, CT: Yale University Press, 2004.

Altschuler, Glenn C., and Jan M. Saltzgaber. *Revivalism, Social Conscience, and Community in the Burned-Over District: The Trial of Rhoda Bement*. Ithaca, NY: Cornell University Press, 1983.

Anderson, Richard Lloyd. *Joseph Smith's New England Heritage*. Rev. ed. Salt Lake City: Deseret Book Co., 2003.

Anderson, Richard L. "Joseph Smith's New York Reputation Reappraised." *BYU Studies* 10, no. 3 (Spring 1970): 283–314.

Anderson, Rodger I. *Joseph Smith's New York Reputation Reexamined*. Salt Lake City: Signature Books, 1990.

Appleby, Joyce. "The Personal Roots of the First American Temperance Movement." *Proceedings of the American Philosophical Society* 141, no. 2 (June 1997): 141–59.

Arrington, Leonard. "James Gordon Bennett's 1831 Report on 'The Mormonites.'" *BYU Studies* 10, no. 3 (Spring 1970): 353–64.

Balik, Shelby M. *Rally the Scattered Believers: Northern New England's Religious Geography*. Bloomington: Indiana University Press, 2014.

Ball, Erica L., Richard Newman, and Patrick Rael. *To Live an Antislavery Life: Personal Politics and the Antebellum Black Middle Class*. Athens: University of Georgia Press, 2012.

Barkun, Michael. *Crucible of the Millennium: The Burned-Over District of New York in the 1840s*. Syracuse, NY: Syracuse University Press, 1986.

Barnes, Gilbert H., and Dwight L. Dumond, eds. *Letters of Theodore Dwight Weld, Angelina Grimké Weld, and Sarah Grimké*. Repr. ed. New York: Da Capo, 1970.

Benson, Lee. *The Concept of Jacksonian Democracy: New York as a Test Case*. Princeton, NJ: Princeton University Press, 1961.

Brooke, John L. *Columbia Rising: Civil Life on the Upper Hudson from the Revolution to the Age of Jackson*. Chapel Hill: University of North Carolina Press, 2010.

Bushman, Richard Lyman. *Joseph Smith and the Beginnings of Mormonism*. Urbana: University of Illinois Press, 1984.

Bushman, Richard Lyman. *Joseph Smith, Rough Stone Rolling: A Cultural Biography of Mormonism's Founder*. New York: Knopf, 2005.

Butler, Diana Hochstedt. *Standing against the Whirlwind: Evangelical Episcopalians in Nineteenth-Century America*. Religion in America. New York: Oxford University Press, 1995.

Butler, Jon. *Awash in a Sea of Faith: Christianizing the American People*. Cambridge, MA: Harvard University Press, 1990.

Campisi, Jack, and William A. Starna. "On the Road to Canandaigua: The Treaty of 1794." *American Indian Quarterly* 19, no. 4 (Autumn 1995): 467–90.

Chapin, David. "The Fox Sisters and the Performance of Mystery." *New York History* 81, no. 2 (April 2000): 157–88.

Conkin, Paul K. *Cane Ridge: America's Pentecost*. Madison: University of Wisconsin Press, 1990.

Cope, Rachel. "'In Some Places a Few Drops and Other Places a Plentiful Shower': The Religious Impact of Revivalism on Early Nineteenth-Century New York Women." PhD diss., Syracuse University, 2009.

Covart, Elizabeth E. "Collision on the Hudson: Identity, Migration, and Improvement of Albany, New York, 1750–1830." PhD diss., University of California, Davis, 2011.

Criales, Jessica Lauren. "Women of Our Nation: Gender, Race, and Christian Indian Identity in the United States and Mexico, 1753–1867." PhD diss., Rutgers University, 2020.

Cross, Whitney. *The Burned-Over District: The Social and Intellectual History of Enthusiastic Religion in Western New York, 1800–1850*. Ithaca, NY: Cornell University Press, 1950.

Darlington, James W. "Peopling the Post-revolutionary New York Frontier." *New York History* 74, no. 4 (October 1993): 343–44.

Davis, Bitton. "Mormonism's Encounter with Spiritualism." *Journal of Mormon History* 1 (1974): 39–50.

Dennis, Matthew. *Seneca Possessed: Indians, Witchcraft, and Power in the Early American Republic*. Philadelphia: University of Pennsylvania Press, 2010.

Densmore, Christopher. "More on Red Jacket's Reply." *New York Folklore* 13, nos. 3–4 (1987): 121–22.

Densmore, Christopher. *Red Jacket: Iroquois Diplomat and Orator*. Syracuse, NY: Syracuse University Press, 1999.

Dorsey, Jennifer Hull. "Conscription, Charity, and Citizenship in the Early American Republic: The Shaker Campaign for Alternative Service." *Church History* 85, no. 1 (March 2016): 140–49.

Eisenstadt, Peter R., and Laura-Eve Moss, eds. *The Encyclopedia of New York State*. Syracuse, NY: Syracuse University Press, 2005.

Ellis, David Maldwyn. "The Yankee Invasion of New York, 1783–1850." *New York History* 32, no. 1 (January 1951): 3–17.

Fahey, David M. *Temperance and Racism: John Bull, Johnny Reb, and the Good Templars*. Lexington: University Press of Kentucky, 1996.

Faulkner, Carol. *Lucretia Mott's Heresy: Abolition and Women's Rights in Nineteenth-Century America.* Philadelphia: University of Pennsylvania Press, 2011.

Fenton, William N. *The Great Law and the Longhouse: A Political History of the Iroquois Confederacy.* Norman: University of Oklahoma Press, 1998.

Field, Peter S. *The Crisis of the Standing Order: Clerical Intellectuals and Cultural Authority in Massachusetts, 1780–1833.* Amherst: University of Massachusetts Press, 1998.

Fluhman, J. Spencer. *"A Peculiar People": Anti-Mormonism and the Making of Religion in Nineteenth-Century America.* Chapel Hill: University of North Carolina Press, 2012.

Folts, James D. "The Fanatic and the Prophetess: Religious Perfectionism in Western New York, 1835-1839." *New York History* 72, no. 4 (October 1991): 357-87.

Ford, Bridget. *Bonds of Union: Religion, Race, and Politics in a Civil War Borderland.* Chapel Hill: University of North Carolina Press, 2016.

Formisano, Ronald P. *For the People: American Populist Movements from the Revolution to the 1850s.* Chapel Hill: University of North Carolina Press, 2008.

Franklin, Brian. "America's Missions: The Home Missions Movement and the History of the Early Republic." PhD diss., Texas A&M University, 2012.

Friend of Man. "Petitions! Petitions!! Petitions!!!" August 2, 1837.

Ganter, Granville, ed. *The Collected Speeches of Sagoyewatha, or Red Jacket.* Syracuse, NY: Syracuse University Press, 2006.

Gaustad, Edwin S., and Leigh E. Schmidt. *The Religious History of America: The Heart of the American Story from Colonial Times to Today.* New York: Harper One, 2002.

Gellman, David Nathaniel. *Emancipating New York: The Politics of Slavery and Freedom, 1777–1827.* Baton Rouge: LSU Press, 2006.

Ginzberg, Lori D. *Untidy Origins: A Story of Woman's Rights in Antebellum New York.* Chapel Hill: University of North Carolina Press, 2005.

Givens, Terryl, and Matthew J. Grow. *Parley P. Pratt: The Apostle Paul of Mormonism.* New York: Oxford University Press, 2011.

Godwin, Joscelyn. *Upstate Cauldron: Eccentric Spiritual Movements in Early New York State.* 2nd ed. Albany: SUNY Press, 2015.

Grainger, Brett Malcolm. *Church in the Wild: Evangelicals in Antebellum America.* Cambridge, MA: Harvard University Press, 2019.

Grow, Matthew J. "A 'Truly Eventful Life': Writing the *Autobiography* of Parley P. Pratt." *Journal of Mormon History* 37, no. 1 (Winter 2011): 153-58.

Harper, Steven C. *First Vision: Memory and Mormon Origins.* New York: Oxford University Press, 2019.

Harper, Steven C. "Missionaries in the American Religious Marketplace: Mormon Proselyting in the 1830s." *Journal of Mormon History* 24, no. 2 (Fall 1998): 1-29.

Haselby, Sam. *The Origins of American Religious Nationalism.* New York: Oxford University Press, 2015.

Hatch, Nathan O. *The Democratization of American Christianity.* New Haven, CT: Yale University Press, 1989.

Hatch, Nathan O. "Mormon and Methodist: Popular Religion in the Crucible of the Free Market." *Journal of Mormon History* 20, no. 1 (Spring 1994): 24–44.

Hillman, Joseph. *The History of Methodism in Troy, New York.* New York: Joseph Hillman, 1888.

Howe, Daniel Walker. "Protestantism, Volunteerism, and Personal Identity in Antebellum America." In *New Directions in American Religious History*, edited by Harry S. Stout and D. G. Hart, 206–35. New York: Oxford University Press, 1997.

Howe, Daniel Walker. *What Hath God Wrought: The Transformation of America, 1815–1848.* New York: Oxford University Press, 2007.

Humez, Jean M. "Weary of Petticoat Government: The Specter of Female Rule in Early Nineteenth-Century Shaker Politics." *Communal Societies* 11 (1991): 1–17.

Humphrey, Thomas J. *Land and Liberty: Hudson Valley Riots in the Age of Revolution.* DeKalb: Northern Illinois University Press, 2004.

Isenberg, Nancy. *Sex and Citizenship in Antebellum America.* Chapel Hill: University of North Carolina Press, 1998.

Jarvis, Brad D. E. *The Brothertown Nation of Indians: Land Ownership and Nationalism in Early America, 1740–1840.* Lincoln: University of Nebraska Press, 2010.

Jessee, Dean C. "Joseph Knight's Recollection of Early Mormon History." *BYU Studies* 17, no. 1 (Fall 1976): 36–37.

Jessee, Dean C., et al., eds. *The Joseph Smith Papers, Documents Series.* 15 vols. Salt Lake City: Church Historian's Press, 2013–2023.

Jessee, Dean C., et al., eds. *The Joseph Smith Papers, Histories Series.* 2 vols. Salt Lake City: Church Historian's Press, 2012.

Jessee, Dean C., et al., eds. *The Joseph Smith Papers, Journals Series.* 3 vols. Salt Lake City: Church Historian's Press, 2008–2015.

Johnson, Curtis D. "'Disordered' Democracies: Gender Conflict and New York Baptist Women, 1791–1830." *Journal of Social History* 47, no. 2 (Winter 2013): 482–506.

Johnson, Paul E. *A Shopkeeper's Millennium: Society and Revivals in Rochester, New York, 1815–1837.* New York: Hill & Wang, 1978.

Johnson, Paul E., and Sean Wilentz. *The Kingdom of Matthias: A Story of Sex and Salvation in Nineteenth-Century America.* New York: Oxford University Press, 1994.

Johnson, Rochelle, and Daniel Patterson, eds. *New Essays on Rural Hours and Other Works.* Athens: University of Georgia Press, 2001.

Johnson, Rochelle, and Daniel Patterson, eds. *Susan Fenimore Cooper: Essays on Nature and Landscape.* Athens: University of Georgia Press, 2002.

Jones, Christopher Cannon. "Methodism, Slavery, and Freedom in the Revolutionary Atlantic." PhD diss., College of William and Mary, 2016.

Jortner, Adam. *Blood from the Sky: Miracles and Politics in the Early American Republic.* Charlottesville: University of Virginia Press, 2017.

Jortner, Adam. *The Gods of Prophetstown: The Battle of Tippecanoe and the Holy War for the American Frontier.* New York: Oxford University Press, 2012.

Jortner, Adam. *No Place for Saints: Mobs and Mormons in Jacksonian America*. Baltimore: Johns Hopkins University Press, 2022.

Juster, Susan. *Doomsayers: Anglo-American Prophecy in the Age of Revolution*. Philadelphia: University of Pennsylvania Press, 2003.

Kappler, Charles J., ed. *Indian Affairs: Laws and Treaties*. 7 vols. Washington, DC: Government Printing Office, 1904.

Kidd, Thomas S. *The Great Awakening: The Roots of Evangelical Christianity in Colonial America*. New Haven, CT: Yale University Press, 2007.

Klein, Milton M., and the New York State Historical Association, eds. *The Empire State: A History of New York*. Ithaca and Cooperstown: Cornell University Press and the New York State Historical Association, 2001.

Klingaman, William K., and Nicholas P. Klingaman. *The Year without Summer: 1816 and the Volcano That Darkened the World and Changed History*. New York: St. Martin's, 2014.

Lerner, Gerda. *The Grimké Sisters from South Carolina: Pioneers for Women's Rights and Abolition*. 2nd ed. Chapel Hill: University of North Carolina Press, 2004.

Mackay, Michael Hubbard. *Prophetic Authority: Democratic Hierarchy and the Mormon Priesthood*. Urbana: University of Illinois Press, 2020.

McBride, Spencer. *The First Vision: A Joseph Smith Papers Podcast*. Podcast audio. January 3, 2020. https://www.josephsmithpapers.org/articles/the-first-vision-a-joseph-smith-papers-podcast.

McCurdy, Charles W. *The Anti-rent Era in New York Law and Politics, 1839–1865*. Chapel Hill: University of North Carolina Press, 2001.

McIntosh, W. H. *History of Monroe County, New York*. Philadelphia: J. B. Lippincott, 1877.

McMillen, Sally G. *Seneca Falls and the Origins of the Women's Rights Movement*. New York: Oxford University Press, 2008.

Medlicott, Carol. *Issachar Bates: A Shaker's Journey*. Hanover, NH: University Press of New England, 2013.

Medlicott, Carol, and Christian Goodwillie. *Richard McNemar, Music, and the Western Shaker Communities: Branches of One Living Tree*. Kent, OH: Kent State University Press, 2013.

Modern, John Lardas. *Secularism in Antebellum America: With Reference to Ghosts, Protestant Subcultures, Machines, and Their Metaphors; Featuring Discussions of Mass Media, Moby-Dick, Spirituality, Phrenology, Anthropology, Sing Sing State Penitentiary, and Sex with the New Motive Power*. Chicago: University of Chicago Press, 2011.

Moore, R. Laurence. *Religious Outsiders and the Making of Americans*. New York: Oxford University Press, 1986.

Moore, R. Laurence. *Selling God: American Religion in the Marketplace of Culture*. New York: Oxford University Press, 1994.

Murphy, Angela F. *The Jerry Rescue: The Fugitive Slave Law, Northern Rights, and the American Sectional Crisis*. Oxford: Oxford University Press, 2016.

Nordhoff, Charles. *The Communistic Societies of the United States*. London: John Murray, 1875.

Noyes, George Wallingford. *Free Love in Utopia: John Humphrey Noyes and the Origin of the Oneida Community*. Edited by Lawrence Foster. Urbana: University of Illinois Press, 2001.

Oberg, Michael Leroy. *Peacemakers: The Iroquois, the United States, and the Treaty of Canandaigua, 1794*. New York: Oxford University Press, 2016.

Olin, Spencer C., Jr. "The Oneida Community and the Instability of Charismatic Authority." *Journal of American History* 67, no. 2 (September 1980): 285–300.

Painter, Nell Irvin. *Sojourner Truth: A Life, a Symbol*. New York: W. W. Norton, 1996.

Porter, Larry C. *A Study of the Origins of the Church of Jesus Christ of Latter-day Saints in the States of New York and Pennsylvania*. Provo, UT: BYU Studies, 2011.

Porterfield, Amanda. *Conceived in Doubt: Religion and Politics in the New American Nation*. Chicago: University of Chicago Press, 2012.

Porterfield, Amanda. *Feminine Spirituality in America: From Sarah Edwards to Martha Graham*. Philadelphia: Temple University Press, 1980.

Pratt, Parley Parker. *The Autobiography of Parley Parker Pratt*. New York: Russell Bros., 1874.

Pritchard, Linda K. "The Burned-Over District Reconsidered: A Portent of Evolving Religious Pluralism in the United States." *Social Science History* 8, no. 3 (Summer 1984): 243–65.

Robie, Harry. "Red Jacket's Reply: Problems in the Verification of Native American Speech Text." *New York Folklore* 12, nos. 3–4 (1986): 99–117.

Rohrer, James R. "The Origins of the Temperance Movement: A Reinterpretation." *Journal of American Studies* 24, no. 2 (August 1990): 228–35.

Rorabaugh, William J. *The Alcoholic Republic: An American Tradition*. New York: Oxford University Press, 1979.

Rowe, David L. *God's Strange Work: William Miller and the End of the World*. Grand Rapids, MI: Eerdmans, 2008.

Rowe, David L. "A New Perspective on the Burned-Over District: The Millerites in Upstate New York." *Church History* 47, no. 4 (December 1978): 408–20.

Ryan, Mary P. "A Women's Awakening: Evangelical Religion and the Families of Utica, New York, 1800–1840." *American Quarterly* 30, no. 5 (Winter 1978): 602–23.

Shafer, Jamie O. "A Propper Yankee in Central New York: The Diary of Mary Bishop Cushman, 1795–1797." *New York History* 79, no. 3 (July 1998): 255–312.

Shalev, Eran. *American Zion: The Old Testament as a Political Text from the Revolution to the Civil War*. New Haven, CT: Yale University Press, 2013.

Sheriff, Carol. *The Artificial River: The Erie Canal and the Paradox of Progress, 1817–1862*. New York: Hill & Wang, 1996.

Silverman, David J. *Red Brethren: The Brothertown and Stockbridge Indians and the Problem of Race in America*. Ithaca, NY: Cornell University Press, 2010.

Skeen, C. Edward. "The Year without a Summer: A Historical View." *Journal of the Early Republic* 1, no. 1 (Spring 1981): 51–67.

Smith, Ellen Wayland. *Oneida: From Free Love Utopia to the Well-Set Table*. New York: Picador, 2016.

Stein, Stephen J. *The Shaker Experience in America*. New Haven, CT: Yale University Press, 1992.

Taylor, Alan. *Divided Ground: Indians, Settlers, and the Northern Borderland of the American Revolution*. New York: Knopf, 2006.

Taylor, Alan. "The Early Republic's Supernatural Economy: Treasure Seeking in the American Northeast, 1780–1830." *American Quarterly* 38, no. 1 (Spring 1986): 6–34.

Taylor, Alan. "The Free Seekers: Religious Culture in Upstate New York, 1790–1835." *Journal of Mormon History* 27, no. 1 (Spring 2001): 44–66.

Taylor, Alan. *William Cooper's Town: Power and Persuasion on the Frontier of the Early American Republic*. New York: Vintage Books, 1995.

Taysom, Stephen C. *Shakers, Mormons, and Religious Worlds: Conflicting Visions, Contested Boundaries*. Bloomington: Indiana University Press, 2011.

Thomas, Benjamin P. *Theodore Weld: Crusader for Freedom*. New Brunswick, NJ: Rutgers University Press, 1950.

Underwood, Grant. *The Millenarian World of Early Mormonism*. Urbana: University of Illinois Press, 1993.

Walker, David. "The Humbug in American Religion: Ritual Theories of Nineteenth-Century Spiritualism." *Religion and American Culture: A Journal of Interpretation* 23, no. 1 (Winter 2013): 30–74.

Wallace, Anthony F. C. *The Death and Rebirth of the Seneca*. New York: Knopf, 1970.

Wellman, Judith. "Crossing Over Cross: Whitney Cross's Burned-Over District as Social History." *Reviews in American History* 17, no. 1 (March 1989): 159–74.

Wellman, Judith. *The Road to Seneca Falls: Elizabeth Cady Stanton and the First Woman's Rights Convention*. Urbana: University of Illinois Press, 2004.

Wergland, Glendyne R. *Sisters in the Faith: Shaker Women and the Equality of the Sexes*. Amherst: University of Massachusetts Press, 2011.

Wonderley, Anthony. "Brothertown, New York, 1785–1796." *New York History* 81, no. 4 (October, 2000): 457–92.

Wonderley, Anthony. *Oneida Utopia: A Community Searching for Human Happiness and Prosperity*. Ithaca, NY: Cornell University Press, 2017.

INDEX

movements, 4,7, 12, 253–56, 383; rebuttal of, 285–89. *See also* Noyes, John Humphrey
Onondaga (nation), 16, 19, 20–22, 63
ordination (ordain), 100–1, 155, 193, 200, 215, 253, 334, 337, 379
orthodoxy, 145, 351

pastors, 114, 134, 137–41, 190–91, 195, 198, 200, 202, 216, 338, 347–48
Peacemakers, 161–65
Pequot, 160
Perfectionists. See Oneida Association
Perkens, Artemesia, 122–23
Phelps, Oliver, 21
Pickering, Timothy, 19–20, 23
Pierson, Elijah, 208, 245–52
Pratt, Parley P., 223–27
prayer: and abolition, 339, 351, 359, 364–67, 368–69, 377; in Baptist trustee minutes, 170–76; and conversion, 199, 213–14; and eschatology, 242; Joseph Smith's, 205; in the Kingdom of Matthias, 246, 248, 250; meetings, 222, 246; in missionary diaries, 41, 44–47, 50, 54, 59, 63, 66, 68; and Presbyterian covenant, 191–93; and revival, 104, 113, 116–17, 120–22, 125, 128–43, 145–49; at Sabbatarian convention, 315, 321; and salvation, 203, 234; and unity, 279–80; in Waterloo Missionary Society Constitution, 82; women praying in meetings, 145, 150–52, 155–56
Presbyterian: and church expansion, 12, 159–60; confession and covenant, 195–97; and education, 163; Episcopalians, 83; and Finney, 9; and the Kingdom of Matthias, 208, 247; missionaries, 4, 80; in mission diaries, 47–48, 51, 57–61, 67; outside New York, 71–72; and revival, 120, 123, 128; Samson Occom, 161. *See also* Synod of Geneva; Synod of Pittsburgh; Smith, Gerrit
priest, 83, 87, 297
priestcraft, 319
priesthood, 63, 100–1, 215, 226, 243
Prior, Edmund, 161–62
prisons, 86, 94–97, 208, 243, 309, 327, 335, 373–74, 378–79
prophecy *or* prophesy: and antislavery, 351; and Joseph Smith, 226; and

revival, 104; and William Miller, 207, 229–34, 239, 241
prophets (prophetic): and antislavery, 351; in Book of Mormon, 214–16; false, 238–42 (rebuttal of Miller); Native American, 101; and revival, 104; and William Miller, 229–33. *See also* Matthews, Robert; Miller, William; Smith, Joseph, Jr.
Protestant: and freedom, 319; mainline, 3, 100, 124, 160, 256, 384; and Millerism, 242; missionaries, 3, 37, 79, 83–84; and new religious movements, 12; and prophecy, 231; revivals, 100; and slavery, 352; and women's ordination, 155

Quakerism (Quakers), 47, 59, 101, 160, 162, 198–99

race, 13, 160, 198–203, 337, 353, 377
real estate, 266, 326
reform (reformer): and abolition, 333–34, 340, 343, 352; and the Burnt-over District, 3–12; Grimké Sisters and, 150, 155–57; 382; land, 323; in mission diaries, 59; movements, 152–54, 382–85; and New York politics, 291–94, 296, 324–25; and Oneida, 288; and Presbyterians, 192; and revival, 9, 110, 125; and Sabbatarianism, 319; and Senecas, 101–2; and temperance, 303, 309; and women's rights, 100, 328, 331. *See also* Smith, Gerrit
reformation, 59, 110, 125, 152–53, 157, 192: temperance, 309; the Reformation, 319
Reformed Baptist Society, 223
Reformed Baptist Society, 219, 223
Remer, Susan, 266–69
revival: aftermath of, 144–50; convention to regulate, 128–43; conversion narratives in, 122–27; defined, 9–10, 99–102 Finney on, 103–16; Grimké sisters on, 155–59; historical background, 99–102; and Latter-day Saints, 205, 222; legacy of Great Awakening, 381, 384–85; in mission diaries, 50, 56–57, 60, 69–70, 88, 93; in New York, 117–21; and New York politics, 334; and Sabbatarianism, 314; and the Second Great Awakening, 3–9; three waves of, 6; and women's rights, 150–54

Printed in the USA
CPSIA information can be obtained
at www.ICGtesting.com
LVHW091218020923
757049LV00002B/99